4WD ADVENTURES
COLORADO

Publisher's Cataloging-in-Publication
(Provided by Quality Books, Inc.)
Massey, Peter Gerald, 1951-
    4WD adventures: Colorado: how to explore the remote grandeur of Colorado
    without getting lost / Peter Massey and Jeanne Wilson—1st edition
    p.   cm.—(4WD adventures; no. 1)
    Includes bibliographical references and index.
    ISBN 0-9665675-5-2
    1. Automobile travel—Colorado—Guidebooks.
    2. Four-wheel drive vehicles. 3. Colorado—Guidebooks.
    4. Trails—Colorado—Guidebooks. 5. Ghost towns—Colorado
    I. Wilson, Jeanne Welburn, 1960- II. Title.
    GV1024.M37 1998   917.88
                    QB198-876

4WD ADVENTURES
COLORADO

HOW TO EXPLORE THE REMOTE GRANDEUR OF COLORADO WITHOUT GETTING LOST

PETER MASSEY AND JEANNE WILSON

SWAGMAN
PUBLISHING

Acknowledgements

During the more than two years it has taken us to research, write, and publish this book, many people have helped us in many ways. We owe them all special thanks.

We would like to acknowledge two members of the Colorado Division of Wildlife: Bob Hernbrode, wildlife program specialist of Watchable Wildlife, for his time and guidance; and Andy Hough, district wildlife manager, for his advice.

Thanks also to Andy Kratz, biologist, and Susan Gray, silviculturist, at the U.S. Forest Service, who provided valuable assistance with the sections on wildflowers and trees.

We would also like to express gratitude to the many others at the U.S. Forest Service, the Denver Public Library, the Colorado Historical Society, the Denver Botanic Gardens, Chatfield Arboretum, and the various Chambers of Commerce throughout Colorado who have given us guidance in our research. Thanks to Mike Foster, Ferdinand Hayden's biographer, for setting us straight on facts about Hayden.

We are grateful to all those who have helped us locate the photographs we have included in the book: Debbie Woods at the Cornell University Division of Ornithology for organizing bird photos; Lori Swingle and Jennifer Thom at the Denver Public Library for helpful assistance with historical photos; the Colorado Historical Society; Erin Wardlow at the Huntington Library in San Marino, California; Jane Kapler Smith at the USDA Forest Service Rocky Mountain Research Station in Montana; Cathy Stewart at the South Rowe Ranger Station in Montana; Tim Hogan at the University of Colorado at Boulder; Robert McCaw; and Lauren Livo.

Thanks to our friend and cousin, Jim Wilson, president of Commonwealth Design Group, who provided valuable assistance with the prepress for this book. We are particularly grateful also for the assistance of Geoff Chettle, Ian McBeath, John Lester, Lee Barker, Stephen Howard, and Peg Anderson without whose help and generosity this project might never have seen the light of day.

Finally, we would like to thank the following for their major contributions to this endeavor:

Graphic Design and Maps: **Deborah Rust Design**
Editing: **Peter Goodwin**
Copyediting and Proofreading: **Alice Levine**
Digital Photograph Retouching: **Will Cousey, The Digital Frontier**
Marketing Consultant: **Judith Appelbaum, Sensible Solutions, Inc.**
Vehicle Maintenance: **Chops**

Publisher's Note: Every effort has been taken to ensure that the information in this book is accurate at press time. Please visit our web site to advise us of any corrections that you identify. We also welcome recommendations for new 4WD trails or other suggestions to improve this book.

Swagman Publishing, Inc.
P.O. Box 519, Castle Rock, CO 80104
Phone: 303.660.3307
Toll-free: 800.660.5107
Fax: 303.688.4388
www.4wdbooks.com

SWAGMAN
PUBLISHING

Contents

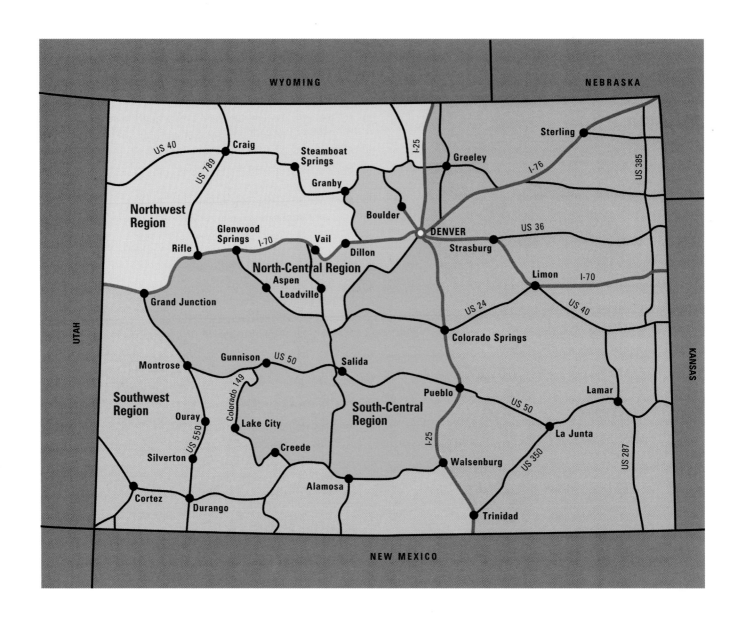

Animas Forks ghost town

Introduction

Four-wheel driving spells freedom and adventure. A four-wheel drive vehicle, whether a sport utility vehicle or a pickup truck, is vastly superior to a normal family sedan when it comes to exploring the sights of Colorado because many of the best sights require you to leave the pavement.

Yet most of the millions of four-wheel drive (4WD) owners do not take advantage of the opportunities their vehicles can provide. If you would like to make more of the off-highway capabilities of your vehicle, then this book is for you.

Four-wheeling helps you to make the most of Colorado's backcountry, opening up a multitude of opportunities:

- explore the grandeur of the Rocky Mountains
- visit ghost towns straight out of the wild West
- step back in history to the remote silver-mining camps of the 1800s
- cross mountain passes used by the American Indians for centuries
- view Colorado's wild animals in their own habitats
- marvel at peaceful alpine meadows, ablaze with summer wildflowers
- enjoy backcountry locations, far from the madding crowd
- access the best locations for other activities—backcountry camping, hiking, mountain-bike and trail-bike riding, hunting, and fishing

We have selected more than seventy 4WD trails to let you escape into the magical Colorado backcountry. All the trails are within the scope of stock sport utility vehicles. They range in difficulty from trails that are suitable for drivers who have never driven off-highway to trails that provide more of a challenge to drivers accustomed to off-highway touring. None is beyond any driver who has some off-highway experience.

The rewards of 4WD touring are immense. We hope all readers are rewarded with as much enjoyment as we have been as they travel to the most spectacular, interesting, and historic locations in Colorado.

Before You Go

Why a 4WD Does It Better

The design and engineering of 4WD vehicles provides them with many advantages over normal cars when you head off the paved road:

- improved distribution of power to the four wheels
- a transmission transfer case, which provides low-range gear selection for greater pulling power and for crawling over difficult terrain
- high ground clearance
- less overhang of the vehicle's body past the wheels, which provides better front and rear clearance when crossing gullies and ridges
- large-lug, wide-tread tires
- rugged construction (including underbody skid plates on many models)

If you plan to use your vehicle for off-highway touring, all of these considerations are important when you are selecting your vehicle; each is considered in detail in this chapter.

In order to explore the most difficult trails described in this book, you will require a 4WD vehicle that is well rated in each of the above features. If you own a 2WD sport utility vehicle or pickup truck, your ability to explore the more difficult trails will depend on conditions and your level of experience.

A word of caution though: whatever type of 4WD vehicle you drive, understand that it is not invincible. Nor is it indestructible or able to go everywhere. A 4WD has a much higher center of gravity and weighs more than a car, with consequent limitations.

Experience is the only way to develop an understanding of your vehicle's abilities and limitations. Therefore, if you are inexperienced, we strongly recommend that you start with trails that have lower difficulty ratings. As you develop an understanding of your vehicle and of your own taste for adventure, you can start to tackle the more challenging trails.

One way to quickly beef up your knowledge, without risking learning from costly or dangerous mistakes, is to undertake a 4WD course taught by a professional. A selection of the courses available can be readily located in the Yellow Pages.

Using this Book

Route Planning

Maps at the beginning of each regional section provide a convenient overview of the area concerned. Each 4WD trail in the region is highlighted in color, as are major highways and towns. This allows you to relate the start and end points of every 4WD trail in this book to the other nearby roads and trails.

By referring to the maps you can plan your overall route to utilize as many 4WD trails as possible. Checking the difficulty rating and time required for each trail then allows you to finalize your plans.

Distances between Colorado towns can be ascertained from the Colorado Distance Chart at the end of this chapter.

Difficulty Ratings

We utilize a point system to provide a guide to the difficulty of each trail. Any such system is subjective and is dependent on the driver's experience level and the road conditions at the time.

We have rated the 4WD trails in this book on a scale of 1 to 10, 1 being passable for a normal passenger vehicle in good conditions and 10 requiring a heavily modified vehicle and an experienced driver who is willing to expect vehicle damage. Because this book is designed for owners of unmodified 4WD vehicles whom we assume do not expect to damage their vehicles, nearly all the trails are rated 5 or lower.

This is not to say that all the trails discussed here are easy. We strongly recommend that inexperienced drivers not tackle any 4- or 5-rated trails before undertaking a number of the lower-rated ones, so that they can gauge their skill level and prepare for the difficulty of the higher-rated trails.

In assessing the trails, we have always assumed good road conditions (dry road surface, good visibility, and so on). The factors influencing our ratings are as follows:

- obstacles such as rocks, mud, ruts, and stream crossings
- the stability of the road surface
- the width of the road and the vehicle clearance between trees or rocks
- the steepness of the road
- the margin of error (for example, a very high, open, shelf road would be rated more difficult even if it was not very steep and had a stable surface)

The following is a guide to the ratings:

Rating 1: Graded dirt but suitable for a normal passenger vehicle. Gentle grades; fairly wide; very shallow water crossings (if any).

Rating 2: High-clearance vehicle preferred. Dirt road but with rocks, grades, water crossings, or ruts that make clearance a concern in a normal passenger vehicle; fairly wide, passing not a concern; mud not a concern under normal weather conditions.

Rating 3: High-clearance 4WD preferred. Rough road surface to be expected; mud possible but easily passable; rocks up to six inches in diameter; loose surface possible; shelf road but wide enough for passing or with adequate pull-offs.

Rating 4: High-clearance 4WD recommended. Rough road surface with rocks larger than six inches possible, but a reasonable driving line available; mud possible but passable; stream crossings up to fifteen inches deep; substantial sections of single-lane shelf road possible; moderate grades; moderately loose surface possible.

Rating 5: High-clearance 4WD required. Rough, rutted surface; rocks up to nine inches possible; mud may be impassable for inexperienced drivers; stream crossings up to twenty-four inches deep; sections may be steep enough to cause traction problems; very narrow shelf road with steep drop-offs likely; tight clearance between rocks or trees possible.

Rating 6: Experienced four-wheelers only. Potentially dangerous; large rocks, ruts, or terraces may need to be negotiated; stream crossings at least twenty-four inches deep and with rapid current, unstable stream bottom, or difficult access; steep slopes, loose surface, and narrow clearance likely; very narrow shelf road with steep drop-offs and challenging road surfaces possible.

Rating 7: Skilled, experienced four-wheel drivers only. Very challenging sections; very steep sections likely; loose surface, large rocks, deep ruts, and tight clearance expected; mud likely to necessitate winching.

Rating 8 to 10: Stock vehicles are likely to be damaged and may find the trail impassable. Well beyond the scope of this book.

Scenic Ratings

If rating the degree of difficulty is subjective, rating scenic beauty is guaranteed to lead to arguments—especially in Colorado, a stunningly beautiful state. However, we have tried to give some guide to the relative scenic quality of the various trails. The ratings are based on a scale of 1 to 10.

Estimated Driving Times

In calculating driving times, we have not allowed for stops. Actual driving time may be considerably longer than indicated, depending on the number and duration of stops. Add more time if you prefer to drive more slowly than good conditions allow.

Current Road Conditions

All the 4WD trails described in this book may be impassable in poor weather conditions. For each trail, we have provided a phone number for obtaining current information about conditions.

Abbreviations

The route directions provided for the 4WD trails in this book use a series of abbreviations.

SO	CONTINUE STRAIGHT ON
TL	TURN LEFT
TR	TURN RIGHT
BL	BEAR LEFT
BR	BEAR RIGHT
UT	U-TURN

Using Route Directions

To help you stay on track, we have described and pinpointed (by odometer reading) nearly every significant feature along the route (intersections, streams, gates, cattle guards, and so on) and have provided directions from these landmarks. Odometer readings will vary from vehicle to vehicle, but you will soon learn to allow for slight variations.

If you diverge from the route, zero your trip meter upon your return and continue the route, making the necessary adjustment to the point-to-point odometer directions. We have regularly reset the odometer readings in the directions, so that you won't have to recalculate for too long.

Directions for traveling the 4WD trails in reverse are printed in blue. When traveling in reverse, read from the bottom of the table and work up.

Route directions include cross-references whenever the current route crosses another 4WD trail included in this book, which allows easy change of route or destination.

Latitude and longitude readings are provided periodically along each trail to facilitate using a Global Positioning System (GPS) receiver. These readings may also assist in finding your location on your maps. The GPS coordinates were taken using the NAD 1927 datum and are in the format dd°mm.mmm'. When loading coordinates into your GPS receiver, you may wish to include only one decimal place, because in Colorado, the third decimal place equals only about two yards and the second less than twenty yards.

Map References

We recommend that you supplement the information in this book with more-detailed maps. Each trail in this book refers to various sheet maps and road atlases that provide the detail necessary to navigate and identify accurately your location on these trails. Typically, the following five references are given:

- U.S. Forest Service Maps—Scale 1:126,720
- U.S. Geological Survey County Series Maps—Scale 1:50,000
- *The Roads of Colorado,* 1st ed. (Fredericksburg, Texas: Shearer Publishing, 1996)—Scale 1:158,400
- *Colorado Atlas & Gazetteer,* 2nd ed. (Freeport, Maine: DeLorme Mapping, 1995)—Scale 1:160,000 and 1:320,000
- *Trails Illustrated* Topo Maps; National Geographic Maps— Various scales, but all contain good detail

We recommend the *Trails Illustrated* series of maps as the best for navigating these trails. They are reliable, easy to read, and printed on nearly indestructible plastic paper. However, the series does not cover all the 4WD trails described in this book.

If *Trails Illustrated* maps are not available, we recommend the U.S. Geological Survey County Series maps. These show the necessary detail without being too detailed. Their main weakness is that some are out of date and do not show the 4WD trails accurately.

The two atlases listed are both useful and have the advantage of providing you with maps of the entire state at a reasonable price. While the atlases do not provide much information for each 4WD trail beyond what we have provided, they are useful if you wish to explore the hundreds of side roads. Of the two, we prefer *The Roads of Colorado*.

U.S. Forest Service maps lack the detail of the other sheet maps and, in our experience, are also out of date occasionally. They have the advantage of covering a broad area. These maps are most useful for the longer trails.

For those who want to navigate with the assistance of their portable computer, Maptech publishes a particularly good series of maps on CD ROM. These are based on the U.S. Geological Survey 7.5°Series Maps—Scale 1:24,000, but they can be viewed on four scales. The 1:100,000-scale series are also included. These maps offer many advantages over normal maps:

■ GPS coordinates for any location can be found, which can then be loaded into your GPS receiver. Conversely, if you have your GPS coordinates, your location on the map can be pinpointed instantly.

■ Towns, rivers, passes, mountains, and many other sites are indexed by name so that they can be located quickly.

■ 4WD trails can be marked and profiled for elevation change and distance from point to point.

■ Customized maps can be printed out.

To cover the entire state of Colorado requires 8 CD ROMs and is therefore expensive, but the CD ROMs can be purchased individually.

At the time this book was researched, this series of CD ROMs could not be used with a laptop computer and a GPS receiver in your vehicle to monitor your location on the map and navigate directly from the display. However, a new version of the software has this capability.

All these maps should be available through good map stores. The CD ROMs are available directly from Maptech (800-627-7236 or on the Internet at www. maptech.com).

Assessing Your Vehicle's Off-Road Ability

Many issues come into the selection of a 4WD vehicle: the normal use of the vehicle and your budget being the two most important. Most of the 4WDs on the market are suitable for even the roughest trails described in this book. Engine power will be adequate in even the least powerful modern vehicle. However, some vehicles are less suited to off-highway driving than others and some of the newest, car-like vehicles simply are not designed for off-highway touring. The following information should allow you to separate the good, the bad, and the ugly.

Differing 4WD Systems

All 4WD systems have one thing in common: The engine can provide power to all four wheels rather than to only two as is typical of the normal family car. However, there are a number of differences in the way power is applied to the wheels.

The other feature that distinguishes nearly all 4WDs from normal passenger vehicles is that the gearboxes have high and low ratios that effectively double the number of gears. The high range is comparable to the range on a normal passenger car. The low range provides lower speed and more power, which is useful when towing heavy loads, driving up steep hills, or crawling over rocks. When driving downhill, the 4WD's low range increases engine braking.

Different makes and models of sport utility vehicles offer different drive systems. Differences between drive systems center on two issues: the way power is applied to the other wheels if one or more wheel slips, and the ability to select between 2WD and 4WD.

Normal driving requires that all four wheels are able to turn at different speeds; this allows the vehicle to turn without scrubbing the tires. In a 2WD vehicle, the front wheels (or rear wheels in a front-wheel-drive vehicle) are not powered by the engine and thus are able to coast at whatever speed is appropriate. The rear wheels are powered by the engine but are able to turn at different speeds due to the action of the differential, which applies power to the faster-turning wheel.

This standard method of applying traction has certain weaknesses. First, when power is applied to only one set of wheels, the other set cannot help the vehicle gain traction. Second, when one powered wheel loses traction it spins, but the other powered wheel doesn't turn. This happens because the differential applies all the engine power to the faster-turning wheel and no power to the other wheels, which still have traction. All 4WD systems are designed to overcome these two weaknesses. However, different 4WDs address this common objective in different ways.

Full-Time 4WD

In order for a vehicle to remain in 4WD all the time without scrubbing the tires, all the wheels must be able to rotate at different speeds. A full-time 4WD system allows this to happen by having three differentials. One is located between the rear wheels, as in a normal passenger car, to allow the rear wheels to rotate at different speeds. The second is located between the front wheels in exactly the same way. The third differential is located between the front and rear wheels to allow different rotational speeds between the front and rear sets of wheels. In nearly all vehicles with full-time 4WD, the center differential operates only in high range. In low range, it is completely locked.

Part-Time 4WD

A part-time 4WD system does not have the center differential located between the front and rear wheels. Consequently, the front and rear drive shafts are both driven at the same speed and with the same power at all times.

This system provides improved traction, because when one or both of either the front or rear wheels slips, the engine continues to provide power to the other set. However, because such a system doesn't allow a difference in speed between the front and rear sets of wheels, the tires scrub when turning, placing additional strain on the whole drive system. Therefore, such a system can be used only in slippery conditions; otherwise, the ability to steer the vehicle will deteriorate and the tires will quickly wear out.

Some vehicles, such as Jeeps with Selec-trac and Mitsubishi Monteros, offer both full-time and part-time 4WD high range.

Switching Between 2WD and 4WD

There are three systems for switching between 2WD and 4WD. The most basic requires stopping and getting out of the vehicle to lock the front hubs manually before selecting 4WD. The second requires stopping but can be effected by merely throwing a lever inside the vehicle (the hubs lock automatically). The third allows shifting between 2WD and 4WD high range while the vehicle is moving. Any 4WD that does not offer the option of driving in 2WD must have a full-time 4WD system.

Limiting Wheel Slippage

4WDs employ various systems to limit wheel slippage and transfer power to the wheels that still have traction. These systems may completely lock the differentials or allow only limited slippage before transferring power back to the wheels that retain traction.

Lockers completely eliminate the operation of one or more differentials. A locker on the center differential switches between full-time and part-time 4WD. Lockers on the front or rear differentials ensure that power remains equally applied to each set of wheels regardless of whether both have traction. Lockers may be controlled manually by a switch or lever in the vehicle, or they may be automatic.

The Toyota Land Cruiser offers the option of having manual lockers on all three differentials, while other brands such as the Mitsubishi Montero offer manual locks on the center and rear differential. Manual lockers are the most controllable and effective devices for ensuring that power is provided to the wheels with traction. However, because they allow absolutely no slippage, they must be used only on slippery surfaces.

An alternative method for getting power to the wheels that have traction is to allow only limited wheel slippage. Systems that work this way may be called limited-slip differentials, posi-traction systems, or, in the center differential, viscous couplings. The advantage of these systems is that the limited difference they allow in rotational speed between wheels enables such systems to be used when driving on a dry surface. All full-time 4WD systems allow limited slippage in the center differential.

For off-highway use, a manually locking differential is the best of the above systems but is the most expensive. Limited slip differentials are the cheapest but also the least satisfactory. For the center differential, the best system combines a locking differential and to enable full-time use, a viscous coupling.

Tires

The tires that came with your 4WD vehicle may be satisfactory, but many 4WDs are fitted with passenger-car tires. These are unlikely to be the best choice because they are less rugged and more likely to puncture on the rocky Col-orado trails. They are particularly prone to sidewall damage. Passenger vehicle tires also have a less aggressive tread pattern than specialized 4WD tires, providing less traction in mud.

For information on purchasing tires better suited to off-highway conditions, refer to the "Special 4WD Equipment" section later in this chapter.

Clearance

The road clearance of different makes of 4WD varies considerably—from less than seven inches to more than ten inches. Special vehicles may have far greater clearance. For instance, the Hummer has sixteen-inch ground clearance. High ground clearance is particularly advantageous on the rockier 4WD trails discussed in this book.

When evaluating the ground clearance of your vehicle, you need to take into account the clearance of the body work between the wheels on each side of the vehicle. This is particularly relevant for crawling over larger rocks. Vehicles with side-steps have significantly lower clearance than those without.

Another factor affecting clearance is the approach and departure angles of your vehicle—the maximum angle that a ridge can make to the flat ground without the front of the vehicle hitting the ridge on approach or the rear of the vehicle hitting on departure. Mounting a winch or tow hitch to your vehicle is likely to reduce your approach or departure angles.

If you do a lot of driving on rocky trails, you will inevitably hit the bottom of the vehicle sooner or later. When this happens, you will be far less likely to damage vulnerable areas such as the oil pan and gas tank if your vehicle is fitted with skid plates. Most manufacturers offer skid plates as an option. They are worth every penny.

Maneuverability

When you tackle some of the tighter switchbacks on Colorado's 4WD trails, you will quickly appreciate that maneuverability is an important criterion when assessing 4WD vehicles. Where a full-size vehicle is forced to go back and forward a number of times to get around a sharp turn, a small 4WD will go straight around. This is not only easier, it is safer.

If your passenger and luggage requirements are such that you prefer a full-size vehicle, all is not lost. The only trail in this book that we have not traveled in our Suburban is Black Bear Pass Road, which is definitely a trail for smaller vehicles. That is not to say that some of the other trails wouldn't have been more easily navigated in a smaller vehicle!

In Summary

Selecting the best 4WD system is, at least partly, subjective. It is also a matter of your budget. However, for the type of off-highway driving covered in this book, we make the following recommendations:

- Select a 4WD system that offers low-range and, at a minimum, has some form of limited slip differential on the rear axle.
- Use light truck, all-terrain tires as the standard tires on your vehicle. Better still, if your budget allows, use a separate set of mud-terrain tires for off-highway use. Whichever type you choose, select a brand with maximum puncture protection, including the sidewalls.
- For maximum clearance, select a vehicle with sixteen-inch wheels, or at least choose the tallest tires that your vehicle can accommodate. If you are going to try the typical rocky Colorado 4WD trails, don't install a sidestep (or, if already fitted, temporarily remove it). If you have the option, have underbody skid plates mounted.
- Remember that narrow shelf roads with very tight switchbacks are more difficult to navigate in a full-size vehicle than in a compact 4WD.

Driving Off-Road

Four-wheel driving involves special driving techniques and road rules. This section is provided as an introduction for 4WD beginners.

4WD Road Rules

To help ensure that these trails remain open and available for all four-wheel drivers to enjoy, it is important to minimize your impact on the environment and not be a safety risk to yourself or anyone else. Remember that the 4WD clubs in Colorado fight a constant battle with the U.S. Forest Service to retain the access that currently exists.

The fundamental rule when traversing the 4WD trails described in this book is to use common sense. In addition to this fundamental rule, special road rules for 4WD trails apply.
- Vehicles traveling uphill have the right of way.
- If you are moving more slowly than the vehicle behind you, pull over to let the other vehicle by.
- Park out of the way in a safe place. Set the parking brake—don't rely on leaving the transmission in park. Manual transmissions should be left in the lowest gear.

In addition to these rules, we offer the following general advice to four-wheel drivers.
- Size up the situation in advance.
- Be careful and take your time.
- Maintain smooth, steady power and momentum.
- Engage 4WD and low-range before you get into a tight situation.
- Steer toward high spots, trying to put the wheel over large rocks.
- Straddle ruts.
- Use gears and not just the brakes to hold the vehicle when driving downhill. On very steep slopes, chock the wheels if you park your vehicle.
- Watch for logging and mining trucks.
- Wear your seat belt and ensure that all luggage, espe-

cially heavy items such as tool boxes or coolers, is secured. Heavy items should be secured by ratchet tie-down straps rather than elastic-type straps, which are not strong enough to secure heavy items if the vehicle rolls.

Tread Lightly!

Remember the rules of the Tread Lightly!® program.
- Become informed. Obtain maps, regulations, and other information from the forest service or from other public land agencies. Learn the rules and follow them.
- Resist the urge to pioneer a new road or trail or to cut across a switchback. Stay on constructed tracks and avoid running over young trees, shrubs, and grasses, damaging or killing them. Don't drive across alpine tundra; this fragile environment may take years to recover.
- Stay off soft, wet roads and 4WD trails readily torn up by vehicles. Repairing the damage is expensive.
- Travel around meadows, steep hillsides, stream banks and lake shores which are easily scarred by churning wheels.
- Stay away from wild animals that are rearing young or suffering from a food shortage.
- Obey gate closures and regulatory signs.
- Preserve America's heritage by not disturbing old mining camps, ghost towns, or other historical features.
- Carry out all rubbish.
- Stay out of designated wilderness areas. They are closed to all vehicles. Know where the boundaries are.
- Get permission to cross private land. Leave livestock alone. Respect landowners' rights.

Special Four-Wheel Driving Techniques

Certain obstacles are particularly likely to be encountered on Colorado's 4WD trails. The following provides an introduction to the techniques required for the most common of these.

Rocks

Tire selection is important in negotiating rocks, particularly the sharp rocks encountered on the typical Colorado mountain 4WD trail. Select a multiple-ply, tough sidewall, light-truck tire with a large-lug tread.

As you approach a rocky stretch, get into 4WD low range to give you maximum slow-speed control. Speed is rarely necessary since traction on a rocky surface is usually good. Plan ahead and select the line you wish to take. If the rock appears to be larger than the clearance of your vehicle, don't try to straddle it. Check to see that it is not higher than the frame of your vehicle once you get a wheel over it. Put a wheel up on the rock and slowly climb it, then gently drop over the other side using the brake to ensure a smooth landing. Bouncing the car over rocks increases the likelihood of damage, as the body's clearance is reduced by the suspension compressing. Running boards also significantly reduce your clearance in this respect.

Steep Uphill Grades

Consider walking the trail to ensure that it is passable, especially if it is clear that backtracking is going to be a problem.

Select 4WD low range to ensure that you have adequate power to pull up the hill. If the wheels begin to lose traction, turn the steering wheel gently from side to side to give the wheels a chance to regain traction.

If you lose momentum, but the car is not in danger of sliding, use the foot brake, switch off the ignition, leave the vehicle in gear (if manual transmission) or park (if automatic), engage the parking brake, and get out to examine the situation. See if you can remove any obstacles, and figure out the line you need to take. Reversing a couple of yards and starting again may allow you to get better traction and momentum.

If you decide a stretch of road is impassably steep, back down the trail. Trying to turn the vehicle around is extremely dangerous and very likely to cause it to roll over.

Steep Downhill Grades

Again, consider walking the trail to ensure that it is passable, especially if it is clear that backtracking is going to be a problem.

Select 4WD low range, in first gear, to maximize braking assistance from the engine. If the surface is loose and you are losing traction, change up to second or third gear. Do not use the brakes if you can avoid it, but don't let the vehicle's speed get out of control. Feather (lightly pump) the brakes if you slip under braking.

Travel very slowly over rock ledges or ruts. Attempt to tackle these diagonally, letting one wheel down at a time.

If the vehicle begins to slide around at the back, gently apply the throttle and correct the steering. If the rear of the vehicle starts to slide sideways, do not apply the brakes.

Mud

Muddy trails are easily damaged, so they should be avoided if possible. If you do need to traverse a section of mud, your success will depend heavily on whether you have open-lugged mud tires or chains. Thick mud fills the tighter tread that is on normal tires, leaving the tire with no more grip than if it were bald. If the muddy stretch is only a few yards long, the momentum of your vehicle may allow you to get through regardless.

If the muddy track is very steep, either uphill or downhill, do not attempt it. Your vehicle is very likely to skid in such conditions and the vehicle may roll or slip off the edge of the road.

When crossing mud:

■ Avoid making detours off existing tracks, so that environmental damage is minimized.

■ Check to see that the mud has a reasonably firm base (tackling deep mud is definitely not recommended unless you have a vehicle-mounted winch—and even then, be cautious because the winch may not get you out).

■ Check to see that no ruts are too deep for the ground clearance of your vehicle.

Having decided that you can get through and having selected the best route, use the following techniques:

■ Select 4WD low range and a suitable gear; momentum is the key to success, so use a high enough gear to build up sufficient speed.

■ Avoid accelerating heavily, so as to minimize wheel spinning and provide maximum traction.

■ Follow existing wheel ruts, unless they are too deep for the clearance of your vehicle.

■ Correct slides by turning the steering wheel in the direction that the rear wheels are skidding, but don't be too aggressive with the amount you correct your steering.

■ If the vehicle comes to a stop, don't continue to accelerate, as you will only spin your wheels and dig yourself into a rut. Try backing out and having another go.

Stream Crossings

By crossing a stream that is too deep, drivers risk far more than water flowing in and ruining the interior of their vehicles. Water sucked into the engine's air intake will seriously damage the engine. Likewise, water that seeps into the air vent on the transmission or differential will mix with the lubricant and may lead to serious problems in due course. On modern vehicles, water that gets into the interior may damage the computerized vehicle management system.

Even worse, if the water is deep or fast flowing, it could easily carry a vehicle downstream and may endanger the lives of the occupants.

The manual for some 4WDs will say what fording depth the vehicle can negotiate safely. If your vehicle's owner's manual doesn't include this information, your local dealer may be able to assist. If you don't know, then you should try to avoid crossing through water that is more than a foot or so deep.

The first rule for crossing a stream is to know what you are getting into. You need to ascertain how deep the water is, make sure that there are no large rocks or holes and that the bottom is solid enough to avoid getting the vehicle bogged, and see that the entry and exit points are negotiable. This may take some time and involve getting wet, but to cross a stream without first properly assessing the situation is to take a great risk.

The secret to water crossings is to keep moving, but not too fast. In shallow water (where the surface of the water is below the bumper), your primary concern is to safely negotiate the bottom of the stream, avoiding any rock damage and maintaining momentum if there is a danger of getting stuck or slipping on the exit.

In deeper water (between eighteen and thirty inches deep), the objective is to create a small bow wave in front of the moving vehicle. This requires a speed that is approximately walking pace. The bow wave reduces the depth of the water around the engine compartment. If the water's surface reaches your tailpipe, select a gear that will maintain moderate engine revs to avoid water backing up into the exhaust; do not change gears midstream.

Crossing water deeper than thirty inches requires more extensive preparation of the vehicle and should be attempted only by experienced drivers.

Snow

The trails in this book are nearly all closed until the snow has melted or been bulldozed. Therefore, the only snow conditions that you are likely to encounter are an occasional snowdrift that has not yet melted or fresh snow from an unexpected storm. Getting through such conditions depends on the depth of the snow, its consistency, the stability of the underlying surface, and your vehicle.

If the snow is no deeper than about nine inches and there is solid ground beneath it, it should not pose a problem. In deeper snow that seems solid enough to support your vehicle, be extremely cautious: If you break through a drift, you are likely to be stuck, and if conditions are bad, you may have a long wait.

The tires you use for off-highway driving, with a wide tread pattern, are probably suitable for these snow conditions. Nonetheless, it is wise to carry chains (preferably for all four wheels) and if you have a vehicle-mounted winch, even better.

It is important to remember how quickly the weather can change in the Colorado high country, even in summer. Pack clothes and other items to ensure your survival if you are caught in a sudden storm.

Sand

As with most off-highway situations, your tires will affect your ability to cross sand. It is difficult to tell how well a particular tire will handle in sand just by looking at it, so be guided by the manufacturer and your dealer.

The key to driving in soft sand is floatation, which is achieved by a combination of low tire pressure and momentum. Before crossing a stretch of sand, you should start by reducing your tire pressure to between fifteen and twenty pounds. If necessary, you can safely go to as low as twelve pounds. As you cross the sand, maintain momentum so that your vehicle rides on the top of soft sand without digging in or stalling. This may require plenty of engine power.

Air the tires back up as soon as you are out of the sand to avoid damage to the tires and the rims. Airing back up requires a high-quality air compressor. Even then, it is a slow process.

The only trail in this book that may necessitate lowering the tire pressure for sand is the Medano Pass road, which ends in the Great Sand Dunes National Monument. If you air down on this trail, a refill station at the national monument is open in the peak season, which may mean that you can avoid buying a portable compressor.

Vehicle Recovery Methods

If you do enough four-wheel driving, you are sure to get stuck sooner or later. The following techniques will help you get back on the go. The most suitable method will depend on the equipment available and the situation you are in—whether you are stuck in sand, mud, or snow, or high-centered, or unable to negotiate a hill.

Towing

Use a nylon yank strap of the type discussed in the "Special 4WD Equipment" section later in this chapter. This type of strap will stretch 15 to 25 percent, and the elasticity will assist in extracting the vehicle.

Attach the strap to a frame-mounted tow hook. Ensure

that the driver of the stuck vehicle is ready, take up all but about six feet of slack, then move the towing vehicle away at a moderate speed (in most circumstances this means using 4WD low range in second gear) so that the elasticity of the strap is employed in the way it is meant to be. Don't take off like a bat out of hell or you risk breaking the strap or damaging a vehicle.

Never join two yank straps together with a shackle. If one strap breaks, the shackle will become a lethal missile aimed at one of the vehicles (and anyone inside). For the same reason, never attach a yank strap to the tow ball on either vehicle.

Jacking

Jacking the vehicle may allow you to pack under the wheel (with rocks, dirt, or logs) or use your shovel to remove an obstacle. However, the standard vehicle jack is unlikely to be of as much assistance as a high-lift jack. We highly recommend purchasing a good high-lift jack as a basic accessory if you decide that you are going to do a lot of serious, off-highway, four-wheel driving.

Tire Chains

Tire chains can be of assistance in either mud or snow. Cable-type chains provide much less grip than link-type chains. There are also dedicated mud chains with larger, heavier links than on normal snow chains. It is best to have chains fitted to all four wheels.

Once you are bogged is not the best time to try to fit the chains; if at all possible try to predict their need and have them on the vehicle before trouble arises.

Winching

Most people using this book will not have a winch. But if you get serious about four-wheel driving, this is probably the first major accessory you will consider buying.

Under normal circumstances, a winch would be warranted only for the more difficult 4WD trails in this book. Having a winch is certainly comforting when you see a difficult section of road ahead and have to decide whether to risk it or turn back. Major obstacles can appear when you least expect them, even on trails that are otherwise easy.

Owning a winch is not a panacea to all your recovery problems. Winching depends on the availability of a good anchor point, and electric winches may not work if they are submerged in a stream. Despite these constraints, no accessory is more useful than a high-quality, powerful winch when you get into a difficult situation.

If you acquire a winch, learn to use it properly; take the time to study your owner's manual. Incorrect operation can be extremely dangerous and may cause damage to the winch or to trees, which are the most common anchors.

Navigation by the Global Positioning System (GPS)

Although this book is designed so that each trail can be navigated by simply following the detailed directions provided, nothing makes navigation easier than a GPS receiver.

The Global Positioning System (GPS) is a satellite-based system consisting of a network of twenty-four satellites, nearly thirteen thousand miles in space, in six different orbital paths. The satellites are constantly moving, making two complete orbits around the earth every twenty-four hours, at about 8,500 miles per hour.

Each satellite is constantly transmitting data, including its identification number, its operational health, and the date and time. It also transmits its location and the location of every other satellite in the network.

By comparing the time the signal was transmitted to the time it is received, a GPS receiver calculates how far away each satellite is. With a sufficient number of signals, the receiver can then triangulate its location. With three or more satellites, the receiver can determine latitude and longitude coordinates. With four or more, it can calculate altitude. By constantly making these calculations, it can calculate speed and direction.

The U.S. military uses the system to provide positions accurate to within half an inch. However, civilian receivers are less sophisticated and are deliberately fed slightly erroneous information in order to effectively deny military applications to hostile countries or terrorists. This degradation of the signal is called Selective Availability (SA). It results in the common civilian receivers having an accuracy of twenty to seventy-five yards.

A GPS receiver offers the four-wheeler numerous benefits:
■ You can track to any point for which you know the longitude and latitude coordinates with no chance of heading in the wrong direction or getting lost. Most receivers provide an extremely easy-to-understand graphic display to keep you on track.
■ It works in all weather conditions.
■ It automatically records your route for easy backtracking.
■ You can record and name any location, so that you can relocate it with ease. This may include your campsite, a fishing spot, or even a silver mine you discover!
■ It displays your position, allowing you to pinpoint your location on a map.
■ By interfacing the GPS receiver directly to a portable computer, you can monitor and record your location as you travel (using the appropriate map software) or print the route you took.

Special 4WD Equipment

Tires

When 4WD touring, you will likely encounter a wide variety of terrain: rocks, mud, talus, sand, gravel, dirt, and bitumen. There is an immense variety of tires on the market, including many specifically targeted at one or another of these types of terrain, as well as tires designed to handle a range of terrain adequately.

Every four-wheel driver seems to have his or her own preference when it comes to tire selection; but most people undertaking the 4WD trails in this book will need tires that can handle all of the above types of terrain adequately.

The first requirement is to select rugged, light-truck tires rather than passenger-vehicle tires. Check the size data on the sidewall: It should have "LT" rather than "P" before the number.

Among light-truck tires, you will have to choose between tires that are designated "all-terrain" and more-aggressive, wider-tread mud tires. Either type will be adequate, especially on rocks, gravel, talus, or dirt. But because mud tires have such an advantage in muddy conditions and soft snow, we have found them the better choice. Muddy, wet, or snowy conditions create the greatest unexpected obstacles on the tracks in this book. However, all-terrain tires will perform significantly better on bitumen, in sand, or on ice.

When selecting tires, remember that they can alter not just traction but also cornering ability, braking distances, fuel consumption, and noise levels. It pays to get good advice before making your decision.

Global Positioning System Receivers

GPS receivers have come down in price considerably in the past few years and are rapidly becoming indispensable navigational tools. Many higher-priced cars now offer integrated GPS receivers; and within the next few years, receivers will become available on most models.

Battery-powered, hand-held units that meet the needs of off-highway driving currently range from less than $100 to a little over $300 and continue to come down in price. Some high-end units feature maps that are incorporated in the display, either from a built-in database or from interchangeable memory cards. However, none of these maps currently include 4WD trails in their database.

If you are considering purchasing a GPS unit, look for the following features:
■ Price. The very cheapest units are likely outdated and very limited in their display features. Expect to pay $125 to $300.
■ The number of channels, which means the number of satellites that the unit tracks concurrently. Many older units have only one channel that switches from one satellite to another to collect the required information. Modern units have up to twelve channels that are each dedicated to tracking one satellite. This provides greater accuracy, faster start-up (because the unit can acquire the initial data it needs much more rapidly), and better reception under difficult conditions, such as when located in a deep canyon or in dense foliage.
■ The number of routes and the number of sites (or "waypoints") per route that can be stored in memory. For off-highway use, it is important to be able to store plenty of waypoints so that you do not have to load coordinates into the machine as frequently. Having plenty of memory also ensures that you can automatically store your present location without fear that the memory is full.

It is also important that the machine can store numerous routes. GPS receivers enable you to combine waypoints to form a route, greatly simplifying navigation. As you reach each waypoint, the machine automatically swaps to the next one and directs you there.

The better units store up to five hundred waypoints and twenty reversible routes of up to thirty waypoints each. Also consider the number of characters a GPS receiver allows you to use to name waypoints. When you try to recall a waypoint, you may have difficulty recognizing names restricted to only a few characters.

■ Automatic route storing. Most units automatically store your route as you go along and enable you to display it in reverse to make backtracking easy.

■ The display. Compare the graphic display of one unit with another. Some are much easier to decipher or offer more alternative displays.

■ The controls. GPS receivers have many functions, and they need to have good, simple controls.

■ Vehicle mounting. To be useful, the unit needs to be located so that it can be read easily by both the driver and the navigator. Check that the unit can be conveniently located in your vehicle. Different units have different shapes and different mounting systems.

■ Position-format options. Different maps use different grids, and you want to be able to display the same format on your GPS unit as on the map you are using, so that cross-referencing is simplified. There are a number of formats for latitude and longitude, as well as UTM (Universal Transverse Mercator) grid, which is used on some maps.

After you have selected a unit, a number of optional extras are also worth considering:

■ A cigarette lighter adapter. Important because GPS units eat batteries!

■ A vehicle-mounted antenna, which will improve reception under difficult conditions. (The GPS unit can only "see" though the windows of your vehicle; it cannot monitor satellites through a metal roof.) Having a vehicle-mounted antenna also means that you do not have to consider reception when locating the receiver in your vehicle.

■ An in-car mounting system. If you are going to do a lot of touring using the GPS, you may want to attach a bracket on the dash rather than relying on a velcro mount.

■ A computer-link cable. Data from your receiver can be downloaded to your PC; or, if you have a laptop computer, you can monitor your route as you go along, using one of a number of inexpensive map software products on the market.

We used a Garmin 45 receiver to take the GPS positions included in this book. This unit is now outdated, but it has served us well for the past five years in our travels throughout the United States and around the world.

Yank Straps

Yank straps are industrial-strength versions of the flimsy tow straps that you may purchase at the local discount store. They are made of heavy nylon, twenty to thirty feet long, two to three inches wide, rated to at least 20,000 pounds, and have looped ends.

Do not use tow straps with metal hooks in the ends (the hooks can become missiles in the event the strap breaks free). Likewise, never join two yank straps together using a shackle.

CB Radios

If you are stuck, injured, or just want to know the conditions up ahead, a citizen's band (CB) radio can be invaluable.

CB radios are relatively inexpensive and do not require an FCC license. Their range is limited, especially in very hilly country, as their transmission patterns basically follow lines of sight. Range can be improved using single sideband (SSB) transmission, an option on the more expensive units. Range is even better on vehicle-mounted units that have been professionally fitted to ensure that the antenna and cabling are matched appropriately.

Winches

There are three main options when it comes to winches: manual winches, removable electric winches, and vehicle-mounted electric winches.

If you have a full-size 4WD vehicle, which may weigh in excess of 7,000 pounds when loaded, a manual winch will be of limited use without a lot of effort and considerable time. However, a manual winch is a very handy and inexpensive accessory if you have a small 4WD. Typically, manual winches are rated to pull about 5,500 pounds.

Electric winches can be mounted to your vehicle's trailer hitch to enable them to be removed, relocated to the front of the vehicle (if you have a hitch installed), or moved to another vehicle. While this is a very useful feature, winches are heavy, so relocating them can be a two-person job. Five-thousand-pound-rated winches weigh only about 55 pounds, while 12,000-pound-rated models may weigh around 140 pounds. Therefore, the larger models are best permanently front-mounted. Unfortunately, this limits their ability to winch the vehicle backwards.

When choosing between electric winches, be aware that they are rated for their maximum capacity on the first wind of the cable around the drum. As layers of cable wind onto the drum, they increase its diameter and thus decrease the maximum load the winch can handle. This decrease is significant: a winch rated to pull 8,000 pounds on a bare drum may only handle 6,500 pounds on the second layer, 5,750 pounds on the third layer, and 5,000 pounds on the fourth. Electric winches also draw a high level of current and may necessitate upgrading the battery in your 4WD or adding a second battery.

There is a wide range of mounting options—from a simple, body-mounted frame that holds the winch, to heavy-duty winch bars that replace the original bumper and incorporate brush bars and mounts for auxiliary lights.

If you buy a winch, either electric or manual, you will also need to buy quite a range of additional equipment so that you can operate it correctly:

■ At least one choker chain with hooks on each end
■ Winch extension straps or cables
■ Shackles
■ A receiver shackle
■ A snatch block
■ A tree protector
■ Gloves

Grill/Brush Bars and Winch Bars

Brush bars protect the front of the vehicle from scratches and minor bumps and also provide a solid mount for auxiliary lights. How much protection from knocks they provide depends on how solid they are and whether they are securely mounted onto the frame of the vehicle. Lighter models may attach in front of the standard bumper, but the more substantial units will replace the bumper. Prices range from about $150 to $450.

Winch bars replace the bumper and usually integrate a solid brush bar with a heavy-duty winch mount. Some have the brush bar as an optional extra to the winch bar component. Manufactures such as Warn, ARB, and TJM offer a wide range of integrated winch bars. These are significantly more expensive, starting at about $650.

Portable Air Compressors

Most portable air compressors on the market are flimsy models that plug into the cigarette lighter and are sold at the local discount store. These are of very limited use for four-wheel driving. They are very slow to inflate the large tires of a 4WD vehicle; to reinflate from fifteen to thirty-five pounds, typically takes about ten minutes for each tire. They are also unlikely to be rated for continuous use, which means that they will overheat and cut off before completing the job. If you're lucky, they will start up again when they have cooled down, but this means that you are unlikely to reinflate your tires in less than an hour.

The easiest way to identify a useful air compressor is by the price—good ones cost $200 and over. Many of the quality units feature a Thomas-brand pump and are built to last. Another good unit is sold by ARB. All these pumps draw between fifteen and twenty amps and thus should not be plugged into the cigarette lighter socket but attached using battery clips. The ARB unit can be permanently mounted under the hood. Quick-Air makes a ten-amp compressor that can be plugged into the cigarette lighter socket and performs well.

Auxiliary Driving Lights

There is a vast array of auxiliary lights on the market today, and selecting the best lights for your purpose can be a confusing process.

Auxiliary lights will greatly improve visibility in adverse weather conditions. Driving lights provide a strong, moderately wide beam to supplement headlamp high beams, giving improved lighting in the distance and to the sides of the main beam. Fog lamps throw a wide-dispersion, flat beam; and spots provide a high-power, narrow beam to improve lighting range directly in front of the vehicle. Rear-mounted auxiliary lights provide greatly improved visibility for backing up.

For off-highway use, you will need quality lights with strong mounting brackets. Some high-powered off-highway lights are not approved by the Department of Transportation for use on public roads.

Packing Checklist

Before embarking on any 4WD adventure, whether a lazy Sunday drive on an easy trail or a challenging climb over rugged terrain, be prepared. The following checklist will help you gather the items you need.

Essential

❒ Rain gear
❒ Small shovel or multipurpose ax, pick, and shovel
❒ Heavy-duty yank strap
❒ Spare tire that matches the other tires on the vehicle
❒ Maps
❒ Emergency medical kit
❒ Bottled water
❒ Blankets or space blankets
❒ Parka, gloves, and boots
❒ Spare vehicle key
❒ Jumper leads
❒ Heavy-duty flashlight
❒ Multipurpose tool, such as a Leatherman

Worth Considering

❒ Global Positioning System (GPS) receiver
❒ A set of light-truck, off-highway tires and matching spare
❒ Hi-Lift jack
❒ Additional tool kit
❒ CB radio
❒ Portable air compressor
❒ Tire gauge
❒ Tire-sealing kit
❒ Tire chains
❒ Handsaw and ax
❒ Binoculars
❒ Firearms
❒ Whistle
❒ Flares
❒ Vehicle fire extinguisher
❒ Gasoline, engine oil, and other vehicle fluids
❒ Portable hand winch
❒ Electric cooler

If Your Credit Cards Aren't Maxed-Out

❒ Electric, vehicle-mounted winch and associated recovery straps, shackles, and snatch blocks
❒ Auxiliary lights
❒ Locking differential(s)

Colorado Distance Chart

	ALAMOSA	ASPEN	BASALT	BRECKENRIDGE	CANON CITY	COLORADO SPRINGS	CORTEZ	CRAIG	CREEDE	CRESTED BUTTE	DEL NORTE	DENVER	DURANGO	FAIRPLAY	FORT COLLINS	GEORGETOWN	GLENWOOD SPRINGS	GRAND JUNCTION	GUNNISON	LAKE CITY	LAMAR	LEADVILLE	LIMON	MARBLE	MEEKER	MONTEZUMA	MONTROSE	OURAY	PITKIN	RANGELY	SAGUACHE	SALIDA	SEDALIA	SILVERTON	STEAMBOAT SPRINGS	STERLING	TELLURIDE	VAIL	WALDEN
ASPEN	163																																						
BASALT	181	18																																					
BRECKENRIDGE	155	99	121																																				
CANON CITY	138	143	162	96																																			
COLORADO SPRINGS	165	158	176	107	48																																		
CORTEZ	194	275	257	318	302	359																																	
CRAIG	279	159	141	145	241	268	377																																
CREEDE	68	200	219	192	175	233	169	337																															
CRESTED BUTTE	150	173	181	148	194	194	228	297	133																														
DEL NORTE	31	163	185	138	196	196	46	261	37	134																													
DENVER	233	164	185	86	116	71	387	234	261	203	224																												
DURANGO	149	245	227	255	273	314	46	297	165	118	91	342																											
FAIRPLAY	134	100	118	21	75	86	297	166	123	144	171	91	252																										
FORT COLLINS	298	219	240	141	181	136	442	288	316	311	288	64	397	146																									
GEORGETOWN	192	115	136	37	133	115	355	202	229	203	202	51	310	64	58	105																							
GLENWOOD SPRINGS	204	41	23	98	193	227	260	184	192	154	184	162	248	51	119	157	128																						
GRAND JUNCTION	250	129	111	185	281	315	200	222	260	442	262	250	169	206	217	157	88	113																					
GUNNISON	122	145	105	137	120	166	219	252	106	28	206	234	170	116	174	193	164	201	128																				
LAKE CITY	119	199	160	192	175	221	163	279	51	82	261	250	174	171	228	164	157	88	55																				
LAMAR	202	302	386	287	160	163	428	396	307	307	315	351	204	234	252	279	451	364	161	321																			
LEADVILLE	135	58	76	41	116	130	298	165	144	135	204	106	253	135	117	87	175	252	62	172	307																		
LIMON	234	247	269	169	120	77	428	298	170	266	234	86	383	55	210	197	146	246	333	119	172	189																	
MARBLE	193	52	34	132	196	262	222	165	135	150	197	215	192	117	239	239	35	122	148	57	398	122	280																
MEEKER	290	111	93	167	263	297	328	48	270	249	232	292	263	153	293	122	70	103	221	164	431	158	315	103															
MONTEZUMA	178	101	122	22	118	134	341	140	105	187	249	73	296	188	183	158	24	187	160	214	274	43	257	134	167														
MONTROSE	188	141	123	203	187	232	140	172	207	94	172	106	296	44	24	183	256	65	66	102	345	183	431	88	160	242													
OURAY	219	175	157	238	221	221	116	204	242	128	242	307	69	217	260	178	291	100	101	137	380	218	423	123	194	277	36												
PITKIN	133	149	132	141	125	170	227	259	193	55	286	197	120	210	265	208	155	27	82	283	121	243	98	201	196	93	128												
RANGELY	342	162	143	216	312	348	283	90	306	243	341	262	363	197	336	119	89	221	232	256	483	206	364	154	55	218	193	158	248										
SAGUACHE	52	126	145	118	101	147	90	306	74	97	352	90	37	155	242	186	197	155	242	96	254	98	219	140	254	141	136	170	81	305									
SALIDA	84	86	105	78	58	103	223	263	223	94	228	148	296	84	155	139	146	202	57	121	216	59	254	139	223	101	133	121	71	265	47								
SEDALIA	213	174	195	96	52	52	385	223	260	232	228	33	362	121	202	176	233	259	202	159	211	116	363	207	240	83	204	259	208	211	157	146							
SILVERTON	197	198	180	260	244	244	94	264	151	166	158	363	48	172	222	211	291	211	159	123	363	180	350	90	349	316	50	59	150	424	66	238	158	372					
STEAMBOAT SPRINGS	258	155	140	103	199	226	264	42	268	295	352	48	361	166	286	90	114	240	295	240	446	245	364	148	90	446	204	257	244	135	221	182	214	291	314				
STERLING	361	282	305	204	244	226	426	361	258	268	342	125	460	172	363	281	201	324	363	295	110	224	123	315	349	245	303	363	295	328	306	266	161	400	291				
TELLURIDE	252	205	187	267	251	251	77	271	158	172	228	460	102	102	166	208	129	130	166	102	409	247	453	152	223	306	50	66	157	72	221	197	379	50	458	481			
VAIL	171	95	83	37	133	133	373	209	181	172	307	102	307	58	134	60	53	148	208	154	303	37	185	95	128	39	238	238	158	135	185	95	112	204	66	261	93		
WALDEN	268	191	166	113	208	108	468	305	277	268	386	148	370	134	100	107	156	243	304	250	349	133	231	178	149	108	287	321	254	206	231	191	180	243	321	344	344	202	59
WALSENBURG	72	204	214	185	90	348	266	354	103	161	164	205	226	103	317	205	404	181	191	168	162	348	227	385	239	282	434	184	125	110	141	269	316	311	257	297	191	130	—

Distances are calculated using major highways.

Along the Trail

Towns, Ghost Towns, and Interesting Places

Alma

The community of Alma was established in 1872. When silver strikes became common in the area and prospectors began traveling over Mosquito Pass from Leadville to seek new claims, Alma became a desirable place to live. Not only silver, but also gold, copper, and lead were to be found in abundance in nearby Mount Bross and Mount Lincoln. A smelter was built as a division of the Boston and Colorado Smelting Works to process the ores from the surrounding mines. Alma became an important smelting center.

In the early days, locals were terrorized by a gang called "The Bloody Espinozas," who hated the Anglos. The Espinozas killed thirty-two victims, six of them from the Alma area. It is not known exactly why the Espinozas felt such hostility, but some people say it was because whites killed their parents. Others say it was because white men stole their land. Alma authorities placed a bounty on the heads of the Espinozas, but somehow the gang managed to evade even the most competent of posses. Finally, an organized party of miners was able to surround and kill all the Espinozas in a surprise attack. They cut off and carried one gang member's head back to Fort Garland to prove victory.

In 1937, the town's main street was nearly destroyed when a fire started in one of Alma's saloons and high winds spread it to a dozen buildings. Alma had no fire department to extinguish the flames. In the smoldering ruins was a local garage that had housed most of the town's automobiles. Most of the buildings you see on Alma's main street today were reconstructed after this fire.

Alma has seen high and low times, but it has never been completely deserted. It is alive today as a small town, still home to many local miners.

GPS COORDINATES: 39°17.03'N 106°03.72'W
TRAIL REFERENCE: North-Central Trail #15, North-Central Trail #18

Alpine Station and Tunnel

Two railroads waged a battle to be the first to connect the Gunnison area to Denver. The Denver & Rio Grande Railroad chose Marshall Pass as its route, so the owner of the Denver, South Park & Pacific Railroad, ex-Governor John Evans, financed a project to tunnel through the Sawatch Range.

A tunnel through the Continental Divide seemed a shorter and more strategic route. Bids were opened to build the Alpine Tunnel in 1879. The bore through the mountain was to be 1,800 feet long. However, the railroad underestimated the severity of the weather, the geologic rock formations at the site, and the difficulty of working at the 11,600-foot altitude, with wind gusts to fifty miles per hour and temperatures at forty degrees below zero.

In 1880, work began, and five hundred laborers worked day and night. Work camps were established at each end of the tunnel. Severe weather conditions and poor working conditions created and exacerbated gigantic labor problems. Workers walked off the site in droves when they experienced the high winds and freezing temperatures they were expected to endure. The railroad recruited workers from the East and Midwest by offering free transportation to Colorado. Over a hundred thousand men were employed, and many worked only a day or two before leaving. Sometimes the entire crew threatened to quit en masse.

The tunnel was bored by July 1881, almost a year behind schedule (which had allowed only six months to complete the project). When the competing Denver & Rio Grande reached Gunnison in early August, the discouraged Denver, South Park & Pacific Railroad company halted the Alpine Tunnel project for about six months. Finally, work continued, and the first train passed through the tunnel in December 1881.

Train exiting the Alpine Tunnel in 1896

The Alpine Station was developed at the west, or Pacific, end of the tunnel, with a bunkhouse where track workers lived, a storehouse, and a section house. The section house included a kitchen, a dining room, a pantry, and several bedrooms. A large stone engine house was built at the station in 1881. Aside from holding six engines, the engine house also contained a large coal bin and a water tank with a 9,516-gallon capacity, a turntable, and a locomotive service area. In 1883, a telegraph office was constructed.

Snowsheds were erected at each end of the tunnel bore to protect the rails. The shed on the Atlantic side was 150 feet in length, and the one on the Pacific side was 650 feet.

Train service through the Alpine Tunnel began in June 1882. The completed project was considered an engineering marvel. At sixteen places on the western descent, walls were laid to provide a shelf for rail construction. The most spectacular shelf is at the Palisades, a mile below the tunnel, where a stone wall 450 feet long, 30 feet high, and 2 feet thick was built from hand-cut stones without mortar. You can see this wall along the drive to the Alpine Tunnel. Over 500,000 feet of California redwood were used to reinforce the tunnel, as workers found loose rock and decomposed granite instead of self-supporting granite. The total cost of the tunnel was over a quarter of a million dollars.

Many problems plagued the Alpine Tunnel during its period of operation. In March 1884, a train whistle caused a severe snowslide that swept away the town of Woodstock and killed many of its residents. In 1906, a fire destroyed the wood buildings at Alpine Station; even the stone buildings were demolished when they collapsed from the intense heat of the blaze. In 1910, several people lost their lives when the tunnel caved in. The tunnel was never reopened.

Inside the Alpine Tunnel in 1975

The first rails were removed in November 1918; however, the rails in the tunnel itself remain in place. Eventually the railroad property was sold.

You can drive to the Alpine Station only from the west side. The telegraph station has been restored, and you can see the ruins of the stone engine house and section house. Volunteers have reconstructed the station platform and relaid 120 feet of the original Denver, South Park & Pacific rails.

GPS COORDINATES: 38°38.44'N 106°24.44'W

TRAIL REFERENCE: South-Central Trail #5, South-Central Trail #8

Alta

Alta was a company town for the Gold King Mine, which was discovered in 1878 and operated as recently as the 1940s. Gold, silver, copper, and lead were mined and transported in aerial tramcars from the Gold King and other mines to the Ophir Loop, two miles further down the mountain.

Alta's Gold King was a very rich mine, but it was expensive to operate because of its high altitude. Fortunately, L. L. Nunn found a way to reduce expenses by bringing electrical power to the mine. In 1881, he organized a contract with the Westinghouse company to construct an electrical plant in Ames, less than three miles away. The plant harnessed the San Miguel River's power, transmitting 3,000 volts of alternating current back up to the Gold King Mine. Encouraged by the success of this first alternating current power transmission plant in America, Nunn expanded his venture to supply the city of Telluride, as well as many nearby mines, and installed transmission lines across Imogene Pass. Subsequently, electricity became widely used in Colorado and the world.

There were three mills at Alta, all of which have burned down. The last one burned in 1945 while seven men were underground. The

View of Alta, circa 1895

superintendent ordered the portal to be dynamited in order to cut off the draft that was feeding the fire, even though his son was one of the men inside.

Amos power station in 1933, built in 1881 to service the Alta Mine

Due to the longevity of the Gold King Mine, Alta thrived longer than most high-country mining towns. Visitors can still see quite a few well-preserved old buildings, including a boardinghouse, cabins, and some more substantial homes. Alta never had a church or a post office.

GPS COORDINATES: 37°53.16'N 107°51.15'W

TRAIL REFERENCE: Southwest Trail #10

Animas Forks

Animas Forks, originally called La Plata City, experienced its first silver strike in 1875. As an enticement to live near timberline and brave the harsh winters, the government offered settlers free lots and aid for building homes.

Within a year, settlers had erected thirty cabins, a post office, a saloon, a general store, a hotel, and two mills; the town boasted a population of two hundred. All the buildings were well constructed, with finished lumber and shingled roofs. The jailhouse, a rough, box-like structure made of two-by-six lumber and consisting of two cells and a jailer's office in front, was a rare exception to the building standard.

In 1877, Otto Mears constructed a wagon road to Eureka, extending it from Silverton to Lake City as a toll road. Animas Forks became an important junction for the roads that headed in all directions to the area's many mining camps. Much of the town's other activity centered on its mill, which treated ore from Red Cloud Mine in Mineral Point.

Snow presented a huge problem for Animas Forks. Although the town was considered a year-round mining community, the population dropped in the

The famous Walsh house in Animas Forks, one of many buildings still standing in the ghost town

wintertime. In 1884, the population reached four hundred in the summer but dropped to a dozen men, three women, and twenty dogs in the winter. A winter storm that same year lasted for twenty-three days.

During the 1880s, telephone lines were installed, running from Lake City and passing over the 12,500-foot Continental Divide near Engineer Pass. Stagecoaches ran daily from Lake City to Silverton via Engineer Pass.

Mrs. Eckard, the first woman in Animas Forks, ran an extremely popular boardinghouse. Eckard won the favor of the local miners by extending them credit. When one freeloader slipped out of town without settling his account for three months' lodging, a vigilante committee set out after him. They caught him in Silverton and threatened to lynch him. He paid up, and no further bad debts were reported!

At its peak, Animas Forks was home to about 1,500 residents. Located at an elevation of 11,584 feet, it once boasted that it was the largest city in the world at this altitude.

Although its prosperity began to wane by the 1890s and the town was nearly deserted by 1901, Animas Forks experienced a resurgence of activity between 1904 and 1916. Otto Mears extended the railroad in 1904 and planned an elaborate system of seven snowsheds to permit the line to operate from Lake City to Silverton. Snowdrifts in the area sometimes piled over twenty-five feet high. When the first big snowslide of the season destroyed the first of Mears's sheds, his idea was abandoned. The remains of this shed are clearly visible along Southwest Trail #4.

A view of Animas Forks in 1875

Animas Forks today

The Gold Prince Mill, constructed in 1904, operated until 1910 and was moved to Eureka in 1917. Animas Forks rapidly declined once more.

In 1942, the railroad tracks were removed and scrapped. The railroad bed became a road again after the tracks were removed.

Today, Animas Forks is a fascinating ghost town, consisting of about a dozen houses. The Columbus Mill still stands, as do several other structures, including an elaborate house with a bay window. The foundations of the Gold Prince Mill remain at the southern end of town.

GPS COORDINATES: 37°55.89'N 107°34.23'W

TRAIL REFERENCE: Southwest Trail #1, Southwest Trail #4, Southwest Trail #5

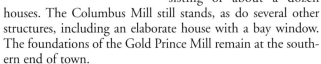

Ashcroft

After silver strikes in 1879, this site was first settled as Castle Forks. Soon renamed Ashcroft, in its early days the town served as the gateway to Aspen for travelers coming over Taylor Pass or Cottonwood Pass. Established at about the same period as Aspen, Ashcroft seemed likely to become the more successful of the two.

The Ashcroft post office was established in 1880. The town had five hotels, a newspaper, a school, a jail, a doctor, a bowling alley, several stores, and many saloons.

In 1881, Horace Tabor (of Leadville) purchased a part share in the Tam O'Shanter silver mine near Ashcroft. It was never a profitable investment, because transporting ore from an elevation of over 13,500 feet proved too difficult and expensive. Tabor and his wife, Baby Doe, enjoyed a lavish home in Ashcroft that served as a pleasant summer retreat and a haven from the Leadville gossip. Baby Doe enjoyed Ashcroft because she was a popular figure there.

Two factors led to the decline of Ashcroft. One was the completion of Independence Pass, which opened accessibility to nearby Aspen. Then, in 1887, the Denver & Rio Grande completed a railway line into Aspen, which encouraged Ashcroft's residents to migrate to Aspen.

One man remained for years after Ashcroft was deserted. If Aspen gossip can be trusted, Jack Leahy (nicknamed "the hermit of Ashcroft") didn't move away until 1935, four years before his death.

In 1974, the Aspen Historical Society leased Ashcroft's town site from the U.S. Forest Service in order to preserve the historic remains. While some of the buildings you see there today are original, others were moved there to replace deteriorated ones so that tourists can safely walk around and explore the resurrected ghost town.

GPS COORDINATES: 39°03.22'N 106°47.94'W

TRAIL REFERENCE: South-Central Trail #27

Aspen

The area in which the town of Aspen is now found was originally home to many Ute Indians. Fear of these tribes kept settlers out of the region until miners spreading out from Leadville found silver veins in the surrounding mountains. Originally named Ute, the city now known as Aspen formed as a mining camp in 1879.

B. Clark Wheeler arrived and platted the town in 1880, naming it Aspen. He had big plans for the town. At that time, the town site was a mix of log cabins, frame structures, and tents. The "business district" consisted of a hotel, a restaurant, an assay office, a few stores, and several saloons.

Aspen quickly began to flourish and prosper with the discovery of mines such as the Smuggler. Other important mines were the Durant, Mollie Gibson, Aspen, and Midnight.

An early prospector sold a half interest in the Smuggler Mine for a burro and fifty dollars. The burro soon died, but the Smuggler went on to produce millions, including the largest silver nugget in the world. The nugget weighed 2,060 pounds and had to be cut down to 1,840 pounds in order to fit through the mine shaft.

The first road into Aspen came across Taylor Pass from Buena Vista. In 1881, Independence Pass opened, connecting Aspen and Leadville and making Aspen much more accessible.

Jerome B. Wheeler (no relation to B. Clark Wheeler), founder of Macy's department stores, is credited with bringing prosperity to Aspen in 1884 with the development of mining interests. He invested much money in Aspen, opened a bank, and purchased a smelter to provide a local market for silver ore. He also established and edited the *Aspen Daily Times* newspaper.

Wheeler backed the construction of the Hotel Jerome (330

East Main Street), which had its grand opening in 1889. He outfitted the lavish three-story hotel with fine European furnishings, electricity, a barber shop, a billiard parlor, and an elegant dining hall. The hotel even had its own greenhouse, where staff gardeners cultivated vegetables and flowers during the winter. A water-powered elevator, which brought guests to the second and third floors, operated until 1952 when it was replaced by an electric one.

Jerome Wheeler also backed the construction of the Wheeler Grand Opera House (330 East Hyman Avenue). The building, with its exquisite woodwork, brass trim, and plush upholstery and curtains, suffered from two fires in 1912 but was refurbished in 1947.

In 1885, Aspen became the first Colorado city to have electric lights. By 1887, two railroads were servicing the community, and during the first month of rail operations more than a million dollars' worth of ore was shipped out of the state. The first of the two railroad lines was a spur of the Denver & Rio Grande narrow-gauge from Glenwood Springs. The other, the Colorado Midland, was a standard-gauge railway and reached Aspen from Leadville through the Hagerman Tunnel. Both railways were a huge benefit to the miners, who had previously paid about fifty to one hundred dollars per ton to transport ore; with the arrival of the railroad, costs were reduced to ten to fifteen dollars per ton.

One merchant, H. P. Cowenhoven, was a popular and good-hearted man who was a "soft touch" for the less fortunate miners. He justified a number of worthless accounts on his books by his theory "The boys have to eat!" One miner with an outstanding tab of four hundred dollars finally settled his bill by paying Cowenhoven with a half share of his Aspen Mine, which he thought was worthless. Needless to say, the mine became extremely successful, and Cowenhoven was made a very rich man.

By 1890, the town reached a population of about twelve thousand residents, making it the third largest city in Colorado. Aspen had four schools, four newspapers, eight churches, three banks, a hospital, nine hotels, five drugstores, six bakeries, nine restaurants, thirty-one saloons, and its own brewery. By 1892, one-sixth of all silver in the United States was mined from the Aspen area.

The silver crash of 1893 had a devastating outcome for Aspen. Over eighteen hundred workers lost their jobs; and within one month, all the mines shut down. The crash dealt a terrible blow to the town's economy, and the population began to plummet. Some of the remaining miners agreed to take pay cuts. The miners who stayed on eventually discovered gold, lead, and copper; but the town did not recover. Aspen came so close to dying with its lack of population in the 1920s that it almost became another of Colorado's ghost towns.

Aspen's first ski resort was established and opened in 1936. Further development of the slopes was abandoned during World War II due to lack of funds. In 1946, a group of developers formed the Aspen Skiing Corporation in order to raise capital and expand development. A 3.5-mile chair lift (the longest in the world at the time) was erected, and over four miles of trails were cleared.

Aspen is currently a world-famous playground for the wealthy. A modern town, it maintains its nineteenth-century Victorian appeal through the numerous buildings and sites listed on the National Register of Historic Places. The ski area continues to be one of the most popular in the world.

GPS COORDINATES: 39°11.44'N 106°49.13'W

TRAIL REFERENCE: South-Central Trail #27

Baldwin

Baldwin came to life in 1897 with the discovery of gold nearby. It shifted to coal mining operations in 1909.

Although it was a prosperous camp, Baldwin was plagued by labor strikes. During one strike union workers killed a "scab." On another occasion, strikers blew up a bridge. On Christmas Eve in 1927, a miner killed a mine superintendent over a labor dispute.

The coal mines closed in the 1940s, and the post office discontinued service in 1949. All residents had moved from Baldwin except one man, who lived there happily until his death in 1967.

Some buildings from Baldwin still exist along Ohio Pass. However, the Gunnison Chamber of Commerce advises that these buildings stand on private property, and trespassing is not allowed.

GPS COORDINATES: 38°45.49'N 107°02.82'W

TRAIL REFERENCE: South-Central Trail #24

Basalt

First known as Frying Pan City, this community was a wild railroad construction town along the Colorado Midland line to Aspen. The name was derived from the phrase "The fishing was so good, the trout jumped out of the river and into the frying pan!"

Frying Pan City became known as Aspen Junction when it became a station stop. It consisted of several saloons, restaurants, stores, and a boardinghouse. Even after the crews moved on to other sites, Aspen Junction remained riotous and was known for its gamblers and seductive ladies.

In 1891, two trains collided just outside of Aspen Junction. A steam valve on one engine broke, and passengers were sprayed with steam and boiling water. Ten died and many others were badly burned in this tragic accident.

Fires throughout the years have taken their toll on the town. In 1892, the train depot was completely destroyed in a fire. Six years later, a kerosene lantern in a boardinghouse exploded, and high winds spread the flames throughout the town. In 1900, a kerosene lamp in a restaurant exploded, and the blaze consumed several buildings.

According to town lore, President Theodore Roosevelt once snubbed Aspen Junction because he felt it did not merit his attention. When he was touring, the town anticipated his arrival by decorating the train station and gathering to cheer him on. Roosevelt, in turn, did not even bother to show himself to the crowd.

Because Aspen Junction was so often confused with Aspen and Grand Junction, in 1894 the town took the name Basalt, after the nearby Basalt Peaks.

Basalt today is a small transportation and ranching town in an attractive setting.

GPS COORDINATES: 39°22.15'N 107°01.96'W

TRAIL REFERENCE: North-Central Trail #16

Boreas

Named for the Greek god of the north wind, Boreas was originally established as a wagon stop for travelers between Breckenridge and Como.

The Denver, South Park & Pacific Railroad narrow-gauge crossed through this route in 1884. A depot, section house, engine house, and other buildings were constructed, as well as a 600-foot snowshed, later extended by another 350 feet. For a while, this railroad run was the highest in America. The steep inclines, sharp curves, and abrupt drop-offs were constantly swept by storms and wind. There were eleven snowsheds along the route, and the grades were so steep that engines were allowed to pull a maximum of only three cars. When the Barnum circus traveled the Boreas route, the engines couldn't pull the heavy cars up the steep grade. The circus was stalled until someone had the brilliant idea to unload the elephants and have them tow the engines to the top.

Snow was a big problem on Boreas Pass. Winter storms began early, and by November, there were often ten feet of snow to contend with. In 1899, a severe winter snowstorm isolated Boreas for one and a half months. No trains ran that year between February and April. Supplies ran short, so two men set out for Como on snowshoes. It was just too cold and too far—their frozen bodies were found buried in the snow.

Even without snow, the Boreas route was treacherous. In 1901, during perfectly fine weather, a runaway train with thirteen cars of ore derailed and crashed. The brakeman was killed.

By 1905, Boreas Station was deserted except for the railroad workers who remained at the pass to keep the tracks clear of snow so the trains could keep operating.

In 1936, two locomotives were descending from the pass at about twenty miles per hour when they hit a frozen snowdrift and plunged down the mountain at Catastrophe Curve. One engine slid two hundred feet from the track, and the other, fifty feet. Temporary tracks had to be built to retrieve the train. A series of cables, ropes, pulleys, and chains were used to stand the trains upright and haul them back up the mountain.

In 1937, the railroad was shut down in South Park and over Boreas Pass. In 1952, the railroad bed was converted to an automobile road on the Breckenridge side; and four years later, it was converted to an automobile road on the Como side.

The walls of a two-story house and a partially roofed shed remain standing atop the pass. In 1996, the section house was rebuilt. When walking around you can also see boards and rotting logs that were once part of the snowsheds. Many other historic items can be found along Boreas Pass between Breckenridge and Como.

GPS COORDINATES: 39°24.64'N 105°58.07'W
TRAIL REFERENCE: North-Central Trail #10

Bowerman

Originally named Nugget City, the camp was laid out in 1903 by J. C. Bowerman, who claimed to have found extremely rich gold deposits nearby. It was incorporated as Bowerman in 1904.

Bowerman, an unlucky prospector, had for years depended on his wife's odd jobs to bring in enough money so they could eat and he could search for minerals. Then, one day, it seemed his luck had changed. Bowerman told his wife that he had struck rich ore, but he wished to keep the find a tight secret in an effort to secure it for himself. His wife, excited by the new discovery, simply could not keep her mouth shut. She boasted to all who would listen that she would soon be rich. Before long, word spread like wildfire, and some five hundred miners rushed the area and swarmed all over her husband's property.

Newspapers announced far and wide that Bowerman had the potential to become the greatest gold camp of the twentieth century. The town sprang up as a result, and contained two hotels, a newspaper, five saloons, five gambling halls, and several other businesses.

In addition to J. C. Bowerman's Independent Mine, several other claims were established; but they produced only low-grade ore. Meanwhile, despite his original declaration that he had found rich gold, Bowerman failed to ship out any ore. He became more secretive, fenced off the property, and would not show the mine to anyone. He came up with all kinds of excuses for his failure to produce.

The five hundred townspeople who had been lured to the area by Bowerman's rich find were bitterly disappointed by their below-average finds. Although some ore was shipped out, even from Bowerman's mine, people began drifting away. By 1910, the mining ended and the town was abandoned.

The site of Bowerman is about three miles north of Waunita Hot Springs. The buildings have been reduced to ruins, some of which are visible from the road but are on private property.

GPS COORDINATES: 38°33.75'N 106°30.69'W
TRAIL REFERENCE: South-Central Trail #3

Breckenridge

Breckenridge was settled after the discovery of placer gold in 1859 and named for President James Buchanan's vice president, John C. Breckinridge. This political maneuver helped speed the establishment of a post office in 1860. However, when the vice president later fell out of favor with the American public, the spelling of the town's name was changed to Breckenridge.

From the beginning, Breckenridge grew quickly and became a convenient center for commerce. Supply wagons constantly rolled in and out of town. Stores, hotels, and saloons sprang up, and the population was soon estimated at nine thousand. The first stagecoach entered Breckenridge in 1860.

When the residents decided they wanted to make Breckenridge the county seat of Summit County instead of nearby Parkville, their methods weren't entirely aboveboard. One night in 1862, Breckenridge townsfolk held a secretive raid on the Parkville city hall, after which all the county records went missing. Some time later, the records were conveniently "discovered" in the new county seat of Breckenridge.

The boom in placer mining lasted only about three years. As in many of Colorado's mining towns, when the gold began to play out, so did the number of residents. By 1866, the population dropped to less than five hundred.

It is rumored that the ensuing silver discoveries in the late

1870s in Breckenridge were completely serendipitous. Supposedly, a gold miner was getting his hair cut one afternoon and chatting with his barber about the massive silver rush in Leadville. It was then that the barber looked down and noticed large amounts of silver dust in his customer's hair.

In the 1880s Breckenridge underwent a second gold boom when prospectors discovered new mines and new techniques for extracting ore from fissures and veins. Dozens of new mines were established in the mountains and gulches near Breckenridge. This helped the population climb back to around two thousand by 1885. The boom was also helped along when the Denver, South Park & Pacific Railroad constructed a Breckenridge depot in 1882.

The town took on a much more permanent look, as log cabins were replaced with attractive Victorian-style homes with gingerbread trim, false-fronted stores, and other commercial buildings styled with elaborate wood trim and attractive architectural detail.

Breckenridge had its share of brothels, but it is interesting to note that most of the prostitutes lived in their own community across the river to the west of town. When miners said they were going "over the Blue," they meant that they were heading to the prostitute district on the other side of the Blue River. Considering that the ratio of men to women in Breckenridge was about thirty to one, the brothels were a welcome outlet for the miners.

Thanks to the railroad and the good roads over Hoosier, Loveland, Argentine, Webster, and Boreas passes, Breckenridge never suffered from transportation problems that plagued many Colorado mountain towns.

Breckenridge's third gold boom occurred in 1898, with the discovery of dredge mining. This type of mining utilized dredge boats, or barges, floated along the rivers and gulches. The residents tolerated the deafening noise caused by the boats because dredge mining provided a number of jobs at a time when mines all over Colorado were going out of business.

One evening in 1898, Pug Ryan and his gang held up the patrons of Breckenridge's elaborate Denver Hotel. Ryan's gang quickly stole the cash from the barroom and were intent on stealing the hotel safe, but one of their guns accidentally discharged, creating havoc. They were tracked to a cabin in Kokomo (between Breckenridge and Leadville), and a bloody shoot-out ensued. Two members of the posse were killed, as were two of Pug Ryan's gang. Ryan escaped and was not captured until four years later, when the tattoo "Pug" on his arm gave him away in Seattle. He was convicted and died in prison in 1931.

Surprisingly, some school children on a picnic discovered the loot from the robbery ten years later. Included in the goods found was a watch belonging to the manager of the Denver Hotel. When he heard of the discovery, he took the first train to Kokomo and dug around in the dirt until he found his stolen diamond stickpin, too.

Winter snowstorms later that same year were particularly difficult for Breckenridge. The railroad tracks were buried so deeply that trains couldn't reach the town for seventy-nine days. Supplies and food ran so low that when the train finally arrived in April with supplies and fifty bags of overdue mail, the townspeople greeted it in wild celebration.

After the third gold boom, the population of Breckenridge fell into decline again. In 1900 the population was listed as down to fewer than one thousand. During World War II, Breckenridge looked very much like a ghost town.

Today, Breckenridge is alive and prospering. The town found new gold in a ski area, developed in 1962. It has since evolved as a world-class resort. While the town still retains much of its Victorian styling and charm, it is now mixed with the towering condos and "Victorianesque" homes of more modern times. The only real telltale sign of the town's rich mining history lies in the countless gravel piles left from the many years of dredging.

GPS COORDINATES: 39°28.93'N 106°02.74'W
TRAIL REFERENCE: North-Central Trail #8, North-Central Trail #10

Bridal Veil Falls

Just off Black Bear Pass, east of Telluride, is a 365-foot high waterfall—the highest in Colorado. On the canyon rim above the falls is a restored hydroelectric plant, built in 1904. Now a National Historic Landmark, it once generated power for nearby mines.

GPS COORDINATES: 37°55.15N 107°46.16'W
TRAIL REFERENCE: Southwest Trail #11, Overlooked from Southwest Trail #8

Buckskin Joe

Buckskin Joe mining camp was founded in 1859 by a group of prospectors led by a trapper named Joe Higgenbottom, nicknamed "Buckskin" because of the deerskin clothing he wore.

It is rumored that a hunter first discovered gold in the area when he shot at his prey and hit a rich gold vein instead, but it is more probable that the find was made by more conventional methods.

The area's best mine was the Phillips, later renamed the Buckskin Joe Mine. News of the Phillips discovery caused miners to pour over the mountains from Leadville with hopes of finding riches in Buckskin Joe. The thriving little town reached its peak in the 1860s with a population of one thousand. Saloons, hotels, and gambling halls provided employment for at least half of the residents, many of whom were women.

Horace and Augusta Tabor were the first managers of the first post office in Buckskin Joe, opened in 1861. The Tabors also ran the general store.

Also in 1861, a devastating outbreak of smallpox hit Buckskin Joe. According to legend, a beautiful dancer named Silverheels—so named because of the silver heels on her dancing shoes—nursed the afflicted miners. Silverheels remained when many others fled town, so that she could cook and clean for the suffering miners. When she eventually caught the virus herself, her beautiful face was disfigured by scars. With her beauty ravaged, she disappeared. The miners later raised about five thousand dollars to show their gratitude, but Silverheels could not be found. Eventually all funds were returned to the donors. It is rumored that a black-veiled woman occasionally turned up at the Buckskin Joe Cemetery to visit the graves of the smallpox victims. Perhaps this was the mysterious Silverheels, visiting the graves of her friends, with her veil in place to cover her disfigured face. No one ever knew, because the woman disappeared before anyone could approach her. Majestic Mount Silverheels was named in her honor.

Although a dozen mills operated in the area during Buckskin Joe's peak years, the high times were short-lived. By 1866, the mines played out. The population dropped, and the county seat moved to Fairplay that same year. The post office remained open until 1873.

Little evidence of the town remains at the original site of Buckskin Joe, because most of the buildings were moved to a tourist park in Fairplay.

GPS COORDINATES: 39°17.48'N 106°05.16'W

TRAIL REFERENCE: North-Central Trail #18

Burrows Park, Tellurium, Sterling, Whitecross

Between Lake City and Cinnamon Pass, a cluster of mining "towns" sprouted up in the alpine meadow of Burrows Park between 1877 and 1880. The park was five miles long and a half-mile wide. The exact locations of the camps are disputed, but the general area is about ten miles southwest of Lake City, at the western end of the valley.

Burrows Park was the name of one of the camps, founded in 1877.

About a mile south of Burrows Park, there was a community named Tellurium. This very small camp had only about a dozen people, who hoped to find tellurium there. The highly optimistic group built an expensive mill. Unfortunately, Tellurium never became prosperous, and it soon was deserted.

Sterling was located a short distance beyond Tellurium, toward Animas Forks.

Nearer the Continental Divide toward Cinnamon Pass, Whitecross was the largest of the settlements and served as the center of activity for the other camps. Whitecross's post office, established in 1880, was first called Burrows Park, after the region. Two years later it was renamed Whitecross.

Many men who lived in this area worked at the Tabasco Mine and Mill, which operated from 1901 to 1904 and was one of the first to use electric alternating current. Tabasco, the Louisiana hot sauce manufacturing company, owned both the mine and the mill. Ruins of the mine are scattered around the summit of Cinnamon Pass.

GPS COORDINATES: 37°56.24'N 107°27.63'W

TRAIL REFERENCE: Southwest Trail #1

Camp Bird

In 1896, Thomas Walsh, an Irishman, discovered very rich gold in Imogene Basin. He immediately purchased more than one hundred claims in the area and consolidated them under the name Camp Bird.

Camp Bird Mine today

Camp Bird, a company town that grew up around the Camp Bird Mine, soon became the second largest gold producer in Colorado, turning out over $1 million per year. The camp had its own post office, which was established in 1898 and discontinued in 1918.

Walsh furnished a boardinghouse for his employees with marble-topped lavatories, electric lights, steam heat, and even a piano. Meals were deliciously prepared and served on china plates.

Winter and snow were always problems for the community. The men often had to tunnel out of their quarters to reach the mine. Snowslides killed several men over the years. It was necessary to construct a two-mile aerial tramway from the mines to the mill. Camp Bird and the Tomboy Mine were linked together by underground tunnels.

Six years after discovering the prosperous mine, millionaire Walsh sold the properties to an English company for $3.5 million cash, a half million in shares of stock, and royalties on future profits. Upon selling the mine, Walsh showed his appreciation to his employees by issuing bonus checks of up to $5,000.

With profits from Camp Bird, Walsh bought a mansion in Washington, D.C., and his wife and daughter hobnobbed with international society. They became "jet-setters" of their era. Walsh's daughter, Evalyn, married Edward B. McLean, whose family owned the *Washington Post* newspaper. As wedding gifts, each family gave the couple $100,000, which they supposedly spent before the honeymoon was over. Evalyn Walsh McLean later purchased the famed Hope Diamond, which is now on display at the Smithsonian Institution.

GPS COORDINATES: 37°58.28'N 107°43.59'W

TRAIL REFERENCE: Southwest Trail #7, Southwest Trail #8

Camp Cochetopa

Camp Cochetopa was an isolated mining camp that sprang up at the site of an old Indian agency in 1880. Originally called Kimbrellville, it was later renamed Cochetopa, after the busy Cochetopa Trail. Cochetopa is a Ute Indian word meaning "buffalo high place" or "pass of the buffalo." The town was reportedly a rather wild place with a number of saloons and its own brewery.

GPS COORDINATES: 38°11.97'N 106°49.63'W

TRAIL REFERENCE: South-Central Trail #21

Capitol City

Rich silver discoveries in 1877 about ten miles west of Lake City brought prospectors to the area. The town of Galena City began as a tent city, but the tents were soon replaced by more permanent structures.

George S. Lee, a miner with grand plans, had the town's name changed to Capitol City because he was certain that Colorado would move its capital to the San Juan Mountains, and he would live in the governor's mansion. To aid in the construction of Capitol City, Lee built a sawmill and planing mill. He also erected the Henson Creek Smelter, one mile below the town, to process ore from the many mines nearby. Additionally, he took over another mill at the other end of town. He seemed to play a part in virtually everything that went on in Capitol City.

A town site of two hundred acres was laid out, and a schoolhouse was built, though the population never exceeded four hundred, with only a handful of students.

Lee built himself a large and elegant house at the edge of town to be the governor's mansion, where he and his wife entertained lavishly. Their home

The house built to be the Colorado governor's mansion, circa 1930

even had a ballroom and orchestra pit. Bricks imported from Pueblo were estimated to have cost a dollar apiece!

However, Lee's efforts did not work out the way he had planned. Capitol City never even became the county seat. His expectations were far too grand, and the ore played out too soon. The town declined in the 1880s and 1890s. The silver crash seemed to signal the end, but the discovery of gold in 1900 revived hopes. These hopes were short-lived though, as the gold proved limited.

GPS COORDINATES: 38°00.47'N 107°27.93'W
TRAIL REFERENCE: Southwest Trail #2

Carson

There were actually two towns named Carson about two miles from each other that were active at different times. The newer one is lower in elevation and was a gold camp. The older one rests atop the Continental Divide and was a silver camp.

The original Carson was one of the most inaccessible mining camps in Colorado and was completely exposed to Colorado's harsh winters. It was first settled in 1882 and named for Christopher Carson, who staked out the Bonanza King Mine, the first claim in the area. During the late 1880s, approximately 100 miners were working 150 claims. The town is believed to have met its demise in the 1893 silver crash, although some gold discoveries may have kept it going a while longer. Little or no evidence of the town remains on this site.

In 1896, the discovery of ores rich in gold spurred the growth and development of "New Carson" on the north side of the Divide. The town became increasingly active throughout the decade, with its population peaking at about five hundred. Much of the activity centered on the Bachelor Mine.

Miners reached Carson from Lake City on the northern side of the Continental Divide by a difficult wagon road up Wager Gulch. In 1887, a road following Lost Creek into town was completed from Creede on the south side.

By 1909, only six prospectors were still working in Carson. The remains of "New Carson" are well preserved, with several buildings still standing today.

GPS COORDINATES: 37°52.13'N 107°21.72'W
TRAIL REFERENCE: Southwest Trail #6

Clark

Clark was dependent upon the nearby Greenville Mine, which produced gold, silver, and copper. In addition to mining, some lumbering was carried out in the area. The post office was established in 1889.

It is not clear whether Clark was named for Rufus Clark, the first postmaster, or Worthington Clark, a property owner with local stagecoach operations.

GPS COORDINATES: 40°42.33'N 106°55.08'W
TRAIL REFERENCE: Northwest Trail #3

Columbine

Columbine was settled in 1897, after the Royal Flush Mine was discovered two miles to the east. The town is nestled in a grove of aspen about four miles north of Hahns Peak and was named for Colorado's state flower.

Columbine's primary industry was centered on the Royal Flush Mine, which operated sporadically over the years. After the Royal Flush Mill closed down in 1918, the town went into decline.

Logging and sheep herding in the area helped support the town for a while. A sheepherder once gambled away his wages and those of two herders who worked for him. Rather than fess up to his men, he killed them and roasted their bodies over a campfire!

Today, a store and a few seasonal cabins and other buildings remain in Columbine. The town functions mainly as a stop for tourists traveling along the forest route.

GPS COORDINATES: 40°51.23'N 106°57.90'W
TRAIL REFERENCE: Northwest Trail #3

Como

Originally Stubbs Ranch, a stage stop for wagons crossing over Boreas Pass into Breckenridge, Como eventually developed and became more diversified. Established in 1873, the town of Como started as a tent community, built by the railroad to house the thousands of workers constructing the Denver, South Park & Pacific Railroad. The many Italian immigrants working on the railroad had named their community after Lake Como in Italy.

Aside from the railroad activity, there was also some coal mining in Como and the surrounding area, which increased as the railroad was being built. In 1893, a huge explosion in the King Cole coal mine killed sixteen miners.

Como was rowdy, with its share of fights and racial bigotry. In 1879, some Chinese miners were brought in to work the coal mines. This incensed the Italians, who beat up the man responsible for offering the employment and then chased the Chinese out of town.

In 1864, a group of outlaws known as the Reynolds Gang robbed a stagecoach of its gold box near Como. One of the bandits was killed by an ensuing posse, and the other five were later shot on their way to jail, evidently for not revealing where the treasure was hidden. As the story goes, the gold was never found, and people still search for the missing fortune.

Although thousands of people passed through Como on their way over Boreas Pass in search of silver and gold riches, the town had an estimated population of only about five hundred permanent residents.

Como experienced a number of fires through the years. In 1896, a fire destroyed the forty-three-room Pacific Hotel. A blaze in 1909 burned down a number of railroad buildings, which were never rebuilt. In 1935, a fire destroyed the wooden section of the railroad's huge roundhouse. The stone portion remains and is listed on the National Register of Historic Places.

The Denver, South Park & Pacific Railroad stopped running in 1937. In 1956, the railroad bed was converted to an automobile road.

GPS COORDINATES: 39°18.64'N 105°53.15'W

TRAIL REFERENCE: North-Central Trail #10

Creede

Creede was named for Nicholas C. Creede, a hard-luck prospector who was exploring the mountains near Wagon Wheel Gap in 1889. Picking at some rocks as he ate his lunch one afternoon, he looked closely at the ore he found and exclaimed, "Holy Moses!" That became the name of the mine he established. The area saw a real boom after that, when word got out that David Moffat, president of the Denver & Rio Grande Railroad, and some other investors purchased the rich claim for $70,000. Before long, a settlement developed in the narrow winding canyon of Willow Creek. This initial settlement was first known as Creede, then Upper Creede, and, finally, North Creede.

Creede saw upwards of two hundred people arriving each day. In the first few months, there were more than ten thousand men, women, and children scouring the mountains in search of a rich claim.

The men mined by day and sought entertainment at night; so flimsy tents became saloons, with boards laid across boxes to constitute drinking bars. Because property on the outskirts of town cost a fraction of the price for real estate in the center of town, some drinking establishments were even set up on poles straddling the creek. The canyon was so narrow, it could facilitate only one main street.

Because of the narrow, deep gorge, Creede was a dangerous place to live. Heavy rains and melting snows often caused water levels to run high. Dangerous flows of water have been known to roar through the area annually. Over the years, numerous floods have washed away buildings and sections of the town. Consequently, many miners built their cabins and pitched their tents as far up the sides of the canyon as possible.

Creede (originally Jimtown) and North Creede are actually about a mile apart from each other. When the population grew south beyond the cliffs, Jimtown was established as the commercial center of the area.

While many people made money on mining claims, an equal number made their fortunes on property claims. They would buy lots and then (with the soaring real estate market) unload them for a beefy profit.

There are some colorful characters associated with Creede. Bob Ford moved to Creede several years after killing Jesse James in Missouri in 1882. A man with a reputation, who considered himself the "boss," Ford was not a popular man. He opened the biggest tent-saloon and gambling house in town, called the Exchange. In June 1892, Edward "Red" O'Kelly ambled into Ford's saloon and gunned him down. Some say that O'Kelly was seeking revenge as a relation of Jesse James, and some say he was settling a gambling debt. The underworld of Creede paid for Ford's funeral; although the service was not much, the wake afterwards became a real party. The revelry lasted for days: Copious quantities of whiskey were served, and people danced on Ford's grave. O'Kelly fled but was arrested and tried for murder in Pueblo. He was sentenced to life in jail at the Canon City penitentiary but was released early in 1900. However, he could not stay out of trouble and was killed three years later by an Oklahoma City police officer.

Above: Creede in 1890, before the fire
Below: After the fire on June 5, 1892

Bat Masterson managed a saloon in town on behalf of a Denver firm. Since the usual way to settle differences in Creede was with guns, when one day a drunk slapped Bat, the hushed saloon ceased drinking to watch the gunman take revenge. Luckily for the drunk, Masterson merely laughed and told him to try again when he was sober.

A branch of the Denver & Rio Grande came through town in 1891. People of all walks of life flooded into the town on every train to the overcrowded region. A melting pot of unique and interesting people, Creede was a fiery town that reached a population of about ten thousand.

More than once, fire took a devastating toll on Creede. In 1892, a saloon fire raged so out of control it burned down the entire business district. Due to the big fire in 1892 and the silver crash of the following year, people began an exodus from Creede in massive numbers. Another fire in 1936 destroyed about one third of the rebuilt business district. Ten years later, a fire burned down the courthouse.

Three hundred people currently live in Creede year-round, but the population swells to about three thousand in the summer. Creede's last mine closed down in the late 1980s, and these days the economy is sustained by tourism. According to the Creede Chamber of Commerce, data indicates a flow of eight to ten thousand tourists in Creede from May to September every summer season.

GPS COORDINATES: 37°50.99'N 106°55.54'W

TRAIL REFERENCE: Southwest Trail #13

Crested Butte

Before the first miners, this area and the surrounding Elk Mountains were inhabited by the Ute Indians and used as summer hunting grounds. Seven years after the 1873 Brunot

Treaty was signed, the town of Crested Butte was laid out and incorporated.

In 1880, Crested Butte already had a population of two hundred fifty, as well as fifty businesses and dwellings. The town also had two-story outhouses that were unique to Crested Butte. The upper level proved functional during the deep winter snows, and since both levels were offset from each other, the outhouses could accommodate two people at the same time.

Although gold discoveries first attracted miners to the area, the town soon flourished as a way station for coaches traveling between Gunnison and Aspen. In 1882, the Denver & Rio Grande laid narrow-gauge railway tracks from Gunnison, and Crested Butte diversified as a supply and railroad center for the area.

A road over Pearl Pass to Aspen was established that same year, but the road was said to have been so rough that wagons occasionally had to be disassembled and lowered down the steep cliffs.

The discovery of coal saw Crested Butte emerge as one of the foremost producers of bituminous coal in the West. Some of the mines were taken over by the Colorado Fuel and Iron Company in 1882. A huge economic boost for Crested Butte, coal mining kept the town going for seventy years.

Crested Butte saw its share of disasters. The Jokerville was an early, ill-fated coal mine owned by the Colorado Fuel and Iron Company. Tragedy struck when a powerful underground explosion claimed the lives of fifty-eight miners. Fire ravaged Crested Butte in 1890, wiping out fifteen of the town's businesses. Damage was high and warranted the establishment of local fire companies and fire hydrants. Another fire broke out three years later; but the water system was frozen, and firefighters had to resort to dynamiting some buildings in order to control the blaze. While this effectively snuffed the fire, the force of the explosions managed to blow out every window in town and blast a gaping hole in the town hall.

When the coal played out, Crested Butte's economy dwindled. In the early 1960s, about ten years after the last mine was closed, things picked up again when enterprising entrepreneurs purchased property on the outskirts of town and developed it into a successful winter ski resort.

In 1974, the entire town of Crested Butte was listed on the National Register of Historic Places. Although Crested Butte has expanded with more modern architecture further up the mountain near the ski resort, the old town continues to thrive and successfully maintains the Victorian charm and appearance it had nearly one hundred years ago.

GPS COORDINATES: 38°52.18'N 106°59.13'W
TRAIL REFERENCE: South-Central Trail #22, South-Central Trail #25, South-Central Trail #26

Crystal

Originally called Crystal City, Crystal began as a silver mining camp in 1880. Early prospectors named the town after the crystal-like quartz they found along the creek.

Crystal Mill in 1893

The trail to Crystal was arduous, leading from Crested Butte over Schofield Pass. The difficulty of traversing this trail made it economically impossible to transport anything but the richest ores in or out of Crystal. Eventually, a better road was constructed, connecting the town with Carbondale.

In the mid-1880s, Crystal had a population of about five hundred. It had a newspaper, a general store, many private homes, several saloons, and the Crystal Club (a men's club), which still stands in town.

The Lead King was the principal mine of the region and continued to produce until 1913. Silver from the Black Queen Mine was exhibited at the Chicago World's Fair in 1893.

Crystal Mill today

Although Crystal survived the silver crash of 1893 by mining other minerals (copper, lead, and zinc) until World War I, its population was reduced to a small number of residents.

The beauty of its location ensured the town's survival. Many of the original cabins have been converted to summer homes, although they still appear much as they did in years past. The much-photographed Crystal Mill remains standing on the outskirts of town, along the Crystal River.

GPS COORDINATES: 39°03.56'N 107°06.14'W
TRAIL REFERENCE: South-Central Trail #22, South-Central Trail #23

Doyleville

Doyleville was originally a 160-acre ranch homestead, owned by Henry Doyle, at the junction of Tomichi and Hot Springs Creek. It was established in 1879 and functioned as a stage stop and supply center on the route from Salida to Gunnison.

The Denver & Rio Grande Railroad began running through Doyleville in 1881. Between then and 1885, over four hundred railway cars of hay and sheep were loaded out of Doyleville each year.

Doyleville was active until the 1950s with a post office, school, train depot, and community hall. Today, there is virtually no evidence of Doyleville's former existence, and the site has reverted to ranchland.

GPS COORDINATES: 38°27.08'N 106°36.47'W
TRAIL REFERENCE: South-Central Trail #21

Durango

Durango was founded in 1880, when the Denver & Rio Grande Railroad platted the site a mile-and-a-half south of Animas City. The depot at this new site attracted most of the population of Animas City to a new home in Durango. Durango was, and is still, a railroad and smelting center.

By 1881, Durango was growing at a rapid rate and boasted 20 saloons, a red-light district, and 134 businesses. Newspaper advertisements declared Durango to be the "Denver of the Southwest," effectively luring about two thousand pioneers to the area.

Durango saw its share of rowdiness and wild-West violence. Brawls and shoot-outs were common, sometimes injuring or killing innocent victims. The members of the Stockton gang were notorious gunslingers who did as they pleased in Durango. They frequently clashed with a rival gang from nearby Farmington. One Christmas season, the Stocktons rode into Farmington all fired up and ready for blood from the Simmons gang. They crashed a local Christmas party, shooting up the place and killing an innocent guest with a stray bullet. The Stockton gang escaped, followed by more bloodshed and shoot-outs.

The people of Durango did what they could to maintain a semblance of law and order. Justice was usually so speedy that sometimes the guilty party would be hanged on the same day he had committed his crime. When the grand opening of the West End Hotel in 1881 had to be delayed because two feuding cowboys shot up the hotel, one of the brawlers was lynched that afternoon. In 1883, citizens thwarted an attempt to rob the Bank of San Juan (1st National Bank today). The town promptly formed a posse, and the culprit was soon captured.

H. A. W. Tabor owned a livery stable and stage line in Durango. It was here that Tabor filed secret divorce papers against his wife so that he could marry Baby Doe. After he had married Baby Doe, his divorce was declared invalid; but because Tabor was both exceedingly rich and a U.S. Senator, he was able to keep his reputation intact.

There is much preserved history in Durango, such as the hundred-year-old Durango & Silverton Narrow Gauge Railroad, which is listed on the National Register of Historic Places. Two historic districts in Durango are recognized by the National Register: Main Avenue Historic District and the East Third Avenue Historic Residential District.

Durango and its surrounding areas have been the settings for a few of Hollywood's memorable scenes. For instance, about twelve miles north of town, crossing the Animas River, is "Bakers Bridge." The chasm provided the setting for Paul Newman and Robert Redford as they made their leap from the cliff into the river in *Butch Cassidy and the Sundance Kid*. Another movie that used the same area for some scenes was *The Naked Spur*.

GPS COORDINATES: 37°16.74'N 107°52.69'W
TRAIL REFERENCE: Southwest Trail #15

Engineer City

Engineer City originated around 1874, when H. A. Woods staked the first claim in the area and named it the Annie Woods Lode. By 1875, the population of prospectors grew to about four hundred.

For a short while, Engineer City prided itself on being the largest city in the state without a saloon. The prospec-

tors were simply too busy looking for silver to spend time in a bar.

In 1875, when Woods overheard some men from Howardsville discussing another claim in the area, he sneaked out and beat them to the area by several hours. He marked the claim and named it the Polar Star, after the cold night air he endured as he traveled through the night to beat the other party. The Polar Star became the best producer in the area.

In 1882, the Frank Hough Mine was discovered. A camp of about fifty men operated it in American Flats on the eastern side of Engineer Mountain. It was closed in 1900, and the ruins of the mine remain.

GPS COORDINATES: 37°58.43'N 107°34.71'W
TRAIL REFERENCE: Southwest Trail #2

Eureka

Eureka was founded in the early 1870s. Although not a boom town, it grew slowly and steadily.

The Sunnyside Mine was located in 1873 and became one of the best producers in the area. Sunnyside Mill was built in 1899, with a three-mile cable tramway connecting the mine to the new mill. The Sunnyside Mill was easily the leading producer of income for the town.

Eureka flourished and boasted a population of two thousand and many stores, meat markets, saloons, and a restaurant. It was incorporated in 1883, making it one of

A view of Eureka and the Sunnyside Mill

only two incorporated towns in San Juan County (Silverton was the other). Eureka had its own post office, and the monthly newspaper, the *San Juan Expositor,* was published there. Otto Mears routed the Silverton Northern Railroad through the town in 1896, further strengthening Eureka's economy.

The Gold Prince Mill was moved to Eureka from Animas Forks in 1917 but did not begin operation until 1918, because it was damaged by fire and had to be rebuilt. Eureka also served the Toltec, the Golden Fleece, the Tom Moore, the Silver Wing, and the Sound Democrat mines. The Sunnyside Mine operated continuously until 1931, when it shut down for a few years and then reopened in 1937. Two years later the miners went on strike, and since an agreement could not be reached, the mine was shut down again.

Toward the end of its operation, the Silverton Northern Railroad's steam engines were replaced by a combination of auto and locomotive parts called the Casey Jones, which could speed down the tracks between Silverton and Eureka in just twenty minutes. To clear snow off the tracks, the Casey Jones carried brooms strapped behind its cowcatcher. Service between Silverton and Eureka ended in 1939 and the railroad was sold and junked in 1942.

The Casey Jones

In 1976, the state of Colorado decided that the town had had no municipal government for the past five years and declared Eureka formally abandoned. Today, only a reconstructed two-story building stands on what was Eureka's flat town site. You also can still see the enormous skeleton of the Sunnyside Mill.

GPS COORDINATES: 37°52.76'N 107°33.88'N

TRAIL REFERENCE: Southwest Trail #4

Fairplay

Fairplay was first established in 1862 as Fair Play. Prospectors, who had just moved on from Tarryall (dubbed "Grab-All") because of greedy miners and claim jumping there, wanted a more civilized and fair-minded mining camp.

The town fell short of its literal name, and people sometimes took justice into their own hands. For instance, in 1879, a judge sentenced a convicted murderer to eight years in jail for getting drunk and shooting a local. The residents were so outraged by the light penalty, they took it upon themselves to seize the killer that night and hang him from the courthouse window until he was dead. When the judge turned up for work the next day, he faced the lifeless body strung up from the second story window and then discovered an extra noose beside the gavel on his desk. Shrewdly realizing that his services were no longer required in Fair Play, the judge promptly caught the first ride out of town.

Fairplay has been the county seat of South Park County since 1867. In 1924, the post office officially changed the city's name from Fair Play to Fairplay.

Fairplay today is an agricultural and ranching community, also serving as a mecca for fishermen, hunters, and tourists. The courthouse, built in 1874, is the oldest still standing in Colorado and is now a library. The town's South Park City Museum is home to thirty old buildings that were moved from Alma, Garo, Leavick, and other places, intermingled with original buildings from Fairplay. They have been restored and filled with thousands of artifacts and furnishings to represent the look and feel of an authentic 1880s Colorado mining town.

GPS COORDINATES: 39°13.48'N 106°0.08'W

TRAIL REFERENCE: North-Central Trail #15, North-Central Trail #17, North-Central Trail #18

Georgetown

Georgetown began as a gold settlement in 1859, when George Griffith from Kentucky found gold there. He brought his brother, their father, George's wife, and a couple of prospectors to the area. They called it George's Town, in honor of George Griffith. The group worked hard to live on the modest amounts of gold they found, despite the large amounts of seemingly worthless (at the time) silver-bearing ore in their lode.

In 1864, plentiful veins of quartz were discovered, creating a boom that brought prospectors pouring into the area. The resulting settlement was called Elizabethtown, in honor of George's wife, Elizabeth. Before long, George's Town and Elizabethtown combined under the name Georgetown, and a post office was established in 1866.

The following year brought the silver explosion. Houses and businesses were erected at a dizzying rate, the streets buzzed with activity, merchants did brisk business, and lots of people were on the verge of becoming very wealthy. Georgetown was known as "the Silver Queen of the Rockies." As it grew, the town acquired an attractive mix of Victorian cottages and a substantial brick business district. Georgetown became the home of many rich men with rich tastes. Large, ornate residences grew in size and ostentation as their owners prospered.

While Georgetown had a wild side—with more than thirty saloons and plenty of red-light houses and gambling dens—it was also a mining town with culture and refinement. Citizens enjoyed two opera houses, met in public halls and a Masonic lodge, and attended society events. Unlike in most other mining camps, families were an integral part of George-

The Georgetown Railroad Loop, circa 1890

town. Schools and churches were constructed from the early days, and homes were built with an air of permanence.

Georgetown is home to many interesting old buildings with their own histories. The Hotel de Paris (now a museum operated by the National Society of Colonial Dames) was a luxurious French inn of outstanding quality that used to accommodate businessmen from the East and Europe while they speculated over mining investments. President Ulysses S. Grant stayed there and was very fond of it. The Hotel de Paris was richly furnished and served exotic foods. The owners bottled their own wine and kept an extensive wine cellar. Fresh fish were kept in an indoor fountain so they could be selected by and prepared for the guests. The Hammill House (now a museum at Argentine and Third Streets) was once a modest home built by mining investor and politician William A. Hammill. As Hammill grew wealthier, his house became more opulent. He added bay windows, a solarium with curved glass panels, a stable, an office, and a six-seat outhouse (with three walnut seats for the family and three pine ones for the servants). The Maxwell House is another immaculately kept Victorian home that was quite modest in its original state and took on a much more lavish appearance as the owner prospered.

In 1884, railroad workers accomplished a true feat of engineering when they completed the Georgetown Loop narrow-gauge between Georgetown and Silver Plume (two miles west). A series of curves constructed in a spiral fashion helped trains gain momentum for the steep grades on the straightaways; in one spot, the railroad actually crossed over itself on a three-hundred-foot trestle. The trip, popular with tourists who wanted to observe the beautiful scenery and experience the thrilling ride, was similar to a roller coaster ride.

After the silver crash of 1893, Georgetown became a sleepy mountain town, although it continued to produce gold and other metals. The railroad was abandoned in 1939; the trestle was dismantled, and the rails were scrapped. However, the entire narrow-gauge railway route between Georgetown and Silver Plume has been reconstructed. Thousands of tourists ride the Georgetown Loop Railroad across the ninety-five-foot Devil's Gate High Bridge between Silver Plume and Georgetown during Colorado's milder months.

Georgetown today is a charming community with interesting architecture and lots of history to observe. The town has been a National Historic Landmark since 1966. In 1970, residents formed the Georgetown Society, which has made an ongoing effort to restore and preserve many of Georgetown's Victorian buildings (including the Hammill House) to their original states.

GPS COORDINATES: 39°42.37'N 105°41.81'W
TRAIL REFERENCE: North-Central Trail #11

Gothic

Named for Gothic Mountain, the town was established in 1879, with the discovery of gold and silver ores in the area. Within four months, nearly two hundred buildings had been erected, including a hotel, three stores, a butcher shop, a barber shop, and a saloon. Millions of dollars' worth of gold and silver ores were extracted from the hills. At its peak, the bustling mining city had a population of around eight thousand.

Gothic gained a reputation as a very wild town with lots of drinking, gambling, and prostitution. When Ulysses S. Grant wanted to see a wild mining town in 1880, he went to Gothic. He reportedly drove his own stage into town and arrived to a riotous celebration.

Gothic's first mayor was elected by a roll of dice between two men. The winner, Garwood Judd, was a saloonkeeper who later earned the reputation of "the man who stayed." He was proud of his title and even nailed a plaque engraved with the phrase over his door.

After gold and silver played out, fortunes receded quickly; by 1884, most of the residents had left town. The city faded as quickly as it had formed. As the last resident of Gothic, Garwood Judd remained all by himself until his death in 1930. His ashes were scattered around the town.

Gothic is now the home of the Rocky Mountain Biological Survey, which studies the wide variety of regional flora and fauna.

A few well-preserved old buildings still stand in Gothic. Set in a beautiful area, the town is experiencing a revival as a summer tourist and residential area.

GPS COORDINATES: 38°57.53'N 106°59.34'W
TRAIL REFERENCE: South-Central Trail #22

Gunnison

Gunnison was named after Captain John W. Gunnison, an army explorer who passed through the area in 1853, leading a group of government engineers in search of the safest and best transcontinental railroad route.

Gold and silver seekers arrived in the 1870s. Valuable ores were found in all directions encompassing Gunnison. With all the mining activity, the town soon became a shipping and supply center. Fortune seekers would stock up in Gunnison before setting out into the mountains.

In 1880, the town became incorporated and was a robust frontier town with a population of ten thousand. As the miners arrived, Gunnison became a wild place. Once, an Alpine Tunnel railway laborer was accused of killing some contractors. He was arrested and taken to his cell, but at midnight a group of vigilantes took him out and lynched him on the main street.

Also in 1880, H. A. W. Tabor established the Bank of Gunnison. He put up capital of $30,000 and served as president. The Tabor family members were stockholders in the bank until 1898.

The Denver & Rio Grande Railroad arrived in Gunnison in the summer of 1881. The line was soon extended to Grand Junction.

Alferd Packer (the admitted cannibal) had his second trial in Gunnison in 1886. He was found guilty of manslaughter and sentenced to forty years in Canon City state penitentiary.

After gold and silver miners exhausted the metals, the town dwindled but did not die. Ranchers moved in, and Gunnison became a cattle and ranching area. The population is not as high as it was during the mining boom, but the town is very much alive. Gunnison is currently the county seat of Gunnison County.

GPS COORDINATES: 38°32.67'N 106°55.58'W
TRAIL REFERENCE: South-Central Trail #24

Hahns Peak

The story of Hahns Peak begins in 1862, the year Joseph Hahn found traces of gold at the base of a volcanic peak. He returned the following year with partners to form a new mining company.

In 1866, there were at least fifty men working the mining district, an estimated forty-seven of whom returned to civilization when the harsh winter set in. Three who kept going were Hahn and his two partners, Doyle and Way. Unfortunately for them, supplies were waning, so Way set out to bring back more provisions. He never returned, and although he lived on for many years, he never explained why he disappeared. Hahn and Doyle nearly starved to death but managed to survive the winter; in April they set out for Empire. Hahn never completed the trip; he died of hunger and exhaustion along the way. A mile later, Doyle, snow-blind and delirious, stumbled into a camp of strangers.

A train at Hancock in 1881

The town of Columbine grew up around Hahns Peak; but mining in the area was never very profitable, and the town faded.

GPS COORDINATES: 40°48.42'N 106°56.61'W
TRAIL REFERENCE: Northwest Trail #3

Hancock

Hancock was named for the Hancock Placer, the first claim in the area. The Denver, South Park & Pacific Railroad established the town in 1880 to support the construction of the Alpine Tunnel. Most of the hundreds of workers employed to build the tunnel lived in Hancock. With five general stores, a hotel, several saloons and restaurants, and two sawmills cutting lumber for the tunnel and railroad, the town supported a population of close to one thousand.

After the Alpine Tunnel was completed in 1881, Hancock became a station on the line to Pitkin, and its Main Street faced the railroad tracks. The population saw a substantial decline

The former railroad bed and a water tank at Hancock in 1940

with the tunnel's completion, but many workers were still needed to keep the tracks clear of heavy snow. Large crews labored constantly throughout winter months.

Hancock's population continued to dwindle when many of the area mines closed down, but the big decline occurred after the collapse of the Alpine Tunnel in 1910. Hancock became a true ghost town. All the buildings have now collapsed, although the structures and foundations are clearly visible in the meadow. The last to fall away was a saloon.

GPS COORDINATES: 38°38.40'N 106°21.64'W
TRAIL REFERENCE: South-Central Trail #5

Henson

Henson was a small camp laid out midway between Lake City and Capitol City, near the Ute-Ulay veins. Little was done to develop claims until after the signing of the Brunot Treaty in 1873.

Named for Henry Henson, the camp became one of the most prosperous in the area after the Henson Creek and Uncompahgre toll road was completed in 1877. Settlers pitched in to extend the road to connect with the Animas Forks road

to Ouray and Silverton. This well-traveled route traversed the Continental Divide at 12,200 feet.

Henson was a rough town. It was never very large, but it was filled with troubles. Shootings and mine accidents were common. The eight doctors in town frequently stayed busy around the clock. A miscalculation in tunneling once caused a terrible gas explosion when mine tunnels of the Ute-Ulay and Hidden Treasure accidentally met, killing thirty-six miners.

Henson also saw a long, bitter, and violent miners' strike. Reportedly, the strike started because the mine owners insisted that all single men board at the company boardinghouse. To protest, miners went on strike. When the owners hired non-union labor to replace the striking miners, violent fights erupted and some scabs were run out of town. The volatility of the situation prompted the governor of Colorado to send four companies of cavalry and two companies of infantry to settle the dispute. The dispute eventually went to trial, and all the miners were forced to leave camp.

Henson's post office, established in May 1883, was closed in November 1913. The buildings still standing in Henson are privately owned, and many are still in use.

GPS COORDINATES: 38°01.23'N 107°22.58'W
TRAIL REFERENCE: Southwest Trail #2

Highland Mary

Highland Mary was actually a town near the Highland Mary Mill and Highland Mary Mine in Cunningham Gulch.

Highland Mary was founded by two enterprising brothers from New York City who decided to go into mining. To figure out where they should begin prospecting, the Ennis brothers consulted a fortuneteller who pointed to a map, marking the area where the two would find treasure. The brothers named the area the Highland Mary and continued to visit the spiritualist for advice. Her instructions regarding where and how to find ore led the brothers on a peculiar and unsuccessful search through the mountains, in which they must have crossed over some rich gold veins without knowing it! Occasionally they made some lucky discoveries, but all too rarely. The Ennises had invested about a million dollars in the mine by 1885, and gave another fifty thousand to the spiritualist. The pair ended up bankrupt; they sold the mine and their elaborate house nearby and returned to New York.

The new owners of the mine prospected using more conventional methods, and Highland Mary immediately began to pay off. It became one of the best mines in Cunningham Gulch. Despite the harsh winters at the mine's elevation of twelve thousand feet, the Highland Mary proved quite worthwhile to the new owners.

All that remains in modern days are ruins of the mill.

GPS COORDINATES: 37°47.37'N 107°34.68'W
TRAIL REFERENCE: Southwest Trail #13

Howardsville

Howardsville was originally named Bullion City for the Bullion City Company, which laid out the town as a promotional settlement in late 1872. However, the following year the residents changed the name to Howardsville, after the individual who built the first cabin on the site in 1872.

Because Howardsville was growing at the same time as nearby Silverton, the two towns became rivals. Howardsville was named the first county seat in Colorado in 1874, but a vote the following year moved the county seat to Silverton.

Howardsville consisted of about thirty buildings and at its peak had about 150 residents. The post office that served Howardsville was claimed to have been the first post office in western Colorado, serving the community from 1874 to 1939.

Howardsville, circa 1873

Some of the old mines in the area included the Pride of the

Howardsville today

West, the Highland Mary, the Little Nation, and the Old Hundred. The Pride of the West Mill has operated intermittently over recent years under various owners. The Old Hundred Mine is privately owned and open for daily tours.

Most of the early buildings of Howardsville are gone today, but a few residents still live in the gulch.

GPS COORDINATES: 37°50.17'N 107°35.64'W

TRAIL REFERENCE: Southwest Trail #4, Southwest Trail #13

Idaho Springs

George Jackson discovered the hot springs around which the town of Idaho Springs grew up when he was scouting for gold and spotted smoke in the distance. Suspecting the smoke came from an Indian campfire, Jackson crept forward to get a closer look and found that it was actually steam rising from a natural hot spring in the frozen ground. Upon closer inspection of the area, Jackson found promising traces of gold in the nearby stream.

Jackson marked his placer discovery and then left it for several months until the ground thawed. In the meantime, he organized a group of miners from Chicago and quietly established the Chicago Mining Company. Upon his return, Jackson and his men found more rich ore. When news of their success got out, other prospectors poured into the area.

In 1859, the town formed a short distance from the original strike and was successively called Jackson's Diggings, Sacramento City, Idahoe City, Idaho Bar, Payne's Bar, and finally, Idaho Springs. It grew so quickly that within just a few months there were 10 saloons, 150 homes, a handful of shops, and a boardinghouse.

Horace Tabor, his wife, Augusta, and their baby son came to Idaho Springs in the early days. Augusta set up a bakery to earn money while Horace prospected. One old prospector ad-

vised Horace to take Augusta to Denver for the winter, where she'd be safe from the inevitable avalanches. When Horace returned to Idaho Springs, he found that the old prospector had jumped his claim. Also living in Idaho Springs at the time were newlyweds Harvey and Baby Doe. They were working the Dictator Mine, which Harvey's father, William, had staked out before he went on to become a banker and a state legislator. Baby Doe later became Tabor's second wife.

The medicinal benefits of the hot springs were recognized early on, and by 1866 two bathhouses had opened to the public. Idaho Springs became a renowned health resort that attracted invalids and tourists alike.

In 1868, stagecoaches began carrying passengers and mail between Idaho Springs and Georgetown. Ten years later, the Colorado Central Railroad completed a narrow-gauge line from Golden to Georgetown, and Idaho Springs became an important stop on the run.

Idaho Springs never did collapse when mining declined, as did many other mining towns. In fact, the town is still very much alive. Because of its good location, accessibility, and diversity of businesses, the town has survived through the years.

GPS COORDINATES: 39°44.56'N 105°31.12'W

TRAIL REFERENCE: North-Central Trail #11

Ironton

After the mining craze around Red Mountain, Ironton was formed in 1883 as a tent colony. At the time, the camp was also called Copper Glen, but that name quickly fell out of use.

Ironton developed into a somewhat refined town. Some merchants of the better stores in Ouray and Silverton opened branches in Ironton. Ironton served as the residential center for workers in the nearby mines, such as the Yankee Girl and the Guston.

Ironton also served as an important stage and supply center for the region. Wagons arrived at regular intervals, and ore wagons headed out from the city continuously. When Otto Mears opened the Rainbow Route, extending his railroad from Silverton, over Red Mountain Pass, through to Ironton in 1889, the town had a grand celebration to welcome it.

Prospectors found gold in nearby mountains, which helped create another rush. New mine shafts were drilled deeper into the mountains. Digging deep mine shafts entailed finding underground water; and unfortunately the water was found to contain deadly sulfuric acid. It often ate through machinery, making equipment maintenance a constant and expensive endeavor.

The mines all closed after the silver crash of 1893, and though most of Ironton's residents moved on to other areas, Ironton remained inhabited until the early 1930s. Some old buildings are left in the area.

GPS COORDINATES: 37°56.13'N 107°40.59'W

TRAIL REFERENCE: Southwest Trail #5

Irwin

See "Ruby and Irwin."

Jefferson

Jefferson was originally a tent colony that grew up when the Denver, South Park & Pacific Railroad arrived in 1879.

Like Fairplay, Jefferson was first settled by prospectors who were disgusted by the greedy miners and claim jumpers in Tarryall (dubbed "Grab-All"). However, Jefferson did not last long as a gold camp, although some prospectors carried out modest mining activity along the Michigan and Jefferson Creeks.

Located at the junction of Georgia Pass (some very rich strikes were made in Georgia Gulch) and the road from Denver to Fairplay, Jefferson was a convenient place for miners to send their ore for shipping via the Denver, South Park & Pacific. It was also a handy supply depot.

The railroad tracks were torn up in the 1930s, but the station still exists, as does a modest little town.

GPS COORDINATES: 39°22.65'N 105°47.97'W

TRAIL REFERENCE: North-Central Trail #9

Kenosha

Kenosha was a railroad stop and post office on the summit of Kenosha Pass. Kenosha is likely to have been named after a tribe of Chippewa Indians.

GPS COORDINATES: 39°24.69'N 105°45.56'W

TRAIL REFERENCE: North-Central Trail #2, North-Central Trail #3

Keystone

Keystone Mountain saw some mining activity in the early 1880s, but Keystone's main role was as a significant transportation center for the mining industry.

The Denver, South Park & Pacific Railroad route from Como, over Boreas Pass, and through Breckenridge terminated in Keystone. A number of wagon roads and mountain passes (Loveland and Argentine) also led to Keystone, allowing miners to ship their ore from the many regional mining camps to connect with the railroad in Keystone. In addition, Keystone loggers were able to ship a significant amount of lumber to the surrounding mining camps.

The railroad company's plans to extend the railroad east over the Continental Divide were never carried out, and Keystone remained the terminus of the line until the tracks were removed in 1937.

Keystone ski area was built some thirty years later, near the old town. Today the resort is one of the most popular in Colorado.

GPS COORDINATES: 39°36.34'N 105°58.47'W

TRAIL REFERENCE: North-Central Trail #5, North-Central Trail #6, North-Central Trail #7

Lake City

In 1871, Henry Henson discovered the Ute-Ulay Mine; but the land belonged to the Indians, who did not take kindly to white trespassers. Henson was unable to develop the property until well after the Brunot Treaty of 1873, as violence with the Indians continued for several years. White settlers clashed violently with the native Indians near Lake City as late as 1879.

In 1874, the Golden Fleece Mine was located; originally named the Hotchkiss Mine, it soon became the best producer in the area. Many other strikes followed, and the development of Lake City was underway. In 1875, Lake City was registered. It was named for nearby Lake San Christobal, which was formed by two massive mud and rock slides: the first around the year 1270 and the second about 350 years later.

Also in 1875, the first stagecoach arrived and began making three trips a week to Saguache. That same year, Harry M. Woods published Lake City's first newspaper, the *Silver World*.

Lake City began to take on a permanent look by its second year. Substantial buildings constructed of attractive frames with gingerbread trim outnumbered log cabins. An influx of women signaled the arrival of families and a civilizing influence. Schools and churches went up; and social activities such as balls, suppers, raffles, and skating parties became popular entertainment. The post office opened with a mail stage to Del Norte.

Lake City was one of the first towns in Colorado to have telephone service. In 1876, Western Union initiated telephone service; and by 1881, service had been extended to Silverton, Ouray, Capitol City, Rose's Cabin, Mineral Point, and Animas Forks. Musicians utilized the telephone service to perform popular telephone concerts for listeners along the various lines!

At its high point, Lake City had around 2,500 residents. Since the town was platted at the junction of two toll roads—Saguache to Silverton and Antelope Springs to Lake City—hundreds of people passed through the community each week. Stagecoaches continued to stop in the city daily.

The wild red-light district on the west of town was known as Hell's Acres. Gambling dens and dance halls were interspersed among the many brothels. Lake City had its rough side: many of its residents were killed in mine accidents, snowslides, and shoot-outs.

In 1882, Sheriff E. N. Campbell and a posse attempted to arrest George Betts and James Browning, two saloonkeepers who moonlighted as burglars. In an ensuing gunfight, the sheriff was killed and others in the posse were wounded. Nonetheless, surviving members of the posse were able to recognize and pursue Betts and Browning. Soon after, the burglars were captured and jailed. Two hundred people met at the murdered sheriff's home and formed a lynch mob. They stormed the jail and strung up Betts and Browning from the Ocean Wave Bridge. The mob left the corpses dangling as a lesson to any others contemplating theft. Both are buried in the Lake City cemetery.

The Denver & Rio Grande Railroad arrived in 1889. There were two trains daily in the 1890s, and ore shipments left regularly.

Lake City experienced a series of economic fluctuations. It suffered greatly after the silver crash of 1893 and went into a long decline, relieved only by subsequent gold and lead production.

After the turn of the century, Lake City was on the decline; but camping, fishing, and hunting helped revive it as a summer community. In 1933, the railroad tracks were sold for scrap.

Lake City never became a ghost town, although its population dwindled and it is currently a sleepy little community. Many buildings were made of stone and still survive. The large stone schoolhouse was built in 1882. The courthouse was built in 1877 and is still used.

(One of the best-known stories about Lake City took place in 1874 and revolves around the infamous Alferd Packer. The activities of this unique cannibalistic scout are described in the section of this book entitled "People.")

GPS COORDINATES: 38°01.76'N 107°18.98'W

TRAIL REFERENCE: Southwest Trail #1, Southwest Trail #2

Looking south on Silver Street, Lake City, in 1894

Leadville

As early as 1860, prospectors staked claims in the California Gulch, which yielded gold for the following six years. The camp was then called Oro City. The miner H. A. W. (Horace) Tabor, along with his wife, Augusta, arrived during a food shortage. Tabor sacrificed his oxen to feed the miners and hence made many friends.

The gold soon played out but was followed by rich discoveries of silver. In 1877, the area's silver boom took flight, and the town began to evolve. Hundreds of prospectors arrived on a daily basis and slept wherever they could. Some slept in alleyways, some in tents, and one saloon even rented out floor space (the owner is said to have saved the tabletops for regular customers). Still, others could not find room in the saloons, and hundreds died of exposure.

Officially named Leadville in January 1878, the town was incorporated the following month. Later that year, two prospectors asked Tabor to lend them seventeen dollars' worth of mining supplies in exchange for a one-third interest in their findings. The two prospectors discovered a mine about a mile up East 7th Street, which they called the Little Pittsburg. It turned out to be one of the richest silver lodes in Colorado and promptly made all three men millionaires. Tabor became Leadville's first mayor that same year.

By the summer of 1879, Leadville's architects and builders had endowed the town with a sophisticated air. The town was quickly blossoming with its nineteen hotels, eighty-two saloons, thirty-eight restaurants, thirteen liquor houses, ten lumber yards, seven smelting and reductions works, two works for ore testing, twelve blacksmith shops, six jewelry stores, three undertakers, twenty-one gambling houses, and thirty-six brothels. The town grew so prosperous that not only miners but also merchants, business owners, and artisans could earn a comfortable living.

Leadville became a place where countless fortunes could be made. Even seemingly barren mines produced. Leadville claimed that in a ten-year period it had created more millionaires than any city in the world. And there were many places for rich men to spend their money. The red-light district along State Street was a notorious haunt for the most infamous of Leadville's early gamblers. It was considered to be one of the most wicked and rowdy areas in the entire West. Easy money inevitably encouraged lawlessness lurking everywhere. Violence, murder, and thievery were prevalent in Leadville. Anyone who flashed a wad of cash could be staked out as prey. It was dangerous to walk the streets at night.

Leadville saw some interesting characters and fortunes come and go. Doc Holliday had a famed dispute with a Leadville bartender. The bartender, who had previously lent Holliday five dollars, demanded to be repaid. He followed Holliday into a saloon and threatened to "lick" him if he did not get his money back right away. Holliday drew his pistol and fired a shot that wounded the bartender in his arm. Holliday was taken into custody, tried, and acquitted.

"Broken Nose Scotty" sold his mining claim for $30,000 while he was in jail for drunkenness. With the proceeds he paid bail for all the other inmates, bought everyone new clothes, and then took them out on the town. Needless to say, before the night was over the group was back in jail for disturbing the peace!

Once, a group of men were digging a grave for their friend when they struck a fortune. Their poor "friend" ended up buried in a snowbank.

Young Margaret Tobin was nineteen years old when she married J. J. Brown. After Brown struck it rich on the Little Jonny Mine, the couple moved to Denver. Mrs. Brown later became famous as a survivor of the *Titanic* and was subsequently known as the Unsinkable Molly Brown.

During its boom years, Leadville's population swelled to somewhere between twenty and forty thousand. It was the second largest city in Colorado.

The Tabor Opera House (310 Harrison Avenue) was opened in 1879 with the financial assistance of Horace Tabor. The Great Houdini, poet Oscar Wilde, and John Philip Sousa's Marine Band are among the famous performers who made appearances there. (It is rumored that Wilde drank the miners under the table at local saloons.)

Tabor was also responsible for construction of the Tabor Grand Hotel, which opened in 1885. Its famous lobby floor was imbedded with silver dollars, and its bar was known as the best-stocked bar in the state. (Renamed the Hotel Vendome in 1894, it still stands at 701 Harrison Avenue.)

Tabor and his wife began to drift apart. A woman of simple taste, Augusta frowned on her husband's free spending and did not enjoy the lavish life the two led after striking it rich. In 1881, Tabor met and romanced beautiful divorcee Elizabeth McCourt Doe (Baby Doe). Their relationship became an open secret, and Tabor and Augusta were divorced the following year. Tabor and Baby Doe were married in an elaborate wedding in Washington, D.C., in 1883.

Ten years later Tabor lost everything in the silver crash, as all his money was tied up in silver investments. Baby Doe remained a devoted wife as Tabor was forced to sell everything—except the Matchless Mine (two miles east on 7th Street), which Tabor strongly believed would once again become valuable. After Tabor's death in 1899, Baby Doe moved into a small shack on the premises. She became a recluse and destitute woman. Thirty-six years later, in March 1935, her lifeless body, dressed in rags, frozen in the shape of a cross, was found at the mine. Surrounding her were scrapbooks with yellowed pages and mementos of the elegant life she had once known.

Businessmen attempting to bring tourists to the community built the Leadville Ice Palace between 6th and 8th Streets during the winter of 1895. The palace covered five acres and cost

Tabor Opera House, Leadville, circa 1879

$40,000. It looked like a castle but was constructed with five thousand tons of ice. Up to 250 men cut the ice and constructed the palace. Inside its five-foot-thick walls were a large skating rink, a ballroom, and a dining room. Leadville held a huge celebration and parade to commemorate the opening day. The railroads even added extra passenger cars to accommodate the flocks of tourists who came to visit the structure. Unfortunately, a mild winter forced the ice to melt early, and the palace was closed after only three months of operation.

After the turn of the century, Leadville's economy was in shambles. Mine production had dropped to a fraction of what it had been, and houses were torn down for firewood. Leadville became a source of illicit whiskey, the county's major source of income during prohibition.

Today Leadville is home to a few thousand residents, but it never did revive. Although it is not an especially pretty town, with a little imagination one can still glimpse the faded splendor of a long-gone era.

GPS COORDINATES: 39°14.91'N 106°17.48'W
TRAIL REFERENCE: North-Central Trail #15, North-Central Trail #16, North-Central Trail #17

London Junction

London Junction was also called Alma Junction and Alma Station. Located at the intersection of Mosquito Pass and the road between Alma and Fairplay, the settlement served as a stop for travelers to and from Leadville and Fairplay as well as a home to those who worked in the nearby London Mines. The McLaughlin stagecoach line ran between Alma and Fairplay, providing transfers at London Junction for travelers heading west.

In 1882, a spur of the London, South Park & Leadville Railroad was completed—a six-mile segment leading from London Junction, through Park City, to the London Mountain mining area. Used for hauling ore from the London

Mine, the spur was abandoned two years later when the mine closed down.

Although London Junction was never incorporated, in 1884 150 people lived there. At its peak, the population reached 300.

Some ruins of the original cabins still remain, and a few residents occupy the area today.

GPS COORDINATES: 39°16.02'N 106°02.68'W
TRAIL REFERENCE: North-Central Trail #15

The London Mines
(North London and South London)

The London Mines were established in the 1870s by London Mines, Inc., a British syndicate. Small settlements grew up in the area to house the miners. A concentration works was constructed at London Junction in 1883 to process ore.

The South London Mine, which opened in 1874, lies on the eastern slope of Mosquito Pass. It was the terminus of the London, South Park & Leadville spur up Mosquito Gulch.

The North London Mine was high on London Mountain (12,280 feet). The mine had its own boardinghouses and an aerial tram, with wooden tram towers that are still visible among the trees. The tram was constructed to span the 3,300-foot distance between the North London Mine and its mill, because a conventional chute was not sufficient. Buildings that remain in evidence at the site include some ruins of cabins and the bunkhouse.

The North London and South London Mines merge via a tunnel beneath them on the interior of London Mountain. Over one hundred miles of tunnels burrow through London Mountain in all directions and have yielded millions of dollars' worth of ore.

GPS COORDINATES: 39°16.93'N 106°09.96'W
TRAIL REFERENCE: North-Central Trail #15

Marble

Marble began as a silver and gold mining camp in the 1870s. The ores were of poor grade, and the mines never became very popular. The area went mostly ignored until the discovery of a huge mountain of pure white, high-grade stone in 1882.

The marble was said to have been of the best quality and in the most plentiful supply in the world. Contractors from Italy traveled to Colorado to lend their knowledge of mining marble quarries.

Transporting the marble presented a major problem. Miners shipped marble to Carbondale by way of wagons and pack trains in summer, and horse-drawn sleds in winter. The marble was heavy and the trip was difficult and slow; thus the cost was high. To counteract these problems, the Colorado Yule Marble Company built the Crystal River and San Juan Railroad into Placita in 1907.

High-quality stone from Marble was used in both the Lincoln Memorial and the Washington Monument. However, the most remarkable stone ever produced was reserved for the Tomb of the Unknown Soldier in Arlington, Virginia. The largest single block of marble ever quarried—it weighed over a hundred tons raw and almost fifty-six tons dressed—took a year to excavate.

The town of Marble has seen a number of fires, avalanches, and mud slides. In 1941, a huge cloudburst sent mud sliding down through the valley like a tidal wave, destroying much of the business district and many homes. In just a few minutes, deep mud and debris filled street after street. The damage was so extensive that the mill was rendered inoperable. Many of the residents left town.

The block of marble that was used for the Tomb of the Unknown Soldier in Arlington Cemetery, ready for shipment east in 1931

There is still plenty of marble left in the area, but demand for marble has tapered off over the years. Genuine marble is used less frequently than it once was, because of the many synthetics, veneers, and other alternatives available. The mill is currently open and operates during summer months under the direction of the Colorado Yule Marble Company.

GPS COORDINATES: 39°04.30'N 107°11.37'W
TRAIL REFERENCE: South-Central Trail #22

Marshall Pass

Marshall Pass, a small railroad town with a post office, sat at the top of Marshall Pass. At 10,846 feet, it was the highest railroad pass and the highest railroad town on the Continental Divide in the 1930s, before the railroad abandoned the run.

GPS COORDINATES: 38°23.50'N 106°14.85'W
TRAIL REFERENCE: South-Central Trail #15, South-Central Trail #16, South-Central Trail #17

Middleton

Two men, named Gotlieb and Konneker, made the first strike in 1893, and the town formed the following year. The site was named for neither of these men; rather, it was named for nearby Middle Mountain, presumably because it was halfway between Howardsville and Eureka.

Middleton was located two miles above Howardsville, where Maggie Gulch enters the Animas Valley. Because the town was too close to other residential towns (such as Silverton, Eureka, and Howardsville), Middleton never really became a permanent community, despite some very well-paying mines there. Middleton was abandoned by the early 1900s.

GPS COORDINATES: 37°51.30'N 107°34.32'W
TRAIL REFERENCE: Southwest Trail #4

Mineral Point

Mineral Point mining camp was founded by prospectors Abe Burrows and Charles McIntyre in 1873. It was located below the crest of Engineer Pass, at an altitude of 11,500 feet.

The discovery of large composites of quartz and other minerals gave the area its name and spurred the influx of numerous miners in search of riches. To generate interest in the camp, promoters of Mineral Point circulated far-fetched advertisements with unrealistic claims and pictures to raise capital. One advertisement depicted a steamship running up the Animas River and streetcars running from Mineral Point to Animas Forks!

In truth, only very mediocre transportation was available, and miners had to use cumbersome wagons or burros to transport their ore. Most was sent either to Silverton via Animas Forks or to Lake City.

The Old Lout was a regional mine that was considered worthless. The mining company sank a three-hundred-foot shaft without finding anything profitable. The mine was on the verge of being abandoned when the miners took one last shot and uncovered a rich body of ore. The mine produced a staggering $85,000 the following month.

Due to the inhospitable winters, the lack of transportation, and the silver crash of 1893, by the mid-1890s Mineral Point was on its way to becoming a ghost camp.

GPS COORDINATES: 37°57.28'N 107°35.80'W
TRAIL REFERENCE: Southwest Trail #2

Monarch

Camp Monarch was established in 1879 after the discovery of numerous local mines, some of which were discovered by Nicholas Creede. Residents of the fledgling community boasted that there were over twenty productive mines within half a mile of the town. The town was located along the Old Monarch Pass, down in a valley about a mile from the current Monarch Pass, or U.S. Highway 50.

In 1880, the tent city began to develop into a town with log cabins and dressed lumber buildings; its name was changed from Camp Monarch to Chaffee City, in honor of Senator Jerome Chaffee. In 1884, the town was renamed Monarch. Monarch's population peaked between two thousand and three thousand.

In the beginning, miners hauled ore to Canon City in wagons, but in 1881, the railroad reached Monarch.

The town fell victim to the silver crash in 1893. People began leaving Monarch, and those who stayed dismantled the buildings for firewood. Later, an avalanche swept away everything that remained.

GPS COORDINATES: 38°32.44'N 106°18.75'W
TRAIL REFERENCE: South-Central Trail #1

Montezuma

Mining strikes in 1865 led to the founding of the Montezuma silver camp, named after the Aztec chief in Mexico. The camp grew slowly, mainly because of its poor accessibility and transportation problems. When the Argentine and Webster passes were built, Montezuma began to expand. Montezuma became a hospitable area, something of a social center for local miners, offering dances, sports, and poker games—which are said to have gone on twenty-four hours a day.

Montezuma reached its peak population of about eight hundred residents around 1880. The town had the normal mining town amenities by this point, including a post office.

The following year, the city was incorporated.

A story is told about two miners who loved the same girl back in Missouri. The two were friendly rivals, each endeavoring to be the first to earn enough money to return home and take her hand in marriage. One night around the campfire, one of the men suddenly realized that he could kill the other and thus double the fortune he could take home. He killed his fellow prospector and set out for Missouri. But by the time he reached there, his crime had been discovered and he was extradited back to Montezuma. En route, he hired a lawyer. When they reached Montezuma, the wedding ceremony had been replaced with a hanging scaffold, and the execution papers were all prepared. While the lawyer presented his case to the town officials, the murderer made his escape and was never heard from again.

Montezuma suffered greatly from the silver crash of 1893, but some residents stayed on and waited for better times to come.

In 1958, a fire started at the Summit House hotel and blazed through town, completely destroying the hotel, the town hall, houses, garages, and other buildings. Almost half of the seventy-five residents were rendered homeless—a week before Christmas.

Montezuma never did totally become a ghost town and today is a pretty mountain town with a few residents. The one-room schoolhouse, which operated from 1884 to 1958, still stands on a slope east of Main Street.

GPS COORDINATES: 39°34.86'N 105°52.04'W
TRAIL REFERENCE: North-Central Trail #5, North-Central Trail #6, North-Central Trail #7

Mosquito

Mosquito was formed after gold was discovered high in the mountains between Leadville and South Park. In 1861, when early settlers met to decide on a name, they supposedly chose the name "Musquito" (originally misspelled) because a mosquito had landed on their pages of notes. While there is some confusion of what area actually constituted Mosquito, it seems that it was the name of the gulch, creek, road, peak, pass, and mining district.

That first year was a busy one for the Mosquito District. The Newland Lode was the first discovery, followed by the Sterling Lode a few months later, then the Lulu and the Orphan Boy. Soon, miners worked about fifty claims in the area, and there was much hope for Mosquito. By September, the town of Sterling was laid out in the Mosquito District near the Orphan Boy Mine. In its time, Sterling was alternatively called Sterling City and Mosquito. In 1862, a post office was established to serve the 250 residents. In this law-abiding community (rare in Colorado at the time), there were no lynchings, no murders, and no gambling.

Mosquito Pass, constructed in the late 1870s, was one of the most important passes in the state and served as the main route to the Leadville boom area. It was nicknamed the Highway of Frozen Death because of the ill-prepared prospectors and travelers too cheap to pay stagecoach fares who met their deaths trekking in subzero temperature and blizzards along the precarious route. A halfway house was built in 1879 as a stage stop and a saloon, where the "ladies" would often await male travelers.

It is not clear why Sterling met its demise. Some speculate that men began leaving for mines in other areas or heading east to fight in the Civil War. The population steadily declined, and by the mid-1870s, fewer than thirty residents remained. Stagecoach service across the pass was discontinued; the pass fell completely into disuse and was closed by 1910.

Mosquito Pass is now open to 4WD traffic, and there is very little evidence of the activity seen in days gone past. The forest has reclaimed much of the area.

GPS COORDINATES: 39°17.95'N 106°09.25'W
TRAIL REFERENCE: North-Central Trail #15

Nathrop

Originally called Chalk Creek, Nathrop came into existence in 1880 as a stage stop and supply center for the area mines. Not a mining community itself, Nathrop developed as a farming town, where the first grist mill (for processing grain) in the Arkansas Valley was constructed.

The Denver & Rio Grande Railroad junction with the Denver, South Park & Pacific was established nearby in 1880. To be closer to the station, the whole town moved one-and-a-half miles.

The town is named for entrepreneur Charles Nachtrieb, part owner in the town site, who also built the town's Gothic Hotel. Nachtrieb met his death in 1881 at the age of forty-eight, when a cowboy gunned him down over a wage dispute.

GPS COORDINATES: 38°44.72'N 106°04.61'W
TRAIL REFERENCE: South-Central Trail #5, South-Central Trail #9, South-Central Trail #10

North Star

Originally called Lake's Camp, the site was founded in 1878 as a camp for the miners at the North Star Mine. Owned by the May-Mazeppa Company, it was considered a "suburb" of Whitepine. The camp, renamed North Star, became its own town and prospered from the mining of galena ore.

After the silver crash in 1893, before the town was properly developed, miners abandoned North Star for areas with promise of gold. However, the North Star Mine reopened a few years later and experienced a new boom. During 1901, men worked the mines day and night. Buildings continued to be erected, including the Leadville House and a post office. Mining declined again, although there has been some resurgence in the twentieth century.

Several buildings are still standing today. The mine is situated on the May-Mazeppa Company's property and may be visited only by special permission.

GPS COORDINATES: 38°32.47'N 106°23.06'W
TRAIL REFERENCE: South-Central Trail #6

Ohio City

In 1880, the town was officially founded as Eagle City at the junction of Gold and Quartz Creeks. It was a silver camp with about fifty tents and log cabins. Later that year, the name was changed to Ohio City, and the population expanded to over 250.

Ohio City's first murder occurred in 1880, when two men had a shoot-out. It seems they had previously engaged in a bitter dispute in Leadville and some months later eyed each other on the street in Ohio City. The two drew their guns, firing off many shots as they approached each other. Both men's aim was so hopeless that bullets sprayed everywhere. All at once, they fired shots that struck each other in the heart. Witnesses reported that the two men were so close when they finally fell, they almost hit each other on the way down!

The Ophir Loop in 1920

A stage line connected Ohio City with Pitkin. The Denver, South Park & Pacific Railroad arrived in Ohio City in 1882. It later continued on to Parlin and Gunnison. While the community benefited from the railroad's arrival, its economy was already in trouble because ore was beginning to dwindle.

The silver crash of 1893 was a severe blow to the community, and miners left town. However, Ohio City was able to survive by switching to gold production in 1896, which continued until 1943.

Today Ohio City has several full-time residents, a post office, a general store, a restaurant, and a hunting lodge. Excellent hunting and fishing in the area have helped the town's survival.

GPS COORDINATES: 38°34.10'N 106°36.61'W
TRAIL REFERENCE: South-Central Trail #7

Ophir and Ophir Loop

Throughout the mining period, the name Ophir referred to two areas near each other. Early settlers named the town after an Old Testament reference to a region rich in gold, in hopes that the nearby mines would bring similar fortunes.

Located at the foot of Ophir Pass, Old Ophir, or just Ophir, was established shortly before Ophir Loop, in 1870. The first claims were staked in 1875, after which time prospectors worked the area sporadically.

By 1885, the population of Ophir grew to two hundred. In three years, it blossomed to five hundred. Ophir had five saloons, several churches, a school, and its own electricity and water works.

The town was often snowbound because of avalanches. In December 1883, a mail carrier named Swen Nilson left Silverton to deliver sixty pounds of Christmas packages and letters to Ophir and was never seen or heard from again. While some people believed he had stolen the mail and fled the county, Swen's brother set out searching. He searched for two years, finally discovering Swen's skeleton with his mail sack still around his neck.

New Ophir, or Ophir Loop, was two miles away from Ophir and founded in the mid-1870s. Although having a railway in this area seemed inconceivable, Otto Mears did not know the word impossible. Getting trains started up the steep grade to Lizard Head Pass was a true feat of railroad engineer-

ing. Mears oversaw the construction of three tiers of tracks with loops crossing above and below each other and trestles as much as one hundred feet high. This difficult project enabled the railroad to run from Telluride to Durango. Two cars of ore were shipped from Ophir Loop each day, and the town accumulated a small population as a few of Ophir's residents moved to be closer to the railroad.

The population of Ophir dwindled after the turn of the century, and the area was close to being a ghost town by 1929. In 1960, it was listed as one of four incorporated towns in the United States with no residents. However, today the town is home again to a number of summer residents.

GPS COORDINATES: Ophir Loop-37°51.56'N 107°51.96'W;
Ophir-37°51.38'N 107°49.89'W
TRAIL REFERENCE: Southwest Trail #9

Ouray

Ouray is located in a beautiful box canyon at the base of steep and colorful mountains. When miners first came to the area in the early 1870s, the land belonged to the Ute Indians. The first mining camp was called Uncompahgre City.

Ute leader Chief Ouray functioned as a peace ambassador between the Indians and the white prospectors. Realizing that the influx of white men was inevitable, Ouray continued his peaceful arbitration between the whites and Utes, saving countless lives. Chief Ouray signed the Brunot Treaty of 1873, giving the San Juan Mountains to the United States. The town's name was changed to honor Chief Ouray in 1876.

In its early days, the town was quite isolated. Roads were so poor that there was little transportation into or out of Ouray. Food was scarce, particularly in winter months. Supplies were hard to get and expensive. The postal service had such difficulties negotiating the roads that mail carriers often arrived behind a team of sled dogs. Since local mines could not afford to ship out all of their ore, they transported only their high-grade ore and had to scrap the lower-grade commodity. Mining implements freighted in were outrageously priced.

By 1877, the town reached a population of eight hundred. Two newspapers were published in Ouray. The printing presses had to be carried over the mountains by wagon train. The people of Ouray used their saloons in more ways than one. Early in the town's history, residents held church services in saloons and used kegs of beer for seating. When Ouray became the county seat a few years later, the Star Saloon was renovated as the first courthouse. The bar was removed, the first floor functioned as city hall, and the second-floor rooms were changed into county offices.

Otto Mears earned his nickname, "Pathfinder of the San Juans," by constructing a toll road in 1881. His ambitious twelve-mile road from Ouray to Red Mountain cost $10,000 per mile to construct. Some sections cost $1,000 per foot!

However, improved accessibility boosted Ouray and its economy. The toll road enabled the mining companies to ship their lower-grade ore at reasonable expense instead of throwing it away. This road was the beginning of Mears's Million Dollar Highway from Silverton to Ouray. He later followed the route with his railroad but could go only as far north as Ironton. Supplies from Ouray reached the northern end of the railroad by wagon. Because Mears still wanted to reach Ouray by train, he began building the Rio Grande Southern from Durango, through Ophir and Ridgway, and into Ouray. This line was completed in 1887.

A stagecoach in front of the Beaumont Hotel in Ouray in 1888

By the 1890s, much of Ouray's downtown area had been replaced with brick and stone buildings. Ouray became one of the most elegant mining towns in the San Juans. The remarkable Beaumont Hotel at Main and 5th Streets, with its three-story rotunda and divided stairway, displayed French architectural influences. The furnishings came from Marshall Fields in Chicago, and the dining room staff was trained at the Brown Palace Hotel in Denver. Its interior was lush and luxurious. Many prominent people stayed there, including Herbert Hoover. The Beaumont has been closed since 1965, but it still stands today.

Thomas Walsh, owner of the Camp Bird Mine, was a miner who struck it rich and became famous. Walsh gave Ouray a 7,500-volume library, although it has been said he was illiterate. The Walsh family became so rich from the Camp Bird Mine that Walsh's daughter, Evalyn, purchased the Hope Diamond. Later, Harry Winston bought the diamond from her and donated it to the Smithsonian Institution.

Today, Ouray is an attractive Victorian town prospering by tourism, particularly during summer months. Its population peaked at around 6,500 in 1890; for the past fifty years it has stabilized at around 2,500. As virtually all of Ouray's major public buildings and commercial structures were constructed over one hundred years ago, the town's appearance is largely unchanged. Some popular vacation activities in the area include hiking, bathing in the Ouray Hot Springs Pool, and exploring countless 4WD routes.

GPS COORDINATES: 38°01.30'N 107°40.29'W
TRAIL REFERENCE: Southwest Trail #2, Southwest Trail #7

Parkville

Parkville, on the south fork of the Swan River, was established after placer gold was found in Georgia Gulch in 1859. It quickly evolved as a mining center, supply town, and hub for social activities. It became *the* mining camp of Summit County.

It is estimated that in the early 1860s as many as 100,000 people lived in Parkville. The post office opened in 1861. There was also a county courthouse, hotels, restaurants, saloons, various stores, a newspaper, and a popular playhouse. The town had a mint that produced gold pieces in denominations of $2.50, $5.00, and $10.00.

Parkville was the county seat of Summit County from 1860 until 1862, when Breckenridge townsfolk decided they wanted to make Breckenridge the county seat. One night a secret raid took place on the Parkville courthouse during which all the county records disappeared. After a number of weeks, the records mysteriously surfaced in the newly constructed county courthouse in Breckenridge. From then on, Breckenridge was the county seat. Because Parkville had already begun to experience its decline, no legal action was taken to have the records or county seat returned.

The post office closed its doors in 1866, after the placer gold played out. Subsequent dredge mining in the area during the 1880s produced massive amounts of tailings, which buried the remains of Parkville in rubble

GPS COORDINATES: 39°29.86'N 105°57.01'W
TRAIL REFERENCE: North-Central Trail #9

Pearl

The brothers Luke, Bill, and Bob Wheeler settled this area in 1884 and founded the Phantom Valley Ranch. A post office was established in 1889. Located in Jackson County, Pearl is a very small town located in a rather desolate, treeless meadow near the Wyoming border. It is unclear whether the town was named for its first postmistress, Pearl Ann Wheeler, or for a daughter of Benjamin Franklin Burnett, a developer.

Copper was discovered nearby in 1894. In the early 1900s, Charles Knapp founded the Pearl Mining and Smelting Company. He bought Pearl, Elms Ranch, and other valuable properties for five million dollars; and Pearl became a company town. Among the businesses in town were two saloons, three hotels, a general store, a blacksmith shop, a printer, and a meat market. Further mining in the area produced silver and gold. The Big Horn Lode was a prominent producer, and the best-known mine was the Zirkel. After mining waned, Pearl developed its livestock and lumber industries, which it continues today.

GPS COORDINATES: 40°59.12'N 106°32.81'W
TRAIL REFERENCE: Northwest Trail #2

Pitkin

Before Pitkin became a town, early prospectors braved the Indian territory to search for silver and gold. Miner Karl Warenski found about $50,000 worth of gold in 1862. The Utes killed one of his miners and chased the terrified party out of the area. Warenski, who had buried his gold, returned eighteen years later to retrieve it.

The first recorded inhabitants arrived in 1878 and set up a gold camp. Originally called Quartzville, the camp was renamed Pitkin in 1879, to honor Governor Frederick Pitkin. It claims to be the first incorporated town on the Western Slope of Colorado.

Pitkin experienced rapid growth; within two years of its founding, its population had ballooned to fifteen hundred, making it the twelfth largest city in Colorado. There were nearly two hundred houses, four hotels, eight restaurants, a dozen saloons, and a bank in Pitkin, as well as a very busy jail. Two stagecoach lines served the town. Gold and silver generated early wealth for the town, with some ore assayed at as much as $20,000 per ton.

The Denver, South Park & Pacific Railroad came to town in 1882; but its arrival was anticlimactic, as it had lost its race to be the first to service the area, and most of the freight carriers and passengers were using the Denver & Rio Grande over Marshall Pass. The Denver, South Park & Pacific's late arrival was caused partly by complications in constructing the Alpine Tunnel.

That same year, Pitkin's mines were starting to face serious problems, too. Gold and silver were playing out and did not justify further development. Frustrated with the low-grade ore, many miners began to leave town for areas of more promise.

Pitkin enjoyed a short silver revival in 1891, but that ended after the crash in 1893. Gold production continued sporadically, but silver mining went into an eclipse.

Pitkin was hit by several disastrous fires, one of which occurred in 1898 and reduced the business section to ashes. The fire was fueled as it spread by illegally stored blasting powder in a general store. Five years later, another fire took out one square block when a drunkard accidentally set the fire with a candle.

By the 1920s, Pitkin was totally dependent on revenue from the timber industry. In 1927, over 150 men worked in the business, shipping over 800 railroad cars out via the Denver, South Park & Pacific Railroad. When the Great Depression hit in 1929, the timber business in Pitkin was seriously affected and ceased operation for several decades.

Today, fewer than one hundred permanent residents live in Pitkin, although the summer population swells to around four hundred. Its principal industries are the state fish hatchery and tourism. Pitkin is a quiet town in a beautiful setting.

GPS COORDINATES: 38°36.53'N 106°31.07'W
TRAIL REFERENCE: South-Central Trail #3, South-Central Trail #7

Placerville

Prospectors panning in the San Miguel River in 1876 found placer deposits in the area, which resulted in the establishment of a tent colony originally called Dry Diggings. By 1877, prospectors had built several cabins, and the area was officially named Placerville.

Placerville's gold deposits were quickly exhausted, and the town went into decline until the Rio Grande Southern laid tracks for its route from Telluride to Ridgway. The depot was about a mile from the original town of Placerville. A general store and saloon sprung up near the depot, and eventually the population of Placerville actually moved the town nearer to the station.

Placerville never was a very successful mining town. In-stead, the town became a ranching town with cattle first and then sheep. Western cattlemen hated sheepherders, so the area saw a violent range war; and several sheep ranchers were killed before the ranchers learned to coexist peacefully. Placerville became a major transportation center for livestock.

In 1919 a fire swept through the town, and many of the buildings were destroyed. The town was subsequently rebuilt with sturdier materials. These days, Placerville is a very small town with only a few residents.

GPS COORDINATES: 38°00.96'N 108°03.13'W
TRAIL REFERENCE: Southwest Trail #8, Southwest Trail #11

Poncha Springs

American Indians discovered and used the numerous medicinal hot springs in the region now called Poncha Springs long before white men settled in the area.

Originally called South Arkansas, Poncha Springs was founded in 1879 and incorporated in 1880. The town's founder, James True, traveled to the area and set up shop when he saw the potential of the area. He laid out Poncha Springs and set up a bank.

Shortly after a dispute between True and his business partners, True's bank caught fire. When True found one of his partners at the scene fighting flames, he immediately presumed him to be an arsonist and shot the fellow on the spot. The town marshal later found an oil-soaked rag among the charred remains, so there was no doubt that the fire had been intentionally set; but the burning question was, Who set it? Some suspected True had set the fire himself to cover up bad management. Nevertheless, True was put on trial and was acquitted of murder.

The town saw the arrival of the Denver & Rio Grande Railroad in 1880. The railroad designated the town Poncha Junction. At that time, the population was around five thousand people, but that figure included a large number of railroad construction workers who continued to labor on Marshall Pass.

Poncha Springs served as a supply center for camps in all directions during the mining boom. It was also an agricultural village. The town's economy was aided by businesses that capitalized on the local hot springs. Entrepreneurs built hotels to create a resort community, drawing in customers for the springs' medicinal and soothing effects.

Poncha Pass Road, which travels south of Poncha Springs, was the first toll road Otto Mears ever built. Although this first attempt was not a huge financial success, it launched Mears into his road-building career.

While Poncha Springs was in danger of being abandoned after 1900 and into the 1930s, residents acted to reverse the decline and today the town is a crossroads center. Poncha Springs is a small and pleasant town with a population of about two hundred.

GPS COORDINATES: 38°30.88'N 106°04.56'W
TRAIL REFERENCE: South-Central Trail #15, South-Central Trail #16

Poughkeepsie

Poughkeepsie was high in the Uncompahgre Mountains, about seven miles south of Ouray. The town's remote location and the poor quality of the roads leading to it hindered development. The winters were so harsh that miners could work only two or three months of the year.

Despite the hardships Poughkeepsie residents had to endure, the town was surprisingly well planned. It had a post office established in 1880, a newspaper called the *Poughkeepsie Telegraph,* stores, restaurants, saloons, and other businesses.

Miners usually sent ore to Lake City or Silverton via rough roads by burro. Transporting the ore in this manner was so difficult and expensive that eventually mine owners decided it wasn't worth it and ceased operations.

GPS COORDINATES: 37°56.02'N 107°37.35'W

TRAIL REFERENCE: Southwest Trail #2, Southwest Trail #5

Powderhorn

The site of Powderhorn was first settled in 1876. For a short while, Powderhorn may have been called White Earth, after a village a short distance away. In 1887, the town had a population of seventy-five.

Two different stories explain how the name Powderhorn may have originated. One says that the town is named for the shape of the valley in which it rests. The other says that the town was named by an early settler who went down to the creek and found a powder horn along the embankment.

Powderhorn did not have any particularly rich mining properties until recently. In modern times, geologists have located a pocket of high-grade columbium (a rare metal-hardening mineral) near Powderhorn that may be the richest in the United States.

Powderhorn became a trading center and tourist resort, catering to visitors to the Cebolla Hot Springs nearby. Powderhorn's 240-acre ski area receives a generous amount of snowfall annually, and the national forest surrounding the mountain is a popular destination for cross-country skiers and snowmobilers.

GPS COORDINATES: 38°16.60'N 107°05.72'W

TRAIL REFERENCE: South-Central Trail #21

Quartz

Quartz was established in 1879 as Quartz Town Company with the discovery of carbonate in the area. Although nearby Pitkin was also originally named Quartz, they were always two separate towns.

In 1882, the Denver, South Park & Pacific Railroad arrived, and the town was given a post office. At the time, there were about one hundred residents. Two boxcars served as a jail.

Quartz was about 2.5 miles above Pitkin at the Alpine Tunnel turnoff. The town site is now grazing range, marked by a U.S. Forest Service sign.

GPS COORDINATES: 38°37.38'N 106°28.56'W

TRAIL REFERENCE: South-Central Trail #7, South-Central Trail #8

Redcliff

Redcliff was established during the Leadville boom, when prospectors sought to find ore in the surrounding areas. Miners discovered gold on Battle and Horn Mountains.

The Meeker Massacre in 1879 terrified new settlers across Colorado. Redcliff residents quickly built a blockhouse where women and children could seek refuge while the men guarded the camp. The Indians, however, never did come to Redcliff.

Redcliff's development was greatly enhanced by the arrival of the Denver & Rio Grande Railroad in the early 1880s. During the construction of the railroad, Redcliff evolved as a commercial center when during the surveying procedure, more local mines were discovered, thus generating new towns. The railroad not only made Redcliff an accessible destination but also provided a reasonable method for receiving supplies and shipping out ore.

The largest camp in the area, Redcliff assumed the role of county seat of Eagle County, which it held for nearly forty years. Redcliff had its own newspaper, an opera house, numerous businesses, saloons, and hotels.

Not long after the Redcliff Cemetery was established, two men who killed each other in a gunfight were brought to town for burial. The locals refused to put murderers alongside the respectable townspeople, so the pair were buried along the roadside.

Mining activity continued until as recently as the late 1970s, when the last mine closed. Today, Redcliff is a modest residential community.

GPS COORDINATES: 39°30.78'N 106°22.03'W

TRAIL REFERENCE: North-Central Trail #12

Rico

Gold was discovered in Rico as early as 1866; but because the Ute Indians were not inclined to share their land, prospectors could not safely search for gold until a few years after the Brunot Treaty was signed in 1873. Rico's boom era officially began in 1878, when some very rich ores were found in the area and the riches warranted braving the miner's fear of the Ute.

Rico (the Spanish word for "rich") was appropriately named: The land provided millions of dollars' worth of minerals and metals over the years.

During 1879, miners poured into Rico, and in a single month more than one hundred cabins and thirty commercial buildings—25 percent of them saloons—were constructed. The population was approximately six hundred.

Later that same year, rumor spread that the Ute were about to attack Rico. The men of the town gathered the women and children and sent them to hide in one of the buildings while the men went on sentry duty around the town. Some men took the task of "guarding" Lovejoy's Saloon and proceeded to barricade it with bales of hay and kegs of beer. Though the Ute never did attack, when a pack train arrived in town during the night, one inebriated guard from the saloon was so startled by the sound of hooves that he shot one of the burros. The only human injury suffered that night belonged to the guard, who was severely beaten by the packer.

Miners lived in continuous fear of the Indians. In 1881, the Ute burned a ranch outside of town, killing all the occupants. The following year, the government sent in troops to eradicate the Indians from the region.

In January 1880, Rico faced a famine because of heavy snow. The town was snowbound; and food, whiskey, tobacco, and other supplies became desperately scarce. When a pack train finally reached town four months later, the driver was able to sell his hundred-pound sacks of flour for thirty-five to fifty dollars each. He disposed of every one of them as quickly as he could unload them.

The Galloping Goose, Ridgway

Rico has remained somewhat isolated because of poor roads and lack of railroad transportation into the town. Shipping ore was so expensive that it consumed a huge percentage of mining profits. Whenever supplies arrived in town via wagon or pack trains, townspeople found reason to celebrate.

In 1891, Otto Mears brought his railroad to Rico, inciting a four-day celebration. Because the railway opened Rico up to the rest of the world, Rico truly began to flourish and has continued to thrive.

Locals tell an interesting story about one of the largest producing mines in Rico, the Enterprise. A man named Swickhimer, who was either a sheriff or handyman, owned the mine. He was convinced that there was ore to be found at the Enterprise, but he and his wife had spent all their savings to purchase the claim. They had no option but to put the mine up for sale. However, Mrs. Swickhimer bought a lottery ticket with the last of their coins, and her winning ticket paid out five thousand dollars! The Swickhimers spent the money on further developing the mine until they struck silver, and their efforts paid off. They sold the Enterprise in 1891 for one-and-a-quarter million dollars!

Rico is not a ghost town in modern times, although it has few residents and many businesses have been boarded up. It has survived because its residents have mined different minerals as the markets fluctuate. Many mines continue to operate in the area, and some optimists claim that Rico's best days are yet to come.

GPS COORDINATES: 37°41.68'N 108°01.85'W

TRAIL REFERENCE: Southwest Trail #15

Ridgway

Ridgway was founded in 1890 as a transportation center, named for R. M. Ridgway, a railroad official.

The Denver & Rio Grande's railway line ran between Ouray and Montrose, with Ridgway located between them. The Rio Grande Southern's Telluride route also passed by Ridgway.

The town attracted swarms of gamblers and con men. Swindlers encouraged bets on fixed horse races and lion hunts. Reportedly, an unfortunate mountain lion was kept tied behind one of Ridgway's saloons. Once a week the lion was released as the subject of a hunt, in which he would be captured and promptly hauled back to the saloon—only to be tethered and forced to await the next week's hunt.

Ridgway became a prosperous town; attractive stone and brick buildings, Victorian-style houses, stores, saloons, and pool halls adorned its streets. Its post office was established in the year the town was founded and still exists.

Bank president C. M. Stanwood pulled off a noteworthy fraud in Ridgway in 1931. He "borrowed" the deposits and contents of customers' security boxes and invested them in the stock market; but the market dropped and most everything was lost. The bank's patrons were wiped out. Some depositors were able to recoup some of their money, but those who lost their securities were unable to retrieve them.

When mining tapered off, the railroad began to suffer economic problems, although it continued to operate. In an effort to cut costs, the railroad introduced the Galloping Goose, a relatively inexpensive construction—part car, part train, with a cowcatcher on the front. The Galloping Goose operated until the early 1950s, and then the train and tracks were disposed of for scrap.

Much of the John Wayne movie *True Grit* was filmed in locations around Ridgway.

Ridgway is alive and well today. The town now consists of a number of homes, modern stores, and other businesses.

GPS COORDINATES: 38°09.09'N 107°45.57'W

TRAIL REFERENCE: Southwest Trail #7, Southwest Trail #8, Southwest Trail #11

Romley

The Mary Murphy and Pat Murphy Mines led to the founding of the town of Romley in the late 1870s. Originally called Morley and also Murphy's Switch, the town changed its name to Romley in 1897. One book theorizes that the name Romley may have originated as a typographical error—an inversion of the first three letters of the name Morley. Colonel B. F. Morley had operated the Murphy mines through the 1890s with great success.

The Mary Murphy Mine was by far the biggest mine in the Alpine district. It is said be named after a kind

View of Romley, circa 1915

nurse in Denver who once cared for the prospector who discovered the mine. The Mary Murphy grew so large that it supported Romley, St. Elmo, and Hancock, making the region quite prosperous.

The Denver, South Park & Pacific Railroad came through town in 1881. A five-thousand-foot tramway was built to transfer ore to the railroad cars.

In 1908, tragedy struck when sparks from a train engine kindled a fire that reduced most of Romley to ashes. When the town was rebuilt, the buildings were painted bright red with white trim, although nobody knows why!

In 1912, five men from the Mary Murphy boardinghouse died of food poisoning. Canned spinach was thought to be the culprit, because after the leavings were thrown out into the garbage heap, five burros died.

The Murphy mines continued to produce until 1926, when the ore ran out. Hundreds of workers had been em-

Romley town site today

ployed in the mines during Romley's boom time, and the town had a population of nearly one thousand.

The buildings of Romley stood until 1990, when bulldozers leveled the dilapidated remains.

GPS COORDINATES: 38°40.72'N 106°22.00'W
TRAIL REFERENCE: South-Central Trail #5

Rose's Cabin

Rose's Cabin was once a lively inn offering food, lodging, and entertainment to miners and travelers.

Corydon Rose was one of the first pioneers to explore the San Juans after a treaty was signed with the Utes in 1873. Rose decided to build an inn to serve the area, locating it about halfway between Ouray and Lake City to provide a convenient stopover for travelers along the route.

In 1877, Otto Mears constructed a toll road between Ouray, Animas Forks, and Lake City, which passed right in front of Rose's Cabin. This increased the inn's business substantially, particularly when the road became the main stage route.

Inside the cabin were twenty-two partitioned bedrooms. Road-weary travelers, exhausted from the rough coach trip, would scurry inside to secure their lodgings. Rose often greeted them heartily at the door in his high hat and long coat. Rose's guests could dine, socialize, quench their thirst at the bar, or perhaps take in a game of poker before retiring for the evening.

The area around the cabin began to grow in population as miners settled there. They built cabins nearby and worked mines in the surrounding hills. It is estimated that about fifty people settled in the vicinity. Rose's Cabin served the community as its local bar, restaurant, hotel, general store, and post office. Rose even kept sixty burros in a stable to ship supplies to the miners and carry their ore down to his cabin.

The cabin was the hive of activity in the region.

With the silver crash of 1893, activity at Rose's Cabin gradually trickled off. By about the turn of the century, need for the lively inn ceased entirely. Only a few traces of the cabin remain. The structure still standing is the old stable; the cabin was situated to the left.

GPS COORDINATES: 37°58.58'N 107°32.20'W
TRAIL REFERENCE: Southwest Trail #2

Ruby and Irwin

The towns of Ruby and Irwin are usually spoken of as a single community, since as each expanded, they grew together and formally united.

Ruby was established in 1879, after silver was discovered at the Ruby Chief Mine. When word spread about the riches found in Ruby, prospectors poured into the camp and built cabins, even with the heavy snow on the ground. They cut down trees for their lumber; and when the snow melted in the spring, ten-foot "stumps" were everywhere!

As the town grew, it was renamed Irwin. It became one of the most important camps in Gunnison County and the principal town in the Ruby mining district. It soon became a supply center for the mining camps surrounding it in the nearby gulches and basins.

Irwin had at least five hundred buildings, including seventy-five businesses. There was a large stamp mill, a sampling works, six sawmills, a bank, three churches, a theater, many hotels, and twenty-three saloons. The main street was a mile long.

Irwin was so bustling that by 1880, lots that had sold the previous year for twenty-five dollars were selling for as much as five thousand dollars.

When rumors spread that there was a plot to assassinate former President Grant in Irwin during a speech, the speech was canceled and Grant was entertained for two days at the Irwin Club, a prestigious, members-only establishment for men, where they met friends to discuss business and social affairs. Other guests of the club included Teddy Roosevelt and Wild Bill Hickok.

The site of Ruby/Irwin is eight miles west of Crested Butte and about thirty miles north of Gunnison. It lies within two miles of the highway, or Kebler Pass, near Irwin Lake. The cemetery, however, is right beside the road. Established in 1879, it was originally known as Ruby Camp Cemetery; but its name was changed in 1885 to the Irwin Cemetery.

As it did for other mining camps, the silver crash of 1893 led to Irwin's demise, although many mines had played out earlier. Miners and investors moved away, and by 1909 Irwin was a ghost town.

GPS COORDINATES: 39°34.26'N 105°52.86'W
TRAIL REFERENCE: South-Central Trail #24, South-Central Trail #25

Saints John

Saints John was originally named Coleyville, after John Coley, who located the first ore in 1863. A slightly more colorful story tells of hunters in the area before Coley who ran out of bullets and resorted to using pieces of rock in their guns instead. Several years later the hunters were in Nevada and noticed a great similarity between the rich ore they saw there and the rocks that they had used as ammunition. They contacted Coley, who set up camp in the area and subsequently located silver ore.

The town was renamed Saints John by Freemasons who gave it the biblical name after John the Baptist and John the Evangelist.

A prospector named Bob Epsey once made an unusual strike. Suffering from a hangover one day, Epsey laid down to sleep it off under a shady tree. When he awoke, he steadied himself by grasping a rock as he stood. When the rock broke off in Epsey's hand, he discovered in it a big chunk of solid ore.

Saints John became a company town when it was taken over by the Boston Silver Mining Association, an East Coast company, in 1872. At great expense, the company erected a sophisticated milling and smelter work, complete with bricks imported from Europe. A few years later it was taken over by the Boston Mining Company. For such a remote mining town, Saints John was exceptionally well endowed, with a 350-volume library (complete with regularly stocked newspapers from Boston and Europe), a boardinghouse, a dining hall, a company store, an assay office, various cabins, and a beautiful superintendent's house with elegant furnishings from Europe and the eastern United States. However, Saints John had no saloon, so the miners regularly traveled down the mountain to Montezuma, where they indulged to their hearts' content in brothels, saloons, and poker dens.

Poor access, harsh winters, and waning silver finds caused the decline of Saints John. The Argentine and Webster Passes were impassable due to snow in the winter and at other times suffered from rock slides. The post office was closed by 1881.

GPS COORDINATES: 39°34.26'N 105°52.86'W

TRAIL REFERENCE: North-Central Trail #6

Salida

When the Denver & Rio Grande Railroad decided to construct a main junction two miles away from the small town of Cleora, residents were devastated because the train would not travel through their town; they unsuccessfully protested the action. A new town, developed at the site of the junction, was to be named South Arkansas. But the postal department rejected that name because it had been given three years earlier to the post office at nearby Poncha Springs. According to town lore, it took two elections and a bribe from the railroad to provide trees for the city streets before residents agreed to incorporate as Salida.

Salida grew quickly, and the residents wanted it to become Colorado's state capital. However, when nearby Buena Vista was named county seat, Salida soon abandoned its capital ambitions.

Colonel Thomas Fauntleroy led U.S. troops in a famous battle against the Ute Indians near Salida in 1885. The troops killed forty Indians and captured many others, thus helping open the territory for white settlement.

Salida's downtown historic district lies off the main highway. The interstate was designed to bypass the downtown area. For a pleasant diversion, drive through town to see some of Salida's turn-of-the-century architecture.

Ranching and farming have always been important to Salida's economy. The town also relies on the trade of passing motorists and travelers, who find it a convenient place to stop and eat or stay overnight. Year-round tourist trade includes sightseeing, river rafting, hunting, and skiing.

GPS COORDINATES: 38°32.18'N 105°59.48'W

TRAIL REFERENCE: South-Central Trail #1, South-Central Trail #15, South-Central Trail #16

Schofield

Prospectors discovered silver in the area as early as 1872, but their fear of Indians deferred permanent settlement for several years. Located eight miles northwest of Gothic, Schofield was platted in August 1879 by B. F. Schofield and his party.

A smelter was built in 1880, and a mill in 1881. By 1882, the town had a population of about four hundred and the usual amenities of a hotel, a restaurant (whose staff had trouble cooking because of the altitude), a general store, a blacksmith shop, and a barbershop.

Schofield, located at the base of Schofield Pass, served as a stagecoach station for people traveling over the pass. Because the pass was so rough and dangerous, few people made the journey unless it was absolutely necessary.

In 1880, former President Ulysses S. Grant and ex-Governor Routt visited Schofield. Grant reportedly rode into town atop a white mule. The residents of Schofield thought that if they could sell shares in one of the local mines to Grant, they could boast that the President owned a mine in Schofield. When that failed, they tried to unsuccessfully "lose" shares to Grant in a poker game—to no avail. Finally, they brought out a big barrel of whiskey, hoping to get Grant drunk and just give him the mining shares! Needless to say, Grant was impressed with Schofield's hospitality, but it is unclear whether he ended up with any claim.

Old Lady Jack was a character who wore a gunnysack as a shawl and claimed to be the niece of Indian scout Jim Bridger. No one could fault Old Lady Jack for uncleanliness: She washed everything—including her firewood and even her multitude of cats, hanging them out to dry by the napes of their necks.

Unfortunately, the ore found around Schofield was poor in quality. Although miners did find some good galena, the inaccessible location and high transportation costs drained off their profits. These factors, coupled with the immense problems of eight-month winters dumping as much as forty feet of snow, led to the demise of Schofield. The post office closed in 1885. Some residents moved down the valley to Crystal, while others left to seek fortunes elsewhere in the state.

The town is now gone, and the lovely area is visited primarily by summer tourists.

GPS COORDINATES: 39°02.49'N 107°03.87'W

TRAIL REFERENCE: South-Central Trail #22

Sherman

Sherman was founded in 1877 and named for an early pioneer. The town grew slowly at first, then expanded quickly in the 1880s. Although several mines in the area yielded large amounts of gold, silver, copper, and lead, the principal mine was the Black Wonder. Located on the north side of town, the Black Wonder produced primarily silver. Sherman's population and prosperity fluctuated with the fortunes of the Black Wonder Mine, which continued to produce into the turn of the century. Most of the mine's ore was transported to smelters in Lake City.

Otto Mears's toll road passed by Sherman. To travel between Sherman and Lake City cost $2.50 and between Sherman and Animas Forks cost $2.00 in either direction. The town was a convenient stagecoach stop since it was located halfway between Animas Forks and Lake City.

Sherman peaked in the mid-1880s, when the summer population reached about three hundred. Because winters were harsh, few stayed in town during those months. After the snow melted in the spring, miners would return to Sherman, repair any damages from the winter snowstorms, and resume their work.

The town had frequent problems with flooding, especially during the spring runoff. Sherman's location—in a valley at the intersection of Cottonwood Creek and the Lake Fork of the Gunnison River—made it particularly susceptible to floods. Around 1900, an ambitious 150-foot dam was constructed upstream to hold back waters. However, only a few days after the dam's completion, runoff from torrential rains flooded the mountainside, ripped the dam to pieces, and swept away much of the town of Sherman.

Like many Colorado mining towns, Sherman was devastated by the silver crash of 1893. The silver devaluation, combined with the wreckage from the big flood, led to Sherman's demise.

By 1925, Sherman was deserted. Travelers to the area can still see some ruins of scattered cabins throughout the lush wooded valley. Because these are on private property, it is necessary to view them from the road only.

GPS COORDINATES: 37°54.17'N 107°25.38'W
TRAIL REFERENCE: Southwest Trail #1

Sherrod

Also called Camp Sherrod and Sherrod Switch, Sherrod was a mining camp named for W. H. Sherrod, a gold and silver miner who found some rich gold and silver ore in the late summer of 1903. Almost immediately after this discovery, the rush to Sherrod was on.

By 1904, Sherrod had two hotels, two stores, a loading station, several log cabins, numerous tents, a depot, and even the *Sherrod News*. The town was a stop on the Denver, South Park & Pacific Railroad and a terminus for the Whitepine stagecoach route over Tomichi Pass.

The tough winters in Sherrod contributed to the demise of the camp. At 12,000 feet, miners were in perpetual danger of snowslides, and the heavy snows prohibited work for long periods of time.

The area's ores soon played out, and Sherrod was a ghost town by 1906. The depot was subsequently moved to Ohio City.

GPS COORDINATES: 38°36.82'N 106°23.40'W
TRAIL REFERENCE: South-Central Trail #5, South-Central Trail #8

Shirley

Shirley was originally a tollgate station on the Mears's toll road. It later functioned as a railroad station on the Marshall Pass route. There was some mining in the area, and a 7.5-mile

aerial tram carried the ore to Bonanza for treatment.

GPS COORDINATES: 38°25.35'N 106°7.67'W
TRAIL REFERENCE: South-Central Trail #15, South-Central Trail #16

Silverton

In July 1860, before the Brunot Treaty, Charles Baker (a native Virginian) and a party of six men explored Ute Indian territory in search of gold. They crossed the peaks of the San Juan Mountain ranges and set up camp in an area they called Baker City or Baker's Park. The miners lived in almost constant dread of the Utes, who were fierce fighters and the original occupants of the land.

When the Brunot Treaty was signed in 1873, the land was opened up for settlement to white men. At this time, twelve houses were recorded in Baker City, and the settlement's name was changed to Silverton. It is rumored that the town earned its name when a prospector exclaimed there was not much gold in the area, but there was "silver by the ton."

Prospectors discovered an enormous number of rich silver properties in the surrounding area, and miners began flooding in from all over.

La Plata Miner, Silverton's first newspaper, was published in 1875. Some of the other early businesses established at the same time were the Greene & Company general store, a general merchandise store, a meat market, a drugstore, an attorney's office, an assay office, a doctor's office, and a post office. There was no jail at this time, and it has been reported that the first lawbreaker was actually chained to the floor of a cabin.

While Greene Street was considered the main commercial district, Blair Street was alive with numerous saloons and the red lights of prostitutes' bordellos. Blair Street became one of the West's most notorious hell-raising areas, twenty-four hours a day, seven days a week. Silverton's thirty-seven saloons and numerous whorehouses lined the several block stretch. It is also reported that the underworld settled in on Blair Street and began to control Silverton. Wyatt Earp ran the gambling rooms for a while at the Arlington, a fancy saloon and gaming hall. Crime was so rampant that local vigilantes could not settle the town, so they hired Bat Masterson from Dodge City to take charge of the Silverton police department. He was able to calm things down a bit but did not close down Blair Street completely because he enjoyed what it had to offer a bit too much.

Up until 1880, Silverton's buildings consisted mainly of all-wood frames. From that time onwards, brick and stone construction became commonplace, and many of the buildings from that era remain. One of Silverton's most elegant establishments, the Grand Hotel at the corner of 12th and Green Streets, opened in 1882. The name of the hotel later changed to the Grand Imperial Hotel. It was a lavish, grandly decorated, three-story showplace.

Because Silverton was situated in a mountain valley, like Ouray it had a problem with transportation over the San Juan ranges. Only the richest gold and silver ores were worth shipping out by pack trains of burros, which brought supplies on the return trip. Because the mountain passes were navigable only in summer, residents had to haul in enough supplies to last the snowy winter months.

Mid-1882 saw the arrival of the Denver & Rio Grande Railroad from Durango. Otto Mears established three other narrow-gauge lines from Silverton, making a total of four railway lines serving Silverton. This solved Silverton's transportation problems and opened it up economically and geographically to the rest of the world. To this day, the Denver & Rio Grande narrow-gauge railway still makes trips between Durango and Silverton during warm months.

The railroad did not guarantee comfortable living in the San Juan Mountains. During the winter of 1884, avalanches blocked the railroad for seventy-three continuous days, leaving Silverton desperate for supplies. Crews of men eventually dug from both directions to clear an eighty-four-foot snowslide. When the train finally reached Silverton, it was met by a cheering crowd of townspeople, many of whom were down to their last morsels of food.

Several wealthy characters lived in Silverton. Thomas Walsh of the Camp Bird Mine had interests there. The Guggenheims accumulated a sizable portion of their fortune from the Silverton area. Lena Stoiber, married to the owner of the Silver Lake Mine, was a rich woman who shared her wealth by piling gifts into her sleigh at Christmastime and delivering toys to the town's children.

Silverton never did become a ghost town. It survived the silver crash of 1893, primarily because gold was discovered in the region. Also, copper and lead were mined locally. The Durango-Silverton narrow-gauge railway attracts tourists to the area and accounts for a major part of Silverton's economy today. Hollywood also discovered Silverton—with its authentic Victorian storefronts still intact and its nineteenth-century train—an ideal site for filming. Such films as *Ticket to Tomahawk, Around the World in Eighty Days,* and *The Naked Spur* were filmed in Silverton.

GPS COORDINATES: 37°48.70'N 107°39.83'W

TRAIL REFERENCE: Southwest Trail #4

Sneffels

During the winter of 1874, several prospectors built a cabin in the region of Sneffels and endured the harsh, snowy winter. As the snow thawed, it was clear they had chosen a very successful locale for mining; so they founded the camp in 1875 and called it Porters. This was before Ouray was founded and several years prior to the first strikes at Camp Bird.

During its peak, as many as three thousand men worked the area's silver and gold mines. Sneffels served as the headquarters for local mines, although some smaller camps were situated around the more distant mines. Some of the profitable mines included the Yankee Boy, the Ruby Trust, the Wheel of Fortune, and the best producer of all, the Virginius Mine.

A shelf road was cut down the mountain to Ouray, passing by the future site of Camp Bird. The narrow ledges and steep grades were dangerous; rock slides and snowslides were frequent.

A mule train preparing for departure from Silverton

In 1884, the Revenue Tunnel was bored three miles into the side of Mount Sneffels, nearly three thousand feet below the original shaft of the Virginius Mine. This venture further enhanced new mining prospects and developed into one of the best mines in the state, known as the Revenue-Virginius. The Revenue Mill was powered by electricity furnished by the stream. When the stream froze in the wintertime, a boiler engine powered the mill.

While the silver crash of 1893 saw the end of some local mines, rich ore and good management kept the Virginius open. Prospectors discovered additional gold veins. Operations were suspended in 1905 for some improvements to the mining works; but in 1906, a fire badly damaged the mine.

In 1909, operations resumed as normal; but the activity was short lived. When miners began sending their ores to the more economical Tomboy Mill on Imogene Pass, the Revenue Mill ceased operations. Ten years later, the mill was destroyed by fire.

The Sneffels post office closed down in 1930. The town experienced a brief revival during the late 1940s when some enterprising folks rehabilitated several of the town's buildings and attempted to get the Revenue Tunnel operating again, but the town was never the same. The Revenue-Virginius properties later became property of Camp Bird.

GPS COORDINATES: 37°58.53'N 107°44.97'W

TRAIL REFERENCE: Southwest Trail #7

St. Elmo

The town site was established in 1880 and incorporated under the name of Forest City. The post office soon insisted that the name be changed to St. Elmo, because other towns had been named Forest City.

St. Elmo's main street around 1880

St. Elmo grew with the success of the Mary Murphy Mine and several other mines in the vicinity. It became a major supply center within the district and served as a convenient stopover for travelers to Tincup, Alpine, and various other mountain passes nearby. Before the railroad's arrival, St. Elmo was a stage stop. With the opening of the Alpine Tunnel by the Denver, South Park & Pacific Railroad in 1882, St. Elmo became a main station on the line.

In its heyday, St. Elmo was a thriving town with a population of about 1,500. It had five hotels, a newspaper, and many other businesses. Although nearby towns had saloons, St. Elmo was considered the best place to spend a Saturday night. The construction workers on the Alpine Tunnel came to St. Elmo for their weekend sprees.

Fire swept through the town in 1890, causing much damage. Two blocks in the business district burned and were never rebuilt.

By 1910, a cave in and lack of freight caused the closure of the Alpine Tunnel. By 1926, it was no longer profitable to continue rail service to St. Elmo. A few residents continued to live in the area, hoping that mining would revive.

By the mid-1950s only two residents remained in the town: Tony and Annabelle Stark, who grew up in St. Elmo and operated a general store (which still stands) from the boom years. They stayed on long after the town faded, living in isolation during the long winters and opening their store to tourists in

St. Elmo today

the summer. After the Starks passed away, St. Elmo assumed the role of a true ghost town.

St. Elmo is one of the best-preserved mining towns in Colorado, with most of the buildings along its main street looking much the same as they did a hundred years ago. It is listed on the National Register of Historic Places and has been the subject of a Historic American Building survey. St. Elmo is a must-see for visitors who want to step back into a wild-West mining town of the 1800s.

GPS COORDINATES: 38°42.23'N 106°20.65'W

TRAIL REFERENCE: South-Central Trail #5, South-Central Trail #9

Steamboat Springs
Named for a nearby spring that once made puffing noises that sounded much like the hoots of a steam train, Steamboat Springs was established in 1875 and incorporated in 1907. The spring was destroyed during the building of the Moffat Railroad in 1908.

Steamboat Springs is very much alive today and is the county seat of Routt County. The biggest industry in Steamboat Springs is the ski resort, which attracts large numbers of tourists to the area each winter.

GPS COORDINATES: 40°29.17'N 106°50.04'W

TRAIL REFERENCE: Northwest Trail #2, Northwest Trail #3

Stunner
Although little is known about Stunner, it is suspected that the first construction occurred in 1882. Both gold and silver were mined in the vicinity, but the remoteness of the camp pre-

vented proper development. No railroad came through Stunner, but the LeDuc and Sanchez Toll Road Company built a road to the area.

Between 100 and 150 people lived in Stunner in its best days. A post office was established in 1890, but the town lasted only a few more years. Stunner's decline began with the high costs of transporting ore from the area's mines and was speeded by the lack of good ores to justify these costs. Because nearby Summitville (on the other side of the range) offered better ore and lower transportation costs, Stunner's population began to dwindle.

There is now nothing left of Stunner. A U.S. Forest Service ranger station and the Stunner Campground are on the site of the old town.

GPS COORDINATES: 39°30.50'N 105°53.50'W

TRAIL REFERENCE: Southwest Trail #14

Summitville
Summitville, on South Mountain, was once the highest of Colorado's major gold camps.

In 1870, miner John Esmund discovered rich ore in abundance near the area that years later would become the Summitville mining camp. After Esmund's initial discovery, he returned to his location several times to extract ore, during which time he failed to file proper paperwork to make the claim legally his. When he showed up at the site in 1873, he found that someone else had established a mine on his spot. The mine, the Little Annie, became the best gold-producing mine in the area. Esmund was discouraged, but he knew there was more gold to be found nearby, so he scoured the hills and located two other sites rich in gold; but this time he filed the paperwork to make the claims lawfully his.

As it turned out, numerous other gold strikes made all of South Mountain practically one giant gold mine. Summitville became a bustling gold camp.

By 1882, Summitville had swelled to a population of over 600; there were several hotels, the *Summitville Nugget* newspaper, saloons, stores, and nine mills at which to process the ore. One of the mining companies set up a pool hall to entertain the men during their free time, especially over the long winter months. This attracted pool sharks from all over the state, who came to match skills with the miners.

Del Norte, about twenty-four miles northeast of Summitville, was an important shipping point, supply center, and stagecoach junction. One of its residents, Tom Bowen, struck it rich with his Little Ida Mine in Summitville. Suave and colorful, Bowen wore many hats; and his skill and luck were legendary. Over the course of his life, Bowen was a judge, an entrepreneur, a lawyer, the governor of Idaho Territory, brigadier general for the Union army, a U.S. Senator, and a very big gambler. Bowen once lost shares of a mining company in a poker game, only to have the winner decide he didn't want the shares. Bowen redeemed the stock for a nominal purchase; and the mine, the Little Ida, later made him very rich. He purchased many other mining properties, including the Little Annie.

In 1885, some of the mines in the area began having financial difficulties, and even the Little Annie could not pay its workers' salaries. Other mines were playing out, so the population of Summitville rapidly declined. By 1889, only about twenty-five residents remained in town.

There were a few short revivals in mining: one in the late 1890s and another in the late 1930s. In recent years, mining started up again with Galactic Resources, Ltd. They suffered heavy losses through 1991 and sold the balance of their mining interests. In 1993, the *Wall Street Journal* reported that Galactic had filed for bankruptcy.

Current operations near Summitville are restricted to the environmental restoration of the area. The U.S. Environmental Protection Agency has ordered a cleanup of high concentrations of copper and minerals distributed in the local water sources through mining procedures. This problem could date back to the earliest mining operations in the 1870s.

Although some of the ghost town's buildings have been torn down to make room for modern-day mining, a number of well-preserved buildings still stand in Summitville. It is an interesting ghost town to explore and photograph.

GPS COORDINATES: 39°30.50'N 105°53.50'W

TRAIL REFERENCE: Southwest Trail #14

Swandyke

Swandyke had its boom in the late 1890s, considerably later than most other Colorado mining camps. The gold camp was actually divided into two sections called Swandyke and Upper Swandyke, about a mile apart, near the Middle Fork of the Swan River.

Stagecoach service connected the camp to Breckenridge and Jefferson; and from there, railroad service ran regularly to Denver.

The population peaked at about five hundred in 1899, when the post office was set up. Many of the camp's families were summer habitants who would move away to avoid the harsh, bitter winters. Some miners, however, chose to remain and work their claims during the cold months. In the winter of 1898, snow began falling one morning and was soon five feet deep on Swandyke. Additional snow fell every day until mid-February. The huge quantities of snow caused a number of avalanches and snowslides, some of which destroyed buildings in the town. One avalanche carried Swandyke's mill from one side of the mountain across a deep gulch, leaving the wreckage on the opposite mountainside.

Swandyke's life span was rather short, partly due to the town's remote location and difficult transportation. Furthermore, mining in Colorado began to decline after the turn of the century, except in extraordinary areas like Creede or Cripple Creek. Swandyke's post office was closed in 1910.

Today, Swandyke is a crumbling Colorado ghost town with a couple of wasted cabins remaining. It is a beautiful location in a remote setting.

GPS COORDINATES: 39°30.50'N 105°53.50'W

TRAIL REFERENCE: North-Central Trail #8

Tarryall

The gold camp of Tarryall was established along Tarryall Creek in July 1859, following the discovery of gold flakes "as big as watermelon seeds." The early prospectors found abandoned log cabins presumed to have belonged to miners a decade earlier, who had been killed by Indians. Hamilton, a sister town, was set up next door.

When word got out about Tarryall's rich placer gold finds, prospectors flocked to the area, and the banks of Tarryall Creek were soon lined with tents. Meanwhile, the original settlers furiously grabbed up all the best sites and became jealous of any newcomers, aggressively running them off. This earned Tarryall a reputation as an inhospitable and greedy place. Prospectors left in disgust, dubbing the camp "Grab-All."

The city was platted in 1861 and became the county seat of Park County for a short while. A private mint was established in the mid-1860s to stamp out $2.50 and $5.00 pieces.

After producing nearly $2 million in gold, the mine played out, and miners moved on. By 1875, both Tarryall and Hamilton were totally deserted. Much of Tarryall and Hamilton were buried under rock prior to World War II as a result of dredging operations along Tarryall Creek.

GPS COORDINATES: 39°07.32'N 105°28.45'W

TRAIL REFERENCE: North-Central Trail #10

Telluride

Telluride began as a small mining camp along the San Miguel River in 1878. The first residents there called it Columbia. Because the post office sometimes confused Columbia with other towns of the same name, the town was renamed in 1881. Telluride, derived from tellurium (a metallic substance that is often attached to silver and gold in their natural states), was an apt name, since tellurium was widespread in the region.

In 1881, business sites in Telluride were being sold for twenty-five dollars, and residential lots went for seventy-five cents. At this time, Telluride had a population of around a thousand people to patronize two grocery stores and a whopping thirteen saloons! Two newspapers were established, and a school district was organized, with classes held in private homes. The following year, the townspeople raised funds to erect the first schoolhouse. The building still stands, but now it serves as Telluride's city hall. The first church was built in 1889, which was followed by a number of others. One unconventional pastor even held services in a local saloon!

Telluride's mountains held fortunes in silver and gold. Zinc, copper, and lead were also mined in the area, but transporting the ores presented a major difficulty. At the Liberty Bell, miners tried to send ore from the mine to the mill downhill on sleds. This failed, because the ore kept falling off the sleds. The miners tried to steady the toboggans by constructing and adding wings, but too many sleds practically flew off the mountainside!

Telluride was isolated, so the townspeople often had trouble obtaining supplies and food. Lack of transportation also made shipping ore to Ouray on burros an arduous task. From Ouray, teams of oxen towed the ore to Alamosa. Finally, the ore traveled on to Denver by rail to reach the smelter.

When Otto Mears brought the Rio Grande Southern Railroad to Telluride in 1890, population growth was colossal, but little did people know what lay ahead of them. "To hell you ride!" the conductor would yell to passengers headed for Telluride.

Telluride was a wild and crazy place, where guns and tempers often got out of hand. The town's three dozen saloons and gambling halls never shut their doors. Telluride's saloon patrons seemed prone to drunken brawls and fights, and gun battles and murders were common. "The Law" itself committed much of the lawlessness. Prostitutes were plentiful, especially along Pacific Avenue. The residents of town tolerated the prostitutes because the bordello madams paid all the town's taxes in regular installments on their behalf.

Butch Cassidy robbed his first bank in Telluride in 1889. Cassidy and two other men held up a bank at the corner of First and Colorado in broad daylight. Although they had three fresh horses waiting for them outside of town, they had no time to make the exchange as they rode for their lives toward Rico with the posse on their tails. Cassidy and his cohorts never were caught for the robbery, but several weeks later three dead horses were found still tied to the tree.

Although Telluride in its early days certainly was not for the faint of heart, it did offer more than saloon fights and gun-slinging bank robbers. The townspeople enjoyed dances, concerts, and various social clubs.

Set magnificently in a box canyon surrounded by snowy mountains and breathtaking waterfalls, Telluride has suffered problems from the elements. Historically, snow piling up in the mountain bowls has presented the greatest threat. In 1902, several men were swept away in an avalanche that also took out the Liberty Bell's tramway. More were killed when a slide buried the rescue party recovering the first bodies. The following day a third slide hit, bringing the death toll to nineteen. It took months to locate all the bodies. Two years later, nearly one hundred people lost their lives in snowslides.

Floodwaters once washed out a dam on the San Miguel River, depositing up to eight feet of mud on the streets and isolating the town for weeks. To counteract this problem, residents constructed a flume leading from the town to the creek so that mud would wash into the creek, sometimes assisted by fire hoses.

Largely because of numerous complicated disputes between labor unions and mining companies, Telluride's economy declined dramatically in the early part of this century. One by one, the mines ceased operation. The most recent to close its doors was the Smuggler Union, renamed the Idarado in the 1970s.

Today, Telluride's gold is the ski industry, which started in the 1970s and has boomed ever since. Thanks to successful efforts at architectural preservation of Victorian houses and other buildings, the town looks much as it did a century ago. Telluride's community is currently prosperous and thriving with year-round resort activities.

GPS COORDINATES: 37°56.26'N 107°48.71'W

TRAIL REFERENCE: Southwest Trail #8, Southwest Trail #9, Southwest Trail #10, Southwest Trail #11

Tincup

Established and laid out after the Gold Cup Mine was discovered in 1879, the town was first named Virginia City. Because other towns had that same name, the post office encouraged the town to change its name. In 1882, it was reincorporated as Tincup.

People flooded into Tincup—one of the wildest and roughest mining camps in Colorado. Its saloons and gambling parlors operated night and day. Drunkenness and shootings were casual occurrences. Tincup was a controlled town, meaning it was ruled by the underworld. Organized crime took charge of all city offices, many saloons, gaming halls, and houses of ill repute. When the first marshal started work in 1880, he was told to see nothing, hear nothing, and do nothing; his first arrest would be his last. He lasted only a few months, because when he went unpaid, he quit. The second marshal occasionally rounded up a few drunks, put them in jail, and then released them. The third marshal decided to harass a saloon owner one night and didn't live long enough to regret it. The fourth marshal went insane and killed himself. The fifth marshal was shot and killed. Quite a record of accomplishment for the lively little town, isn't it?

By 1882, Tincup had several thousand residents and was the biggest silver producer in the Gunnison area. It was a supply center and social center for the area, despite lacking a railroad. The absence of good transportation forced miners to cart out their ore by pack train. Eventually, construction of the Alpine Tunnel brought the railroad to nearby Pitkin.

By 1884, Tincup suffered a mild recession, partially due to high transportation costs. Tincup strengthened again and even managed to survive through the silver crash of 1893 with its gold and silver production.

The town's fortunes continued into the twentieth century, only to end dramatically in a fire that burned the town to the ground in 1906. The fire started in a store that sold kerosene. As it spread, the flames destroyed everything for one city block. The town was rebuilt, but it never fully recovered. Another fire in 1913 started at a saloon and went on to heavily damage several other buildings.

Tincup Town Hall, built in 1906

After the Gold Cup Mine closed in 1917, Tincup declined rapidly. All the working mines in the area shut down, and in 1918 Tincup's post office closed.

The Tincup cemetery has four sections, on separate knolls. One section is for Protestants, another for Catholics, and another for Jews. By far the largest is Boot Hill, where those who had no religion and died with their guns blazing and boots on were buried.

Today the town is supported by tourism and offers many fine opportunities for fishing and backcountry camping. It is a summer resort community with many buildings restored as residences and businesses.

GPS COORDINATES: 38°45.27'N 106°28.77'W

TRAIL REFERENCE: South-Central Trail #7, South-Central Trail #9

Tomboy

The Tomboy Mine, located in 1880 by Otis C. Thomas, was situated high above Telluride. Tomboy was Thomas's nickname.

For several years there was little activity at Tomboy because it was so difficult to reach. However, after the silver crash in 1893, prospectors struck gold at the Tomboy, and the mine began to produce handsomely.

At its peak, the mining camp supported about nine hundred people. Although Tomboy's residents relied on Telluride for supplies, they did not necessarily turn to Telluride for entertainment. About halfway between the Tomboy and the Smuggler Mine was a renegade district called The Jungle, offering a mix of brothels, poker dens, and saloons.

In 1897, the Tomboy Mine was sold to the Rothschilds of London for two million dollars. At this time, the mining camp was booming. It continued to produce for several years but began to decline around the turn of the century. Mining operations ceased entirely in 1928.

There is still much to see at the Tomboy site. The area is littered with ruins of many old buildings and evidence of mining activity, with beautiful views and spectacular scenery all around.

GPS COORDINATES: 37°56.18'N 107°45.23'W

TRAIL REFERENCE: Southwest Trail #8

Tomichi

First called Argenta, Tomichi Camp was laid out because of silver finds in the area in 1880. The town of Tomichi developed around the successful Magna Charta Tunnel, which was the best-producing silver mine in the area. Before long, the town's population swelled to nearly 1,500. A smelter was constructed to serve the Magna Charta Tunnel and the other local mines. Unfortunately, it was destroyed by fire in 1883.

The silver crash in 1893 drastically reduced the town's population. All the nearby mines were closed except the Eureka, which operated until 1895.

In 1899, a huge avalanche struck the town, destroying all the buildings and mine machinery. Five or six people were killed, and all the survivors left the town.

Only a few foundations remain at the town site, about two miles north of Whitepine. A large metal sign marks the site.

GPS COORDINATES: 38°34.26'N 106°22.17'W

TRAIL REFERENCE: South-Central Trail #6

Waunita Hot Springs

Ute Indians were the first to enjoy this region's many hot springs (there are nearly one hundred springs in the area).

First named Tomichi (meaning boiling) Hot Springs, the lower springs were later called Elgin in 1882. The settlement had a post office and a two-story hotel with a mineral bath

A view of Tomboy as it once was; the remains of many of the structures are still in evidence today

that was reported to relieve rheumatism, arthritis, and other illnesses.

The upper springs were called Waunita and developed by Colonel Moore in 1879 to include a hotel, a restaurant, and a post office. The town was named for an Indian maiden: According to a Shoshoni legend, the beautiful Indian maiden Waunita roamed the valley for days, weeping and grieving the death of her love, a Shoshoni warrior who had been killed in battle. After Waunita died of a broken heart, the hot springs appeared wherever her tears had fallen.

In 1916, Dr. Charles Gilbert from Chicago started a hot springs resort that became world famous. He built cottages and a large hotel. Guests arrived from all over the world to seek relief from various diseases in the hot springs. The resort boomed until Gilbert died in 1927, but went into decline soon after. It never recovered, although several attempts were made. Today Waunita Hot Springs operates as a private dude ranch.

GPS COORDINATES: 38°30.85'N 106°30.41'W

TRAIL REFERENCE: South-Central Trail #3

Webster

Located near the foot of the Kenosha and Webster Passes, Webster was established in 1877 and named for William Emerson Webster. William Webster, along with the Montezuma Silver Mining Company, was responsible for the construction of Webster Pass from Handcart Gulch to Montezuma.

By 1879, the Denver, South Park & Pacific Railroad reached Webster, and the town became a shipping point. At that time, the railroad did not venture over Kenosha Pass (only 9,950 feet), so Webster was the end of the line. Supplies and passengers intending to go further south had to terminate and find another method of transportation.

Miners, railroad workers, prostitutes, con men, and fortune seekers all poured through Webster. It became a rough, violent town where disorder and shootings were commonplace. The cemetery had two sections; one was a crowded "boot hill."

Although thousands of people flooded through Webster, it had only one hotel. The proprietor rented floor space and blankets when he ran out of beds. When customers outnumbered blankets, the proprietor collected blankets from snoring patrons and reissued them numerous times during the night.

Webster met its demise for two reasons. First, better routes than Webster Pass were established through the mountains. Second, the railroad eventually made it over Kenosha Pass, thus allowing travelers to reach their destinations conveniently by train.

GPS COORDINATES: 39°27.39'N 105°43.23'W

TRAIL REFERENCE: North-Central Trail #2, North-Central Trail #3

Weston

Originally a well-used Indian trail, Weston Pass quickly became a popular wagon road for prospectors when gold was discovered south of Leadville. Early prospectors called it the California Gulch toll road.

In 1859, Philo M. Weston arrived in Colorado and purchased a 480-acre ranch that straddled the California Gulch toll road—soon to become Weston Pass toll road. By 1862, Weston and his wife had set up a roadside hotel.

During Leadville's heyday, Weston Pass may have been the busiest road in Colorado. Reportedly, a steady flow of wagons, stages, and animals over the pass stirred up a permanent cloud of dust that resembled a dense fog.

The actual town of Weston was established as the Denver, South Park & Pacific Railroad extended toward Leadville in 1879. Weston was a tent town for the railroad, and it served as a shipping point to take cargo up and over the pass. During the boom, piles of freight were always waiting to be transported. Colonel Robert J. Spotswood controlled the flow of traffic and freight traversing the pass. Three forwarding and commission houses held a monopoly on wagons, horses, and burrows crossing the pass.

At its peak, the busy little town had eleven restaurants that catered to the many passersby. Several saloons operated day and night. In 1879, the county issued liquor licenses to establishments along the road. One of these was known as Park Place, or simply Clara's kitchen. It served up cooked meals to hungry travelers making the laborious trip over Weston Pass. One notable customer was Charles Dow, a wealthy New Yorker who later established the Dow-Jones Stock Market Index. He described his meal as excellent—lacking style but with great variety and quality.

The road over the pass was so busy that in the narrow sections traffic jams and even bloody stage crashes were commonplace. The poor animals that towed heavy wagons for miles, sometimes with loads of up to six thousand pounds, lived a brutal existence. Carcasses of the beasts of burden littered the side of the road.

After the railroad reached Buena Vista and Leadville, the need for Weston passed. Very little evidence of the town remains.

GPS COORDINATES: 39°02.69'N 105°55.20'W
TRAIL REFERENCE: North-Central Trail #17

Whiskey Park / Elkhorn

The discovery of gold around Hahns Peak led to the settlement of a mining camp called Elkhorn, also known as Whiskey Park, in the 1890s. Reports heralded rich lodes of precious metals in the area, and a population of about one hundred sprang up around the Elkhorn Mine. Although the mine produced some good ore, most was lower grade. The boom was very short-lived.

For a while Elkhorn survived on other industries such as lumber, agriculture, and dairy farming, but today there is little or nothing left of Elkhorn.

GPS COORDINATES: 40°58.29'N 105°55.03'W
TRAIL REFERENCE: Northwest Trail #3

Whitepine

Prospectors began arriving in Whitepine in 1879, and the town was founded in 1880. The primary mines in the area were the North Star and the May-Mazeppa.

The Whitepine and Tomichi stagecoach service to Sargents started in 1881. That same year, the Denver & Rio Grande railroad service commenced.

The town thrived throughout the 1880s and was considered a sociable, bustling place. The population of Whitepine reached about three thousand.

Despite high expectations, none of the area mines produced much, and with the silver crash of 1893, the town was doomed. By the following year, Whitepine was virtually deserted. The town saw a brief resurgence of activity in 1901.

Whitepine experienced a comeback when lead, zinc, and copper were mined during World Wars I and II, mainly at the Akron Mine. The Akron Mine hit a high point in 1948, when it reached production of one hundred tons per day. By then the North Star and May-Mazeppa mines were back in production with some lead and zinc mining.

Whitepine opened a ski area in 1946 with an 1,800-foot rope tow. After just two years, the tow was dismantled and moved.

Whitepine is now primarily a summer residence, with many reconstructed miners' cabins.

GPS COORDINATES: 38°32.55'N 106°23.59'W
TRAIL REFERENCE: South-Central Trail #6

Wild Irishman

The Wild Irishman was a silver-producing mine in the late 1870s. It remained a camp and never did formally incorporate as a town. The camp had no church or school. Several cabins were situated around the mine so that the miners could be close to their work. The Wild Irishman camp is typical of a number of camps where men and their families worked during the mining boom.

The ruins of the Wild Irishman Mine are still in evidence in a beautiful timberline meadow along the Saints John and Glacier Ridge road.

GPS COORDINATES: 39°33.59'N 105°53.22'W
TRAIL REFERENCE: North-Central Trail #6

Woodstock

Woodstock was initially established as a silver mining camp in 1881. It is a mysterious town with a tragic end.

Located below the Palisades of the Denver, South Park & Pacific Railroad, Woodstock reached its peak population of seventeen in 1881, the same year the train came to town.

In the spring of 1884, a giant avalanche, perhaps caused by a train whistle, destroyed the town and killed fourteen people. Six of those who died were children. A rescue party traveled from Pitkin in temperatures near forty degrees below zero. The rescue party dug up what bodies they could find and brought them back to Pitkin on sleds. Woodstock was never rebuilt.

GPS COORDINATES: 38°37.09'N 106°23.53'W
TRAIL REFERENCE: South-Central Trail #8

People

Explorers and Surveyors

Antoine Robidoux

In about 1823, the frontiersman Antoine Robidoux traveled from his native Missouri to Santa Fe, where he settled temporarily. In 1825, he moved north, crossing Cochetopa Pass, recording the first vehicular crossing of the Continental Divide in Colorado, to establish a trading post on the Gunnison River.

Antoine Robidoux

Zebulon Pike

Zebulon Montgomery Pike was the first official explorer of Colorado. When the United States purchased the Louisiana Territory in 1803, the eastern boundary was not established. France and the United States considered the territory to include everything east of the Continental Divide, but Spain contended that its land extended north to the Arkansas River. This dispute was not settled until 1819.

The lack of knowledge about the land the United States had purchased led to the formation of the Lewis and Clark expedition. The following year, Pike was sent to explore the source of the Mississippi. He returned, having incorrectly concluded that Lake Cass was the source of the great river.

Zebulon Pike

In 1806, Pike was sent with a party of twenty-two men to examine the extent of the southwestern part of the Louisiana Purchase. During the course of this expedition, he discovered Pikes Peak but failed in his attempt to climb it. He did not name the peak; John Frémont named it, following what had become common usage. Pike also discovered the Royal Gorge, the upper waters of the South Platte, South Park, and several important passes, including Medano Pass.

Pike served as brigadier-general in the War of 1812. He won a brilliant victory at the Battle of York when the United States besieged Toronto, only to be killed when an abandoned British powder magazine exploded. He was thirty-four years old when he died.

Jim Bridger

Jim Bridger was one of the most famous and most able mountain men of the American western frontier. In 1830, he became one of the organizers of the Rocky Mountain Fur Company. He trapped in the headwaters of the Missouri; then, in 1834, he traveled through present-day Colorado to trap in the Southwest, extending his knowledge of the vast region. Bridger is credited with the discovery of the Great Salt Lake in 1842, though he believed it to be the Pacific Ocean.

Jim Bridger

Bridger married three times to women of three different Indian tribes: Flathead, Ute, and Shoshone. He was a valuable scout, because of his exact knowledge of the Colorado region and his knowledge of Indian sign language.

Bridger died on his farm near Little Santa Fe, Missouri, in 1881, aged seventy-seven.

John Frémont

John Charles Frémont was known as "the Pathfinder" for his western explorations of 1842-1854. Following early military training, he married Jessie Benton, daughter of the influential senator, Thomas Hart Benton. Frémont gained prominence as an explorer in 1842 when, with Benton's sponsorship, he was given the assignment of surveying the Oregon Trail up the Platte River to South Pass. With the assistance of Kit Carson, he established the best route to Oregon.

In his second expedition in 1843-1844, Frémont explored a massive circle of the least-known parts of the West: from the Colorado Rockies north to the South Pass, northwest to the Columbia, south along the Cascade and Sierra Nevada ranges into California, and southward before turning east across the desert to the vicinity of Salt Lake, and thence east across the Colorado Rockies.

John Frémont

In 1845, Frémont's third expedition followed the Arkansas River, crossed the Rockies, explored the upper Colorado River, crossed the desert west of Salt Lake, and finally crossed the Sierra Nevada range. Frémont participated in the recapture of California during the Mexican War. He became embroiled in military politics and was found guilty of disobedience and mutiny. The sentence was overturned by President Polk, but Frémont resigned from the army anyway.

In 1848 he led his fourth expedition, which sought to open a trail across the Rockies through the San Juan Mountains. This ambitious project led to the death of eleven of his thirty-three men when they were trapped by heavy snow. In 1853, Frémont led his fifth expedition, crossing the Rockies in midwinter to California.

Frémont served as U.S. senator from the new state of California, and in 1856 he was defeated in the presidential election as the first candidate of the Republican party. Business failures, including a disastrous transcontinental railroad project, made Frémont a near-pauper. Congress finally granted him a pension for his explorations only three months before his death.

Edward Beale

Beale graduated from Annapolis, served as a naval officer, and, after leaving the navy, was surveyor general of California and Nevada. He supported the formation of a camel corps to facilitate army transportation and supply in the arid Southwest. In 1858, he led an expedition using his camels from the Colorado River to New Mexico, a trip he believed confirmed the

Edward Beale

camel's value as a means of transportation in the region.

Beale died in Washington, D.C., in 1893, aged seventy-one. He remained a lifelong friend of John Frémont, Kit Carson, and other frontiersmen with whom he had worked.

John Gunnison

Gunnison was the last official explorer before Colorado's gold rush period. He was a graduate of West Point and served as a captain for the U.S. Topographical Engineers.

John Gunnison

Early in 1853, Gunnison was assigned to conduct a government railroad survey across central Colorado and Utah. By October, the thirty-seven-man party with its eighteen wagons of supplies had explored the northern end of the San Luis Valley, threaded Cochetopa Pass, followed the Gunnison River to the site of Grand Junction, and crossed into Utah to reach the Sevier River. Here Gunnison and seven others were purportedly attacked and killed by Paiutes, although some have suggested the attacking party was a combined force of Indians and Mormons. Gunnison was forty-one when he was killed.

John Wesley Powell

Powell was an artillery officer in the Civil War, who lost an arm at Shiloh and attained the rank of major by the end of the war.

Powell spent the winter of 1869 with the Ute chiefs Antero and Douglas and learned to speak the Ute language. During this time, he conceived the idea of exploring the great rivers in the area by boat.

In 1869, financed by the Smithsonian Institution, Powell and eleven others, with four boats loaded with provisions, explored both the Green and Colorado Rivers before reaching the Grand Canyon in August. One man quit the expedition early; three others, refusing to risk the danger of the rapids through the final stretch of the canyon, climbed the canyon walls, only to be slain by Indians. The remainder of the party reached the quieter lower Colorado River in safety.

John Wesley Powell

Powell's further explorations, conducted for the federal government in the 1870s, added to the information on public lands in the Rocky Mountain area and laid the groundwork for subsequent irrigation and conservation projects.

Powell's expeditions sparked his interest in and study of the American Indians, which led to his classification of their languages.

Powell was appointed the first director of the U.S. Bureau of Ethnology in 1879 and also served as director of the U.S. Geological Survey from 1881 to 1892.

Ferdinand Hayden

Ferdinand Vandeveer Hayden was born in Westfield, Massachusetts, on September 7, 1828, and raised on a farm near Rochester, New York, before graduating in medicine from Albany Medical College in New York.

On his first expedition, Hayden accompanied F. B. Meek to the Dakota Badlands in 1853. During the next three years, he made a series of expeditions of the upper Missouri River into Montana. In 1858 he undertook the geological exploration of Kansas, and in the following year he returned to Montana for a similar geological survey.

Following Civil War service as a surgeon in the Union Army, Hayden was appointed a professor at the University of Pennsylvania; but he continued his exploration of the American West, undertaking a geological survey of Nebraska in 1867.

In 1869, Hayden was placed in charge of the forerunner of the U.S. Geological Survey and made his first expedition to Colorado. During the next eight years, he was responsible for the systematic, scientific investigation of Colorado west of the Continental Divide. He directed parties of surveyors, artists, and scientists who made a detailed record of the topography

Hayden survey party, 1872; Ferdinand Hayden is third from left (seated)

of the region, including a great number of the routes that are contained in this book. He published this record in *The Geological and Geographical Atlas of Colorado and Portions of Adjacent Territory* in 1877. The information was instrumental to the settlement of Colorado and the development of railroad and mining activity.

The establishment of Yellowstone National Park in 1872 followed Hayden's survey of the area the previous year and his support for the proposal upon his return.

Hayden was an initial appointee to the U.S. Geological Survey when it was established in 1879, but was forced to retire due to ill health in 1886. He died the following year, aged fifty-nine.

Prospectors, Miners, and Road Builders

Nicholas C. Creede

Nicholas Creede was born William Harvey in Fort Wayne, Indiana, in 1842. He changed his name and headed west after his girlfriend married his brother.

Creede worked at odd jobs as he traveled across Illinois to Iowa, where he joined the Union Army as a scout in the Civil War. As a scout, Creede trained his eyes to observe small details on his long treks into the wilderness; he trained his body to endure all sorts of weather, surviving on only small rations of food. The experience proved to be good preparation for the man whose next occupation was scouting the countryside in search of riches in the earth.

Creede spent the next decade as a less-than-successful

prospector. In 1878, he turned up a little silver float in what later became Monarch, west of Salida; and another strike a few months later netted him a quickly spent $13,000. These mines are speculated to have been the Monarch and the Madonna. Creede continued to search for riches and was not discouraged. He traveled southward from Salida, prospecting until he came to Wagon Wheel Gap, where he accepted a job as a ranch hand. He was determined to find pay dirt in his spare time. In 1889, when Creede was forty-seven years old, he found specks of silver float along Willow Creek. It was enough to cause him to follow the creek for another mile or so upstream into a steep and narrow canyon where the silver particles appeared to concentrate. Creede scaled the sheer canyon wall with great difficulty, until he reached a small ledge where he stopped to catch his breath and have a bite to eat. As his sharp eyes surveyed the rock around him, he chipped into a section and hollered, "Holy Moses! Chloride of silver!"

Nicholas Creede

The Holy Moses lode was a vein of silver ore five feet wide; and with three hired men, Creede worked it until winter set in. Back at the ranch bunkhouse, Creede realized that he needed capital and a railroad to get the ore to the smelter as cheaply as possible. Creede decided to visit David Moffat, president of the Denver & Rio Grande Railroad in Denver, to discuss both issues.

Moffat was impressed with Creede's findings. After investigating the facts, Moffat bought the Holy Moses for $70,000 and put Creede on the payroll as a prospector, with a guaranteed salary and a one-third interest in future discoveries.

Nicholas Creede wasted no time getting back to prospecting in the mountains. He soon found another lode, whereupon he immediately sent a letter of resignation to Moffat. Creede hired miners, dug shafts, and in December, when Moffat's Denver & Rio Grande Railroad reached the junction of Willow Creek, sent wagonloads of his ore off to the smelter. This time, when Moffat volunteered to buy him out, Creede refused. Creede knew he was onto a good thing, and he was right; in the first year, he took two million dollars out of his Amethyst Mine.

The silver crash of 1893 did not affect Nicholas Creede at all. He had already made his fortune by selling his investments the previous year. Unfortunately, the cowboy millionaire only had five years to enjoy his wealth. In the late fall of 1892, Creede, upon advice from his doctors, was forced to leave his home in Colorado and move to Los Angeles.

Creede's retirement was not completely easy, as he and his wife decided to divorce after years of bickering. In late 1896, Creede gave his wife $20,000 and moved her back to her family home in Alabama for what he hoped would be the last of her. She was back in six months, hounding him for more money. Creede became increasingly depressed, and in 1897 a servant found him dead of a morphine overdose.

Otto Mears

Otto Mears was born in Russia in 1840 and was orphaned at the age of four. Various relatives took care of him, first in Russia, then in England, then in New York, and finally in San Francisco when he was twelve. When he arrived in San Francisco to live with an uncle, he found that the uncle had left for the gold rush in Australia; Mears was on his own.

He drifted through the mining camps of Nevada before serving in the First California Volunteers in the Civil War. In 1863-1864, he served under Kit Carson in the Indian Campaign against the Navajos.

After the war, Mears first went to Santa Fe before moving to Colorado, where he opened a store in Saguache. He prospered and expanded his business interests. He farmed in the San Luis Valley and operated a sawmill and a grain mill.

To expand market access for his wheat, Mears constructed a road over Poncha Pass. The government gave permission for this road to become a toll road. This was the beginning of Mears's reputation as the Pathfinder of the San Juans.

By the time he was finished, Mears had built 450 miles of roads in the region. (See map on page 58.) His most famous road is what has become known as the Million Dollar Highway, U.S. Highway 550 between Silverton and Ouray.

As the railroads expanded in Colorado, Mears naturally expanded his interests into railroad construction. In partnership with the Denver & Rio Grande Railroad, he built a network of four narrow-gauge rail lines. In 1887, he built the main line from Durango to Rico, over Lizard Head Pass on what is now Colorado Highway 145, descending with the aid of the Ophir Loop and proceeding to Placerville, Ridgeway, and south to Ouray.

Otto Mears

Mears learned the Ute language and was friendly with Chief Ouray. He served as an interpreter in the Brunot Treaty negotiations. Following the Meeker Massacre, he assisted Chief Ouray in freeing the women captives. This led Mears to work with Ouray to negotiate the resulting Washington Treaty, which was signed in March 1880. In June, Mears was chosen by President Hayes as one of five commissioners to implement the treaty. In 1884, he was elected to the Colorado legislature and became influential in the Republican Party.

Mears suffered heavily in the silver crash of 1893, with many of his enterprises being jeopardized or bankrupted. In 1907, Mears returned to Silverton and remained there until his retirement to Pasadena, California, in 1917. He died there on June 24, 1931, at the age of ninety-one.

Horace Tabor, Augusta Tabor, and Baby Doe

Horace Austin Warner Tabor was born in Vermont in 1830. He rose to enormous riches and became an inspiration to every gold and silver seeker in the West. Unfortunately, he sank back to poverty before his life was over.

The son of a tenant farmer and a mother obsessed with religion, H. A. W. Tabor found his first job as a stonemason. He married his boss's homely, no-nonsense

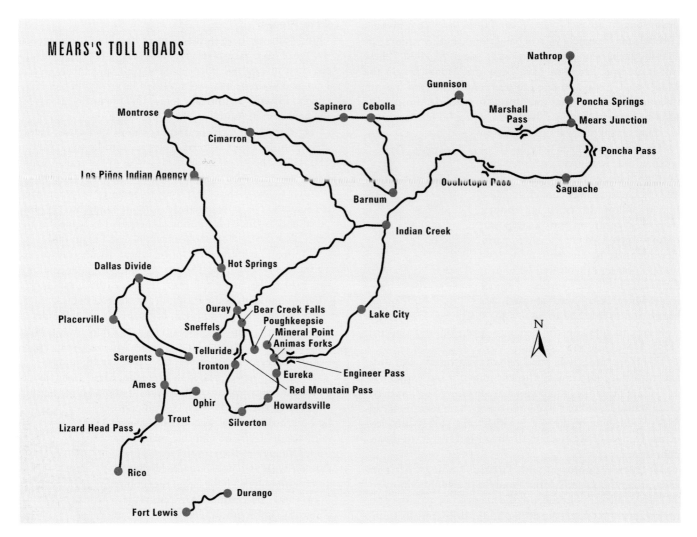

daughter, Augusta Pierce. In 1859 they set off together to find a fortune in the Colorado gold rush.

Horace, Augusta, and their son spent the next nineteen years traveling and prospecting between various mining camps in Colorado, from Idaho Springs to Oro City, trying to make enough money to survive. The Tabors operated a succession of shops, run by Augusta, who also sold her bakery goods and took in boarders to support Horace while he prospected.

Horace Tabor

By 1878, Tabor had made money from his shops and had become mayor of Leadville. At that time, he occasionally grubstaked other prospectors (provided supplies in return for a share in their profits), which brought him instant wealth when two men whom he had given sixty-four dollars' worth of provisions in exchange for a one-third interest in their strikes discovered a silver lode. Tabor immediately bought all shares of the Little Pittsburgh and in six months netted half a million dollars.

For a while, everything Tabor touched seemed to turn to silver; even his seemingly worthless or overpriced investments, such as the Matchless Mine, made him increasingly richer. He

felt the urge to splurge and spent his money on everything from opera houses in Leadville and Denver to silk nightshirts with huge diamond buttons. He loved dining on oysters and drinking champagne at Leadville's Saddle River Café, which was where he met and fell in love at first sight with Baby Doe.

Born Elizabeth Nellis McCourt in Oshkosh, Wisconsin, Elizabeth was nicknamed Baby by her brother, James. In 1877, beautiful, blonde Elizabeth abandoned her dreams of becoming an actress to marry Harvey Doe, a good-looking mama's boy who was also son of the mayor. Because of Harvey's possessive mother, the marriage seemed doomed from the beginning, as Harvey's mother faked heart attacks and pretended she was dying in order to get his attention. Since "Papa" Doe

Augusta Tabor

owned some mining interests near Idaho Springs, Baby persuaded her husband to seek their fortunes in the West.

Baby was so intent on getting rich, she even donned miner's pants and dug for ore alongside Harvey when his efforts were ineffective. She didn't care what people who talked about her "lewd" behavior thought of her. Their mine made them money for a while, but then failed to produce. They had money problems, and Harvey began to drink heavily.

Baby met another man named Jake Sandelowski and bore a stillborn baby that was believed to have been his. She divorced Harvey in 1880 and went to Leadville in pursuit of a new life. In Leadville, she met up again with Sandelowski, who had money to show her the best restaurants and entertainment spots in town. He became a good friend to her.

Baby Doe's strong desire for riches drove her to pursue Horace Tabor, then forty-nine, married, and worth millions of dollars. On the night they met at the Saddle River Café, Tabor fell hard for her; and within five days, she became his mistress. Tabor's millions hypnotized Baby Doe, but over time she fell deeply in love with him.

Augusta was left out of Horace's new rich life and began to feel lonely, unwanted, and bitter. She resented being ignored after she had lovingly stayed with him through their lean years, and she wanted to live a simple life with her husband in Leadville.

Tabor entered politics and became lieutenant governor of Colorado from 1879 to 1883. In 1883, he was named to fill a thirty-day term in the U.S. Senate. It was rumored that Tabor was viewed as a vulgar, uncouth, and low-class man and tolerated in Washington only because of his great wealth.

Baby Doe

Horace Tabor married Baby Doe while in Washington, D.C., in one of the most flamboyant weddings of all time. Even President Chester Arthur attended, along with many other prominent men whose wives snubbed Baby Doe and stayed away. Tabor's divorce from faithful Augusta to marry Baby Doe was a scandal that tarnished Tabor's reputation in both Washington and Colorado.

The next ten years were full of riches and happiness for Baby Doe and Horace Tabor, although they were scorned by Denver society. They spent money on every whim they had.

Tabor, by some accounts, was an incompetent man in his business dealings; despite his amassed fortunes, his gullibility and wild spending caused him to steadily lose everything. Tabor thought he owned overseas holdings, but in fact, his money had been swindled. The silver crash of 1893 saw Tabor lose the last of his investments, except for the Matchless Mine, which by that time was full of water and worthless.

In 1898, Tabor became a postmaster in Denver and lived on a small salary. He became ill and was destined to die the following year in utter poverty. Before he died, he told his wife to hold on to the Matchless Mine and never sell it. She lived in exile in a cabin at the mine and was deserted by her family.

In 1935, Baby Doe was found frozen to death at age eighty-one. She was dressed in rags, penniless among the many mementos of her wealthy years.

Thomas Walsh

Thomas Walsh was born in Ireland and came to America in 1869 at the age of nineteen. He was a carpenter who worked his away across America by building bridges.

Walsh spent some time prospecting in the Black Hills of South Dakota. By 1878 he had moved on to Leadville and made some money in mining and even more from owning the Grand Hotel.

In Leadville, Walsh married Carrie Bell Reed, a schoolteacher. She was a charming woman, who as a youngster had taught herself to have a graceful, gliding walk by practicing with a glass of water balanced on her head.

The silver crash of 1893 wiped out everything the Walshes had, so they packed up and moved to Ouray, where most of the silver mines had recently been abandoned.

Walsh, convinced there was gold to be mined in the San Juans, began exploring the deserted mines. In 1896, he found that samples from mine dumps in the Imogene Basin had strong gold showings, so he quietly purchased more than one hundred claims in the area for next to nothing.

Walsh consolidated his properties as Camp Bird (supposedly named after a jay that stole his lunch one day), reinvesting the first mining profits straight back into further development. Walsh built a smelter and a two-mile tram to bring ores down from the mines.

Camp Bird grew up as a company town. Walsh provided unusual luxury for his miners. They ate from china plates, slept in enameled iron beds, and enjoyed electric lights, steam heat, modern plumbing, and marble-topped lavatories! Walsh also supplied a reading room and stocked it with magazines and newspapers.

By 1900, Walsh's 103 mining claims were producing between $3 and $4 million annually. By 1902, Walsh had accumulated claims covering 1,200 acres. He was netting about $95,000 a month from the mines.

Thomas Walsh

Later that year, Walsh sold Camp Bird to the Rothschilds of London for $3.5 million in cash, $0.5 million in stock, and 25 percent royalty on future profits (excluding then-proven reserves).

Walsh moved to Washington, D.C., where he and his family became popular and prominent society figures. President McKinley appointed Walsh as commissioner to the Paris Exposition, and the family sailed to Europe, where they became friends with King Leopold of Belgium.

Back in Washington, Walsh built a sixty-room mansion at 2020 Massachusetts Avenue, where he and Carrie entertained with elaborate dinners, receptions, and soirees. His daughter, Evalyn, married wealthy Edward B. McLean, whose family owned the *Washington Post* and *Cincinnati Enquirer* newspapers.

Evalyn's father told her to choose a wedding present (in addition to the cash gifts he had given her), and she opted for the 92.5-carat Star of the East diamond for $120,000. She later purchased the famous Hope diamond, which is now on display at the Smithsonian.

Walsh died in 1910 after making $10 million from his mining interests.

Lawmen, Gunfighters, and Outlaws

Bob Ford

Born in Virginia in 1861, Bob Ford became an outlaw and Jesse James's assassin, for which he earned the sobriquet "that dirty little coward who killed Mr. Howard."

In 1882, Bob Ford had only just joined Frank and Jesse James's gang when he shot Jesse James in the back of the head in order to collect the reward money offered by the governor of Missouri. He was convicted and then pardoned for the murder. The shooting was so unpopular with the people of Missouri that Ford was forced to leave town.

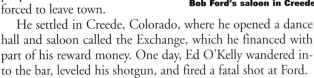
Bob Ford's saloon in Creede, where he was shot to death

He settled in Creede, Colorado, where he opened a dance hall and saloon called the Exchange, which he financed with part of his reward money. One day, Ed O'Kelly wandered into the bar, leveled his shotgun, and fired a fatal shot at Ford.

Little is known about O'Kelly except that he was a native of Missouri; it is suspected that he was a distant relation to Jesse James or that James was his hero.

Ford was not especially popular in Creede—particularly because he acted as if he were boss of the town, when he was generally considered a repulsive criminal. According to Creede town lore, the townspeople celebrated for three days and three nights after Ford's funeral, with plenty of whiskey and dancing on Ford's grave.

Bob Ford

O'Kelly's sentence for killing Ford was life in jail. However, he was paroled after only eight years and released in 1900. Three years after his release, he was shot to death by an Oklahoma City police officer.

Doc Holliday

John Henry "Doc" Holliday was born in Georgia in 1851. He went to dental school in Pennsylvania and returned home to establish a practice for a short time.

When he developed a bad case of tuberculosis (the disease that killed his mother), he decided to move to the American West, hoping the drier climate would improve his health problems. This was the onset of Holliday's transition from a respectable citizen into a notorious, hard-drinking gunfighter, gambler, and con man.

In the West, Holliday worked at several professions: dentistry, gambling, pandering, and stage robbery. He was also suspected of committing at least one train robbery.

As Holliday got sicker, he became progressively more quarrelsome and continued to drink heavily. He was a feisty, hot-tempered man who never backed away from a fight. Few people were silly enough to challenge him; he had killed many men, several of them lawmen.

Doc Holliday

In 1887, Holliday moved to Glenwood Springs, hoping the mineral springs would help cure the tuberculosis that was slowly killing him. His health was so bad that he died in bed later that year at age thirty-five.

Holliday is buried in the Glenwood Springs cemetery on the hill overlooking the town, and his ornate tombstone is decorated with engravings of six-shooters and playing cards.

Bat Masterson

Blue-eyed William Barclay "Bat" Masterson was known as a dapper lawman. Born November 1853 in Quebec, he was originally christened with the name Bartholomiew. He later changed it to William Barclay Masterson and used the nickname "Bat."

When he was eighteen, Masterson moved to Wichita, Kansas, and then to Dodge City the next year, along with his brothers. He tried several professions, from railroad construction worker to buffalo hunter, from Indian fighter to civilian scout.

In 1877, Masterson operated a saloon in Dodge City, while also serving as an assistant sheriff to Charles Bassett. In September of that year, Masterson was appointed a city policeman. He later succeeded to the position of sheriff and held this office from January 1878 to January 1880.

In 1879, while still sheriff of Dodge City, Masterson was recruited by the Atchison, Topeka, and Santa Fe Railroad in its fight with the Denver & Rio Grande Railroad over the right of way through the Royal Gorge of the Arkansas River. He recruited thirty heavily armed men to assist him in this endeavor, but the dispute was settled without bloodshed and Masterson returned to Kansas.

Masterson ventured back to Colorado to investigate mining opportunities, but disappointedly returned to Dodge City a few months later. After that, he spent time in Tombstone, Arizona, before returning to Dodge to assist his brother in a dispute with Al Updegraff and A. J. Peacock, which led to one of Dodge City's more famous gunfights.

Bat Masterson

Masterson was recruited from Dodge to become town marshal of Silverton in an effort to restore order to the town after two outlaws murdered a marshal on Blair Street. The town had become notoriously rowdy, and and someone needed to take control.

Under Masterson's rule, shoot-outs, drunken brawls, and the undesirable element disappeared from Silverton. However, Masterson did not close down the red-light district of Blair Street, since he was known to enjoy district's saloons, gambling, and girls.

In 1882, Masterson served as the marshal at Trinidad. In 1884, he was appointed marshal of La Junta, but served for only five weeks. He then returned to Dodge City, where he first tried his hand as a sportswriter, then briefly served as deputy sheriff, and refereed a prize fight. In 1886, when the saloons in Dodge were closed down, Masterson moved to

Denver. He was married in 1891.

Masterson arrived in Creede, Colorado, in 1892, during the early days of the town, to manage the Denver Exchange, a high-class drinking and gambling establishment. Masterson tolerated no troublemakers and allowed no gunplay inside. The ex-lawman was good at setting the rules and being in command.

Masterson was always known for being well groomed and dressing well; he was considered a dandy, though no one is recorded to have told him so! When he was running the Denver Exchange, he usually wore an impeccable ensemble—such as a lavender corduroy suit, white shirt, and black string tie. A style of hat named after Masterson is still sold.

In 1902, Masterson moved to New York City, where Theodore Roosevelt appointed him deputy U.S. marshal. He became interested in writing and published a series of his articles, *Famous Gunfighters of the Western Frontier*. He became a sportswriter for the *Morning Telegraph* and eventually served as the sports editor. For the next few years, he drank heavily. His fiery temper occasionally got him into trouble. He died at his desk of a heart attack in 1921.

Alferd Packer

Alferd Packer was born in Pennsylvania. He served for a short time in the Union army during the Civil War and was discharged due to "disability."

Packer, like many other men of his era, migrated westward with hopes of finding fabulous riches at the end of his arduous journey. He never made a fortune; he simply bummed around the mining camps, prospecting on occasion.

In November 1873, Packer led a party of twenty-one men from Provo, Utah, to prospect in the San Juan Mountains of Colorado.

Two months later, the group reached Ute Chief Ouray's winter camp at the junction of the Uncompahgre and Gunnison Rivers, near Montrose. Chief Ouray was friendly to the men and tried to warn them of the severe blizzards that regularly bombarded the mountains in the wintertime. Ouray tried to persuade the men to stay with him and his people to wait out the season. After a few days, Packer and five men decided they would continue their journey in search of gold, departing on February 9. The other sixteen men remained with Chief Ouray.

According to Packer, for some unknown reason, his group left camp with rations of only seven days' worth of food for one man. It did not take the six men long to go through such a small supply, so after nearly a week, Packer separated from the group and ventured off in search of food.

In April, Packer arrived alone at the Los Piños Indian Agency on Cochetopa Creek, carrying with him money and possessions from the other men in his party. The authorities' suspicions were aroused, and they questioned Packer about the fate of his five companions.

Packer claimed his companions had deserted him. He told the authorities that when he returned to camp after his fruitless search for food, he found one man sitting near the fire roasting a piece of meat cut from the leg of another man. Another three corpses lay near the fire; the head of each one had

been bashed by a hatchet. Packer claimed that when the man saw him, he stood with his hatchet in hand, and Packer shot him through the belly.

In time, Packer finally admitted to killing the men and eating their bodies. He escorted a search party to recover the remains, but he quit the search before locating the bodies.

Packer was arrested and jailed in Saguache but escaped before he could be tried. Nine years later, he was arrested in Wyoming, where he had been living under another name.

In April 1883, following a trial in Lake City, Packer was found guilty and sentenced to hang the following month. An angry mob wanted to lynch him immediately, so he was moved to Gunnison for safekeeping.

Packer won a retrial, and his sentence was reduced to forty years at the State Prison in Canon City for manslaughter. He had served almost fifteen years when Governor Thomas pardoned him in 1901. As part of the pardon agreement, Packer moved to Denver, where for a while he worked as a doorman at the *Denver Post*'s offices.

Alferd Packer

In April 1907, Packer died and was buried in Littleton Cemetery. A memorial plaque marking the site of the murders overlooks Lake San Christobal on Cannibal Plateau.

Preachers and Townspeople

Father Dyer

Reverend John L. Dyer preached from the pulpit of various midwestern churches. He was a forty-year-old widower when John M. Chivington, a Methodist minister from Kansas, recruited him to carry the word of God to men in the Colorado gold rush.

In 1860, with only fifteen dollars in his pockets, determined Father Dyer departed on his journey to preach the gospel to the prospectors and miners in Colorado's mountain camps. He made his way on foot, as money was too dear to spend on luxuries such as a horse or wagon. He stopped wherever he could to preach and pass the hat to gatherings of settlers.

When Father Dyer neared Denver, it is rumored that someone stole his last two dollars; but he philosophized that he was no worse off than if someone had stolen his last five hundred dollars.

If Father Dyer didn't have a

Father Dyer

building to speak in, he had the congregation sit outside on logs. He occasionally held services in saloons, requesting only that alcoholic beverages be removed from the shelves before the service began. Dyer's fire-and-brimstone approach to preaching appealed to the miners; he fired up his congregations with fear and wonderment.

Father Dyer found that donations were sometimes hard to come by. After one of his five-hundred-mile, two-month-long treks, he collected a measly total of only forty-three dollars. Although Dyer was prepared to be poor, since poverty went with preaching, he somehow had to keep himself alive while carrying forth the word. He fortified his existence by delivering mail, selling newspapers, and prospecting part-time.

Dyer was a tough man, not to be deterred from his calling by Colorado's severe winters. He made ski-snowshoes eleven feet long to enable him to trek with the mail across the snowdrifts. He became known as the Snowshoe Itinerant. Dyer nearly lost his life more than once from being caught in blizzards.

On one of his trips over Boreas Pass to Breckenridge in 1880, Father Dyer was looking downward rather than heavenward when he discovered gold. It made possible the first church in Breckenridge. Dyer built a cabin near the Warrior's Mark Mine, and the camp became known as Dyersville. Located at the top of Indiana Gulch, neither the camp of Dyersville nor the mine ever amounted to much. Father Dyer stayed in Dyersville for just a short time before moving back to Breckenridge, as by then he was nearly seventy and did not have the energy he once had.

Annabelle Stark

Annabelle Stark who grew up in Salida, Colorado, was a college-educated woman with beauty, charm, and a flair for fashion.

Annabelle's mother had been caring for Annabelle's two brothers in St. Elmo; after her mother's death, Annabelle moved there to cook and care for her brothers.

Annabelle Stark's store, circa 1930

Annabelle was a kind woman who took care of others in the town when they were sick or feeble. She became known as the "Queen of St. Elmo" and was popular throughout the community.

One winter, snow blocked the Alpine Tunnel to such an extent that supplies could not get through to the town. Annabelle took it upon herself to bake bread for twelve consecutive days so that the crews clearing the tracks could have something to eat.

As St. Elmo went into decline and the population moved away, Annabelle and her brother Tony (the other brother had

Annabelle Stark's store today

passed away years before) stayed on. Tony ran the post office until it was closed in 1952. As St. Elmo's last two residents, Annabelle and Tony rented out cabins and ran a general store that catered to tourists during the summers. At all other times of the year, Tony and Annabelle were isolated from the rest of the world.

In 1958, Annabelle was in-jured, and her brother had to seek help to save her life. When help arrived, they discovered both Stark siblings suffering from malnutrition and living in filth. Annabelle's once lovely hair was so dirty that it had to be cut to remove an ingrown ribbon.

Hundreds of newspapers, bones, decayed food, and clothing were piled throughout their home. There were even bags full of silver dollars.

Both Annabelle and Tony were hospitalized in Salida; Tony died within a few weeks, but Annabelle lingered on for several years and died in a Salida nursing home.

Events

The American Indians in Colorado

Prior to the Formation of the Colorado Territory

In the eighteenth century, the eastern plains of what was to become Colorado were controlled by the Kiowa-Apache and, south of the Arkansas River, the Comanche. The vast area west of the Front Range was almost entirely controlled by various bands of Ute, who had lived there for approximately ten thousand years, longer than any other tribe lived within the future boundaries of Colorado.

Several small areas were controlled by other tribes. The area north of the Green River, in the northwest corner of the state, was the southeastern border of the Northern Shoshone lands. The Pawnee had a presence in the Platte River area, in the northeast portion of the state. The Jicarilla Apache lands extended up from New Mexico into the San Luis Valley.

Ute domination of the entire area west of the eastern slope of the Rockies did not alter in the period leading up to the establishment of the Colorado Territory in 1861. But there were many migrations occurring on the eastern plains.

As white settlement pushed the eastern tribes west, the Apache, the Comanche, and the Pawnee were gradually dislodged from Colorado land and replaced by the Arapaho and Cheyenne.

The Arapaho had originally come from the Great Lakes region. Sometime in the early 1800s, pressure from the Sioux, who were in turn under pressure from their traditional enemies the Chippewa, created a general migration west. Concurrently, the Cheyenne, who in the late 1700s had gained use of horses and had become nomadic buffalo hunters, were also being pushed west from the Great Lakes region.

In the 1830s, the Cheyenne split into two groups. One group became allies of their former enemies, the Sioux. The other, the Southern Cheyenne, migrated to eastern Colorado and made war against the Kiowa-Apache and Comanches. The Arapaho had also split into two groups during the early 1800s, and the Southern Arapaho formed a loose alliance with the Southern Cheyenne. These allied tribes took over most of the eastern plains of Colorado.

Then, in 1840, the Cheyenne and Arapaho made a peace settlement with the Kiowa-Apache and Comanche, which meant that the Kiowa-Apache and Comanche were able to retain a presence in the southeast corner of the state, south of the Arkansas River.

The Arapaho and Cheyenne tribes would occasionally venture into the mountains to collect poles for their teepees or lodges; when deer, elk, and buffalo became scarce in the mountain parks, the Ute would descend to the plains in search of further herds to hunt. All these tribes were great warriors, and there was constant tension and intermittent warring between the Ute and the alliance of the Cheyenne and Arapaho.

This, then, was the state of affairs around the time that the Colorado Territory was formed in 1861.

Wars and Treaties

In 1859, the Pikes Peak gold rush erupted, and thousands of white prospectors and settlers poured across Cheyenne and Arapaho territory. From his appointment in 1862, Governor Evans sought to open up eastern Colorado to these white settlers; but the two tribes refused to sell their lands and move to reservations. Evans decided to force the issue through what became known as the Cheyenne-Arapaho War, or the Colorado War, of 1864-1865.

The first shot in the war came when territorial military commander Colonel John Chivington launched a surprise attack against the Arapaho and Cheyenne camped at Sand Creek. The ensuing battle, which came to be known as the Sand Creek Massacre, left two hundred Indians dead and many others wounded and mutilated; many women were raped. Only ten soldiers lost their lives. In response, the Indians raided white settlements and twice attacked Julesburg. These attacks further fueled public support for a policy of extermination. After many more encounters, a treaty was negotiated in 1865; but the last battle on the Colorado plains was not fought until 1869.

During this period, the Ute maintained an uneasy peace with the whites who were slowly encroaching on their lands. The initial fur trapping and prospecting had not greatly affected the Ute way of life, but numerous gold discoveries from 1858 to 1860 led to greater incursions of white settlers into Ute territory.

In 1868, in response to the influx of miners and continued pressure for land to settle, a treaty known as the Kit Carson Treaty was negotiated by Chief Ouray, whereby the Ute gave up their land in the central Rockies and San Luis Valley and agreed to be settled on 16 million acres of land in western Colorado. Two agencies, the White River Agency and the Los Piños Agency, were established in 1869 to maintain the reservation and to distribute the promised $50,000 worth of supplies to the Ute every year.

Early prospecting efforts into the San Juan Mountains, the heartland of the Uncompahgre Ute, were slowed not so much by the Kit Carson Treaty or the fearsome reputation of the Ute, but by the lack of early success in finding gold and the intrusion of the Civil War.

However, in the early 1870s, pressure from mining increased dramatically. Discoveries at Henson and in the Animas River Valley and prospecting in many other areas led to yet another treaty and further loss of land by the Ute. The Brunot Treaty, signed by Chief Ouray and other Ute chiefs in Washington in 1873, ceded the San Juan region from their reservation.

The Meeker Massacre

When Colorado achieved statehood in 1876, the miners and settlers again sought to have the treaties renegotiated. The political slogan became "The Utes Must Go."

Chief Ouray recognized the futility of resisting white expansion but was unable to control all the bands of Ute. The White River Ute especially resented the Brunot Treaty, which Ouray had been instrumental in negotiating.

Nathan C. Meeker was appointed the Indian agent of the White River Ute in 1878. He was convinced that for their own good the Ute should give up hunting for agriculture and the Christian religion. When Meeker plowed the grazing land used by the Ute horses, a medicine man, Chief Johnson, attacked him. In response to this attack, in September 1879, federal officials sent in 150 troops under the command of Major Thomas Thornburgh.

Chief Douglas and Chief Jack considered the calling of troops an act of war. Ute scouts warned the army not to enter reservation lands, which was prohibited by treaty agreement. The soldiers continued and were attacked. Major Thornburgh was killed and his troops besieged until Captain Francis S. Dodge and his cavalry of "Buffalo Soldiers" rescued them.

At the agency, the Ute burned the agency buildings, killed Meeker and the other white men, and took Meeker's daughter, his wife, and another woman into the mountains and held them captive for twenty-three days.

Ouray acted swiftly to negotiate the release of the white women, but the political storm that ensued could not save the Ute from losing their reservation lands. After weeks of testimony in Washington before congressional committees, the Washington Treaty was signed in 1880 by Chiefs Ouray, Shavano, Antero, and others. It was necessary for three-quarters of the Ute males to sign this new treaty for it to come into effect. Otto Mears was appointed commissioner to secure the signatures.

Chief Ouray in 1877

In August 1880, before all the signatures were obtained, Ouray died at the age of forty-six. Within a year, all the Ute were removed to reservations in Utah and southwestern Colorado.

Land developers and settlers gathered in Gunnison in the summer of 1881, waiting for the last of the Ute to vacate the old reservation, which they did on September 7, 1881. In 1882, Congress declared the Ute lands public and open for filing, but many settlers had already moved in and laid out towns.

The Silver Crash of 1893

In the eighteenth century, currencies were typically backed by one or more precious metal. All major countries chose either gold or silver, or a combination of the two, as the basis of their currency. At the time, it was a major political issue both in Europe and in the United States; most countries changed their policy more than once during the course of the 1700s and 1800s.

Adherents of the system believed that it stabilized not only the prices of gold and silver but also the value of all commodities, thereby simplifying foreign exchange. Most economists came to oppose the practice.

In 1792, Secretary of the Treasury Alexander Hamilton led the U.S. Congress to adopt a bimetallic monetary standard, meaning that both gold and silver were used to back the currency. Silver dollars contained 371.25 grains, and gold dollars 24.75 grains—a 15:1 ratio.

One of the difficulties of this system is that as the relative market value of gold or silver changes, one coin becomes more valuable than the other; the more valuable coin's circulation decreases as people melt it down and sell the metal and use the less-valuable coin for commerce. A metal's market value can change because of major discoveries of one of the metals, or because of one nation's changing its policy about the value of a metal backing its currency.

In 1834, the United States was forced to change the gold content of its coins, because France changed its policy. The U.S. ratio of silver to gold was increased to 16:1.

The Californian and Australian gold rushes in 1849 and 1850 resulted in the relative price of gold declining. The value of the silver in silver dollars became greater than the face value of the coins, resulting in widespread melting down of silver dollars. During the course of the Civil War, silver dollars disappeared from circulation; and in 1873, the United States moved to a gold standard, eliminating the free coinage of silver.

Subsequently, the large discoveries of silver in Colorado led to the price of silver falling below the old mint price and created a political clamor for the government to revert to the old policy that supported the silver price. In 1878, Congress responded by reintroducing the minting of silver dollars but restricted silver purchases to between $2 million and $4 million per month. This was insufficient to quiet the clamor, and in 1890 Congress passed the Sherman Silver Purchase Act to provide for the purchase of $4.5 million per month. This resulted in the immediate increase in the price of silver from 84¢ to $1.50 per ounce, which had a dramatic effect on the silver miners in Colorado; times were booming.

However, the act caused the U.S. Treasury to start stocking silver bullion, since the value of silver decreased as increasing amounts were discovered. The government's stockpiling led to a lack of confidence in the currency and caused speculators to hoard gold, thus depleting U.S. reserves.

On August 7, 1893, President Cleveland called an emergency session of Congress and repealed the Sherman Act. This reduced demand for silver by $4.5 million per month, and the price of silver crashed. Overnight, many Colorado mines became unprofitable and ceased operations. Populations moved, and many silver mining towns were doomed to become ghost towns.

In 1896, the presidential election was fought on the issue of gold versus silver. William Jennings Bryan supported silver, but William McKinley won. In 1900, McKinley succeeded in passing the Gold Standard Act, which led to further decline in the depressed silver price, more mine closures, and more ghost towns in the West.

In 1967, the United States eliminated the gold backing from the currency; by 1970, all silver content had been eliminated from U.S. coins, and the government sold the remaining silver reserves.

Mining Operations

Gold and silver deposits are frequently found together. They are formed when molten minerals are forced up from deep within the earth into the bedrock. Usually gold and silver also exist with other minerals such as pyrite (fool's gold) and galena (which has a silvery appearance). Commonly, the host rock is quartz.

Over time, erosion breaks down the rock deposits and the gold is freed and left in pure form. Water then disperses the free gold along stream beds. In its free form, gold exists in a variety of shapes: nuggets, scale, shot, grains, dust. These free deposits are known as "placers" when the gold is found in stream beds or along stream banks. A deposit of gold that is still contained in a rock formation is called a "lode."

Placer Mining

Because placers are relatively easy to find, they are normally the first gold deposits discovered in any area. Miners typically follow the placers upstream to the mother lode.

Placer mining is the simplest form of mining operations, since it merely involves separating the free gold from the dirt,

Gold dredge #3 near Breckenridge

mud, or gravel with which it is mixed. The process takes a number of forms:

- simple panning
- sluicing to process a larger volume, using the same principle as panning
- dredging to process even larger volumes of rock (Dredge mining utilizes a power-driven chain of small buckets mounted on a barge, leaving in its wake squalid piles of washed rock to mark its course for decades to come. Processing tons of rock and soil quickly, dredges overcame the problem of large quantities of low-grade gravel. Dredges could move up to three-quarters of a million yards of earth per annum.)
- hydraulic mining (used where the ancient riverbeds had long since disappeared, leaving the gold on dry land and some distance from any existing stream. Hydraulic mining uses hoses to bring water from up to three miles distant and wash away the extraneous material to recover the gold.)

Placer mining was known as "poor man's mining," because panning a creek could be done with very little capital. Colorado's placer production has been nearly all gold.

Hard-Rock Mining

Hard-rock mining involves digging ore out of the ground and recovering it from the quartz (or other minerals) surrounding it.

Magazine illustration of mining operations, published in 1884

Hard-rock mining in its simplest form involves tunneling horizontally under the vein (either directly or from an initial vertical shaft), then digging out the ore into mine cars placed beneath it. In the 1800s, mining cars were pulled by mules along tracks laid in the mines. If the mine incorporated a vertical shaft, then a hoist would lift the ore to the surface. Digging the shafts was made much easier during the 1870s, when hand drilling techniques were made obsolete by machine drills and dynamite.

Once extracted from the mine, the gold had to be separated from the host rock. To do this economically in the latter half of the nineteenth century, mining companies made use of stamp mills. Large structures that processed the ore in stages, stamp mills required water and a downhill slope. Milling involved progressively crushing the ore, then processing it chemically to extract the precious metal. Mine workers brought the ore into the mill and fed it into a stamper, which weighed up to a ton. The stamper crushed the host rock; then a slurry of the crushed ore and water was fed over a series of mercury-coated amalgamation plates, which captured the precious metal.

Because hard-rock mining required substantial capital, only large mining corporations normally undertook hard-rock mining operations. The men who worked the mines were employees of the larger corporations.

Animals

Mammals

Bighorn Sheep

Bighorn sheep are grayish-brown with yellowish-white rump patches and short brown tails. Some have whitish fur around their muzzles, eyes, bellies, and calves. They have muscular bodies and thick necks. Ewes weigh around 150 pounds, and rams range from 150 to 250 pounds. Both the male and female have horns that grow continually and never molt. The male's are massive and coil up and back over his ears, down and forward in a "C" shape, up to forty inches long. The ewe's horns are thin and only slightly curved— no more than a half curl.

Bighorn sheep

Bighorn sheep are active by day, dwelling on cliffs, mountain slopes, and rolling foothills. They feed on a wide variety of grasses and shrubs.

Rams challenge each other by having butting contests in which they simultaneously charge each other. Their combined speed can be more than forty miles per hour just before impact, and their foreheads meet with a crack that can be heard a mile away. These contests can last for as long as twenty hours. Horn size determines status among rams, but these ramming contests establish hierarchy among the rams with horns of similar size.

Many bighorns have died from diseases contracted from domestic livestock; the bighorn population has suffered greatly. Relocation programs and efforts to reduce competition with livestock have successfully recovered some of the herds.

Bison

The bison has an imposing appearance, with its dark brown shaggy hair, woolly mane, massive head, high shoulders, short legs, and long, tufted tail. Bison are the largest terrestrial animals in North America. Cows range in weight from eight hundred to one thousand pounds, and bulls can weigh well over two thousand pounds. Both sexes have short, black, sharply curved horns with pointy tips.

Bison are herd animals, grazing in groups of at least a dozen but also in massively larger herds. Grazing animals, bison feed mainly on grasses and shrubs. In winter, they clear snow from vegetation with their hooves and heads. Most active in early morning and late afternoon, they rest in the midday heat, chewing cud or dust-bathing. Bison are good swimmers, so buoyant that their heads, humps, and tails remain above water.

When frightened, bison will stampede, galloping at high speeds. Because they are unpredictable at all times, do not approach bison too closely for any reason.

Males may battle each other in an attempt to mate with a cow. Fights can involve butting, horn locking, shoving, and hooking. When butting, males walk to within twenty feet of each other, raise their tails, and charge. Their foreheads collide with the force

Bison

of freight trains and, without apparent injury, they continue charging until one animal gives up.

Once, the North American population of bison was estimated to be seventy million. However, a mass extermination by white men began around 1830, encouraged by the government in an attempt to subdue the Indians. Today's bison population is estimated at approximately thirty thousand. You are unlikely to encounter bison on the open range as you travel the routes in this book. They are only found in national parks, refuges, game farms, and the like.

Black Bear

Black bears can actually be black, brown, or cinnamon. Approximately 60 percent of the Colorado black bear population is brown. The bears' bodies are powerful and densely furred, with slight shoulder humps, small rounded ears, small eyes set close together, and five dark, strongly curved front claws on each foot. Females range in weight from 120 to 200 pounds, and males range from 200 to 400 pounds.

Nocturnal and solitary, black bears are fairly common in Colorado's high country. They stay in forested habitats throughout the year, although they can sometimes be seen on open slopes searching for fresh greens. They usually make their dens in tree cavities, under logs, in brush piles, or under buildings, lining them with leaves or grass. Black bears are omnivorous; they eat both plants and animals. They feast on grasses, sedges, berries, fruits, tree bark, insects, honey, eggs, fish, rodents, and even miscellaneous garbage. In the fall they go into a feeding frenzy to gain as much weight as possible to get them through their winter hibernation, often adding a four-inch layer of fat to keep them warm and nourished.

During hibernation, black bears crawl into their dens, and their bodies go dormant for the winter; they do not eat, drink,

urinate, or defecate during their long sleep. Their kidneys continue to make urine, but it is reabsorbed into their bloodstream. They awaken by an internal clock in the spring and wander out in search of food.

The black bear has a lumbering walk but can actually travel up to thirty miles per hour in a bounding trot. Black bears are powerful swimmers, able fishers, and agile tree climbers.

Black bears breed in the summer; the females undergo a phenomenon in which the fertilized

Black bear

egg passes into the uterus but changes very little until late fall, when it implants and then begins to grow quickly. Females commonly give birth to a litter of one to five young in January or February.

Bobcat

Bobcats are a reddish-tawny color, with dark spots on their body and legs. Their ears are slightly tufted. Their bellies are usually buff and spotted. They have short, stubby tails with three horizontal, dark stripes. Females range in weight from fifteen to twenty-five pounds, and males range from twenty to thirty-five pounds.

The most common wildcat, bobcats live in virtually every habitat in Colorado below ten thousand feet—from dry, rocky

mountainsides to forests and rocky or brushy arid lands. Because of their secretive nature, bobcats are seldom seen.

Bobcats feast mostly on rabbits, ground squirrels, mice, birds, insects, lizards, and frogs. They are efficient predators who have keen eyes and ears to locate prey in poor light. They stalk and move at blinding speed for short distances to pounce and make the kill.

Bobcat

Solitary animals, the sexes come together only for mating. Litters of two or three kittens are born in April and May in maternity dens of dry leaves in hollow logs and under rock ledges or fallen trees. The bobcat population is currently stable, although trapping by humans once nearly decimated the species.

Cougar, Mountain Lion, Puma

These wildcats have grayish-, yellowish-, or reddish-brown fur, with buff areas on their bellies, necks, and faces. They are feline in appearance, with long, heavy legs; padded feet; retractable claws; black-tipped tails; small, round heads; short muzzles; small, rounded ears; supple bodies; strong legs; and

long tails. The females range in weight from 80 to 150 pounds, and males range from 120 to 180 pounds. Cougars are good climbers and jumpers, able to leap more than twenty feet.

Elusive and rarely seen, cougars are territorial loners who live in the wilderness throughout the mountains, foothills, and canyons. Carnivorous eaters, they thrive on large mammals such as deer and elk as well as on porcupine, mice, rabbits, and grouse. They locate prey, slink forward close to the ground, then spring onto

Cougar

their victims' backs, holding and biting the neck. They may bury the "leftovers" of a large kill and return one or more times to eat.

The cougars breed in pairs, and females with young move together. Each has its home range and rarely ventures outside it. Cougars breed every other year, and although there is no fixed breeding season, it often occurs in winter or early spring. Their maternity dens are lined with vegetation and may be located in caves, in thickets, under rock ledges, or in similarly concealed, protected places. Two to four spotted kittens are born in maternity dens from May to July.

Coyote

The coyote is grayish-brown with rusty or tan fur on its legs, feet, and ears. Canine in appearance, with pointed muzzles and bushy tails, coyotes range in weight from thirty to fifty pounds.

Their tracks appear much like those of a domestic dog but in a nearly straight line; hind feet usually come down in foreprints, with four toes per print.

Coyotes can be found in every type of habitat in Colorado—from the eastern plains to the slopes of the alpine tundra. Coyotes inhabit the deepest wilderness as well as the suburbs of Denver. Coyotes rarely seek shelter and remain in dens only when they have pups. They are both carnivores and

Coyote

scavengers with an opportunistic variety of diet including rabbits, mice, squirrels, birds, frogs, snakes, grasshoppers, fruits, berries, and sheep and other domestic livestock. In winter they often eat carrion from larger animals, especially deer, as an important food source.

They are vocal animals whose call is commonly heard at dusk or dawn, consisting of a series of barks and yelps, followed by a prolonged howl and short yaps. Coyotes howl as a means of communicating with each other; one call usually prompts other coyotes to join in, resulting in a chorus audible for significant distances.

They are stealthy runners and can cruise at twenty-five to thirty-five miles per hour, making leaps as high as fourteen feet. They hunt singly or in pairs, acting as a relay team to chase and tire their prey.

Coyotes are monogamous and often mate for life. Their maternal dens are usually found or dug by the female under large boulders, in caves, on hillsides, or along river embankments. The openings, or mouths, of these dens usually measure several feet wide and are often marked by a mound of earth and tracks. Unless disturbed, a coyote might use the same den from year to year. Coyotes breed in February, March, and April, and give birth to a litter of four or more pups by May.

The population of coyotes is flourishing, despite the popular demand for their fur in the 1970s and 1980s. Their main enemies are humans.

Elk

Elk are large deer with brown bodies, tawny-colored rumps, thick necks, and sturdy legs. Cows range in weight from five hundred to six hundred pounds, and bulls range from six hundred to one thousand pounds. Only the males have antlers, which they shed each year.

From the eastern foothills to the western border of Colorado, elk are often found in the timberline or in grassy clearings just below the timberline. They remain in herds throughout the year and feed on grasses, shrubs, and trees.

In the late summer and early fall, bulls display behavior caused by their high levels of testosterone: They begin thrashing bushes and "bugling"— making a sound that begins as a bellow, changes to a shrill whistle or scream, and ends with a series of grunts. This vocalization broadcasts a bull's presence to other bulls and functions as a call of domination to the cows. Bulls become territorial and make great efforts to keep the cows

Elk

together (a harem may consist of up to sixty cows), mating as they come into heat and keeping other bulls at distance. Bulls often clash antlers in mating jousts but are seldom hurt.

Calves are born in the late spring after a gestation period of about nine months.

Colorado has the largest elk population in the United States.

Fox

Four types of foxes live in Colorado: the swift fox, kit fox, red fox, and gray fox.

The *swift fox* has yellow eyes and buff yellow fur, with grayish areas above, and white chins, throats, and bellies. Most have a black tip on their tails. Swift foxes are the smallest of Colorado's foxes, weighing three to six pounds and measuring fifteen to twenty inches long, with ten-inch tails. This fox is found primarily in eastern regions of Colorado in plains, short-grass prairies, and open desert areas. Swift foxes live in

underground dens with several entrances and sometimes settle in old badger or marmot dens. They eat rodents and insects. In winter, they can catch food under the snow. Swift foxes can run up to twenty-five miles per hour, hence their name. Because they are trusting and easily killed, swift foxes are currently in danger of extinction. Trapping, shooting, poisoning, and automobiles are the major causes of mortality. Captive breeding programs are under way to reestablish the swift fox in portions of its historic range and its future depends on our ability to preserve its habitat.

The *kit fox* is very similar in appearance to the swift fox, except that it has a longer tail and larger, more closely set ears. Kit foxes live in the desert shrublands of western and southwestern Colorado.

Red foxes are rusty red in color, with white underparts, chins, and throats. Their tails are very bushy, long, and red, with white tips. Their lower legs and feet are black. The red fox weighs eight to twelve pounds and measures about two feet long with a fifteen-inch tail. This animal is the most common fox in Colorado, partly because of its adaptability to a wide variety of habitats. They are found in all types of habitats, from alpine tundra to farmland to forests. Red foxes are primarily nocturnal, elusive animals, making them difficult to observe. Their favorite foods are voles and mice, followed by almost anything that is available—including rabbits, birds, reptiles, fruits, berries, eggs, insects, and carrion from larger animals. An adult red fox can eat up to one hundred mice per week. Red foxes have keen hearing and can listen for burrowing or gnawing animals underground and then dig into the soil or snow to capture them. They continue to catch food even when they are full, burying the excess in the dirt or snow for later. For years, unregulated trapping took a heavy toll on the red fox population, but the collapse of the fur industry has improved matters. With poultry farms being made nearly predator-proof, farmers kill fewer foxes. The red fox's range is expanding, although competition with the coyote may have a restraining effect.

Red fox

The *gray fox* is recognizable by its salt-and-pepper gray coat, its rust-colored legs and feet, its white throat and belly, its black-tipped tail, and the dark streak down its spine. The gray fox weighs seven to thirteen pounds and is about twenty-two to thirty inches long with a ten- to fifteen-inch tail. This animal prefers heavier cover and is more nocturnal than the red fox, so it is rarely seen. It lives in wooded and brushy slopes in the valleys, north to the Wyoming border. The gray fox is the only fox that commonly climbs trees and has been known to rest, hide, or escape into them. Gray foxes sometimes raise their young in large, hollow trees, some of which have entrance holes as high as twenty feet. More often, dens are located among rocks, in cliffsides, or in hollow trees or logs. Because the gray fox's pelt is undesirably bristly, it has never been heavily hunted or trapped for its fur. Like the other foxes, their worst enemies are humans.

Mountain Goat

Mountain goats have white shaggy hair all over their bodies, with longer hair under their chins to form a beard. They have black eyes, noses, hooves, and horns. Their bodies are compact, and their legs are short. Nannies weigh around 150 pounds, and billies weigh from 200 to 325 pounds. Both females and males have smooth, backward-curving horns, although the male's are much larger. Because horns grow continuously throughout the animal's lifetime and are never shed, the older males tend to have largest horns.

Mountain goats are found in the highest, most inhospitable, remote places in Colorado. They are hardy animals who live

Mountain goat

throughout the year on alpine cliffs and meadows, even when temperatures drop far below zero, winds gust up to one hundred miles per hour, and blizzards rage. Mountain goats feed on grasses, sedges, and other green plants.

Their hooves, with rubbery soles for traction, are well adapted for traversing rocky peaks. Their bodies are slender, so they can traverse narrow mountain ledges. Short legs and powerful shoulder muscles allow the goat to ascend steep, rugged terrain. Their shaggy outer layer of hair creates insulation from the extreme cold with protective long, hollow strands; while their inner layer of hair is more like a thick woolen sweater.

Mountain goats follow a social hierarchy. The older, stronger goats dominate, followed by aggressive adult females, followed by two-year-old males, two-year-old females, yearlings, and kids. Adult males are subordinate to other classes, except during rutting. In breeding season, rival billies threaten each other; but the threats do not always result in a fight.

The mountain goat is not native to the Rocky Mountains but was successfully introduced to the area by humans.

Mule Deer

Gray in winter, the mule deer's coat changes to reddish-brown in summer. Some have a whitish throat and rump patch. Their tails are either black-tipped or black on top. Mule deer have large, mule-like ears that move almost constantly. They are

Mule deer buck

medium-sized deer with stocky bodies and long, slim, sturdy legs. Does range in weight from 100 to 180 pounds, and bucks range from 150 to 400 pounds. Only the buck has antlers; he sheds them in the winter and begins to grow another set in the spring.

The most common large mammal in Colorado, mule deer can be found in dense populations throughout the state, particularly in abundance in the San Juans, Rockies, and Sangre de Cristos. They tend to spend the summers on high mountain pastures, alpine meadows, and sometimes logged areas. The onset of winter snowstorms causes them to migrate to lower slopes, where food supplies are more abundant. Mule deer's summer forage includes grasses, sagebrush, serviceberry, and chokecherry. In winter they browse on twigs, shrubs, and acorns. They are most active in the mornings, evenings, and moonlit nights.

The mule deer's social group generally consists of the doe and her fawn or twins, while bucks are often solitary. In November, bucks become increasingly active and intolerant of each other, sometimes engaging in conflict or vigorous fights wherein each tries, with antlers enmeshed, to force down the other's head. Injuries are rare, and usually the loser withdraws.

Mule deer breed in mid-November; fawns usually arrive in June, July, and August, with spotted coats for camouflage. A doe giving birth for the first time normally produces a single fawn, whereas an older doe tends to have twins.

Pronghorn

Pronghorns are pale or reddish-tan in color on the upper body and outer legs, with two white bands across the throat, a white rump patch, white chest, white lower sides, and white inner legs. The buck has vertical black markings from eyes to snout and along the sides of the throat. Does range in weight from 75 to 110 pounds, and bulls range from 110 to 130 pounds. Both sexes have sets of horns; the doe's are seldom longer than three or four inches, but a buck's horns can grow as long as twenty inches, curving back and slightly inward.

Pronghorns are common and highly visible in open, rolling plains or grasslands. Active night and day, they alternate bits of sleep with watchful feeding. Pronghorns feed on

Pronghorns

grasses and forbs in summer and sagebrush and other shrubs in winter.

They are the fastest animal in the Western Hemisphere and have been clocked at eighty miles per hour, although forty-five miles per hour is more usual. The pronghorns run with their mouths open, not from exhaustion but to gasp extra oxygen. When it senses danger, a pronghorn snorts and erects the white hairs on its rump (twice as long as the body hairs), which creates a flash of white as it flees and warns other pronghorn of danger. If a surprise attack forces a pronghorn to fight rather than flee, it uses its sharp hooves, which can effectively drive off a coyote.

Adult bucks establish territories in March and hold them through the September breeding season. Throughout the spring and summer, non-territorial bucks gather into bachelor herds, while the does and fawns drift on and off the territories. By late September, territorial bucks try to hold groups of does and fawns on their territories for breeding and keep other bucks away. These territories are abandoned after the breeding season; horns are shed; and all ages and both sexes congregate on winter range. The young are usually born in April, May, and June.

Pronghorn populations were reduced to less than twenty-five thousand in the mid-1920s due to the fencing of range land, which hampered migration and foraging (pronghorns cannot leap fences like deer—they crawl under them instead). With management and transplantation of herds by game departments, the pronghorn population is steadily increasing, and current estimates are at more than five hundred thousand.

Raccoon

Raccoons have salt-and-pepper coloring with black masks across their eyes and black-and-white-ringed tails. Raccoons appear slightly hunchbacked. They are about two feet long, with a ten-inch tail. They range in weight from ten to twenty-five pounds.

Raccoons are found near water, living in dens in hollow trees, logs, rock crevices, or ground burrows. They live in lower elevations throughout Colorado. They feed mostly along streams, lakes, or ponds; and their favorite foods include fruits, nuts, grains, insects, eggs, and fish. They appear to wash their food before eating it but are actually feeling for the edible parts.

Raccoons do not hibernate but may sleep for several days during cold weather.

Raccoon

Raccoons give birth in April and May to litters of between two and seven young. Naturalists estimate that there are fifteen to twenty times as many raccoons now than there were in the 1930s.

River Otter

Dark brown in color, with silvery fur on their underparts, river otters have long, cylindrical bodies; small, rounded ears; large noses; small, beady eyes; long whiskers; and thick, furry tails. River otters are about three feet long, with ten- to eighteen-inch tails; they range in weight from ten to twenty-five pounds.

River otters live in large rivers, streams, or beaver ponds throughout Colorado, especially in the north. They enjoy a variety of food but feed primarily on fish, frogs, and aquatic invertebrates. River otters can stay under water for two to three minutes, because their pulse slows and skin flaps close over their ears and nostrils. They have powerful feet and webbed toes to propel them through the water. Stiff whiskers help them hunt by feel under water. Cold waters do not bother them, because their dense fur and oily underfur does not allow water to reach their skin.

River otters tend to use beaver and muskrat burrows as their own. They are very playful animals who spend much time frolicking and chasing each other.

River otter

Pups are born in litters of one to four in March, April, and May—furry, blind, and helpless. River otters were reintroduced in several places in Colorado in 1976.

White-Tailed Deer

White-tailed deer are grayish-brown in winter and reddish-brown in summer. Their tails are white below and brown above. The white-tailed deer has small ears and a slim, graceful appearance. Does range in weight from 120 to 180 pounds, and bucks range from 150 to 400 pounds. Only the buck has antlers; he sheds them in the winter and begins to grow another set in the spring.

White-tailed deer are occasionally found in farmlands, but they prefer a somewhat denser woodland habitat in riparian areas. These deer are adaptable to live near human communities, but are timid and elusive—primarily nocturnal. White-tailed deer forage on a variety of foods—including shrubs, trees, acorns, or

White-tailed deer buck

grass—according to what is in season. They also enjoy garden vegetables (corn, peas, lettuce, apples, herbs) and other agricultural items.

When nervous, the white-tailed deer snorts through its nose and stamps its hooves; when spooked, it raises its white tail, thus alerting other deer of danger. They are good swimmers, can run thirty to forty miles per hour, and can jump thirty feet horizontally and over eight feet vertically.

White-tailed deer breed in much the same manner as mule deer, except that buck fighting is less common. They are fewer in population than mule deer and are altogether absent from western Colorado.

Rodents

Although rodents are mammals, they have been categorized separately for ease of reference.

Beaver

Beavers are very large rodents with thick brown fur; chunky bodies; short legs; rounded heads; small, rounded ears; yellowish-orange front incisors; webbed hind feet; and flat, hairless, paddle-shaped tails. Their weight ranges from thirty to sixty pounds.

Throughout Colorado, beavers live in lakes, streams, ponds, and rivers from four thousand feet to timberline. They eat bark and twigs. Since they do not hibernate, they collect large caches of twigs and branches to eat in their lodge during the winter.

Beaver

Beavers have thick layers of fat and waterproof fur, so icy waters don't bother them. They have skin flaps that close over their ears and nostrils when submerged and webbed feet for swimming. Their eyes have a clear membrane cover that allows them to see in water and protects their eyes from floating debris. A beaver can remain submerged for up to fifteen minutes before coming up for air.

Beavers build dams of sticks and mud across streams and slow rivers. They gnaw down trees, strip them, cut them into small sections, and weave them into the dam, holding the logs in place with mud. They also build lodges with one or more entrances below water and the living chamber well above waterline.

Beavers mate for life, which can be as long as twenty years. Furry beaver kits are born in the lodges in spring, with their eyes open.

The beaver population almost died out during the nineteenth century because of unregulated trapping for their fashionable fur (used primarily for hats). However, due to fashion changes and the Colorado legislature placing the beaver on a list of protected animals, the beaver population has been reestablished and is thriving.

Chipmunk

Several varieties of chipmunks in Colorado share similar characteristics and are not easily discerned from each other. Ranging in color from chestnut to yellowish-gray to light gray, chipmunks are small rodents with dark and light stripes on their face. Dark stripes line their backs from the neck to the base of the tail, with white stripes running parallel on the back portion only. The palest chipmunks tend to be found in arid environments. They measure about three to six inches long,

Chipmunk

with three- to four-inch tails, and weigh a mere one to four ounces.

Chipmunks are active during the day and hibernate in winter. They eat a variety of vegetation, including seeds, leaves, fruits, flower components, and other plants. They have large, fur-lined internal cheek pouches used for carrying food. Chipmunks stow away a great deal of their food; instead of relying on stored body fat to sustain them during hibernation, they awaken periodically throughout winter and early spring to eat from their caches.

They dig burrows and line them with grass underneath rocks, logs, and roots; these burrows become the nests where they have their young. Babies are born blind and naked after a gestation period of about thirty days.

Cottontail, Rabbit

One of the most abundant animals in nature, cottontails are very similar in appearance and behavior to hares (jackrabbits), except that they tend to be smaller and have shorter ears, smaller feet, and shorter hind legs. They do not turn white in winter. Of the several types of cottontail in Colorado, the *desert cottontail* is found in the southwest and the eastern plains; the *eastern cottontail* is found in woodlands in the east; and the most common cottontail in the Rockies is the *mountain cottontail*, also called *Nuttall's cottontail*.

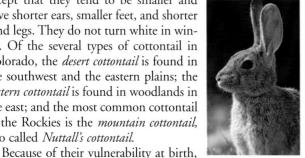

Mountain cottontail

Because of their vulnerability at birth, cottontails are born in maternal nests, which the pregnant female finds and prepares about a week before giving birth. She locates a suitable spot where brush or high grass provides protection and makes a saucer-like depression in the ground, lining it with her own downy fur, soft grasses, and leaves. Adults may have three or four litters per year in a good habitat. Unlike hares, cottontails are born naked, with their eyes closed.

Hare, Jackrabbit

Hares are very similar in appearance to cottontails (rabbits), but they tend to be larger and have longer ears, bigger feet, and longer back legs. It is suggested that hares got the name "jackrabbit" because their large ears resemble those of jackasses. Their fur is a mottled gray and brown in summer. It be-

comes almost pure white in northern areas of the state in winter, while in the south it gets paler but still holds tinges of brown and gray. Does (females) are larger than bucks, which is unusual in mammals. Their weight varies from three to ten pounds.

Snowshoe hare

Colorado's three species of hare are the *white-tailed jackrabbit* (found in mountain parks and shortgrass prairies), the *black-tailed jackrabbit* (found in semi-desert country in western and southern Colorado, as well as eastern plains), and the *snowshoe hare* (found mainly in sub-alpine forests).

In summer, jackrabbits eat mostly green plants, such as clover and flowers. In winter, they rely more on shrubs. Their huge ears are so sensitive that they can detect the muted sound of a coyote as its fur brushes against the grass. When threatened, they first freeze, laying their ears back to be less conspicuous, their coat assisting with the camouflage. If this fails, they can move from a hiding place like lightning, at speeds up to thirty-five miles per hour, and change direction instantly.

Unlike cottontails, young hares are born fully furred, with their eyes open. The female puts each young hare into an individual form, or depression, in the ground, thus decreasing a predator's chance of taking her entire litter. She keeps her distance by day and comes several times to nurse at night so that she attracts less attention.

Marmot, Rockchuck

Brown to yellowish-brown with yellowish bellies, marmots have heavy bodies with short legs, small ears, and bushy tails. Marmots range in weight from five to ten pounds and measure one to two feet in length, with a five- to seven-inch tail. They are the largest ground-dwelling squirrels in the region.

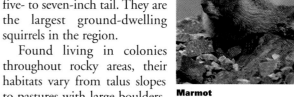

Marmot

Found living in colonies throughout rocky areas, their habitats vary from talus slopes to pastures with large boulders. They feed on grass and plants. Sunbathing on rocks is a favored pastime; while the group enjoys the activity, at least one marmot stands guard to warn the others of danger. When danger approaches, the sentry lets out high-pitched chirps so that the group can scurry to safety.

These burrowing animals spend as much as eight months of the year underground and begin hibernation as early as September. In April and May, females give birth to three to six naked and blind young in their grass-lined dens.

Pika

These small rodents have short, dense, gray-brown fur; round bodies; short legs; large heads; short, rounded ears; and no visible tail. They are small and mouse-like, about eight inches long and four to seven ounces in weight.

Pikas live in colonies found in rocky fields and talus slopes above 8,500 feet in alpine and subalpine meadows throughout

Pika

Colorado. Pikas feed on a variety of grasses, sedges, and forbs. They spend most of the summer gathering great quantities of vegetation and storing it for winter. They clip off bits and carry it back to rock piles where they spread it out to dry in the sun. If rain threatens before the stacks are cured, the pika carries its harvest one mouthful at a time to the shelter of a rocky burrow. It is not uncommon for one pika to store as much as four bushels.

When not foraging, pikas like to find a safe perch near an escape route and keep an eye out for predators. Active during the day, pikas blend with the rocks, yet their characteristic squeak gives them away every time. You can often hear a pika before you see it, although it is usually difficult to tell the direction from which the sound comes. Uttered at the first sign of danger, the call is picked up by other pikas and echoed throughout the colony.

Instead of hibernating for winter, the pika is active all year, moving around beneath the rocks in tunnels dug through the snow. It lives off the caches of food gathered in the summer.

Pikas usually mate in the early spring, producing a litter in May or June; a second litter may be produced in late summer.

Porcupine

Porcupines are gray-brown, with chunky bodies, high arching backs, and short legs. Yellowish hair covers long quills all over their backs, rumps, and tails. These rodents measure up to two feet in length, with an eight-inch tail, and range in weight from ten to twenty-eight pounds. Next to the beaver, they are the largest rodents in Colorado.

Found in nearly all forested areas throughout the state, porcupines are active year-round. Porcupines feast on green plants, grass, and leaves in summer and tree bark in winter. They are slow-moving animals with poor eye-

Porcupine

sight, yet they are equipped with thousands of barbed quills for protection against predators. Contrary to popular belief, porcupines do not throw their quills; quills are released from the porcupine's body and penetrate the enemy's skin. Not only are quills hard to pull out, they readily work themselves in

further. This can produce painful and fatal results.

Porcupines are primarily nocturnal, but they can occasionally be seen resting in treetops during the day. They make their dens in logs or caves and use them for sleeping and birthing.

Kits are born May and June, after a gestation period of seven months. They are born headfirst, with quills aimed backwards.

Prairie Dog

The prairie dog varieties described below are roughly the same size: one to two-and-a-half pounds, about one foot tall. Prairie dogs are active during daylight hours only, and they are most energetic at dawn and dusk. They feed on grass, plants, and insects, with a particular fondness for grasshoppers.

Black-tailed prairie dogs, found in the grasslands of the eastern plains of Colorado, are the most common variety. They are brownish-yellow on the back and sides, with whitish bellies, small ears, and black-tipped tails. Black-tailed prairie dogs are social animals who live in colonies, or "prairie dog towns," composed of several families. On purely a friendly level, they approach each other and touch noses and incisors to "kiss." They communicate by barking a variety of different sounds and groom each other socially—not as an act of courtship.

Prairie dog

Black-tailed prairie dogs retreat to their burrows for brief periods during warm summer days to escape the afternoon heat or for longer periods of time when the weather is severely cold. They do not hibernate but go dormant in bitter winter weather, arousing to feed during warm spells.

They give birth in their burrows to one litter of deaf, blind, and hairless pups in April, after a gestation period of about thirty days.

White-tailed prairie dogs are fawny-colored, sprinkled with black on the back and sides, with whitish bellies, small ears, and white-tipped tails. They are similar to black-tailed prairie dogs, except they are slightly smaller, less social, and they hibernate from fall to spring. They live at higher elevations on plains in the northwestern portion of Colorado.

Their pups are born in April, after a gestation period of about thirty days. They vacate their burrows in May and June, and their dens are taken over by other animals.

Gunnison's prairie dogs are a yellowish color, mixed with black, with slightly paler bellies, and short, white-tipped tails. The smallest of the prairie dog species found in Colorado, they live in high mountain valleys and plateaus of the Rocky Mountains in southwestern and central Colorado at elevations of 6,000 to 12,000 feet.

Gunnison's prairie dogs are less social than the two types discussed above, with smaller communities that are considerably less developed. Their modes of communication include a distinctive danger call that is often repeated and gets louder as the urgency intensifies.

Females typically give birth to one litter in May, after a gestation period of twenty-seven to thirty-three days.

Squirrel

The most abundant ground squirrel in Colorado, the *rock squirrel* is also the largest. Rock squirrels are mottled gray-brown in front and darker behind, with buff bellies. Their tails are long and bushy with sprinklings of brown and buff edges. True to its name, the rock squirrel dwells in rocky locales—such as cliffs, canyon walls, talus slopes, and boulder piles—and digs its den in the ground below.

Rock squirrels dine on berries, nuts, plants, or carrion and often collect food to transport and store back in their dens. They are often seen sitting on or running among rocks, but they are also good tree climbers.

Abert's squirrel

Vocalizations include an alarm call, which is short and followed by a lower-pitched trill. They have a sharp, sometimes quavering whistle.

Females normally bear two litters during the year, one in late spring or early summer and the other in late summer or early fall.

Abert's squirrels (also called *tassel-eared squirrels*) have grizzled gray, black, or reddish sides and backs, with white or black bellies. They can also be solid black in Colorado.

The Abert's squirrel is a large tree squirrel with very distinctive tasseled ears (less tufted in summer). They live in ponderosa pine forests, feeding on pine cones, bark, buds, and twigs of the trees. They build nests of twigs in the trees, where they sleep at night, court, mate, and raise their young.

Abert's squirrels do not hibernate; they remain in their nests during cold weather and venture out to recover stored food below. Mating chases last all day in late winter, during which males frantically chase the females around. A litter of about four young is usually born in April or May, after a gestation period of about forty-six days.

The *red squirrel* (also called *pine squirrel* or *chickaree*) is a small tree squirrel found in Colorado's high country. Its coat is flecked rust-red in the summer and gray-red in the winter. Red squirrels are seven to eight inches long, with bushy four- to six-inch tails.

The red squirrel is the smallest tree squirrel, yet the most common in Colorado's Rocky Mountains. They enjoy opportunistic varieties of nuts, seeds, eggs, pine cones, and fungi. They often have a preference for a favorite feeding stump or branch, where you might find piles of cones or seed pods. In the fall, they stow large quantities of food in caches in the ground, in hollow trees, and in other spots. They do not hibernate in winter. Red squirrels make nests of grass and shredded bark in tree cavities or branches. Litters of young are born in April and May, after a gestation period of thirty-five days; sometimes mothers bear a second litter in August or September.

Snakes

Bullsnake

Also called gopher snakes, bullsnakes are found throughout Colorado in a wide range of habitats below 8,500 feet. They tend to live in riparian areas, forests, canyons, and shrubby areas. Large snakes, they can grow to a length of 36 to 110 inches.

Bullsnakes are often mistaken for rattlesnakes because of their similarity in appearance and behavior. When cornered or disturbed, a bullsnake will often hiss and coil, shaking its tail like a rattlesnake, even striking. Yet, the formidable-looking snake is harmless. Unlike the rattler, the bullsnake is a constrictor, wrapping its coils around its prey and squeezing it to death. Bullsnakes avoid the hottest hours of the day by staying in the shade and moving about early and late in

Bullsnake

the day. They hibernate from October to April in deep dens in cracks of rocks or in caves. Bullsnakes are known to share their dens with other snakes, such as rattlesnakes, milk snakes, and garter snakes.

Garter Snake

Four types of garter snake found in Colorado are the *black-neck, western terrestrial, plains,* and *common garter snake.* The most abundant species is the western terrestrial, which is distributed throughout most of Colorado but absent from the northeastern portion of the state. The moderately slender bod-

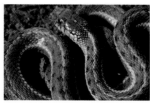
Garter snake

ies of adults range from 24 to 42 inches in length. Their coloring is brown to gray, with a gray and tan checkerboard pattern that darkens and becomes obscure with age. They have light stripes down the sides of their bodies, which become less prominent with age. There is also a distinctive light stripe down the back of some individuals. Western terrestrial garter snakes feed on snails, slugs, earthworms, fish, various small reptiles, and small rodents. When captured, they emit an unpleasant fluid from vent glands.

Milk Snake

Milk snakes have vivid buff, black, and red horizontal stripes around their bodies. Adults reach a maximum total length of about 36 inches. They are often confused with the deadly coral snake, a species not found in Colorado. Milk snakes are found in a wide range of habitats throughout most of the state. In southeastern Colorado, they are most likely to be found at elevations below 8,000 feet and in western Colorado, below 6,000

Milk snake

feet. A constrictor, the milk snake kills its prey by squeezing. Milk snakes are frequently lured to farms, ghost towns, and abandoned buildings by their favorite food, rodents.

Western Rattlesnake

Western rattlesnakes are found in virtually every terrestrial habitat throughout Colorado, from grasslands, sand hills, rocky areas, riparian vegetation, mountain and semidesert shrublands, to open coniferous forests. Only perennially wet areas seem to be avoided. They live at maximum elevations of about 9,500 feet.

The western rattlesnake is typically greenish yellow with darker blotches (although individual colors will vary, depending on how long it has been since the last molt), triangular head, narrow neck, and ranges from fifteen to sixty-five inches, including the obvious rattle on the end of its tail.

Western rattlesnakes live in prairie dog burrows or crevices during winter and emerge for spring-summer activities in May. In hot summer weather they usually prowl at dusk and at night. Pores in their heads pick up scents and heat to help detect prey. The snake kills its prey by injecting it with venom through hollow fangs that snap downward and forward as it strikes.

Western rattlesnake

To human beings, a western rattler's bite is painful and can cause infection and illness, although there have been few fatalities documented among bitten adults. According to the Colorado Department of Health, only four people have died from snakebites in the state between 1970 and 1987. They are not aggressive snakes, although they usually rattle and assume a coiled, defensive posture when approached. If left alone, they normally crawl away and seek a hiding place. Exercise caution in tall grass, rocky areas, and around prairie dog towns, especially in the mornings and evenings and after summer thunderstorms.

Birds

Black-Billed Magpie

One of the most commonly seen birds in Colorado, this bird's black and white coloration and long tail make it easy to identify. It lives anywhere from cities to wilderness areas, and it eats almost anything, thriving by being adaptable. It is a big, flashy, boisterous, and loud bird, with a reputation for raiding the nests of other birds, picking sores of cattle, and attacking the eyes of injured animals. Magpies are found all over Colorado year-round, but mainly at elevations lower than ten thousand feet. Their sturdy nests, made of mud and reeds, are used from year to year; they also mate with the same partners from year to year.

Black-billed magpie

Eagle

The two eagles in Colorado are the golden eagle and the bald eagle. The bald eagle is primarily a winter visitor, arriving around November. Eagles are noted for their strength and keen vision. They have large, heavy, hooked bills and strong, sharp claws called talons. They are usually brown, black, or gray, sometimes with markings on the head, neck, wings, or tail. The bald eagle is not really bald; it was named for its white head.

Bald eagle

The rest of its plumage is brown, except for its white tail. Eagles prey on small animals such as fish, rodents, birds, and snakes. They have very sharp eyesight and hunt while soaring high in the air or watching from a high perch, swooping down to make the kill with their powerful talons. The eagle makes its nest, or aerie, high in a tree or on a rocky ledge where it cannot be reached by other animals, since young eagles remain helpless for a long period. Each year the birds add new material to the nest. The largest known nest ever measured was twenty feet deep and nearly ten feet wide.

Gray Jay

This bird is ten to thirteen inches long, with gray and white plumage, and no crest on its head. Mainly found year-round in coniferous forests in the mountains from 8,500 feet to timberline, the gray jay is not very afraid of humans. This resourceful little bird has learned that people can mean food. It sometimes eats out of human hands, steals food, or even pries open containers. On their own, gray jays eat seeds, small birds, carrion, and insects.

Gray jay

The gray jay is one of five jays found in Colorado. The others are the *Steller's jay* (dark crest, metallic blue, equally bold), *pinyon jay* (grayish-blue, timid, lives in pinyon pines), *blue jay* (deep blue, found in urban areas), and *scrub jay* (low elevations in oak stands).

Great Horned Owl

The great horned owl is the largest, most commonly seen and widespread of the owl species in Colorado. It has been found throughout Colorado in areas ranging from cottonwood groves to coniferous forests below ten thousand feet. It has long ear tufts and yellow eyes. At night you can sometimes hear its deep, resonating hoots. They are skilled hunters, well-equipped for killing their prey. They use their sharp talons to grip prey such as rabbits, weasels, squirrels, and birds in a deadly lock. The owls have a wide range of vision: Their necks can swivel nearly 180 degrees, and they can practically see in the dark.

Great horned owl

Hummingbird

The name hummingbird originates from the noise these birds' wings make in flight. Hummingbirds are the smallest of all birds and are only a few inches long. They feed on nectar, although they also regularly consume small insects. They obtain nectar by inserting their bills and tongues into a flower, thus accumulating pollen on their bills and heads; this pollen is then transferred from flower to flower. Hummingbirds are strong fliers and have exceptional flight characteristics for

Hummingbird

birds: They can hover and also fly backwards. The rate of their wing beats is extremely rapid, reaching as high as eighty beats per second. Some hummingbirds save energy on cool nights by lowering their usually high body temperature until they become sluggish and unresponsive, a condition termed torpor. In contrast, during daylight hours hummingbirds are often very active and can be highly aggressive, sometimes attacking much larger potential predators, such as hawks and owls.

Mountain Bluebird

These beautiful, sky-blue birds are primarily summer residents in western Colorado. Most arrive by mid-March. They normally take over nests abandoned by woodpeckers because their beaks are not strong enough to hollow out their own cav-

Mountain bluebird

ities. Their survival today is difficult, as the logging industry cuts down many standing dead trees that they would normally use as homes. They readily adapt to whatever homes they can find, including chipmunk burrows, abandoned car bumpers, and fence posts in open areas.

Mountain Chickadee

The mountain chickadee is a year-round resident in the Colorado mountains. It is a small, energetic bird that sings

Mountain chickadee

its name: "Chick-a-dee-dee-dee." It must consume nearly its body weight in seeds and insects each day just to stay alive because of its amazingly fast heart rate of five hundred beats per minute. During cold Colorado weather, it puffs out its feathers so it resembles a fluffy ball with a beak.

Northern Flicker

The northern flicker, a type of woodpecker, can be identified in flight by a flash of salmon-red color under its wings and tail. Viewed at rest, the northern flicker has a brown crown, a brownish body, and a red streak behind the bill. The birds are found mainly in coniferous forests and aspen

Northern flicker

stands. They have powerful beaks to make nesting holes in trees. They eat mostly insects, especially ants.

Ptarmigan

Ptarmigans are stocky members of the grouse family that inhabit tundra, moors, and alpine areas. They have short, rounded white wings, extensively feathered toes, and upper tail coverts that extend to the tip of the tail. Males have red "combs" above their eyes. Ptarmigans undergo seasonal col-

White-tailed ptarmigan

or changes: In winter their white plumage matches the snow, and in summer their mottled brown plumage blends with the vegetation. Their camouflage is a good thing for their protection, because their stubby wings prohibit them from flying very far. They eat berries, buds, and leaves and fall prey to hunters, foxes, and owls.

Red-Winged Blackbird

These birds are one of the most common breeding birds in Colorado, found at elevations to about nine thousand feet. They are about eight or nine inches long and black with crimson shoulder patches, bordered with yellow. The red coloration serves as a flag used in courtship and also in aggression. They enjoy marshes, wet-

Red-winged blackbird

lands, and open fields but migrate in late September to spend their winters in warmer areas, even as far south as Costa Rica.

Plants

Alpine Zones (above 11,500 feet)

Alpine plants grow in conditions that are so harsh even the trees cannot survive. They grow above timberline in a variety of habitats, ranging from the delicate sod of alpine meadows to boulder fields to talus slopes and mountain lakes and ponds.

Since the tundra receives very little precipitation, alpine plants have adapted with strong roots that reach deep down, allowing them to feed on the scarce nutrients and moisture in the soil. Their lengthy roots further assist to protect them against arctic winds, serving as an anchor. Short stems allow them to hug the ground and reduce wind resistance.

When alpine plants flower, their blooms are often full-sized with brilliant displays—typically during June or July when they receive maximum daylight. Most are perennials (which last from year to year); annuals simply do not have time to start from seeds and complete a full life cycle before the brief growing season comes to an end.

Marsh Marigold, Elk's Lips

Marsh marigolds are found high in the mountains in small

Marsh marigolds

pools or wet areas that are often the result of early spring runoff. These low plants each bear just one white flower one to two inches across, with many yellow stamens. The leaves are heart-shaped. Sometimes marsh marigolds push up through the snow and bloom very early in the season. Height: 3 to 10 inches.

Moss Campion

Not truly a moss, this common mat-forming plant grows close to the ground and has many densely crowded, woody branches. Its many pink, rose, or white flowers do not bloom until the plant is about ten years old. Moss campion spreads like blankets across rocky ridges and slopes. Height: less than 1 inch.

Moss campion

Sky Pilot, Skunkweed

These plants emit a skunk-like odor that comes from the leaves and stems when they are crushed. The bluish-purple flowers actually have a sweet, pleasant smell. Bell-shaped flowers grow in crowded clusters around the head, blooming from June to August. They are often found growing on rocky slopes. Height: 4 to 12 inches.

Sky pilot

Subalpine Zones (to about 11,500 feet)

Subalpine plants are found midway between alpine regions and the mountain forests. They often have an even shorter growing period than alpine plants, since snow tends to stay longer in areas protected from wind and sun.

Dogtooth Violet, Avalanche Lily, Glacier Lily

This is not a violet, but actually a lily that is found in moist meadows, growing in large patches near melting snowdrifts. It has one or more yellow blossoms that curve backward from the stem. The flowers appear very early, sometimes even pushing up through the snowbanks. This plant is edible and serves as food to many mountain animals, including bears. Height: 6 to 18 inches.

Dogtooth violet

Globeflower

This plant resembles the marsh marigold and also grows in marshy areas and wet meadows. The easiest way to tell a globeflower plant from a marsh marigold is by the yellow color and its three, jagged-edged leaves. Globeflowers bloom from May to August. Height: 10 to 18 inches.

Globeflower

Parry Lousewort

These unusual-looking plants have yellow blossoms atop a stalky stem with sharp-toothed leaves. If you use your imagination, the cluster of flowers somewhat resembles an ear of corn, interspersed with tiny green leaves between the kernels. The unusual name apparently comes from an early superstition that animals could acquire lice from eating the plant. Lousewort is found on open slopes and in meadows. Height: 4 to 12 inches.

Parry lousewort

Parry Primrose

The deep magenta flowers of this plant have yellow "eyes." They rest atop a vertical stem, with all the leaves sprouting from the base, rising nearly as tall as the flower and emitting an unpleasant odor. The height of Parry primrose is unusual, considering the elevation at which they grow. Found in rock crevices, meadows, bogs, and along streams and other moist areas, they bloom from July to August. Height: 10 to 24 inches.

Parry primrose

Purple Fringe

Purple fringe is a beautiful, dense spike of bluish-purple flowers. Plants have several stems, varying in height but rarely exceeding one foot. Purple fringe blooms early in the season and into the summer. It is common in rocky or gravely meadows and dry slopes. Height: 4 to 12 inches.

Purple fringe

Snowball Saxifrage

There are a number of saxifrage varieties that grow in Colorado. The snowball saxifrage has a cluster of white flowers atop a leafless vertical stem that, from a distance, resembles a ball of snow. It grows in the moist crevices of boulders and can actually break the rocks apart! It blooms in midsummer. Height: 2 to 12 inches.

Snowball saxifrage

Montane Zone (8,000–10,000 feet)

Plants in the montane (mountain) zone have a short growing season. They grow often on steep, rocky hillsides and have to compete with trees and shrubs for nutrients in the soil.

Colorado Columbine

Although red and yellow columbines also grow in the region, the Colorado columbine is the state flower. It has five bluish-lavender petals and five white ones. The blue is symbolic of Colorado's blue skies, and the white represents snow. Columbines like moist soil and are found in ravines, rocky slopes, aspen groves, and forest clearings. They bloom from early summer to midsummer. Height: 4 to 24 inches.

Colorado columbine

Monkshood

This creamy white and bluish-violet flower has two tiny petals under a hood. Monkshood is poisonous and was once used as a medicine to lower fevers. It grows in meadows and other moist sites and normally blooms in midsummer or late summer. Height: 24 to 72 inches.

Monkshood

Yellow Monkeyflower, Wild Lettuce

Yellow monkeyflower

These low, creeping plants have bright yellow blooms and grow in masses. The petals have tiny orange or reddish-brown spots. This plant is also called wild lettuce, because Native Americans and early settlers ate the bitter leaves. The blooming season is usually from May to August. Height: 4 to 18 inches.

Foothills (5,500–8,000 feet)

Foothills are very hospitable areas for plants to grow for several reasons. They generally get plenty of water and nutrients due to snowmelt and rain runoff from the mountains. The mountains also provide them with extra protection from winds and storms.

Goldenrod, Yellowweed

Goldenrod

Goldenrod is a genus in the sunflower family. It typically has a slender, unbranched stem with short-stalked or stalkless leaves and small, yellowish flower heads in complex clusters. It is one of the later-blooming plants, usually blooming around July to September. Height: 12 to 72 inches.

Pasqueflower

This is a large, solitary, blue, white, or purple flower that measures two to two-and-a-half inches in diameter. Six petals

Pasqueflower

curve up and around the greenish-yellow centers. The leaves have a feathery appearance, but since the flower usually opens before the leaves, early in the season it can be mistaken for a globeflower. Pasqueflowers grow in meadows and hillsides in fairly deep soil. The blossoms may emerge from March to June. Height: 2 to 16 inches.

Rocky Mountain Phlox

These sweet-smelling plants have many little flowers, half an inch to one inch long, varying in color from white to pink, blue, or lavender. They grow on shrubby slopes; several stems spread around and over

Rocky Mountain phlox

rocks and gravel to form a deep rooting system. They bloom from May to July. Height: 6 to 12 inches.

Shooting Star, Birdbill

The shooting star looks like a colorful rocket. It has backward-

Shooting star

curving magenta petals with a yellow circle in the center, pointing down to form the nose. There is a rosette of leaves around the base of the stalk. Elk, deer, and cattle graze on the young shoots, which are found growing in rich soil and partial shade along streams and in wet meadows during June and July. Height: 6 to 16 inches.

Plains (below 5,500 feet)

Plants in this area have to survive drastic changes in weather, from cold winters to hot summers, with long periods of drought. They can be found in eastern Colorado and in some pockets of the western part of the state. Many of these plants have few leaves in order to conserve root moisture. Some protect themselves with thorny or tough leaves that animals won't eat.

Milkweed

Milkweed

Milkweeds have small but complex flowers in rounded clusters that vary from white or yellowish to red or purplish, with paired leaves and fruit pods filled with seeds. The sap has toxic properties, which are destroyed by boiling; Native Americans used to cook and eat the shoots, leaves, buds, flowers, and seed pods. Milkweeds are commonly found in clumps beside streams, ditches, and roadsides. Height: 18 to 72 inches.

Prickly Pear

This cactus has round pads with prickly spines coming out of

Prickly pear

the body, which is covered with a thick layer of wax to prevent water evaporation. Its flowers may be red, purple, or yellow; the blooms appear from May to June and last only a few days. It has edible fruit, which is pear-shaped and spine-covered and has a sweet flesh. Height: 3 to 15 inches.

Salsify, Goat Dandelion

Salsify

This plant looks much like a tall, large dandelion after it goes to seed. Its yellow flowers bloom in the morning and close by noon. Salsify is not a plant native to Colorado—it was brought by European settlers as a garden vegetable. Height: 12 to 18 inches.

Multiple Life Zones

These plants can grow in a variety of situations and environments all around Colorado. They may vary in appearance slightly, depending on elevation, climate, rainfall, and exposure to sunshine.

Indian Paintbrush

Indian paintbrush

Indian paintbrush flowers are small, modified leaves called "bracts," which have colorful tips of fiery orange, pink, maroon, red, or yellow, giving the appearance of a dipped paintbrush. The roots of these plants steal food from other plants. Native to slopes and meadows, this plant blooms from May to September. Height: 12 to 36 inches.

Mountain Candytuft

Candytuft is a small herb belonging to the mustard family. It has clusters of small, white, four-petaled flowers on top of

Mountain candytuft

the stems. Oval leaves surround the stem's base; and tiny, arrow-shaped leaves adorn the stem farther up. Candytufts are very common plants that are able to grow in thin soil or around rocks. Sometimes they bloom near snowbanks in alpine regions. Height: 1 to 5 inches.

Mountain Harebell

Harebell

The mountain harebell has violet-blue, bell-like flowers that hang downward to protect its pollen in the rain. It typically has round leaves (although the alpine variety can have heart-shaped or grass-like leaves) attached at the base of the stem. The stems support just one full-sized or oversized blossom. Mountain harebells are found from the foothills to timberline and their season and size varies, according to elevation and location. Height: 4 to 12 inches.

Shrubby Cinquefoil, Yellow Rose

Shrubby cinquefoil

These shrubs have yellow flowers that measure about one inch across, with five petals each. Cinquefoils keep their leaves in winter; big game animals eat them when food is scarce, although they don't enjoy the taste. Cinquefoils are found in open woods and meadows from June to August. Height: 12 to 36 inches.

Yarrow

Yarrow

Yarrow is an aromatic herb in the daisy family. The white flowers grow in flat clusters; the leaves are dissected into many fine segments, giving a feathery or fern-like appearance. Yarrow is commonly found in all zones. Height: 6 to 10 inches.

Trees

Aspen

Aspen have smooth, cream-colored bark with green, heart-shaped, deciduous leaves that turn brilliant gold in the fall. Older trees are dark at the base. Aspen grow from forty to seventy feet tall and one to two feet in diameter. They are normally found in montane and subalpine elevations up to timberline, in dry, cool places, often close to clean, flowing water. Groves of these trees allow sunlight to penetrate to the forest floor, thus encouraging diverse plant growth and providing food and shelter for numerous wildlife species.

Aspens with fall foliage

Blue Spruce

Blue spruce trees are sometimes confused with the engelmann spruce, but are distinguished by having larger cones and growing at a lower altitude. Blue spruce trees are normally found at elevations below 9,000 feet. The pyramid shape characterizes them, as do stiff, blue-green-gray needles and scaly bark. Blue spruces produce pale brown cones, hanging in separate clusters on the same tree, mainly in the upper portion, up to four inches long. Many reach heights of over one hundred feet. This is Colorado's state tree.

Blue spruce cones

Blue spruce

Bristlecone Pine

Bristlecone pines are evergreens with short, green, needle-like leaves that grow in bundles of five. They are crowded in a long, dense mass curved against the twig, in a manner that resembles the tail of a fox. The trees have a clear, sticky resin on the cones and needles that becomes white with age. The cones are dark brown, from two to four inches long, cylindrical, and covered in spiny scales. They are usually found at elevations above 9,000 feet, on steep slopes and in areas with high winds and little rainfall. Bristlecone pines vary in height from sixty feet to as short as three feet at higher elevations. The stubby needles may be retained for twenty to thirty years before being replaced. Bristlecones grow slowly and can take up to three thousand years to reach their full height. Some bristlecone pines are among the oldest trees in the world.

Bristlecone pine

Bristlecone pine cones

Cottonwood

Cottonwoods are deciduous members of the poplar family, with smooth, grayish-green bark that is often deeply furrowed on older trees. Their foliage is dark, shiny green above and paler below, turning dull yellow in the fall. Sometimes confused with aspen, the plains cottonwood is distinguished by larger, coarser, more deeply toothed, heart-shaped leaves; cottonwoods are also larger than aspens and have coarser bark, except when young. Narrowleaf cottonwood leaves are pointed at the tip, almost willow-like, with a long oval shape. Cottonwoods like moist soils and are often found near mountain streams and in coniferous forests. This handsome hardwood grows at elevations from 5,000 to 9,000 feet and usually reaches a height between forty and sixty feet.

Cottonwood

Douglas Fir

The Douglas fir is a conical evergreen with thick, furrowed, corky, dark red-brown bark. It has flattened, needle-like leaves and red-brown oblong cones that have three-pronged tongues sticking out between the cone scales. At the end of the twig there is usually one, though sometimes more than one, cone-shaped, sharp-pointed bud, brownish-red in color. These long-lived conifers grow in vast forests often in pure stands, with well-drained soil. They are among the world's most important timber trees. Douglas firs are often used for reforestation. They are usually found at elevations of 6,000 to 9,000 feet and range in height from sixty to ninety feet.

Douglas fir

Douglas fir cones

Engelmann Spruce

These evergreens are large trees with dark or blue-green needles and a dense, narrow, conical crown of branches in close rows. The branches are horizontal, often short, dense, and drooping, with cones less than two inches long. Straight, tall, and slender, Engelmann spruces are shaped vaguely like church spires—about one to two-and-a-half feet in diameter, growing upwards of fifty to eighty feet, in groves very close together. At high altitudes, the Engelmann is dwarfed, straggling, and naked on the windward side; but when growing in the open, it retains its lower branches more completely and takes on more ample outlines. It is normally found between 9,000 feet and timberline. Its needles, twigs, and seeds provide food to a variety of wildlife.

Engelmann spruce

Engelmann spruce cones

Juniper

Rocky Mountain junipers are also called mountain red cedars. They are stout, spreading, bushy trees with minute gray-green leaves that are blunt and grow close to the twig. Berries are blue in color, about a fourth of an inch in diameter, containing one or several seeds. Junipers range in height from ten feet in exposed situations to as tall as thirty feet in sheltered canyons, where the limbs might tend to droop like those of a weeping willow. Junipers are often found growing near pinyon trees (the Forest Service refers to the two together as P & J). The berries serve as an important food source to some birds and small wildlife.

Juniper

Lodgepole Pine

The bark of lodgepole pine trees is thin and loosely scaly. The foliage is yellow-green. The trees have yellow-brown, egg-shaped cones that range in length from three-fourths inches to two inches. These resin-sealed cones remain on the trees for many years. In the event of a forest fire, the resin melts away causing the cones to open and distribute the seeds to regenerate the species. These trees vary enormously in size, from fifteen to eighty feet high. They may be tall with a narrow, conical, dense crown or remain small with a broad, rounded crown. The taller trees look like fields of evenly spaced telephone poles, with little separating them but fallen needles. They grow smaller at higher elevations, where winds twist them into gnarled, bent shapes. Lodgepole pines are found primarily from 8,000 to 11,000 feet.

Lodgepole pines

Lodgepole pine cones

Pinyon Pine

Pinyons are small, bushy evergreen trees with short trunks and compact, rounded crowns. The gray to red-brown bark is rough and scaly. Needles range from three-fourths inches to two inches long, usually two to a bundle, with blue-green foliage on the younger trees and dark, yellow-green foliage on more mature ones. Cones are one to two inches and have edible seeds that are eaten raw or roasted, known as Indian nuts or pine nuts. Pinyon pines range in height from ten to thirty-five feet. They are usually found in open woodlands (often with juniper) in the foothills at elevations of 6,000 to 8,000 feet.

Pinyon pine

Pinyon pine cone

Ponderosa Pine

Also called western yellow pine, ponderosa pines have long needles (three to seven inches) that grow in clusters of two or three. The bark of young trees is dark brown and furrowed, while older trees develop orange, flaky bark. The cones are red-brown and spiky, about three to five inches long. The ponderosa pine grows sixty to ninety feet tall and is usually found at lower altitudes of 6,000 to 8,500 feet.

Ponderosa pine

Pondersoa pine cones

The Southwest Region

Trails in the Southwest Region

- **SW 1** Cinnamon Pass Road
- **SW 2** Engineer Pass Road
- **SW 3** North Fork Cutoff
- **SW 4** Silverton to Animas Forks Ghost Town
- **SW 5** California Gulch and Corkscrew Gulch Trail
- **SW 6** Carson Ghost Town Trail
- **SW 7** Yankee Boy Basin Road
- **SW 8** Imogene Pass Road
- **SW 9** Ophir Pass Road
- **SW 10** Alta Ghost Town Trail
- **SW 11** Black Bear Pass Trail
- **SW 12** Bullion King Lake Trail
- **SW 13** Cunningham Gulch and Stony Pass Trail
- **SW 14** Summitville Ghost Town Trail
- **SW 15** Bolam Pass Road
- **SW 16** Uncompahgre Plateau Trail

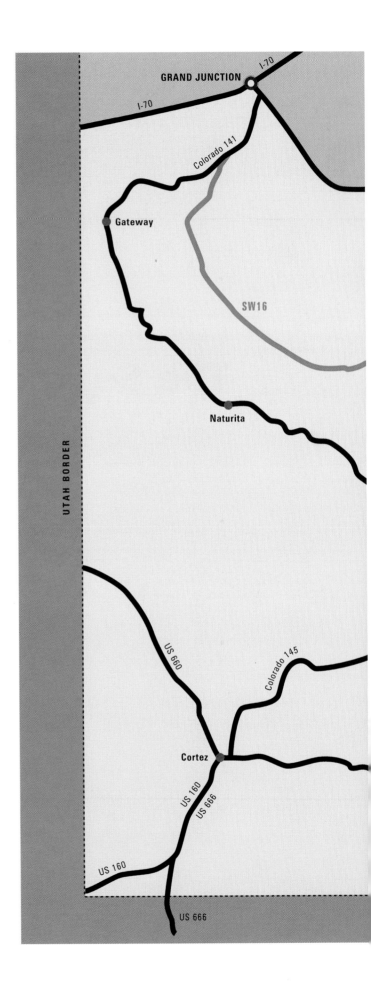

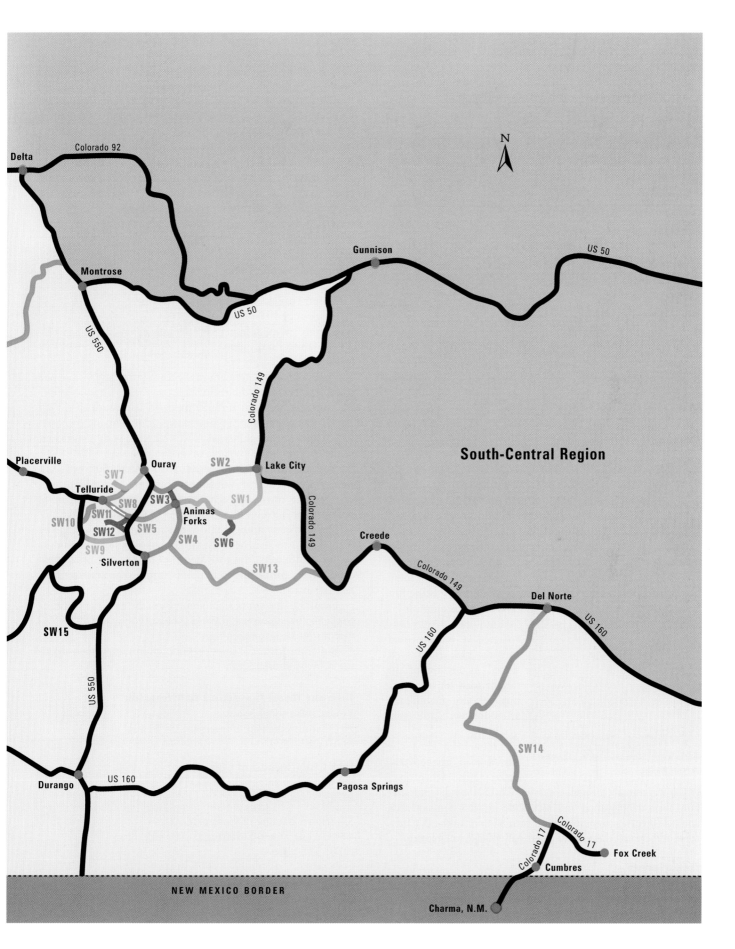

Delta

Colorado 92

N

Montrose

Gunnison

US 50

US 50

US 550

Colorado 149

South-Central Region

Placerville

Ouray

SW2

Lake City

SW7

Telluride

SW3

SW1

SW8

Colorado 149

Animas
Forks

SW10

SW11

SW12

SW5

SW4

SW6

Creede

SW9

Silverton

SW13

Colorado 149

Del Norte

SW15

US 160

US 160

SW14

US 550

Durango

US 160

Pagosa Springs

Colorado 17

Colorado 17

Colorado 17

Fox Creek

Cumbres

NEW MEXICO BORDER

Charma, N.M.

Cinnamon Pass Road

Starting Point:	Lake City
Finishing Point:	Animas Forks
Total Mileage:	26.8 miles
Unpaved Mileage:	20.4 miles
Driving Time:	2 hours
Pass Elevation:	12,620 feet
Usually Open:	Late May to late October
Difficulty Rating:	3
Scenic Rating:	9

Special Attractions

- Animas Forks ghost town.
- Part of the Alpine Loop, with many historic mining towns.
- Moderately easy 4WD trail opened by snowplow early in the season.
- Wonderful, varied scenery.

History

The Ute Indians used this pass road before white exploration of the area. In the early 1860s, Charles Baker used the pass on his journey into the San Juans when he claimed to have found gold, triggering a minor gold rush. In 1873, Albert Burrows further explored the area; and in the following year, the Hayden Survey party crossed the pass.

In the mid-1870s, Washington bureaucrats came to the conclusion that because the pass was not on the Continental Divide, the mail service should be able to cross it all year long; they awarded a contract on just that basis, despite it being impossible to accomplish!

American Basin

Enos Hotchkiss constructed a wagon road over the pass in 1877. It served as an important freight road for a period, but was not maintained after the ore in the area declined.

From Lake City, the paved road extends past Lake San Christobal, which was initially formed in about A.D. 1270 by the Slumgullion Slide, a huge mud and rock slide. A second major slide about 350 years ago completed the formation of Lake San Christobal and created the second largest natural lake in Colorado.

Description

Today Cinnamon Pass Road is a seasonal, moderately easy 4WD road. It is part of the historic and majestic Alpine Loop. The other half of the loop is Engineer Pass Road (Southwest Trail #2). These two roads form the backbone of a network of roads throughout the region.

Cinnamon Pass Road is the easier of the two, but in the peak summer months both are extremely popular 4WD routes.

The scenery varies from the rugged alpine environment of year-round snow and barren talus slopes near the summit to the wildflower-covered valleys and rushing streams draining the melting snow. At either end of the route are wonderful, historic towns, one a ghost town, the other very much alive.

Initially, the gravel road is an easy, maintained road. After entering the Gunnison National Forest, the road is intersected by Wager Gulch Road on the left. This road (Southwest Trail #6) goes to the ghost town of Carson and continues over the Continental Divide.

Burrows Park

Three miles further along County 30 is the intersection with County 35—a short side road leading to the site of Sherman. While the remains of the town are clearly visible, the forest has reclaimed the entire area.

After the Sherman turnoff, the road narrows into a shelf road overlooking the canyon. However, it remains comfortably wide even for full-sized 4WD vehicles, with a sufficient number of pull-offs available to facilitate passing.

A short distance further, the road enters Burrows Park Basin—the region of Whitecross, Burrows Park, Tellurium, and Sterling townships. The road passes the two remaining buildings of Burrows Park (and a new public toilet).

About three and one-half miles further, after passing the turnoff to the American Basin, which is renowned for its spring wildflowers, the road becomes more difficult as it ascends above timberline into alpine tundra vegetation and offers expansive views.

From the summit of Cinnamon Pass, the road descends into the picturesque ghost town of Animas Forks, which has numerous buildings remaining.

Bulldozers clear the snow on Cinnamon Pass, usually opening it by Memorial Day.

Current Road Condition Information

San Juan National Forest
701 Camino del Rio, Durango, CO 81301
(970) 247-4874

Lake City Chamber of Commerce
3rd and Silver Streets, Lake City, CO 81235
(970) 944-2527

Silverton Chamber of Commerce
414 Greene Street, Silverton, CO 81433
(970) 387-5654

Map References

USFS Uncompahgre NF or Gunnison NF
USGS Hinsdale County #1

SW TRAIL #1: CINNAMON PASS ROAD

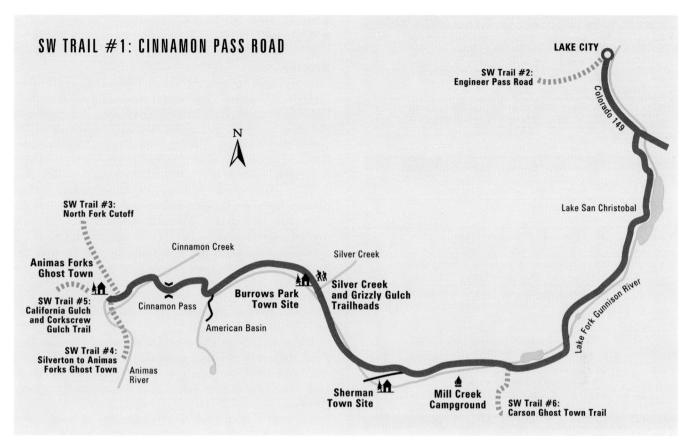

San Juan County
Trails Illustrated, #141
The Roads of Colorado, p. 115
Colorado Atlas & Gazetteer, pp. 67, 77

Route Directions

▼ 0.0		In front of the Lake City Information Center at 306 Silver (main) Street, zero trip meter and proceed south on Silver Street.
14.2 ▲		End at Lake City Information Center.
GPS: N 38°01.76′ W 107°18.98′		
▼ 0.1	TL	Onto 2nd Street.
14.0 ▲	TR	Onto Silver (main) Street.
▼ 0.2	TR	Onto Gunnison Avenue (Colorado 149) toward Cinnamon Pass.
14.0 ▲	TL	Onto 2nd Street.
▼ 2.4	TR	Follow Alpine Loop Drive sign.
11.8 ▲	TL	Onto Colorado 149.
▼ 6.4	BR	Before bridge. Follow Alpine Loop sign onto unpaved road.
7.8 ▲	BL	Bridge on right. Turn onto paved road.
▼ 9.1	SO	USFS Williams Creek Campground on right.
5.1 ▲	SO	USFS Williams Creek Campground on left.
▼ 11.3	SO	Intersection with Southwest Trail #6: Carson Ghost Town Trail via Wager Gulch on left.
2.9 ▲	SO	Track to Carson ghost town on right through Wager Gulch.
GPS: N 37°54.39′ W 107°21.60′		
▼ 11.5	SO	Cross over bridge.
2.7 ▲	SO	Cross over bridge.
▼ 12.5	SO	Public toilets on left.
1.7 ▲	SO	Public toilets on right.

▼ 13.1	SO	Mill Creek BLM campground on left.
1.1 ▲	SO	Mill Creek BLM campground on right.
▼ 14.2	BR	Intersection with County 35 on left to Sherman town site. Follow sign to Cinnamon Pass and Silverton. Zero trip meter.
0.0 ▲		Continue on main road toward Lake City.
GPS: N 37°54.21′ W 107°24.68′		
▼ 0.0		Continue on main road toward Cinnamon Pass.
7.5 ▲	SO	Intersection with County 35 to Sherman town site on right. Zero trip meter.
▼ 0.5	SO	Cross bridge.
7.0 ▲	SO	Cross bridge.
▼ 3.9	SO	Cross over Silver Creek.
3.7 ▲	SO	Cross over Silver Creek.
▼ 4.0	SO	Burrows Park town site. Grizzly Gulch (left) and Silver Creek (right) trailheads. Public toilets.
3.5 ▲	SO	Burrows Park town site. Grizzly Gulch (right) and Silver Creek (left) trailheads. Public toilets.
GPS: N 37°56.24′ W 107°27.63′		
▼ 5.5	SO	Mine on right.
2.0 ▲	SO	Mine on left.
▼ 6.3	SO	Cattle guard.
1.3 ▲	SO	Cattle guard.
▼ 6.4	SO	Creek crossing.
1.1 ▲	SO	Creek crossing.
▼ 7.1	SO	Track on left leads to mines.
0.4 ▲	SO	Track on right leads to mines.
▼ 7.4	SO	Creek cascade on right flows underneath road.
0.2 ▲	SO	Creek cascade on left flows underneath road.
▼ 7.6	BR	Intersection. Posted sign reads "4WD recommended past this point." American Basin on left. Zero trip meter.
0.0 ▲		Continue on main road toward Lake City.

GPS: N 37°55.87' W 107°30.80'			
▼ 0.0			Continue on main road toward Cinnamon Pass.
	2.2 ▲	BL	Intersection. American Basin on right. Zero trip meter.
▼ 0.4		SO	Cross over creek.
	1.8 ▲	SO	Cross over creek.
▼ 0.5		SO	Deserted cabin on right and then Tabasco Mill ruins.
	1.6 ▲	SO	Tabasco Mill ruins and then deserted cabin on left.
▼ 2.2		SO	Summit of Cinnamon Pass. Zero trip meter.
	0.0 ▲		Continue on main road toward Lake City.
GPS: N 37°56.03' W 107°32.25'			
▼ 0.0			Continue on main road toward Animas Forks.
	2.8 ▲	SO	Summit of Cinnamon Pass. Zero trip meter.
▼ 0.1		BL	Track on right.
	2.7 ▲	BR	Track on left.
▼ 0.7		SO	Cross over Cinnamon Creek.
	2.1 ▲	SO	Cross over Cinnamon Creek.
▼ 1.6		SO	First view of Animas Forks in the distance.
	1.2 ▲	SO	Last view of Animas Forks.
▼ 2.1		UT	Intersection. Continue on Cinnamon Pass Road. Track straight ahead is Southwest Trail #3: North Fork Cutoff.
	0.7 ▲	UT	Intersection. Follow switchback toward Cinnamon Pass. Straight ahead is Southwest Trail #3: North Fork Cutoff.
▼ 2.5		UT	Intersection. Go toward Animas Forks. Silverton is straight ahead.
	0.3 ▲	UT	Intersection. Follow switchback toward Cinnamon Pass. Silverton is straight ahead.
GPS: N 37°55.78' W 107°33.90'			
▼ 2.8			Cross bridge into Animas Forks and end at intersection. Southwest Trail #4 to Silverton is to the left. To the right is Southwest Trail #5: California Gulch and Corkscrew Gulch Trail.
	0.0 ▲		At three-way intersection in Animas Forks, zero trip meter and proceed across bridge toward Cinnamon Pass.
GPS: N 37°55.89' W 107°34.22'			

SOUTHWEST REGION TRAIL # 2

Engineer Pass Road

Starting Point:	**Ouray**
Finishing Point:	**Lake City**
Total Mileage:	**30.9 miles**
Unpaved Mileage:	**27.2 miles**
Driving Time:	**3 hours**
Pass Elevation:	**12,750 feet**
Usually Open:	**Mid-June to early October**
Difficulty Rating:	**4**
Scenic Rating:	**10**

Special Attractions

■ Part of the historic Alpine Loop, with many famous mining sites.
■ Driving through the twenty-foot deep channel in the snow early in the season.
■ Spectacular Rocky Mountain scenery.
■ Whitmore Falls.

History

Six years before building the Million Dollar Highway between Ouray and Silverton, Otto Mears extended his toll road from Saguache to Lake City, on through to Ouray. This connected the towns and mining camps in the area (which included Silverton, Animas Forks, Mineral Point, Capitol City, Engineer City, and many others) with Saguache, which was the closest major supply center.

From its completion in August 1877, this road was an important stage route between the two settlements, as well as the main route for freight wagons and mule trains servicing the needs of the thousands of miners in the area by this time.

Within three years, the route had daily stages run by the Rocky Mountain Stage and Express Company.

Description

This route commences south from Ouray on the Million Dollar Highway, US 550.

If you wish to avoid the hardest section of Engineer Pass Road, the route can be commenced at Silverton by taking the road to Animas Forks (Southwest Trail #4) and then the North Fork Cutoff (Southwest Trail #3) to connect with Engineer Pass Road.

The turnoff from US 550 onto Engineer Pass Road is well marked with a National Forest access sign. This 4WD track gets straight down to business. In fact, the next five miles are the hardest of the entire trip. Sections of the road are steep and rough. It is also narrow with sheer drop-offs. While it may appear threatening at first, it is readily passable for 4WD vehicles if taken slowly and carefully.

Empire Chief Mill

A tip for those who are nervous about driving shelf roads and encountering oncoming vehicles: Leave early. This road is popular, and oncoming 4WD vehicles will be encountered frequently later in the day, as those traveling from Lake City are descending. Pull-offs are reasonably frequent, should you need to let a vehicle pass.

At the 1.6-mile point, you pass the Mickey Breene Mine, which was discovered in 1890. The mine yielded high-grade ore and produced copper and silver.

About two and one-half miles from US 550, the road intersects with the Poughkeepsie road. This road is difficult and should be taken only by those willing to risk vehicle damage.

From the Mineral Point turnoff, the terrain starts to clear, with numerous open, although boggy meadows. The climb continues to Engineer Pass at 12,750 feet.

From the summit, the road descends through the southern edge of American Flats and past the site of Engineer City.

SW TRAIL #2: ENGINEER PASS ROAD

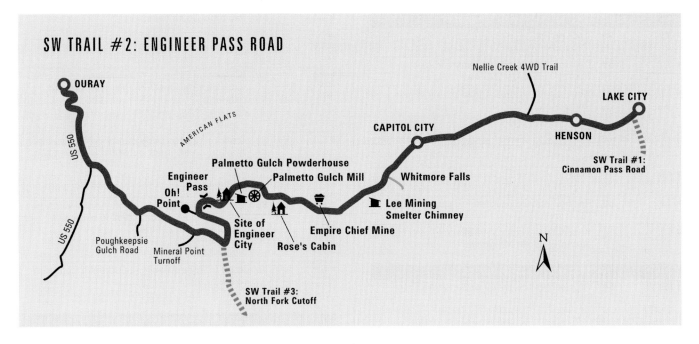

From this point, the road follows the path of Henson Creek all the way to Lake City.

About two miles after the summit, there is a scenic old cabin beside the creek at Palmetto Gulch; shortly after that, a bridge crosses the creek at what was the site of the Palmetto Gulch Mill. From this point, the road is passable by passenger vehicles.

The road passes close by Rose's Cabin, which was an important way station on the stage route. The remains of the buildings can still be seen.

Less than a mile further is the Empire Chief Mill that was worked from January to March 1929, when an avalanche killed four men and destroyed most of the buildings.

A few miles on, a sign marks a short walking trail down to the beautiful Whitmore Falls. Though short, the hike back up is strenuous.

The original Capitol City, with its grand aspirations to be the state capital, is now reduced to the remains of the post office. However, the town site is on private land, and new homes continue to be built there.

Henson was built around the productive Ute-Ulay Mine, which was established before the Brunot Treaty with the Indians in 1873. Today the land is all private, with many buildings still existing. At the end of Henson Creek Canyon lies Lake City.

Bulldozers plow portions of Engineer Pass, which is usually opened around mid-June. When the road crews get through, they leave in their wake a narrow channel through the snow, with walls of snow up to twenty feet high on either side.

Current Road Condition Information

San Juan National Forest
701 Camino del Rio, Durango, CO 81301
(970) 247-4874

Lake City Chamber of Commerce
3rd and Silver Streets, Lake City, CO 81235

(970) 944-2527

Silverton Chamber of Commerce
414 Greene Street, Silverton, CO 81433
(970) 387-5654

Map References

USFS Uncompahgre NF or Gunnison NF
USGS Hinsdale County #1
Ouray County #2
San Juan County
Trails Illustrated, #141
The Roads of Colorado, p. 115
Colorado Atlas & Gazetteer, pp. 67, 77

Route Directions

▼ 0.0		In front of Beaumont Hotel at 5th and Main in Ouray, zero trip meter and proceed south out of town, remaining on US 550.
3.7 ▲		End in front of Beaumont Hotel at 5th and Main in Ouray.
		GPS: N 38°01.30' W 107°40.29'
▼ 3.7	TL	National Forest access sign on right. Engineer Mountain Road and Alpine Loop signs are at the dirt track entrance. Zero trip meter.
0.0 ▲		Proceed on US 550 toward Ouray. Paved road.
		GPS: N 37°59.26' W 107°39.01'
▼ 0.0		Proceed along jeep trail.
7.0 ▲	TR	Intersection with US 550. Zero trip meter.
▼ 1.6	SO	Mickey Breene Mine ruins on left.
5.4 ▲	SO	Mickey Breene Mine ruins on right.
▼ 1.7	SO	Private road on left.
5.3 ▲	SO	Private road on right.
▼ 2.0	SO	Diamond Creek crossing. Track on right to backcountry campsites.
5.0 ▲	SO	Track on left to backcountry campsites. Diamond Creek crossing.
▼ 2.4	TL	Poughkeepsie Gulch 4WD trail to the right.
4.6 ▲	BR	Intersection with Poughkeepsie Gulch 4WD trail on the left.

GPS: N 37°58.01' W 107°37.60'

▼ 3.4		SO	Track on left.
	3.6 ▲	SO	Track on right.

▼ 3.7		SO	Track on right to backcountry campsites.
	3.3 ▲	SO	Track on left to backcountry campsites.

▼ 4.2		SO	Miner's cabin on left. Tracks on left to Des Ouray Mine.
	2.8 ▲	SO	Tracks on right to Des Ouray Mine. Cabin on right.

▼ 4.4		SO	Track on right. Stay on main road.
	2.6 ▲	SO	Track on left. Stay on main road.

▼ 4.6		SO	Track on right to backcountry campsites.
	2.4 ▲	SO	Track on left to backcountry campsites.

▼ 5.0		SO	Track on right to backcountry campsites.
	2.0 ▲	SO	Track on left to backcountry campsites.

▼ 5.1		TL	Intersection: Signpost to Mineral Point. Follow sign to Engineer Mountain.
	1.9 ▲	BR	Intersection.

GPS: N 37°57.72' W 107°35.71'

▼ 5.2		SO	View across the valley to San Juan Chief Mill.
	1.8 ▲	SO	View across the valley to San Juan Chief Mill.

▼ 5.8		SO	Public restrooms on right.
	1.2 ▲	SO	Public restrooms on left.

▼ 6.1		SO	Tracks on right lead to series of open mine portals.
	0.9 ▲	SO	Tracks on left lead to series of open mine portals.

▼ 7.0		TL	Intersection with Southwest Trail #3: North Fork Cutoff. Signs indicate Silverton and Animas Forks to the right. Lake City via Engineer Pass to the left. Zero trip meter.
	0.0 ▲		Continue toward Ouray.

GPS: N 37°57.42' W 107°34.47'

▼ 0.0			Continue on main road toward Engineer Pass.
	6.1 ▲	TR	Three-way intersection. Straight ahead is Southwest Trail #3: North Fork Cutoff, which leads to Animas Forks and Silverton. Zero trip meter.

▼ 0.8		UT	Follow sign to Engineer Pass. An unmarked track is straight ahead.
	5.3 ▲	UT	Unmarked track is straight ahead.

▼ 1.9		SO	Road on left to Oh! Point.
	4.2 ▲	SO	Road on right to Oh! Point.

▼ 2.3		BR	Summit of Engineer Pass. Two walking track trailheads are at summit: Bear Creek and Ridge Stock Driveway. Follow sign to Lake City.
	3.8 ▲	BL	Summit of Engineer Pass. Two walking track trailheads are at summit: Bear Creek and Ridge Stock Driveway.

GPS: N 37°58.46' W 107°35.08'

▼ 2.5		SO	Frank Hough Mine remains and American Flats.
	3.6 ▲	SO	Frank Hough Mine remains and American Flats.

▼ 2.8		SO	Site of Engineer City.
	3.3 ▲	SO	Site of Engineer City.

▼ 3.2		SO	Horsethief Trail walking track on left.
	2.9 ▲	SO	Horsethief Trail walking track on right.

▼ 3.4		SO	Palmetto Gulch Powderhouse and mine remains on right. Track on right to open mine shaft.
	2.7 ▲	SO	Track on left to open mine portal. Palmetto Gulch Powderhouse and mine remains on left.

▼ 4.4		SO	Palmetto Gulch cabin.
	1.7 ▲	SO	Palmetto Gulch cabin.

▼ 4.6		SO	Thoreau's Cabin on left.
	1.5 ▲	SO	Thoreau's Cabin on right.

▼ 4.8		SO	Bridge and Palmetto Gulch Mill remains. 2WD vehicles sufficient from this point onward.
	1.3 ▲	SO	Palmetto Gulch Mill remains and bridge. 4WD vehicles recommended beyond this point.

▼ 5.1		SO	Track on right to backcountry campsites along Henson Creek. Track networks with next two entries.
	1.0 ▲	SO	Track on left to backcountry campsites along Henson Creek.

▼ 5.4		SO	Track on right goes to same vicinity as previous. Also goes across creek to Hurricane Basin and past a mine.
	0.7 ▲	SO	Track on left to backcountry campsites along Henson Creek.

▼ 6.1		BL	Road to Rose's Cabin site on right. Zero trip meter.
	0.0 ▲		Continue along main road toward Engineer Pass.

GPS: N 37°58.58' W 107°32.20'

▼ 0.0		SO	Continue along main road toward Lake City.
	14.2 ▲	BR	Road to Rose's Cabin site on left. Zero trip meter.

▼ 0.1		SO	Public restrooms on right.
	14.1 ▲	SO	Public restrooms on left.

▼ 0.8		SO	Empire Chief Mine and Mill on left.
	13.3 ▲	SO	Empire Chief Mine and Mill on right.

▼ 1.2		SO	Waterfall on right.
	12.9 ▲	SO	Waterfall on left.

▼ 2.4		SO	Smelter chimney on right from the Lee Mining and Smelter Company.
	11.7 ▲	SO	Smelter chimney on left from the Lee Mining and Smelter Company.

▼ 3.4		SO	Whitmore Falls walking track on right.
	10.8 ▲	SO	Whitmore Falls walking track on left.

▼ 4.5		SO	Corral on right.
	9.6 ▲	SO	Corral on left.

▼ 5.0		SO	Capitol City town site. Private land and new homes.
	9.1 ▲	SO	Capitol City town site.

GPS: N 38°00.35' W 107°28.05'

▼ 5.1		BR	Bridge, then signpost on left indicating road to N. Henson Road via Matterhorn Creek and Uncompahgre Peak.
	9.0 ▲	BL	Walking trails on right, then bridge.

▼ 7.1		SO	Bridge and track on right.
	7.0 ▲	SO	Bridge and track on left.

▼ 8.6		SO	Open mine portal on left along road.
	5.5 ▲	SO	Open mine portal on right along road.

▼ 8.9		SO	Public restrooms on left.
	5.2 ▲	SO	Public restrooms on right.

▼ 9.0		SO	4WD track on left leads to Nellie Creek trailhead and Uncompahgre Peak.
	5.1 ▲	SO	Track on right leads to Nellie Creek trailhead and Uncompahgre Peak.

GPS: N 38°01.22' W 107°23.97'

▼ 10.3		SO	Town of Henson.
	3.7 ▲	SO	Town of Henson.

▼ 10.7		SO	Open mine portal on left along road.
	3.4 ▲	SO	Open mine portal on right along road.

▼ 11.5		SO	Alpine Gulch trailhead on right.
	2.6 ▲	SO	Alpine Gulch trailhead on left.

▼ 13.0	SO	Ruins of old mill on left.
1.2 ▲	SO	Ruins of old mill on right.
▼ 14.1	TR	Stop sign in Lake City. At next intersection, TL onto Silver Street.
0.1 ▲	TR	Onto Second Street then TL at next intersection.
▼ 14.2		End in front of the Lake City Visitor Information Center at 306 Silver Street.
0.0 ▲		In front of the Lake City Visitor Information Center at 306 Silver (main) Street, zero trip meter and proceed south.

GPS: N 38°01.76′ W 107°18.98′

SOUTHWEST REGION TRAIL #3

North Fork Cutoff

Starting Point:	Cinnamon Pass Road
Finishing Point:	Engineer Pass Road
Total Mileage:	2 miles
Unpaved Mileage:	2 miles
Driving Time:	20 minutes
Route Elevation:	11,800 feet
Usually Open:	Late May to late October
Difficulty Rating:	3
Scenic Rating:	4

Description

This route is straightforward and is included in this book to allow more flexibility in undertaking the Alpine Loop, which primarily consists of Engineer Pass Road and Cinnamon Pass Road. By linking these two roads, the Alpine Loop can be started or finished from any of three towns: Lake City, Ouray, or Silverton.

The North Fork Cutoff usually opens before the summit of Engineer Pass is cleared, allowing access to the western end of Engineer Pass Road, which can be used as a route between Ouray and Animas Forks.

Although the route includes sections of shelf road, it is not very narrow and has a reasonable number of pull-offs. However, it is sufficiently rough to require a high-clearance vehicle.

Current Road Condition Information

San Juan National Forest
701 Camino del Rio, Durango, CO 81301
(970) 247-4874

Map References

USFS Uncompahgre NF or Gunnison NF
USGS San Juan County
Trails Illustrated, #141
The Roads of Colorado, p. 115
Colorado Atlas & Gazetteer, p. 77

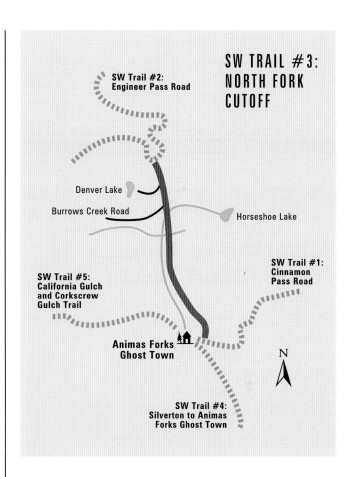

SW TRAIL #3: NORTH FORK CUTOFF

Route Directions

| ▼ 0.0 | | At the intersection of Cinnamon Pass Road and North Fork Cutoff, 0.7 miles from Animas Forks, zero trip meter and proceed north. |
| 2.0 ▲ | | End at intersection with Cinnamon Pass Road. Bear left to Lake City. Bear right to Animas Forks. |

GPS: N 37°56.02′ W 107°34.10′

▼ 0.3	SO	Mine on left.
1.7 ▲	SO	Mine on right.
▼ 0.4	SO	Tram cables overhead.
1.6 ▲	SO	Tram cables overhead.
▼ 0.6	SO	Track on right.
1.4 ▲	SO	Track on left.
▼ 0.9	SO	Open mine portal in mountainside on the left.
1.1 ▲	SO	Open mine portal in mountainside on the right.
▼ 1.0	SO	Cross over creek.
1.0 ▲	SO	Cross over creek.
▼ 1.2	SO	Cross over creek.
0.8 ▲	SO	Cross over creek.
▼ 1.4	BR	Open mine portal on left. Track on left leads to mines along Burrows Creek and dead-ends in approximately 2 miles. Follow sign to Engineer Pass and Alpine Loop.
0.6 ▲	BL	Track on right leads to mines along Burrows Creek and dead-ends. Open mine portal on right.

GPS: N 37°56.91′ W 107°34.53′

| ▼ 1.6 | SO | Track on left to Denver Lake, cabin, and mine. Cross over creek. Track on right. |
| 0.4 ▲ | SO | Track on left. Cross over creek. Track on right to Denver Lake, cabin, and mine. |

▼ 1.7	SO	Mine ruins on right.
0.3 ▲	SO	Mine ruins on left.
▼ 2.0		End at intersection with Southwest Trail #2: Engineer Pass Road. Left goes to Ouray. Right goes to Engineer Pass and Lake City.
0.0 ▲		At the intersection of Engineer Pass Road and North Fork Cutoff, zero trip meter and proceed south along North Fork Cutoff.

GPS: N 37°57.41′ W 107°34.48′

SOUTHWEST REGION TRAIL #4

Silverton to Animas Forks Ghost Town

Starting Point:	**Silverton**
Finishing Point:	**Animas Forks**
Total Mileage:	**12.1 miles**
Unpaved Mileage:	**10.0 miles**
Driving Time:	**45 minutes**
Highest Elevation:	**11,370 feet**
Usually Open:	**Mid-May to late October**
Difficulty Rating:	**1**
Scenic Rating:	**8**

Special Attractions

■ Animas Forks, one of Colorado's best ghost towns.
■ The extremely historic road following the old railway grade, with innumerable points of historic interest.

History

This route commences at Silverton, a well-preserved, historic mining town that was founded in 1873. It is the terminus for the famed Durango and Silverton Narrow Gauge Railroad, which is extremely popular with tourists in the summer months.

From Silverton, the route follows the Animas River as it passes numerous mines that line the sides of the area known as Bakers Park, which extends all the way to Eureka. The park was named after Charles Baker, one of the first explorers in the area, who triggered a minor gold rush into territory still defended by the Ute Indians in the early 1860s.

At the six-mile point is the town site of Middleton, a small mining camp in the late 1800s, of which nothing remains.

At the 7.7-mile point is the town site of Eureka. The road on the right was Saguache Street and led into the center of town. The square building is the restored water tank; the room below was used as the town jail. The foundations of several other buildings are evident.

The massive foundations that rise up the mountainside on the other side of the Animas River are the remains of the Sunnyside Mill. The Sunnyside Mine, located in Eureka Gulch behind the mill, was discovered in 1873. By 1910 it consisted

of ten miles of tunnel and employed three hundred miners. The first wooden mill opened in 1899 to the left of the existing foundations, which belong to the second Sunnyside Mill (which started production in 1918). The second mill incorporated much of the dismantled Gold Prince Mill, relocated from Animas Forks.

About half a mile from Eureka, the ruins of a boardinghouse and a bridge across the Animas River can be seen on the right. The boardinghouse was built in 1907 to house the workers from the Tom Moore Mine.

The road at this point follows the old Silverton Northern Railroad line built by Otto Mears in 1903-1904. Four hundred men worked on this railroad line; it had an average grade of 7 percent, which resulted in the train having a maximum speed of only four miles per hour in the steeper sections, despite pulling a maximum of only two loaded cars.

The other natural obstacle that challenged the railroad was snow. On the left of the road can be seen the remnants of one of the snowsheds built by Otto Mears to protect the railroad from the snowslides prevalent in the area. Despite Mears's best endeavors, nature proved too strong an adversary, and the snowsheds were destroyed in the first winter. High operating costs and declining mineral production led to the closure of the railroad in 1916.

Across the river from the snowshed can be seen the remnants of the last toll road built by Otto Mears in the mid-1880s—the only one he lost money on.

As you cross the Animas River on the entry into Animas Forks ghost town, the foundations on the right are the remains of the Gold Prince Mill, the largest concentrating mill in Colorado when it was built in 1904.

On the left is the location of the railroad turntable used to turn around the steam engine of the Silverton Northern Railroad for the return to Silverton.

Further into Animas Forks, a number of buildings remain to the left of the road. The most famous of these is the two-story Walsh House, with the front bay window. This was home of William Duncan, built in 1879. It has been specu-

Silver Lake Mill, built in the 1890s and twice destroyed by fire before being closed finally in 1914.

lated that Thomas Walsh's daughter stayed there when writing her father's biography and also that Walsh rented a room there in his younger (and poorer) days. It is extremely unlikely that either story is true.

The buildings across the Animas River as you leave town are the Columbus Mine and Mill, built in about 1880. This mill ceased operations in 1948.

Description

The entire route is an easy, well-maintained, gravel road suitable for passenger vehicles under good conditions.

Current Road Condition Information

San Juan National Forest
701 Camino del Rio, Durango, CO 81301
(970) 247-4874

Silverton Chamber of Commerce
414 Greene Street, Silverton, CO 81433
(970) 387-5654

Map References

USFS Uncompahgre NF or San Juan NF
USGS San Juan County
Trails Illustrated, #141
The Roads of Colorado, pp. 115, 131
Colorado Atlas & Gazetteer, p. 77

Route Directions

▼ 0.0		From the Silverton City Hall at Greene (main) Street and 14th Street, zero trip meter and proceed northeast out of town.
7.8 ▲		End in front of the Silverton City Hall at Greene and 14th Streets.
		GPS: N 37°48.79′ W 107°39.72′
▼ 0.2	**BR**	Road forks. Bear right onto Colorado 110. Remain on paved road.
7.6 ▲	**BL**	Road forks. Bear left and remain on paved road.
▼ 0.4	**SO**	Campground on the right.
7.4 ▲	**SO**	Campground on the left.
▼ 0.5	**SO**	Lackawanna Mill on right across the river. Cemetery on hill on left.
7.3 ▲	**SO**	Cemetery on hill on right. Lackawanna Mill on left across the river.
▼ 0.7	**BR**	Road fork entering on left.
7.0 ▲	**BL**	Road fork entering on right.
▼ 1.6	**SO**	Aspen Mine ruins on right across the river.
6.2 ▲	**SO**	Aspen Mine ruins on left across the river.
▼ 1.7	**SO**	On the right side of the road, in the distance about 3 miles east, the tramhouse and boardinghouse of the Old Hundred Mine are evident about three-quarters of the way up Galena Mountain.
6.1 ▲	**SO**	The tramhouse and boardinghouse of the Old Hundred Mine are evident on the left, in the distance about 3 miles southeast, three-quarters of the way up Galena Mountain.
▼ 2.0	**SO**	Silver Lake Mill on right. It was dismantled in 1938.
5.8 ▲	**SO**	Silver Lake Mill on left.
▼ 2.1	**SO**	Pavement ends. Track to Arrastra Gulch on right.
5.7 ▲	**SO**	Paved road. Track to Arrastra Gulch on left.

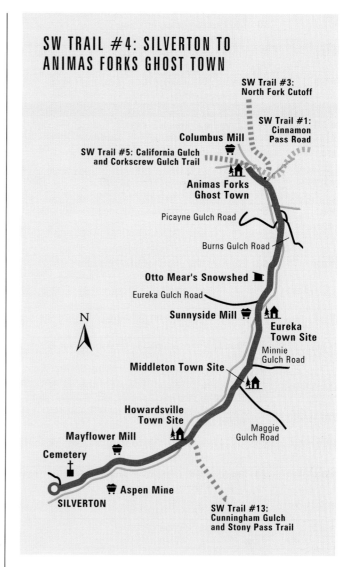

SW TRAIL #4: SILVERTON TO ANIMAS FORKS GHOST TOWN

▼ 2.2	**SO**	Mayflower Mill and tram on left.
5.6 ▲	**SO**	Mayflower Mill and tram on right.
▼ 3.8	**SO**	Little Nation Mine on right, halfway up the mountainside.
4.0 ▲	**SO**	Little Nation Mine on left, halfway up the mountainside.
▼ 4.0	**SO**	Bridge across the Animas River.
3.8 ▲	**SO**	Bridge across the Animas River.
▼ 4.2	**SO**	Bridge across Cunningham Creek, then turnoff for Southwest Trail #13: Cunningham Gulch and Stony Pass Trail on the right. Town site of Howardsville. Little Nations Mill.
3.6 ▲	**SO**	Little Nations Mill. Town site of Howardsville. Turnoff for Southwest Trail #13: Cunningham Gulch and Stony Pass Trail on the left. Bridge across Cunningham Creek.
		GPS: N 37°50.06′ W 107°35.68′
▼ 6.0	**SO**	Maggie Gulch turnoff on right. Town site of Middleton. Public toilets on right.
1.8 ▲	**SO**	Public toilets on left. Town site of Middleton. Maggie Gulch turnoff on left.
▼ 6.6	**SO**	Cross over creek. Minnie Gulch turnoff on right.
1.2 ▲	**SO**	Minnie Gulch turnoff on left. Cross over creek.

▼ 6.7	SO	Track to campsites on right.
1.1 ▲	SO	Track to campsites on left.
▼ 7.7	BL	Entry to Eureka town site on right. Campsites.
0.1 ▲	BR	Entry to Eureka town site on left. Campsites.
▼ 7.8	SO	Bridge over Animas River. Zero trip meter.
0.0 ▲		Continue along main road.

GPS: N 37°52.76′ W 107°33.92′

▼ 0.0		Continue along main road.
4.3 ▲	SO	Bridge over Animas River. Zero trip meter.
▼ 0.1	BR	Sunnyside Mill on left.
4.2 ▲	BL	Sunnyside Mill on right.
▼ 0.3	SO	Turnoff to Eureka Gulch on left.
4.0 ▲	SO	Turnoff to Eureka Gulch on right.
▼ 0.5	SO	Historic boardinghouse for mine workers on right.
3.7 ▲	SO	Historic boardinghouse for mine workers on left.
▼ 1.0	SO	Log remains of a snowshed built by Otto Mears on left.
3.3 ▲	SO	Log remains of a snowshed built by Otto Mears on right.
▼ 1.8	SO	Silver Wing Mine on right.
2.5 ▲	SO	Silver Wing Mine on left.
▼ 2.7	SO	Remains of dam used to feed the Silver Wing Mine.
1.6 ▲	SO	Remains of dam used to feed the Silver Wing Mine.
▼ 2.8	SO	Turnoff to Picayne Gulch on left. Track on right crosses Animas River and joins the road to Burns Gulch.
1.5 ▲	SO	Track on left crosses Animas River and joins the road to Burns Gulch. Turnoff to Picayne Gulch on right.
▼ 2.9	SO	Track on left. Cross over Animas River. Turnoff to Burns Gulch on right.
1.4 ▲	SO	Turnoff to Burns Gulch on left. Cross over Animas River. Track on right.
▼ 3.5	SO	Cross over Cinnamon Creek
0.8 ▲	SO	Cross over Cinnamon Creek
▼ 3.6	BL	Proceed toward Animas Forks. Cutoff to Cinnamon Pass Road on right. Public restrooms on left.
0.7 ▲	BR	Public restrooms on right. Cutoff to Cinnamon Pass Road on left. Proceed on main road toward Silverton.
▼ 3.9	SO	Cross over Animas River. Gold Prince Mill ruins on right.
0.4 ▲	SO	Gold Prince Mill ruins on left. Cross over Animas River.
▼ 4.1	SO	Public restrooms on right. Animas Forks jailhouse site behind the restrooms.
0.2 ▲	SO	Animas Forks jailhouse site behind the public restrooms on left.
▼ 4.3		Animas Forks ghost town. Bridge across Animas River is on the right, leading to Southwest Trail #1: Cinnamon Pass, and Southwest Trail #2: Engineer Pass. The Columbus Mill is straight ahead.
0.0 ▲		At the bridge over the Animas Forks River at the north end of Animas Forks, zero trip meter and proceed south toward Silverton.

GPS: N 37°55.89′ W 107°34.22′

California Gulch and Corkscrew Gulch Trail

Starting Point:	**Animas Forks**
Finishing Point:	**US 550**
Total Mileage:	**11.3 miles**
Unpaved Mileage:	**11.3 miles**
Driving Time:	**2 1/2 hours**
Pass Elevation:	**California-12,930′ Hurricane-12,407′**
Usually Open:	**Mid-June to late October**
Difficulty Rating:	**4**
Scenic Rating:	**9**

Special Attractions

- A moderately challenging 4WD trail that can be taken as an adjunct to the more-famous Alpine Loop.
- Spectacular scenery.

Description

This route departs to the northwest of Animas Forks and is clearly marked to California Gulch.

California Gulch road is a relatively gentle road, entirely above timberline, with numerous mine remains and open mine portals in evidence.

The road ascends to California Pass, which provides spectacular views down onto Lake Como, Poughkeepsie Gulch, the road back to Animas Forks, and across to Hurricane Pass.

The Corkscrew Gulch road is the harder section of this

Como Gulch and Poughkeepsie Gulch 4WD trail

route and traverses quite different terrain. There is a series of tight switchbacks along a narrow shelf road. At times, the road is steep, and passing other vehicles can be difficult. Remember that the vehicle traveling uphill has the right of way, but common sense and courtesy should always prevail.

From the summit of California Pass, the Corkscrew Gulch road continues to afford scenic views as it overlooks, and then descends to, the pine forest below timberline. As you approach Red Mountain, there is a beautiful view of the brilliant red valley and slopes of Red Mountain that gave it its name.

The road is usually open from mid-June to late October, but snow often remains along the side of the road throughout the summer. This trail will be muddy early in the season.

SW TRAIL #5: CALIFORNIA GULCH AND CORKSCREW GULCH TRAIL

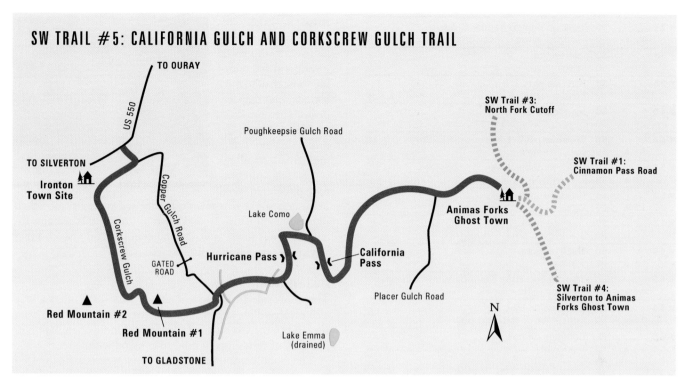

Current Road Condition Information

San Juan National Forest
701 Camino del Rio, Durango, CO 81301
(970) 247-4874

Silverton Chamber of Commerce
414 Greene Street, Silverton, CO 81433
(970) 387-5654

Map References

USFS Uncompahgre NF or Gunnison NF
USGS San Juan County
Ouray County #2
Trails Illustrated, #141
The Roads of Colorado, p. 115
Colorado Atlas & Gazetteer, p. 77

Route Directions

▼ 0.0 — At the bridge over the Animas River at the north end of Animas Forks, zero trip meter and follow signs to California Gulch. Cross over the West Fork of Animas River, past the Columbus Mine and Mill on the right.

4.2 ▲ — End at bridge in Animas Forks.

GPS: N 37°55.89′ W 107°34.22′

▼ 0.5	SO	Bagley Mine and Mill on right.
3.6 ▲	SO	Bagley Mine and Mill on left.
▼ 0.7	BL	Track to Bagley Mill on right.
3.5 ▲	BR	Track to Bagley Mill on left.
▼ 1.0	BR	Intersection: Track on left goes to Placer Gulch.
3.1 ▲	BL	Intersection: Track on right goes to Placer Gulch.
▼ 1.1	BR	Track on left to cabin.
3.1 ▲	BL	Track on right to cabin.
▼ 1.5	SO	Vermillion Mine and Mill ruins on right.
2.7 ▲	SO	Vermillion Mine and Mill ruins on left.

▼ 1.7	SO	Burrows Mine ruins on right.
2.4 ▲	SO	Burrows Mine ruins on left.
▼ 2.9	SO	Cross over creek.
1.3 ▲	SO	Cross over creek.
▼ 3.0	SO	Open mine portal on right side of road.
1.2 ▲	SO	Open mine portal on left side of road.
▼ 3.4	UT	Intersection.
0.8 ▲	UT	Intersection.
▼ 3.5	SO	Road joins on left.
0.7 ▲	BL	Fork in road.
▼ 3.6	SO	Mine on right.
0.6 ▲	SO	Mine on left.
▼ 3.8	UT	Summit of California Pass. The lake you look down upon is Lake Como.
0.4 ▲	UT	Summit of California Pass.

GPS: N 37°55.02′ W 107°36.91′

| ▼ 4.2 | BL | Intersection. Follow signs to Silverton and Corkscrew Gulch. Poughkeepsie Gulch and Lake Como are to the right. Zero trip meter. |
| 0.0 ▲ | | Continue along main track. |

GPS: N 37°55.26′ W 107°37.26′

▼ 0.0		Continue along main track.
7.1 ▲	BR	Intersection. Track to Poughkeepsie Gulch and Lake Como are to the left. Zero trip meter.
▼ 0.5	SO	Summit of Hurricane Pass.
6.6 ▲	SO	Summit of Hurricane Pass.

GPS: N 37°55.18′ W 107°37.55′

▼ 0.7	SO	Open mine portal on right.
6.4 ▲	SO	Open mine portal on left.
▼ 1.2	SO	Intersection. Road on left.
5.9 ▲	SO	Intersection. Road on right.
▼ 1.3	SO	Cross over creek. Mine on right.
5.8 ▲	SO	Mine on left. Cross over creek.
▼ 2.3	BR	Fork in the road. Road on left goes to Gladstone. Proceed toward Corkscrew Gulch.
4.8 ▲	BL	Fork in the road. Road on right goes to Gladstone. Proceed toward Animas Forks.

▼ 2.4	**SO**	Track on right to Copper Gulch.	
4.7 ▲	SO	Track on left to Copper Gulch.	
▼ 3.4	**SO**	Intersection.	
3.7 ▲	SO	Intersection.	
▼ 3.5	**SO**	Pond on right.	
3.6 ▲	SO	Pond on left.	
▼ 4.3	**SO**	Sign to US 550.	
2.8 ▲	SO	Sign to Gladstone and Silverton.	
▼ 4.4	**BR**	Cabin on left.	
2.7 ▲	BL	Cabin on right.	
▼ 5.1	**SO**	Cross through creek.	
2.0 ▲	SO	Cross through creek.	
▼ 5.5	**SO**	Cross through creek.	
1.6 ▲	SO	Cross through creek.	
▼ 5.6	**SO**	Track on right.	
1.5 ▲	SO	Track on left.	
▼ 6.0	**SO**	Track on right.	
1.1 ▲	SO	Track on left.	
▼ 6.5	**SO**	Track on left is the North Pipeline trailhead.	
0.6 ▲	SO	Track on right is the North Pipeline trailhead.	
▼ 6.8	**SO**	Continue on trail.	
0.3 ▲	SO	Sign reads "Corkscrew Gulch 4x4 only."	
▼ 6.9	**BL**	Continue on trail.	
0.2 ▲	BR	Sign indicates Brown Mountain left; Corkscrew Gulch right.	
▼ 7.1		Cross bridge and end at US 550. Ouray is to the right and Silverton is to the left.	
0.0 ▲		Begin at the sign for the Idarado Mine and its mine tailings on US 550, approximately 7.7 miles from Ouray and approximately 15 miles from Silverton. Zero trip meter and proceed east over plank bridge.	

GPS: N 37°56.33′ W 107°40.27′

Carson Ghost Town Trail

Starting Point:	**Intersection of Wager Gulch Road (FR 568) and Cinnamon Pass Road**
Finishing Point:	**Carson Ghost Town**
Total Mileage:	**3.7 miles**
Unpaved Mileage:	**3.7 miles**
Driving Time:	**30 minutes (one-way)**
Township Elev.:	**12,350 feet**
Usually Open:	**Mid-June to late September**
Difficulty Rating:	**4**
Scenic Rating:	**9**

Special Attractions

■ Well-preserved ghost town of Carson.
■ Views from the Continental Divide.

History

Following the discovery of silver at Carson in 1881, a wagon road was built to service the mines, leading from the Gunnison

River to Lake City. Carson was very close to the Continental Divide and was one of the most remote mining camps in Colorado. The silver crash of 1893 led to its demise, and no buildings remain standing.

Carson ghost town, nestled in Wager Gulch

In 1896, prospectors discovered gold in the area, and a new town was built at a lower elevation than the original. It is this second town of Carson that remains today as a ghost town. It was abandoned in 1903; the road that serviced it also fell into disuse.

Description

This short side trip from Cinnamon Pass Road offers a very well-preserved ghost town, spectacular panoramic views from the crest of the Continental Divide, and more often than not, a section of very slippery mud to contend with.

The route commences from Cinnamon Pass Road, 15.4 miles from Animas Forks and 11.3 miles from Lake City. A sign that reads "Wager Gulch/Carson" marks the turnoff.

The road is initially fairly steep but reasonably wide and has an adequate number of pull-offs. Occasional rocks in the road and eroded surfaces can require care in selecting the right line, but the road should not be too rough for a normal 4WD vehicle.

The most difficult problem can be mud. The first two miles of this trail are usually spotted with muddy sections. The sur-

face is firm, but it can be very slippery and wheel-rutted. Getting adequate traction depends on the weight of your vehicle, the state of the road on the day you attempt it, and, most importantly, the tires you are using. Exercise care in order

Stalls in the Carson ghost town stables

to avoid oncoming vehicles that can have difficulty steering or stopping on the downhill slope.

Once past the mud, the road is straightforward. A visit to Carson and the views from the Continental Divide make it all worthwhile.

The Continental Divide is just over a mile past the creek crossing at Carson. From the Continental Divide, you need to retrace your steps and return to Cinnamon Pass Road because the route deteriorates into walking trails on the south side of the divide.

Current Road Condition Information

Gunnison National Forest
Taylor River District
216 N. Colorado, Gunnison, CO 81230
(970) 641-0471

SW TRAIL #6: CARSON GHOST TOWN TRAIL

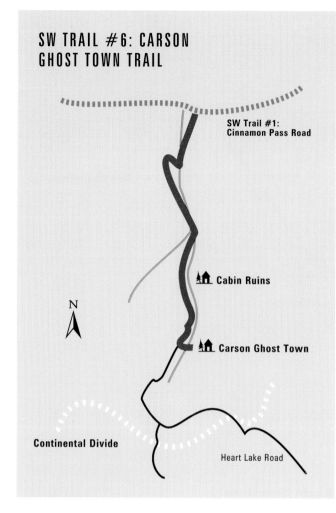

SW Trail #1: Cinnamon Pass Road

🏚️ **Cabin Ruins**

🏚️ **Carson Ghost Town**

N

Continental Divide

Heart Lake Road

Map References
USFS Uncompahgre NF or Gunnison NF
USGS Hinsdale County #1
Trails Illustrated, #141
The Roads of Colorado, pp. 115, 131
Colorado Atlas & Gazetteer, p. 77

Route Directions

▼ 0.0		At intersection of Carson turnoff (FR 568) with Cinnamon Pass Road, zero trip meter and proceed toward Carson. This intersection is 11.3 miles from Lake City.
	GPS: N 37°54.39′ W 107°21.60′	
▼ 0.1	**BL**	Series of private driveways.
▼ 0.7	**SO**	Creek crossing.
▼ 1.7	**BR**	Fork in road. Continue uphill.
▼ 2.2	**SO**	Creek crossing.
▼ 2.8	**SO**	Cabin ruins on left.
▼ 3.5	**BL**	Fork in road. Turn toward Carson ghost town. Straight ahead will lead across the Continental Divide and to the site of Old Carson.
▼ 3.6	**SO**	Cross through creek.
▼ 3.7	**BL**	Carson town site with many well-preserved structures.
	GPS: N 37°52.13′ W 107°21.72′	

Yankee Boy Basin Road

Starting Point:	Ouray
Finishing Point:	Yankee Boy Basin
Total Mileage:	9.1 miles
Unpaved Mileage:	8.6 miles
Driving Time:	1 hour (one-way)
Usually Open:	Mid-June to early October
Difficulty Rating:	3
Scenic Rating:	8

Special Attractions
- Historic mines and old mining camps.
- Canyon Creek shelf road.
- Abundant wildflowers in Yankee Boy Basin.

History
Gold and silver were discovered in Yankee Boy Basin in 1875, and the township of Sneffels was founded in the same year. The area had a number of extremely successful mines, particularly the Virginius, the Atlas, and the Revenue.

The silver crash led to the closure of many of the mines, but the town limped on. In 1930, the post office was finally closed. Some of the buildings were still inhabited in the 1940s, but the town was only a shadow of its former self.

Description
Yankee Boy Basin is a very popular location during the peak summer months for both sightseers and hikers.

It provides a short, varied 4WD trail that is a good introduction to four-wheel driving. It offers rugged scenery, historic mines, deserted town sites, and wonderful natural beauty, including alpine meadows that are covered with wildflowers in the late spring.

About five miles from Ouray, the route offers a spectacular shelf road as you travel above Canyon Creek. The road is well maintained and relatively wide.

From Camp Bird, the route takes you through a fairly wide, flat valley to the Revenue Mine and Mill and the old mining town of Sneffels, which can be viewed from the road but is on private property.

About half a mile further, the road forks, with the road to Governor Basin turning off to the left and the road to Yankee Boy Basin to the right. Until this

Camp Bird Road

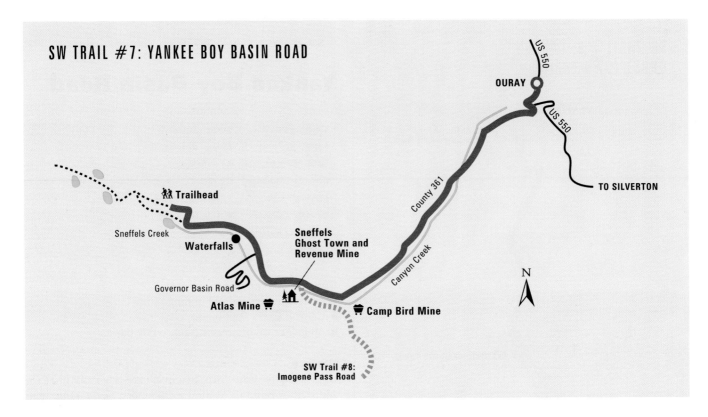

point, the road is negotiable by passenger vehicles; further on it is 4WD.

The Governor Basin 4WD trail is a narrow shelf road that is much more difficult than the Yankee Boy road. Passing is difficult in many sections, and snow can block the road late into summer, necessitating the sometimes difficult job of turning around. Nonetheless, for those with the experience and nerve, the Governor Basin road offers some majestic scenery and historic mines (difficulty rating: 5).

The road continuing into Yankee Boy Basin takes you past Twin Falls and numerous mines as you travel alongside Sneffels Creek to the end of the trail, some two miles further. Peaks ranging in height from Stony Mountain at 12,698 feet to Mount Sneffels at 14,150 feet surround the basin. The abundant wildflowers include columbine, bluebells, and Indian paintbrush.

There are numerous backcountry camping sites along this route, but camping is not permitted within a quarter mile of Sneffels Creek in Yankee Boy Basin and the tributary creek from Governor Basin. Also, camping is not allowed on private lands without written permission. Firewood is scarce in the basin, so if you are planning on camping, we recommend that you either bring some with you or use a gas stove.

Current Road Condition Information

Uncompahgre National Forest
Ouray Ranger District
2505 South Townsend Avenue, Montrose, CO 81401
(970) 240-5300

Map References

USFS Uncompahgre NF

USGS Ouray County #2
Trails Illustrated, #141
The Roads of Colorado, p. 115
Colorado Atlas & Gazetteer, pp. 66, 76

Route Directions

▼ 0.0		In front of Beaumont Hotel at 5th Avenue and Main Street in Ouray, zero trip meter and proceed south out of town.
6.4 ▲		End at Beaumont Hotel in Ouray at 5th Avenue and Main Street.
GPS: N 38°01.30' W 107°40.29'		
▼ 0.5	**TR**	Toward Box Canyon Falls on Camp Bird Road, County 361.
5.9 ▲	**TL**	On US 550 toward Ouray.
▼ 0.6	**BL**	Box Canyon Falls on right. Bear left.
5.8 ▲	**BR**	Box Canyon Falls on left. Bear right.
▼ 2.4	**SO**	Bridge over Canyon Creek. Campsites.
4.0 ▲	**SO**	Campsites. Bridge over Canyon Creek.
▼ 3.1	**SO**	Camping on the left and right.
3.3 ▲	**SO**	Camping on the left and right.
GPS: N 38°59.61' W 107°42.02'		
▼ 3.3	**SO**	Bridge over Weehawken Creek.
3.1 ▲	**SO**	Bridge over Weehawken Creek.
▼ 5.0	**SO**	Camping on the left and right.
1.4 ▲	**SO**	Camping on the left and right.
▼ 5.1	**SO**	Camp Bird Mine turnoff to the left.
1.3 ▲	**SO**	Camp Bird Mine turnoff to the right.
▼ 5.7	**SO**	Canyon wall dramatically overhangs the road.
0.7 ▲	**SO**	Canyon wall dramatically overhangs the road.
▼ 6.2	**SO**	Track on right.
0.2 ▲	**SO**	Track on left.
▼ 6.4	**SO**	Intersection. Southwest Trail #8: Imogene Pass Road on left. Track on right. Zero trip meter.
0.0 ▲		Continue along road toward Ouray and US 550.

		GPS: N 37°58.53' W 107°44.70'
▼ 0.0		Continue along road toward Yankee Boy Basin.
	SO	Intersection. Southwest Trail #8: Imogene Pass Road on right. Track on left. Zero trip meter.
▼ 0.1	SO	Road on right.
▼ 0.3	SO	Revenue Mine and Sneffels site on left. Track on right.
▼ 0.5	SO	Road on right.
▼ 0.7	BR	Numerous campsites on left and right. Atlas Mine ruins on left across the river. Go past the information board.
		GPS: N 37°58.67' W 107°45.36'
▼ 0.9	BR	Road forks. Governor Basin road is to the left.
		GPS: N 37°58.73' W 107°45.52'
▼ 1.2	SO	Closed track on left.
▼ 1.3	SO	Dual waterfall view on left.
▼ 1.5	SO	Private road on left. Walker Ruby Mining.
▼ 1.6	SO	Public restrooms on left.
▼ 1.7	SO	Short road on left goes to a mine portal and then rejoins the main track.
▼ 1.9	SO	Cross through creek. Yankee Boy Mine and tailing dump on right. Track on left rejoins from the previous entry.
▼ 2.1	SO	Tracks on left and right.
▼ 2.7		End of track. Zero trip meter for return.
		GPS: N 37°59.45' W 107°46.76'

SOUTHWEST REGION TRAIL #8

Imogene Pass Road

Starting Point:	**Yankee Boy Basin Road**
Finishing Point:	**Telluride**
Total Mileage:	**12.8 miles**
Unpaved Mileage:	**12.2 miles**
Driving Time:	**2 1/2 hours**
Pass Elevation:	**13,114 feet**
Usually Open:	**Late June to late September**
Difficulty Rating:	**4**
Scenic Rating:	**10**

Special Attractions

- The highest pass road in the San Juan Mountains, with spectacular scenery and a wealth of historic interest.
- The ghost town of Tomboy.
- Views of Bridal Veil Falls and the switchbacks of Black Bear Pass Trail.

History

The Imogene Pass Road was built in 1880 to access Ouray from the Tomboy Mine. It was named for Imogene Richardson, the wife of one of Thomas Walsh's partners in the Camp Bird Mine.

Wires carrying the first commercial transmission of alternating-current electricity were strung across this pass in the 1890s. The power was generated in Ames and transmitted to Ouray.

Following the silver crash in 1893, the Tomboy Mine and township were saved when residents concentrated on gold production.

In 1901, the Western Federation of Miners called their first strike in the Telluride area. This strike was successful, and non-union laborers were chased out of Tomboy over Imogene Pass. In 1903, the Tomboy Mill again began to use non-union labor, and a second strike was called. The mine owners requested Governor Peabody to call out the state militia, and the governor, in turn, called on President Roosevelt to send federal troops. The U.S. army stayed away, but when five hundred state troopers arrived the violence soon escalated. The union even brought in a hired gun, Harry

Tomboy town site

Orchard, whom they had previously commissioned to assassinate the governor of Idaho. On union orders, he attempted to murder Governor Peabody, but the plot failed. With the area under military rule, the union and the strike were broken. The union labor was run out of town but set up camp at Red Mountain and plotted to recapture Tomboy and Telluride. Fort Peabody was constructed at the top of the pass in 1903 to protect against such an attack. The attack never occurred.

The Tomboy Mine was sold for $2 million to the Rothschilds of London in 1897 and continued to operate until 1927.

The route was reopened as a 4WD road in 1966, following the efforts of various 4WD clubs.

Description

Imogene Pass is the second highest pass road in the United States and provides a wonderfully scenic route through the San Juan Mountains. The route passes two major mining camps: Camp Bird and Tomboy. The ghost town of Tomboy is one of the better ghost towns to visit in the area as many of its buildings still stand above their foundations.

From the Yankee Boy Basin turnoff, the road deteriorates and becomes 4WD. The track passes through the forest and the Imogene Creek Valley. There are a number of creek crossings as the track proceeds toward the pass, although none should prove to be any problem for a 4WD.

The road narrows for the final ascent to the pass, but there are adequate pull-offs available for passing.

About two miles from the pass, the track enters the ghost town of Tomboy, 2,880 feet above Telluride,

Social Tunnel

three miles distant, with its numerous historic remains. Although the buildings of Tomboy continue to deteriorate from the onslaught of harsh weather, Tomboy remains one of the

SW TRAIL #8: IMOGENE PASS ROAD

better ghost towns to explore.

Some two miles past Tomboy, the road passes through Social Tunnel, a short passage through a rock outcrop that provides a popular photo opportunity. This point also provides spectacular views of the switchbacks on Black Bear Pass Trail and both Ingram Falls and Bridal Veil Falls.

Current Road Condition Information

Uncompahgre National Forest
Norwood Ranger District
1760 Grand Avenue, Norwood, CO 81423
(970) 327-4261

Map References

USFS Uncompahgre NF
USGS Ouray County #2
San Miguel County #3
Trails Illustrated, #141
The Roads of Colorado, p. 115
Colorado Atlas & Gazetteer, p. 76

Route Directions

▼ 0.0		At intersection of Southwest Trail #7: Yankee Boy Basin Road and Imogene Pass Road (FR 869), zero trip meter and proceed across bridge over Sneffels Creek. Track on right, bear left.
5.3 ▲		Track on left. Cross bridge over Sneffels Creek. End at intersection with Southwest Trail #7: Yankee Boy Basin Road.
		GPS: N 37°58.53' W 107°44.70'
▼ 0.2	SO	Track on right—no access.
5.1 ▲	SO	Track on left—no access.
▼ 0.4	SO	Creek crossing.
4.9 ▲	SO	Creek crossing.
▼ 0.8	SO	Old cabin on left.

4.5 ▲	SO	Old cabin on right.
▼ 1.2	BR	Private road to Camp Bird Mine on left.
4.1 ▲	BL	Private road to Camp Bird Mine on right.
▼ 1.5	SO	Imogene Creek cascading down through valley on left.
3.8 ▲	SO	Imogene Creek cascading down through valley on right.
▼ 1.9	SO	Track on right. Old sign to Imogene Pass. Cross through Imogene Creek. Cascade on left. Another track on right goes to an old log building and mine.
3.4 ▲	SO	Track on left goes to an old log building and mine. Cross through Imogene Creek. Track on left.
▼ 2.0	SO	Spectacular view of Imogene Creek cascading into valley.
3.3 ▲	SO	Spectacular view of Imogene Creek cascading into valley.
▼ 2.3	SO	Cross bridge over Imogene Creek. Track on left to Richmond Basin.
3.0 ▲	SO	Track on right to Richmond Basin. Cross bridge over Imogene Creek.
		GPS: N 37°57.22' W 107°43.45'
▼ 2.7	SO	Track on right to buildings and mine. Cross through creek.
2.6 ▲	SO	Cross through creek. Track on left to buildings and mine.
▼ 2.9	SO	Track on right. Follow Imogene Pass sign.
2.4 ▲	SO	Track on left.
▼ 3.0	BR	Series of tracks, continue to the right.
2.3 ▲	SO	Roads rejoin on the right.
▼ 3.1	SO	Roads rejoin on the left.
2.2 ▲	BL	Roads on the right.
▼ 4.1	SO	Cross through creek.
1.2 ▲	SO	Cross through creek.
▼ 4.4	SO	Cross through creek.
0.9 ▲	SO	Cross through creek.
▼ 5.2	BR	Track on left to Ptarmigan Lake.
0.1 ▲	BL	Track on right to Ptarmigan Lake.
▼ 5.3	SO	Summit of Imogene Pass. Zero trip meter.
0.0 ▲		Continue along main road.
		GPS: N 37°55.88' W 107°44.07'
▼ 0.0		Stay on main road and proceed downhill.
7.5 ▲	SO	Summit of Imogene Pass. Zero trip meter.
▼ 1.2	SO	Track on left. Stay on main road.
6.3 ▲	SO	Track on right. Stay on main road.
▼ 1.4	SO	Cross over drainage.
6.1 ▲	SO	Cross over drainage.
▼ 1.5	SO	Tracks on right.
6.0 ▲	SO	Tracks on left.
▼ 1.7	SO	Stone building remains on left.
5.8 ▲	SO	Stone building remains on right.
▼ 1.8	UT	Overlook of Tomboy mining township.
5.7 ▲	UT	Overlook of Tomboy mining township.
▼ 2.1	SO	Tomboy site.
5.4 ▲	SO	Tomboy site.
		GPS: N 37°56.18' W 107°45.23'
▼ 2.4	SO	Mill, bridge over creek.
5.1 ▲	SO	Bridge over creek and then mill.
▼ 2.5	SO	Track on right.
5.0 ▲	SO	Track on left.
▼ 3.0	BR	Track on left.
4.5 ▲	BL	Track on right.

▼ 3.1		SO	Bridges over two creeks.
	4.4 ▲	SO	Bridges over two creeks.
▼ 3.3		SO	Tomboy Mine remains.
	4.2 ▲	SO	Tomboy Mine remains.
▼ 3.8		SO	Colorful mine buildings.
	3.7 ▲	SO	Colorful mine buildings.
▼ 4.3		SO	Social Tunnel.
	3.2 ▲	SO	Social Tunnel.
▼ 6.6		SO	Seasonal closure gate.
	0.9 ▲	SO	Seasonal closure gate.
▼ 6.9		UT	Onto Gregory Avenue at intersection with North Oak. Then turn right onto North Fir.
	0.5 ▲	TL	Onto Gregory Avenue. Then U-turn to the right at North Oak.
▼ 7.1		TR	Intersection of N. Fir and W. Colorado.
	0.4 ▲	TL	Intersection of N. Fir and W. Colorado.
▼ 7.5			End at Visitor Information Center on W. Colorado (main street) in Telluride.
	0.0 ▲		From Visitor Information Center on W. Colorado (main street) in Telluride, zero trip meter and proceed east.

GPS: N 37°56.37' W 107°49.15'

SOUTHWEST REGION TRAIL #9

Ophir Pass Road

Starting Point:	Colorado 145 and FR 630, south of Telluride
Finishing Point:	US 550 (between Ouray and Silverton)
Total Mileage:	9.8 miles
Unpaved Mileage:	9.8 miles
Driving Time:	1 3/4 hours
Pass Elevation:	11,789 feet
Usually Open:	Mid-June to October
Difficulty Rating:	3
Scenic Rating:	8

Special Attractions

- Driving through the twenty-foot-high channel in the snow early in the season.
- The long, narrow shelf road set into the talus slope on the west side of the pass.
- Varied scenery, with exceptional views from near the summit toward the west.

History

This route was first called the Navajo Trail and was a well-used Indian hunting trail. The remains of an Indian camp were still visible near the pass in the 1880s.

Trappers were the first white men to use the pass. Explorers and prospectors followed them in the 1860s, and the road across the pass developed as a recognized route. In the mid-1870s after the Brunot Treaty opened up the region, a wagon road was built across the pass. The wagon road was converted into a toll road in 1880. When Otto Mears built his railroad through the area in 1891, the need for the pass road began to decline.

The current 4WD road was opened in 1953.

Description

The turnoff from Colorado 145 at the site of the Ophir Loop starts this track; but it is not well marked, so we recommend that you measure the distance from Telluride on your odometer. Those with GPS receivers will be glad to

The Ophir Pass Road in early June

have the benefit of modern technology.

Across the highway from the start of this trail is a short road to the township of Ames, the site of the first commercial, alternating-current electricity generating plant in the United States.

As you leave the old township of Ophir, the road starts to ascend immediately through scenic woods and aspen stands.

As the ascent continues, the road rises above the timberline and becomes a narrow shelf road cut into the talus slope with some tight switchbacks and high, steep drop-offs. This section is the most difficult part of the route. For a short section, passing requires careful negotiation. Traveling slowly and carefully, moderately experienced drivers should not have any difficulty.

The road is certainly easier than Black Bear Pass Trail, but those who are tempted to take the route too lightly should heed the lesson offered by the remains of a wrecked vehicle that rolled off the road at this point.

From the summit of the pass to US 550, the route is much easier. While the road is wider and the footing more sound, it remains a shelf road for much of the balance of the journey.

The varied scenery offers some particularly panoramic views on the west side. The east

A pack train on Ophir Pass Road in 1920

side is more heavily wooded than the west side, and the wildflowers in the valley add color.

The intersection with FR 820 offers an alternative route to US 550. The road is about 1.5 miles long and at times provides a challenging crossing through Mineral Creek. It joins US 550 0.7 miles north where the main route intersects.

Where the main route joins US 550, Ouray is about eight-

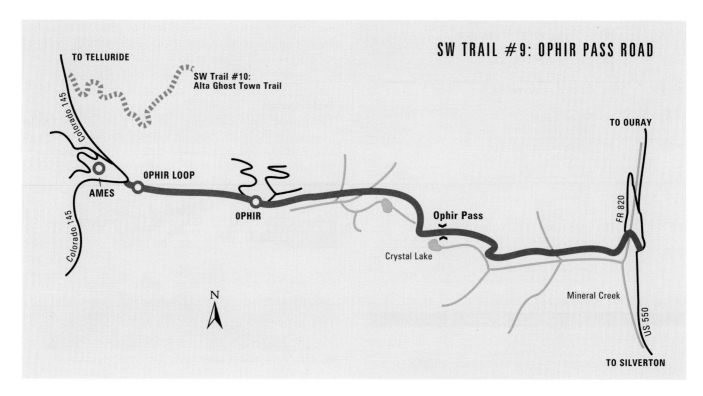

een miles north and Silverton five miles south.

The road opens in early to mid-June each year. The snowplow only clears the east side of the pass to the summit. When the road is first opened, the plow leaves a narrow channel through the snow for 4WDs to travel—the sides are up to twenty feet high.

Current Road Condition Information

San Juan National Forest
701 Camino del Rio, Durango, CO 81301
(970) 247-4874

Map References

USFS Uncompahgre NF or San Juan NF
USGS San Miguel County #3
       San Juan County
Trails Illustrated, #141
The Roads of Colorado, pp. 114-115
Colorado Atlas & Gazetteer, p. 76

Route Directions

▼ 0.0			At intersection of Colorado 145 and FR 630 at Ophir Loop (no signpost, but opposite the Ames turnoff), zero trip meter and turn onto FR 630 heading east toward Ophir. This is 10 miles from the Telluride Visitor Center.
5.7 ▲			End at intersection of Colorado 145 and FR 630 at Ophir Loop.
GPS: N 37°51.74′ W 107°52.11′			
▼ 0.6		SO	Seasonal gate.
5.1 ▲		SO	Seasonal gate.
▼ 2.0		SO	Seasonal gate. Enter town of Ophir. Follow sign to Ophir Pass.
3.7 ▲		SO	Leave Ophir. Seasonal gate.
▼ 2.1		BR	Road forks. Then Ophir Pass sign.
3.6 ▲		BL	Road forks.

▼ 2.6		BL/TR	Stay on main road.
3.1 ▲		TL/BR	Stay on main road.
▼ 2.7		SO	Leaving town on Ophir Pass Road.
3.0 ▲		SO	Enter Ophir town limits.
▼ 3.2		SO	Track on right.
2.4 ▲		SO	Track on left.
▼ 3.7		SO	Two tracks on left.
2.0 ▲		SO	Two tracks on right.
▼ 3.8		SO	Track on left.
1.9 ▲		SO	Track on right.
▼ 4.1		SO	Track on left.
1.6 ▲		SO	Track on right.
▼ 4.2		SO	Tracks on left and right. Track on right goes to the lake and campsites.
1.5 ▲		SO	Track on left goes to the lake and campsites. Tracks on right.
▼ 5.7		SO	Summit of Ophir Pass. Zero trip meter.
0.0 ▲			Continue along main track toward Ophir.
GPS: N 37°51.00′ W 107°46.72′			
▼ 0.0			Continue along main track.
4.1 ▲		SO	Summit of Ophir Pass. Zero trip meter.
▼ 0.5		SO	Tracks on left.
3.6 ▲		SO	Tracks on right.
▼ 1.0		UT	Track on left.
3.1 ▲		BL	Track on right.
▼ 3.2		SO	Track on right.
0.9 ▲		SO	Track on left.
▼ 3.7		SO	Columbine Lake Trail on left (FR 820).
0.4 ▲		SO	Columbine Lake Trail on right (FR 820).
▼ 3.9		SO	Cross bridge.
0.2 ▲		SO	Cross bridge.
▼ 4.1			End at intersection with US 550.
0.0 ▲			From intersection of US 550 and San Juan County 8 (FR 679), zero trip meter and proceed along County 8 toward Ophir.
GPS: N 37°50.84′ W 107°43.44′			

Alta Ghost Town Trail

Starting Point:	Telluride
Finishing Point:	Alta Lakes
Total Mileage:	12.4 miles
Unpaved Mileage:	4.2 miles
Driving Time:	1 hour (one-way)
Town Site Elevation:	11,100 feet
Usually Open:	Mid-June to October
Difficulty Rating:	2
Scenic Rating:	8

Special Attractions
- Alta, a well-preserved ghost town.
- The picturesque Alta Lakes.

History
The Alta Mine was discovered in 1878, and the more successful Gold King Mine was discovered the following year. Both mines produced gold, silver, lead, and copper; thus Alta was able to survive the silver crash of 1893. There were three mills in Alta, all of which burned down. The last burned in 1945 and led to the tragic death of seven miners.

The Gold King Mine was able to operate profitably only

Alta Lakes

because the lawyer who represented the mine, L.L. Nunn, pioneered the use of alternating-current electricity, which he transmitted from Ames. The success of this early venture led Nunn to build the transmission line over Imogene Pass. His plant pioneered the commercial production of alternating-current electricity, which was supported by George Westinghouse against the strong opposition of Thomas Edison.

Description
FR 632, an unpaved road from Colorado 145 to the township of Alta, is well maintained and in good conditions can be traveled easily by passenger cars.

FR 632 meets Colorado 145 1.7 miles north of the intersection with the start of the road to Ophir Pass (Southwest Trail #9). On the western side of Colorado 145 at the Ophir

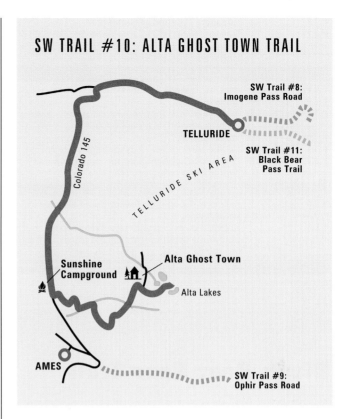

SW TRAIL #10: ALTA GHOST TOWN TRAIL

Pass turnoff is the road to the township of Ames, where the electricity for Alta was generated.

A short way above the Alta ghost town are the very scenic Alta Lakes, located at timberline. The lakes have good picnic facilities and public toilets.

The road to the lakes is also easy, but the road that encircles the lakes can be extremely rutted and muddy. This section of road would have a difficulty rating of 5.

A number of maps suggest that there is a road from the Alta Lakes to the Telluride ski area. However, when we were last there, this road had been blocked off. We were not able to confirm that this road would be reopened.

Current Road Condition Information
Uncompahgre National Forest
Norwood Ranger District
1760 Grand Avenue, Norwood, CO 81423
(970) 327-4261

Map References
USFS Uncompahgre NF
USGS San Miguel County #3
Trails Illustrated, #141
The Roads of Colorado, p. 114
Colorado Atlas & Gazetteer, p. 76

Route Directions

▼ 0.0		In front of the Telluride Visitor Information Center on W. Colorado (main street) in Telluride, zero trip meter and proceed west out of town.
		GPS: N 37°56.37' W 107°49.15'
▼ 3.1	TL	Follow Colorado 145 south toward Ophir.

▼ 7.8	SO	Sunshine Campground on right.
▼ 8.2	TL	National Forest access sign on right (FR 632) toward Alta Lake Road and Alta Lakes. Unpaved. Zero trip meter.

GPS: N 37°53.02' W 107°53.25'

▼ 0.0		Proceed toward Alta on FR 632.
▼ 2.9	SO	Track on right.
▼ 3.0	SO	Track on left with private property sign. Gate. Sign to stay on designated roads.
▼ 3.0	SO	Track on right.
▼ 3.4	SO	Private track on left. Private track on right.
▼ 3.7	BR	Ghost town of Alta. Zero trip meter at small sign for Alta Lakes.

GPS: N 37°53.13' W 107°51.28'

▼ 0.0		Follow track on right toward Alta Lakes.
▼ 0.3	BL	Road forks.
▼ 0.5		Road forks. End at Alta Lakes. There are numerous spots for picnics and tracks winding around the lakes.

GPS: N 37°52.83' W 107°50.87'

SOUTHWEST REGION TRAIL #11

Black Bear Pass Trail

Starting Point:	Ouray
Finishing Point:	Telluride
Total Mileage:	25.2 miles
Unpaved Mileage:	10.1 miles
Driving Time:	2 1/2 hours
Pass Elevation:	12,840 feet
Usually Open:	Mid-July to late September
Difficulty Rating:	6
Scenic Rating:	10

Special Attractions

■ Expansive views of Telluride, nestled in the valley four thousand feet below.

■ Ingram and Bridal Veil Falls.

■ The challenge of completing a difficult 4WD trail.

History

Black Bear Pass has also been known as Ingram Pass, after J. Ingram, who discovered the Smuggler Union Mine in 1876. Although Black Bear Pass is now the name commonly used, it has not been accepted by the U.S. Geological Survey Board on Geographical Names.

Black Bear Pass Trail was developed in the late 1800s to provide access to the Black Bear Mine. In the early 1900s, it fell into disrepair and was reopened as a 4WD road in 1959 only through the efforts of the Telluride Jeep Club.

Description

The one-way Black Bear Pass Trail is one of the more difficult 4WD trails included in this book. It can be dangerous and has claimed many lives during the past thirty years. Just how dif-

ficult you will find it depends on your vehicle, your 4WD experience, and current road conditions. We have included it here for drivers who wish to try a more demanding road and because it is justly famous for its scenery.

The trail is not suitable for a full-sized vehicle, due to the very tight switchbacks on the steep, western side of the pass. It is the only trail in this book that we have never traveled in our Suburban. Taken slowly and carefully in a small vehicle, this pass should not be beyond the abilities of any driver who has com-

Hydroelectricity power station at the top of Bridal Veil Falls

fortably undertaken a broad selection of the easier trails included in this book.

The portion of the trail that earns its difficulty rating stretches from the summit of the pass to the U-turn at the entrance to the power station at Bridal Veil Falls about four miles below. This section is one way and can only be traveled from east to west.

From the Million Dollar Highway, US 550, the road starts its climb toward the pass. About a mile before the summit of the pass, the road flattens out, leading through lovely meadows with little alpine lakes and waterfalls in beautiful tundra countryside.

At the summit, a network of tracks provides a multitude of wide, panoramic views. The abundance of tracks makes it difficult to identify the main track down to the west side; but by looking down into the valley (to the northwest of the summit), you can easily see the road you need to take.

Dropping down from the pass, the road heads into a treeless alpine valley but remains quite easy. The water crossings may be of concern to some drivers, but the base is sound and should pose little problem when taken carefully. Some slipping on the talus surface must be anticipated.

Up to this point, the degree of difficulty would be rated at only 3. As you will have noticed, though, the spectacular views are already evident.

The road continues to get rougher and more difficult as you descend. Obstacles that may prove too challeng-

The Black Bear Pass 4WD trail crosses directly beneath Ingram Falls

ing for inexperienced four-wheelers include tight, off-camber switchbacks, loose talus, and narrow shelf roads with thousand-foot-plus drop-offs. Because of the difficulty of this section of road, local 4WD rental businesses do not permit their vehicles to cross this pass.

The very tight switchbacks commence about two miles below the summit. The road has a formidable reputation, and when you get to these switchbacks, it is easy to see why. One

SW TRAIL #11: BLACK BEAR PASS TRAIL

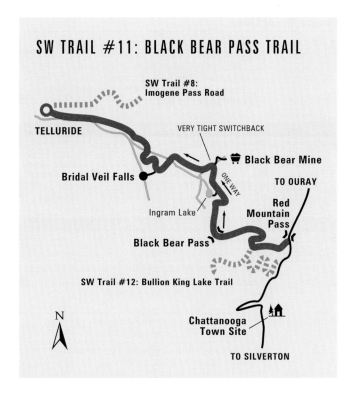

switchback is particularly notorious and is justly considered impassable for full-sized vehicles. A short distance further, the road crosses the creek directly above Ingram Falls.

The route provides many scenic views of Bridal Veil Falls and the early hydroelectric power station. Numerous mines and tramways are evident during the journey down into Telluride.

We think this is one of the great 4WD roads of Colorado. Although experienced four-wheelers may not find it as difficult as it is reputed to be, we are sure they will consider it a great drive.

Current Road Condition Information

Uncompahgre National Forest
Norwood Ranger District
1760 Grand Avenue, Norwood, CO 81423
(970) 327-4261

Map References

USFS Uncompahgre NF or San Juan NF
USGS San Juan County
San Miguel County #3
Trails Illustrated, #141
The Roads of Colorado, pp. 114-115
Colorado Atlas & Gazetteer, p. 76

Route Directions

▼ 0.0		In front of Beaumont Hotel at 5th and Main in Ouray, zero trip meter and proceed south out of town onto US 550.
GPS: N 38°01.30′ W 107°40.29′		
▼ 12.9	TR	Onto Black Bear Pass Trail (FR 823), just beyond the summit marker of Red Mountain. The track is marked only by a small, brown 4WD signpost. Zero trip meter.
GPS: N 37°53.81′ W 107°42.78′		

▼ 0.1	SO	Mine remains.
▼ 1.0	BR	Road forks. To the left is Southwest Trail #12: Bullion King Lake Trail.
▼ 1.2	BR	Track on left. Waterfall on right.
▼ 1.3	SO	Track on right.
▼ 2.9	BL	Road forks.
▼ 3.2		Summit of Black Bear Pass. Zero trip meter.
GPS: N 37°53.99′ W 107°44.52′		
▼ 0.0		Proceed from the summit on main track, heading northwest down the hill.
▼ 1.6	SO	Track on left to Ingram Lake.
▼ 1.8	SO	Spectacular view of Telluride on left.
▼ 2.1	BL	Track on right goes to Black Bear Mine. Cross through creek.
▼ 2.6	SO	Very tight downhill switchback.
▼ 2.8	SO	Mine portal on the right side of road.
▼ 3.2	SO	Mine on left.
▼ 3.3	SO	Cross through Ingram Creek at Ingram Falls. Mine ruins.
GPS: N 37°55.34′ W 107°45.60′		
▼ 4.1	UT	One-way sign. End of difficult section. Closed driveway to old power station on left.
▼ 4.7	SO	Mine entrance (closed) on right.
▼ 5.0	SO	Parking at Bridal Veil Falls.
▼ 5.5	SO	Cross Ingram Falls runoff.
▼ 5.8	SO	Cross over creek.
▼ 6.4	SO	Tracks on left and right.
▼ 6.5	BL	Entrance to Pandora Mill on right (no access).
▼ 6.6	SO	Tailing ponds on left and Pandora Mill on right.
GPS: N 37°55.84′ W 107°46.70′		
▼ 6.9	SO	Road changes from dirt to paved surface.
▼ 8.0	SO	Telluride Cemetery on right.
▼ 8.4	SO	Enter Telluride's main street (W. Colorado).
▼ 9.1		End at Visitor Information Center on W. Colorado (main street) in Telluride.
GPS: N 37°56.37′ W 107°49.15′		

SOUTHWEST REGION TRAIL #12

Bullion King Lake Trail

Starting Point:	**Side road off Black Bear Pass Trail**
Finishing Point:	**US 550**
Total Mileage:	**2.8 miles (one-way)**
Unpaved Mileage:	**2.8 miles**
Driving Time:	**1/2 hour**
Pass Elevation:	**12,400 feet**
Usually Open:	**Mid-July to late September**
Difficulty Rating:	**3**
Scenic Rating:	**7**

Special Attractions

■ Attractive, panoramic scenery.
■ Small alpine lakes.

Description

Most maps do not show this road, and those that do are not accurate.

This road can be used as a side route of Black Bear Pass

SW TRAIL #12: BULLION KING LAKE TRAIL

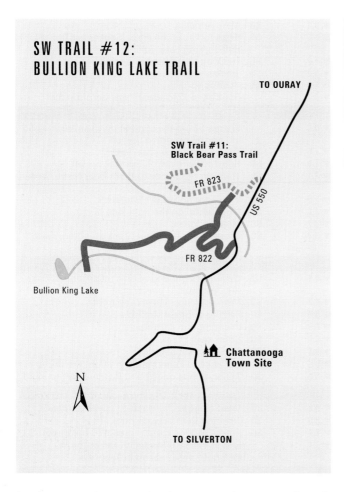

TO OURAY

SW Trail #11: Black Bear Pass Trail

FR 823

US 550

FR 822

Bullion King Lake

Chattanooga Town Site

N

TO SILVERTON

Trail or as an alternative for those not wishing to tangle with Black Bear—one of the most notorious 4WD roads in the San Juans. It provides some wonderfully panoramic scenery and an opportunity for a short hike to a few small, tranquil alpine lakes at the end of the trail.

The route commences one mile along Southwest Trail #11: Black Bear Pass Trail. It includes a section of narrow shelf road, a hundred feet or more above Porphyry Gulch Creek, which is sound but provides little opportunity for passing oncoming vehicles. It therefore pays to look ahead and let any oncoming vehicles come through before proceeding.

Taking a side road toward Silverton rather than returning all the way to Black Bear Pass Trail can vary the return trip.

Current Road Condition Information

Uncompahgre National Forest
Ouray Ranger District
2505 South Townsend Avenue, Montrose, CO 81401
(970) 240-5300

Map References

USFS San Juan NF
USGS San Juan County
Trails Illustrated, #141
Colorado Atlas & Gazetteer, p. 76

Route Directions

| ▼ 0.0 | | Begin at the intersection of US 550 and Southwest Trail #11: Black Bear Pass Trail (FR 823), just south of the summit marker of Red Mountain. The track is marked only by a small, brown 4WD signpost. Zero trip meter and proceed along FR 823. |
| 2.8 ▲ | | End at intersection with US 550. |

GPS: N 37°53.81′ W 107°42.78′

▼ 0.1	SO	Mine remains.
2.7 ▲	SO	Mine remains.
▼ 1.0	BL	Road forks. Black Bear Pass Trail continues on the right fork.
1.8 ▲	BR	Intersection. Southwest Trail #11: Black Bear Pass Trail. Left goes to Black Bear Pass.

GPS: N 37°53.70′ W 107°43.51′

▼ 1.1	SO	Cross through creek.
1.7 ▲	SO	Cross through creek.
▼ 1.3	SO	Track on left to campsite. Then cross through creek.
1.5 ▲	SO	Cross through creek. Track on right to campsite.
▼ 1.4	SO	Track on left to campsite on cliff.
1.4 ▲	SO	Track on right to campsite on cliff.
▼ 1.5	BR	Track on left to campsite. Then alternate route from US 550 enters on left.
1.3 ▲	BL	Alternate route from US 550 enters on right.
▼ 2.3	SO	Mine remains on the left. Cross through creek. Mine remains on the right.
0.5 ▲	SO	Mine remains on the right. Cross through creek. Mine remains on the left.
▼ 2.6	SO	Cross through creek.
0.2 ▲	SO	Cross through creek.
▼ 2.7	SO	Waterfall on right.
0.1 ▲	SO	Waterfall on left.
▼ 2.8		Road comes to an end. Follow walking path to Bullion King Lake. Zero trip meter.
0.0 ▲	UT	Turn around and proceed back down the mountain away from Bullion King Lake.

GPS: N 37°53.16′ W 107°44.42′

▼ 0.0	UT	Turn around and proceed back down the mountain away from Bullion King Lake.
2.8 ▲		Road comes to an end. Follow walking path to Bullion King Lake. Zero trip meter.
▼ 0.1	SO	Waterfall on left.
2.7 ▲	SO	Waterfall on right.
▼ 0.2	SO	Cross through creek.
2.6 ▲	SO	Cross through creek.
▼ 0.5	SO	Mine remains on the left. Cross through creek. Mine remains on the right.
2.3 ▲	SO	Mine remains on the left. Cross through creek. Mine remains on the right.
▼ 1.3	BR	Fork in road. Left reconnects with Black Bear Pass Trail.
1.5 ▲	BL	Fork in road.
▼ 1.6	BR	Track on left.
1.2 ▲	BL	Track on right.
▼ 2.2	SO	Campsite on right.
0.6 ▲	SO	Campsite on left.
▼ 2.7	SO	Fork in road to private cabin.
0.1 ▲	BR	Fork in road to private cabin.
▼ 2.8		End at US 550.
0.0 ▲		At the intersection of US 550 and FR 822, zero trip meter and proceed west on FR 822.

GPS: N 37°53.33′ W 107°43.12′

Cunningham Gulch and Stony Pass Trail

Starting Point:	Howardsville
Finishing Point:	Colorado 149 between Lake City and Creede
Total Mileage:	37.7 miles
Unpaved Mileage:	37.2 miles
Driving Time:	3 1/4 hours
Pass Elevation:	12,588 feet
Usually Open:	Mid-June to late October
Difficulty Rating:	5
Scenic Rating:	9

Special Attractions

- A varied and scenic 4WD trail.
- A challenging stream crossing.
- Relative solitude; this trail has less traffic than many others in the peak summer months.

History

Cunningham Gulch is named for Major Cunningham, who brought a party of mining investors from Chicago through the area. Stony Pass was named by common usage to describe the rocky pass. It was also known as Hamilton Pass, after the builder of the first wagon road over the pass, and Rio Grande Pass.

The Stony Pass crossing is of extremely high historic interest. The Utes used the trail for centuries, and Spanish artifacts have also been found in the area. The pass is believed to have been discovered in 1860 by Charles Baker, who led a party of prospectors to the area, well before the Brunot Treaty officially opened the territory in 1873.

Major E. M. Hamilton built a wagon road along the route in 1872, which was improved seven years later. The route was heavily used during this period by stagecoaches and as the major supply line for the four thousand mines that were operating in the area.

When the railroad reached Silverton in 1882, the pass was used less often. However, the route remained open and at one point in the early 1900s was classified as a state highway. Eventually, it was completely abandoned, until the Forest Service reopened it in the 1950s as a 4WD recreational route.

Description

The route is a long 4WD trail with varied scenery. It sees light use compared to other, better known routes in the San Juans during summer. It is usually open by the middle of June.

The road starts at Howardsville, between Silverton and Animas Forks, as an attractive 2WD road, running alongside Cunningham Creek up Cunningham Gulch. Within a couple of miles it becomes steeper, narrower, and rougher as it climbs up a ledge overlooking the gulch. It soon narrows to the width

of one vehicle, with occasional pull-offs for passing.

As the road approaches the summit of Stony Pass, it levels out into a beautiful alpine valley with typical vegetation and many wildflowers. The open portals of mines and decaying cabins are still in evidence.

From the pass, the road tracks the edge of the Weminuche Wilderness Area and follows the headwaters of the Rio Grande River. At around the ten-mile point, the road offers great access to some scenic and quiet fishing spots.

The road from the summit has a relatively gentle grade. The biggest potential problems in the first ten miles of the descent are mud and occasional shallow creek crossings. The few rough stretches are relatively short.

At the 11.8-mile point is the Pole Creek crossing, which is the deepest of all the stream crossings covered in this book. Early in the season, we advise you to start this trail in the morning because snowmelt causes the creek to rise significantly throughout the day. Late in the day, this crossing could cause vehicle damage. Later in the season, the creek can still be two feet deep, but the bottom is sound. With good tires and a slow, steady pace, 4WD vehicles should have no problem crossing.

The degree of difficulty of the next few miles is a matter of how long it has been since the last rain. When wet, the road can be very muddy. Assess the situation and proceed cautiously when crossing the creeks; sharp approach and departure an-

One lonely miner's cabin and some of the many mines near the summit of Stony Pass

gles at these crossings can hang up your vehicle. The trail winds through forest in this section, so once it gets muddy, it can stay that way for some time. Clearance between the trees is narrow at times, and the road even has a couple of short, rocky sections.

Current Road Condition Information

San Juan National Forest
701 Camino del Rio, Durango, CO 81301
(970) 247-4874

Map References

USFS Uncompahgre NF
Rio Grande NF

USGS San Juan County
Hinsdale County #2
Mineral County #1

Trails Illustrated, #140, #141
The Roads of Colorado, pp. 131-132
Colorado Atlas & Gazetteer, pp. 77-78

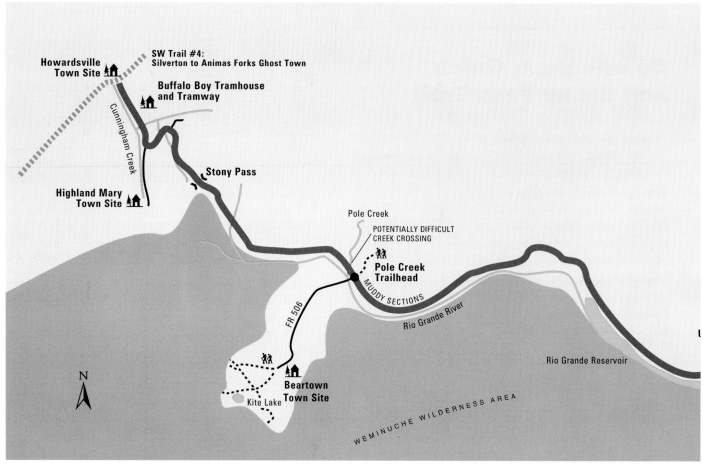

Route Directions

▼ 0.0		At intersection of Southwest Trail #4 and the turnoff to Cunningham Gulch in Howardsville, zero trip meter and proceed toward Cunningham Gulch and Stony Pass.
5.8 ▲		End at intersection with Southwest Trail #4.

GPS: N 37°50.12' W 107°35.69'

▼ 0.2	BR	Fork in road. Left goes to Old Hundred Mine.
5.6 ▲	SO	Road on right to Old Hundred Mine.
▼ 1.0	SO	Old Hundred Mine and Mill on left.
4.8 ▲	SO	Old Hundred Mine and Mill on right.
▼ 1.3	SO	Site of Green Mountain Mill on right.
4.5 ▲	SO	Site of Green Mountain Mill on left.
▼ 1.5	SO	Buffalo Boy Tramhouse and Tramway on left.
4.3 ▲	SO	Buffalo Boy Tramhouse and Tramway on right.
▼ 1.7	BR/BL	Follow sign to Creede via Stony Pass on County 3. Road enters on left and goes to Old Hundred Mine. Then road forks and the track on right goes to the town site of Highland Mary in 3.4 miles.
4.1 ▲ BL/BR		Intersection. Roads enter on left and right. Continue on middle road.
▼ 2.5	SO	Cross through creek.
3.3 ▲	SO	Cross through creek.
▼ 3.2	BR	Short track on left.
2.6 ▲	BL	Short track on right.
▼ 3.3	BR	Track on left.
2.5 ▲	BL	Track on right.
▼ 3.5	BL	Cross under tramway. Track entering on right.
2.3 ▲	BR	Track entering on left. Cross under tramway.
▼ 3.7	SO	Small bridge over creek.

2.1 ▲	SO	Small bridge over creek.
▼ 4.0	SO	Cross over creek. Small track on right.
1.8 ▲	SO	Small track on left. Cross over creek.
▼ 4.7	SO	Small track on right.
1.1 ▲	SO	Small track on left.
▼ 5.8	SO	Summit of Stony Pass. Zero trip meter.
0.0 ▲		Continue along road.

GPS: N 37°47.75' W 107°32.93'

▼ 0.0		Continue along road.
6.2 ▲	SO	Summit of Stony Pass. Zero trip meter.
▼ 0.2	SO	Cabin and mine tracks on right.
6.0 ▲	SO	Cabin and mine tracks on left.
▼ 1.0	SO	West Ute Creek and Ute Creek trails.
5.2 ▲	SO	West Ute Creek and Ute Creek trails.
▼ 1.3	SO	Cross over creek.
4.9 ▲	SO	Cross over creek.
▼ 3.6	SO	Cross over creek.
2.6 ▲	SO	Cross over creek.
▼ 5.3	SO	Track to river on right.
0.9 ▲	SO	Track to river on left.
▼ 5.4	SO	Pass through fence line.
0.8 ▲	SO	Pass through fence line.
▼ 6.0	SO	Cross through Pole Creek. Beware that this crossing may be deep.
0.2 ▲	SO	Cross through Pole Creek. Beware that this crossing may be deep.

GPS: N 37°45.86' W 107°28.00'

▼ 6.2	BL	Intersection. FR 506 on right goes to Beartown site and Kite Lake. Zero trip meter.

SW TRAIL #13: CUNNINGHAM GULCH AND STONY PASS TRAIL

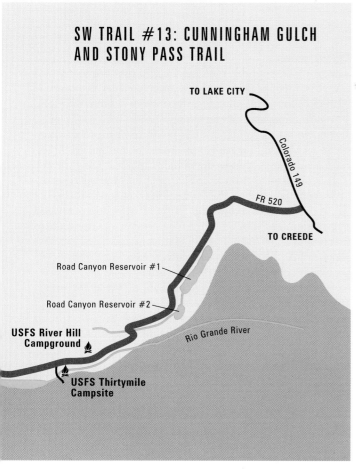

TO LAKE CITY

Colorado 149

FR 520

TO CREEDE

Road Canyon Reservoir #1

Road Canyon Reservoir #2

Rio Grande River

USFS River Hill Campground

USFS Thirtymile Campsite

0.0 ▲		Continue toward Stony Pass and Silverton.
GPS: N 37°45.72' W 107°27.97'		
▼ 0.0		Continue toward Rio Grande Reservoir and Creede. Pole Creek Trail is on left.
16.2 ▲	SO	Pole Creek Trail on right. Intersection. FR 506 on left goes to Beartown site and Kite Lake. Zero trip meter.
▼ 0.7	SO	Cross through creek.
15.5 ▲	SO	Cross through creek.
▼ 1.0	SO	Gate.
15.2 ▲	SO	Gate.
▼ 2.1	SO	Cross through Sweetwater Creek.
14.1 ▲	SO	Cross through Sweetwater Creek.
▼ 2.3-2.5	SO	Beaver ponds and dams on right.
13.7-13.9 ▲	SO	Beaver ponds and dams on left.
▼ 2.9	SO	Cross through creek.
13.3 ▲	SO	Cross through creek.
▼ 3.0	SO	Water crossing. This can be deep.
13.2 ▲	SO	Water crossing. This can be deep.
▼ 3.2	SO	Cross through creek.
13.0 ▲	SO	Cross through creek.
▼ 3.5	SO	Cross through creek.
12.7 ▲	SO	Cross through creek.
▼ 4.3	SO	Cross through creek.
11.9 ▲	SO	Cross through creek.
▼ 4.4-4.8	SO	Series of water crossings. None difficult.
11.4-11.8 ▲	SO	Series of water crossings. None difficult.
▼ 5.0	SO	Cattle guard. Cross through creek.
11.2 ▲	SO	Cross through creek. Cattle guard. Sign reads "Brewster Park."

▼ 5.7	SO	Track on right to river.
10.5 ▲	SO	Track on left to river.
▼ 6.5	BR	Track on left. Cross through creek.
9.7 ▲	SO	Cross through creek. Track on right.
▼ 6.7	SO	Track to campsites on right.
9.5 ▲	SO	Track to campsites on left.
▼ 7.1	SO	Track on right.
9.1 ▲	SO	Track on left.
▼ 7.9	SO	Lost Trail Creek trailhead on left. Cattle guard.
8.3 ▲	SO	Cattle guard. Lost Trail Creek trailhead on right.
▼ 8.3	SO	Bridge over creek. Lost Trail Campground on right.
7.9 ▲	SO	Lost Trail Campground on left. Bridge over creek.
▼ 9.1	SO	Ute Creek trailhead on right. Public restrooms.
7.1 ▲	SO	Public restrooms. Ute Creek trailhead on left.
▼ 10.1	SO	Cattle guard. Overlook to Rio Grande Reservoir.
6.1 ▲	SO	Overlook to Rio Grande Reservoir. Cattle guard.
GPS: N 37°44.99' W 107°19.87'		
▼ 13.2	SO	Track on right to reservoir. Public restrooms available.
3.0 ▲	SO	Track on left to reservoir. Public restrooms available.
▼ 14.2	SO	Seasonal closure gate. Track on right to Rio Grande Reservoir (no access).
2.0 ▲	SO	Track on left to Rio Grande Reservoir (no access). Seasonal closure gate.
GPS: N 37°43.35' W 107°16.00'		
▼ 14.8	SO	Turnoff on right to USFS Thirtymile Campground, Weminuche trailhead, Thirtymile Resort, and Squaw Creek trailhead.
1.4 ▲	SO	Turnoff on left to USFS Thirtymile Campground, Weminuche trailhead, Thirtymile Resort, and Squaw Creek trailhead.
▼ 16.2	SO	USFS River Hill Campground. Zero trip meter.
0.0 ▲		Continue along main road toward Stony Pass.
GPS: N 37°43.81' W 107°13.86'		
▼ 0.0		Continue along main road.
9.5 ▲	SO	USFS River Hill Campground. Zero trip meter.
▼ 1.2	SO	Cattle guard. Road on left to Sawmill Canyon.
8.3 ▲	SO	Road on right to Sawmill Canyon. Cattle guard.
▼ 2.8-4.8	SO	Road Canyon Reservoirs #1 and #2 on right.
4.7-6.7 ▲	SO	Road Canyon Reservoirs #1 and #2 on left.
▼ 3.3	SO	USFS campground.
6.2 ▲	SO	USFS campground.
▼ 3.6	SO	Seasonal gate.
5.9 ▲	SO	Seasonal gate.
▼ 4.4	SO	Public toilets.
5.1 ▲	SO	Public toilets.
▼ 5.1	SO	Public toilets.
4.4 ▲	SO	Public toilets.
▼ 6.2	BR	Fork in the road.
3.3 ▲	BL	Track on right.
▼ 6.8	SO	Cattle guard.
2.7 ▲	SO	Cattle guard
▼ 9.0	SO	Pavement begins.
0.5 ▲	SO	Unpaved road.
▼ 9.5		Cattle guard. Stop sign. End at intersection with Colorado 149. Lake City is approximately 32 miles to the left; Creede is approximately 20 miles to the right.
0.0 ▲		At intersection of Colorado 149 with FR 520, zero trip meter and proceed onto FR 520. Creede is approximately 20 miles east.
GPS: N 37°47.41' W 107°07.71'		

Summitville Ghost Town Trail

Starting Point:	**Intersection of Colorado 17 and FR 250**
Finishing Point:	**Del Norte**
Total Mileage:	**68.8 miles**
Unpaved Mileage:	**57.9 miles**
Driving Time:	**4 hours**
Pass Elevation:	**Stunner-10,541'; Elwood-11,630'**
Usually Open:	**Early July to late October**
Difficulty Rating:	**2**
Scenic Rating:	**6**

Special Attractions

- The well-preserved ghost town of Summitville.
- An easy 4WD trail that is not heavily used.

History

The first road over Stunner Pass was constructed by the LeDuc and Sanchez Toll Road Company, which was formed for the purpose in 1884. The road was built as a freight route to service the mines that had started activity in the early 1880s. Mining activity was short-lived, and by the early 1890s, the area was almost deserted. However, the route has been maintained for recreational access to the area.

The U.S. army constructed Elwood Pass Road in 1878 to connect Fort Garland and Fort Harris in Pagosa Springs. In the 1880s, mining began in the area, and significant deposits of

Miners' boardinghouse at Summitville ghost town

gold and silver were found. Summitville ghost town is the best-preserved of the mining camps from this period; numerous buildings still stand.

Gold was discovered in the Summitville area in 1870, and hundreds of prospectors descended on the area. At its peak, the town had a population of more than 600 and had 2,500 mining claims staked. It boomed during the 1880s and produced a fortune for Tom Bowen, who became a leading figure

in Colorado politics and a great rival of Horace Tabor. The town was in decline by 1890 and deserted by 1893.

Description

The first section of this route via FR 250 over Stunner Pass is a well-maintained dirt road. The pass stretches between the Alamosa River to the north and the Conejos River to the south.

It offers a peaceful journey through gentle, rolling hills, interspersed with rock formations and overlooks that provide wonderful views along the valley and across the mountains. Abundant aspen groves spangle the hillsides in gold during the fall. The area also offers many accessible campsites and hiking trails.

In good conditions, the Stunner Pass section (FR 250) of this route warrants a difficulty rating of only 1. The Elwood Pass section (FR 380) is more difficult and causes this route to be rated at 2; but although FR 380 is higher, narrower, and rougher than FR 250, it is a relatively easy route and should provide no obstacles for a 4WD vehicle.

The area offers an extensive network of 4WD and hiking trails. Mining activity has continued in the Summitville area until recent times, although presently operations are restricted to an EPA-mandated clean-up of the mine remains.

Current Road Condition Information

Rio Grande National Forest
Del Norte Ranger District
13308 West Hwy 160, Del Norte, CO 81132
(719) 657-3321

Map References

USFS Rio Grande NF
USGS Conejos County #1
Rio Grande County #1
Rio Grande County #2
Trails Illustrated, #142
The Roads of Colorado, pp. 133-134 , 149-150
Colorado Atlas & Gazetteer, pp. 79, 89

Route Directions

▼ 0.0		At intersection of Colorado 17 and FR 250, zero trip meter. There is a signpost for Platoro. Turn onto the unpaved road.
16.1 ▲		End at intersection of Colorado 17 and FR 250.
		GPS: N 37°07.98' W 106°21.01'
▼ 6.0	SO	Cattle guard. USFS Spectacle Lake Campground.
10.1 ▲	SO	USFS Spectacle Lake Campground. Cattle guard.
▼ 6.3	SO	USFS Conejos Campground.
9.8 ▲	SO	USFS Conejos Campground.
▼ 7.4	SO	Intersection. FR 855 on left goes to Rybold Lake and No Name Lake.
8.7 ▲	SO	Intersection. FR 855 on right goes to Rybold Lake and No Name Lake.
▼ 8.8	SO	Cattle guard.
7.3 ▲	SO	Cattle guard.
▼ 10.8	SO	Southfork trailhead.
5.3 ▲	SO	Southfork trailhead.
▼ 11.1	SO	Intersection. Track on left for fishing access. Public restrooms.
5.0 ▲	SO	Intersection. Track on right for fishing access. Public restrooms.

▼ 11.8	SO	Cattle guard.
4.3 ▲	SO	Cattle guard.
▼ 13.2	SO	Valdez Creek Campground.
2.9 ▲	SO	Valdez Creek Campground.
▼ 13.8	SO	Trail Creek backcountry camping area.
2.3 ▲	SO	Trail Creek backcountry camping area.
▼ 13.9	SO	Track on right.
2.2 ▲	SO	Track on left.
▼ 14.2	SO	Cattle guard.
1.9 ▲	SO	Cattle guard.
▼ 16.1	SO	Track on left is FR 100 to Lake Fork Ranch. Zero trip meter.
0.0 ▲		Proceed along main road.

GPS: N 37°17.87′ W 106°28.63′

▼ 0.0		Proceed along main road.
12.0 ▲	SO	Track on right is FR 100 to Lake Fork Ranch. Zero trip meter.
▼ 0.6	SO	Cattle guard.
11.4 ▲	SO	Cattle guard.
▼ 0.8	SO	USFS Lake Fork Campground.
11.2 ▲	SO	USFS Lake Fork Campground.
▼ 1.6	SO	Beaver Lake trailhead.
10.4 ▲	SO	Beaver Lake trailhead.
▼ 3.5	SO	Fisher Gulch.
8.5 ▲	SO	Fisher Gulch.
▼ 4.1	SO	Track on right is FR 260 to Robinson Gulch.
7.9 ▲	SO	Track on left is FR 260 to Robinson Gulch.
▼ 4.7	SO	Cattle guard.
7.3 ▲	SO	Cattle guard.
▼ 6.1	SO	Intersection. Platoro on left.
5.9 ▲	SO	Intersection. Platoro on right.
▼ 6.5	SO	Track on left to Mix Lake Campground.
5.5 ▲	SO	Track on right to Mix Lake Campground.
▼ 7.6	TR	T-intersection. Left goes to Mix Lake and Platoro Reservoir.
4.4 ▲	TL	Intersection.
▼ 8.6	BL	Stunner Pass (unmarked). FR 257 on right goes to Lilly Pond and Kerr Lake.
3.4 ▲	BR	FR 257 on left goes to Lilly Pond and Kerr Lake. Stunner Pass (unmarked).

GPS: N 37°21.73′ W 106°33.44′

▼ 11.7	SO	Bridge over Alamosa River. Campsites.
0.3 ▲	SO	Campsites. Bridge over Alamosa River.
▼ 12.0	UT	Intersection. Straight goes to Monte Vista. Zero trip meter.
0.0 ▲		Continue on FR 380.

GPS: N 37°23.04′ W 106°33.95′

▼ 0.0		Continue on FR 380.
11.7 ▲	UT	Intersection. Straight goes to Monte Vista. Zero trip meter.
▼ 0.3	SO	USFS Stunner Campground on left. Old cabin on right is part of Stunner town site.
11.4 ▲	SO	Old cabin on left is part of Stunner town site. USFS Stunner Campground on right.

GPS: N 37°22.88′ W 106°34.21′

▼ 0.9	SO	Cattle guard.
10.8 ▲	SO	Cattle guard.
▼ 1.1	SO	Drainage ford.
10.6 ▲	SO	Drainage ford.
▼ 2.1	SO	Track on right.
9.6 ▲	SO	Track on left.
▼ 2.4	SO	Track on right.
9.3 ▲	SO	Track on left.

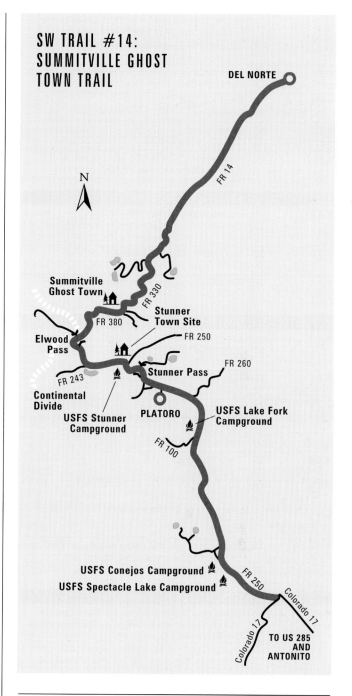

SW TRAIL #14: SUMMITVILLE GHOST TOWN TRAIL

DEL NORTE

FR 14

Summitville Ghost Town

FR 330

Stunner Town Site

FR 380

FR 250

Elwood Pass

FR 260

FR 243

Stunner Pass

Continental Divide

USFS Stunner Campground

PLATORO

USFS Lake Fork Campground

FR 100

USFS Conejos Campground

USFS Spectacle Lake Campground

FR 250

Colorado 17

Colorado 17

Colorado 17

TO US 285 AND ANTONITO

▼ 4.0	SO	Lake DeNelda on left (private property).
7.7 ▲	SO	Lake DeNelda on right (private property).
▼ 4.1	BR	Intersection. Dolores Canyon Road, Treasure Creek Road, and Lake Annella are straight ahead. Turn toward Summitville and US 160.
7.6 ▲	TL	Intersection. Dolores Canyon Road and Treasure Creek Road are to the right. Proceed toward Platoro.
▼ 4.6	SO	Cattle guard.
7.1 ▲	SO	Cattle guard.
▼ 6.5	SO	Track on right.
5.2 ▲	SO	Track on left.
▼ 7.7	SO	Crater Lake hiking trail on left.
4.0 ▲	SO	Crater Lake hiking trail on right.
▼ 8.4	SO	Intersection. Track and Continental Divide Trail

			on left. Elwood Pass is a short distance along it. Straight ahead is South Fork sign.
3.3 ▲		SO	Intersection. Track and Continental Divide Trail on right. Elwood Pass is a short distance along it.
▼ 8.7		SO	Elwood Cabin on right. Track FR 3802A on left.
3.0 ▲		SO	Elwood Cabin on left. Track FR 3802A on right.
▼ 9.6		SO	Track on right.
2.1 ▲		SO	Track on left.
▼ 9.8		SO	Cattle guard.
1.9 ▲		SO	Cattle guard.
▼ 11.7		TR	Intersection. Summitville ghost town to the right. Southfork to the left. Zero trip meter.
0.0 ▲			Proceed toward Platoro.

GPS: N 37°25.75' W 106°37.70'

▼ 0.0			Proceed toward Summitville.
2.5 ▲		TL	Intersection. Southfork to the right. Platoro to the left. Zero trip meter.
▼ 2.0		SO	Summitville Historic Mining Town sign.
0.5		SO	Summitville Historic Mining Town sign.
▼ 2.5		BL	Summitville visitor information board. Zero trip meter.
0.0 ▲			Continue on route.

GPS: N 37°25.93' W 106°35.94'

▼ 0.0			Continue on route.
26.5 ▲		BR	Summitville visitor information board. Zero trip meter.
▼ 0.1		TL	Turn onto FR 330.
26.4 ▲		TR	Intersection with FR 244.
▼ 0.3		SO	Intersection. Go toward Del Norte. Wightman Fork is to the right and forks off from the mining entrance.
26.2 ▲		SO	Intersection.
▼ 0.6		SO	Track on right.
25.9 ▲		SO	Track on left.
▼ 1.7		SO	Track on left.
24.8 ▲		SO	Track on right.
▼ 2.7		SO	Track on left.
23.8 ▲		SO	Track on right.
▼ 7.8		TR	Intersection. Crystal Lakes and South Fork to the left. Follow toward Del Norte.
18.7 ▲		BL	Intersection. Crystal Lakes and South Fork to the right.

GPS: N 37°29.31' W 106°32.81'

▼ 9.3		TL	Cattle guard. Intersection. Fuches Reservoir and Blowout Pass to the right. Follow road to Del Norte (FR 14).
17.2 ▲		TR	Intersection. Fuches Reservoir and Blowout Pass straight on. Follow FR 330. Cattle guard.
▼ 11.0		SO	Road on left.
15.5 ▲		SO	Road on right.
▼ 11.2		SO	Cattle guard.
15.3 ▲		SO	Cattle guard.
▼ 12.3		SO	Track on right to campsite.
14.2 ▲		SO	Track on left to campsite.
▼ 13.0		SO	Track on left is FR 331 to Bear Creek.
13.5 ▲		SO	Track on right is FR 331 to Bear Creek.
▼ 14.0		SO	Track on right.
12.5 ▲		SO	Track on left.
▼ 14.3		SO	Track on right.
12.2 ▲		SO	Track on left.
▼ 14.4		SO	Track on right.
12.1 ▲		SO	Track on left.
▼ 15.1		SO	Seasonal gate.
11.4 ▲		SO	Seasonal gate.

▼ 15.2		SO	Cattle guard.
11.3 ▲		SO	Cattle guard.
▼ 15.6		SO	Pavement begins. Bridge.
10.9 ▲		SO	Bridge. Unpaved.
▼ 24.4		SO	Road 14A forks off on left.
2.1 ▲		SO	Road 14A on right.
▼ 26.5			End at intersection of FR 14 and US 160 in Del Norte.
0.0 ▲			At intersection of FR 14 and US 160 in Del Norte, zero trip meter and proceed along FR 14. Sign reads "National Forest Access, Pinos Creek Rd, Summitville."

GPS: N 37°40.75' W 106°21.66'

SOUTHWEST TRAIL #15

Bolam Pass Road

Starting Point:	Silverton
Finishing Point:	Intersection of Colorado 145 and FR 578
Total Mileage:	45.7 miles
Unpaved Mileage:	24.3 miles
Driving Time:	2 1/2 hours
Pass Elevation:	11,340 feet
Usually Open:	Early July to October
Difficulty Rating:	2
Scenic Rating:	7

Special Attractions

- Attractive stream valley through the Purgatory ski area.
- Historic mining area of special significance in the effort to develop the first atomic bomb during World War II.

History

The Ute Indians used Bolam Pass long before miners entered the area in the early 1860s. In 1881, the pass was surveyed as a railroad route. The road was improved during World War II to provide access to the Graysill Mine.

This mine produced the vanadium and uranium used in the first atomic bombs. It continued to supply these substances for this purpose until 1963. At its peak, there were 450 working claims in the area, but only about twenty men endured the harsh winters (not to mention the odorless, tasteless, radioactive radon gas), enabling the mine to remain in production year-round.

Description

The route commences in Silverton and follows US 550, the Million Dollar Highway, south for twenty-one miles to the Purgatory ski resort. The route passes through the resort and its network of paved roads without signs to guide you. An unpaved road exits the resort area and travels through the winter ski runs.

Numerous camping spots with good creek access lie off the road for about ten miles from the Purgatory ski resort.

Until the creek crossing 9.9 miles from the resort, the road is a well-maintained, unpaved, passenger-vehicle road. From this point, it gets narrower and rougher but remains an easy road for 4WD vehicles.

At the 16.1-mile point from Purgatory ski resort, the road passes the one remaining building (and a Forest Service information board) from the Graysill Mine.

A mile and one-half further, past an attractive alpine lake, is Bolam Pass, at which point the road traverses a relatively level ridge through open meadows and patches of forest. This section affords pleasant views of adjoining hillsides and many wildflowers in the alpine meadows.

After about two miles, the road starts its descent and grows rougher, with considerable erosion evident. It is not difficult, but it does require caution.

Some twenty-two miles from the Purgatory ski resort, the road returns to easy passenger-vehicle conditions and follows Barlow Creek as it descends into the valley.

Current Road Condition Information

San Juan National Forest
701 Camino del Rio, Durango, CO 81301
(970) 247-4874

Map References

USFS San Juan NF
USGS San Juan County
La Plata County #2
Dolores County #3
San Miguel County #3
The Roads of Colorado, p. 130
Colorado Atlas & Gazetteer, p. 76

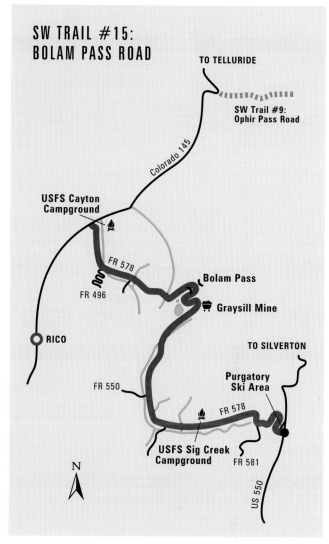

SW TRAIL #15: BOLAM PASS ROAD

Route Directions

▼ 0.0			In front of the Silverton Visitor Center (at the intersection of Greene Street and US 550), zero trip meter and proceed south on US 550.
	21.0 ▲		End at the Silverton Visitor Center.
		GPS: N 37°48.29' W 107°40.18'	
▼ 21.0		TR	Into Purgatory ski resort and zero trip meter.
	0.0 ▲		Continue along US 550 toward Silverton.
		GPS: N 37°37.71' W 107°48.59'	
▼ 0.0			Keep to the right.
	8.4 ▲	TL	Onto US 550. Zero trip meter.
▼ 0.3		SO	Intersection. Dirt road enters from the right.
	8.1 ▲	SO	Intersection. Remain on paved road.
▼ 0.4		TR	Paved road continues to the left. Follow unpaved road.
	8.0 ▲	TL	Onto paved road.
▼ 1.0		SO	Hermosa Travel board to the right has a map posted. Sign to Bolam Pass.
	7.4 ▲	BR	Continue toward Purgatory Ski Resort.
▼ 2.1		BR	Track on left.
	6.3 ▲	BL	Track on right.
▼ 3.1		BR	Elbert Creek Road on left to Cafe de Los Piños. Follow Hermosa Creek Trail.
	5.3 ▲	BL	Elbert Creek Road on right to Cafe de Los Piños. Stay on main road.
▼ 3.5		BL	Intersection. Remain on FR 578.
	4.9 ▲	BR	Intersection. Remain on FR 578.

▼ 4.4		SO	Intersection.
	4.0 ▲	SO	Intersection.
▼ 4.8		SO	Access to trout streams.
	3.6 ▲	SO	Access to trout streams.
▼ 6.6		SO	USFS Sig Creek Campground.
	1.8 ▲	SO	USFS Sig Creek Campground.
▼ 6.7		SO	Track on left.
	1.7 ▲	SO	Track on right.
▼ 7.5		SO	Track on left to campsites.
	0.9 ▲	SO	Track on right to campsites.
▼ 7.6		SO	Cross over creek.
	0.8 ▲	SO	Cross over creek.
▼ 8.4		SO	Road on left crosses through East Fork of Hermosa Creek to Hermosa Creek trailhead FR 577. Follow sign toward Bolam Pass. Zero trip meter.
	0.0 ▲		Continue along route.
		GPS: N 37°37.92' W 107°54.95'	
▼ 0.0			Continue along main road.
	7.9 ▲		Road on right. Zero trip meter.
▼ 0.4		SO	Cattle guard.
	7.5 ▲	SO	Cattle guard.
▼ 0.7-1.6		SO	Numerous campsites.
	6.4-7.2 ▲	SO	Numerous campsites.

Uncompahgre Plateau Trail

Starting Point:	Montrose, at the intersection of US 550 (Townsend Ave.) and Jay Jay Road	
Finishing Point:	Intersection of Colorado 141 and County 26.10 road (FR 402)	
Total Mileage:	90.3 miles	
Unpaved Mileage:	85.6 miles	
Driving Time:	4 hours	
Pass Elevation:	9,120 feet	
Usually Open:	Mid-June to late November	
Difficulty Rating:	2	
Scenic Rating:	7	

Special Attractions

- Views from the Uncompahgre Plateau, particularly from Windy Point.
- An extensive network of 4WD trails.
- Good backcountry camping.

History

Columbine Pass, named for the Colorado state flower, which used to grow in abundance here, is located on the Uncompahgre Plateau and was crossed by the Hayden Survey expedition in the mid-1870s. The plateau was an important summer hunting ground for the Ute Indians for thousands of years prior to the Washington Treaty of 1880.

Description

This route starts at the intersection of US 550 and Jay Jay Road, 4.7 miles northwest of the National Forest office in Montrose (2505 S. Townsend). The next five miles involves a considerable number of intersections, so care is necessary to navigate correctly. At the end this section of the route, you should turn on to Rim Road. There are more-direct routes from Montrose, but this route offers the more varied and interesting views.

Initially, Rim Road is a well-maintained, wide 2WD road that provides some good views over the local ranch land and the San Juan Mountains in the distance to the south. There are also numerous small side roads: stay on the main road in each case. Further along the road, there are some sections that are rocky, but they will not pose any problems. The road travels along the rim of a canyon and provides good views down to the floor below.

After turning on to FR 402 (Divide Road), you will pass numerous camping sites, which are heavily used in hunting season, and an extensive network of 4WD side roads, many of which can be very muddy. FR 402 is wide and well maintained and suitable for passenger vehicles in dry conditions.

▼ 1.5	SO	Cross through creek.
6.4 ▲	SO	Cross through creek.
	GPS: N 37°38.80′ W 107°55.65′	
▼ 2.2	SO	Intersection. FR 550 on left has signs to Rico and Hotel Draw via Scotch Creek. Follow FR 578 toward Bolam and Rico via Barlow Creek.
5.7 ▲	SO	Intersection on right to Rico and Hotel Draw. Remain on FR 578.
▼ 2.9	SO	Cattle guard.
3.4 ▲	SO	Cattle guard.
▼ 3.5	SO	Cross through creek.
4.4 ▲	SO	Cross through creek.
▼ 5.7	SO	Cross over creek.
2.2 ▲	SO	Cross over creek.
▼ 5.8	SO	Cross through creek.
2.1 ▲	SO	Cross through creek.
▼ 6.2	SO	Cross over creek.
1.7 ▲	SO	Cross over creek.
▼ 7.6	SO	Cross over creek.
0.3 ▲	SO	Cross over creek.
▼ 7.7	SO	Graysill Mine ruins on right.
0.2 ▲	SO	Graysill Mine ruins on left.
▼ 7.9	SO	Cabin and historic marker. Zero trip meter.
0.0 ▲		Continue along main road.
	GPS: N 37°42.82′ W 107°53.93′	
▼ 0.0		Continue along main road.
8.4 ▲	SO	Cabin and historic marker. Zero trip meter.
▼ 0.3	SO	Lake on left.
8.1 ▲	SO	Lake on right.
▼ 0.4	SO	Track on right is FR 578B.
8.0 ▲	SO	FR 578B on left.
▼ 1.4	SO	Bolam Pass summit (unmarked).
7.0 ▲	SO	Bolam Pass summit (unmarked).
	GPS: N 37°43.15′ W 107°53.89′	
▼ 2.3	TR	Cross over creek. Intersection.
6.1 ▲	TL	Intersection. Cross over creek.
▼ 4.6	SO	Cross through creek.
3.8 ▲	SO	Cross through creek.
▼ 4.8	SO	Track on left to creek.
3.6 ▲	SO	Track on right to creek.
▼ 5.0	SO	Cabin.
3.4 ▲	SO	Cabin.
▼ 5.8	SO	Cross over creek.
2.6 ▲	SO	Cross over creek.
▼ 5.9	SO	Intersection with FR 496 on left.
2.5 ▲	SO	Intersection with FR 496 on right.
▼ 6.9	SO	Barlow Lake on right.
1.5 ▲	SO	Barlow Lake on left.
▼ 8.1	BL	FR 476 Intersection on right. USFS Cayton Campground.
0.3 ▲	BR	USFS Cayton Campground. FR 476 on left.
	GPS: N 37°46.15′ W 107°58.91′	
▼ 8.4		Bridge over Dolores River. End at intersection with Colorado 145 (paved).
0.0 ▲		At intersection of Colorado 145 and FR 578, zero trip meter and proceed along FR 578. Cross bridge over Dolores River.
	GPS: N 37°46.14′ W 107°59.25′	

The views to the west, down into the valley below, are particularly scenic.

As you descend from Uncompahgre Plateau, the scenery changes to the red rock walls of Jacks Canyon before connecting with Colorado 141 in the vast Unaweep Canyon. From here, the road travels along the path of East Creek before crossing the Gunnison River and joining US 50. Gunnison is approximately twenty-four miles from the intersection with Colorado 141, at the start of the paved road.

Current Road Condition Information

Uncompahgre National Forest
Ouray Ranger District
2505 South Townsend, Montrose, CO 81401
(970) 240-5300

Map References

USFS Uncompahgre NF
USGS Montrose County #1
Montrose County #2
Mesa County #6
The Roads of Colorado, pp. 81, 97-98, 114
Colorado Atlas & Gazetteer, pp. 54-56, 65-66

Route Directions

▼ 0.0		At intersection of US 550 and Jay Jay Road, turn west (left, if coming from Montrose).
5.0 ▲		End at intersection with US 550.
GPS: N 38°31.91′ W 107°56.19′		
▼ 0.1	SO	Cross railroad tracks. Name of road changes to Menoken Road.
4.9 ▲	SO	Cross railroad tracks.
▼ 1.4	SO	Cross over bridge and then a second bridge.
3.6 ▲	SO	Cross over two bridges.
▼ 1.6	BL	Fork in road; go left onto South River Road.
3.4 ▲	BR	At fork in the road.
▼ 2.0	BR	County 5975 is on the left.
3.0 ▲	BL	County 5975 is on the right.
▼ 2.9	BL	Intersection. Remain on paved road.
2.1 ▲	BR	Intersection.
▼ 3.5	TL	Stop sign at intersection. Turn onto County 5850.
1.5 ▲	TR	Intersection. Turn onto South River Road.
GPS: N 38°31.56′ W 107°59.68′		
▼ 3.9	TR	Onto Kiowa Road.
1.1 ▲	TL	Onto County 5850.
▼ 4.7	BL	Bear left, then cross bridge. Bear left again onto unpaved road named Shavano Valley Road.
0.2 ▲	BR	Onto Kiowa Road. Then cross bridge and bear left again.
▼ 5.0	TR	Onto Rim Road. Zero trip meter.
0.0 ▲		Continue to the left.
GPS: N 38°30.92′ W 108°00.54′		
▼ 0.0		Proceed along Rim Road.
13.1 ▲	TL	Intersection. Zero trip meter.
▼ 1.7	SO	Track crosses road.
11.4 ▲	SO	Track crosses road.
▼ 2.2	SO	Track on right.
10.9 ▲	SO	Track on left.
▼ 2.5	SO	Track on right. Note: From this point, there will

be numerous side tracks, but remain on Rim Road.

10.7 ▲	SO	Track on left.
▼ 3.0	SO	Track on right goes into canyon.
10.2 ▲	SO	Track on left goes into canyon. Note: From this point, there will be numerous side tracks, but remain on Rim Road.
GPS: N 38°29.14′ W 108°02.50′		
▼ 5.7	SO	Cross under high voltage wires and cross cattle guard.
7.5 ▲	SO	Cattle guard. Cross under high voltage wires.
▼ 9.7	BL	Cattleyards on left, then fork in road.
3.5 ▲	BR	Fork in the road, then cattleyards on right.
▼ 12.2	SO	Cattleyards on left, then cattle guard.
0.9 ▲	SO	Cattle guard, then cattleyards on right.
GPS: N 38°24.43′ W 108°04.21′		

Jacks Canyon

▼ 13.1	TR	T-intersection with Old Highway 90. Turn right and go through seasonal closure gate. Zero trip meter.
0.0 ▲		Turn onto Rim Road.
GPS: N 38°21.79′ W 108°02.94′		
▼ 0.0		Proceed along Old Highway 90.
23.6 ▲	TL	Intersection. Zero trip meter.
▼ 0.4	SO	Cross over East Fork of Dry Creek.
23.2 ▲	SO	Cross over East Fork of Dry Creek.
▼ 5.8	SO	USFS Silesca Ranger Station on left.
17.8 ▲	SO	USFS Silesca Ranger Station on right.
▼ 7.9	SO	FR 402 on left (Dave Wood Road and Norwood).
15.7 ▲	SO	FR 402 on right.
GPS: N 38°19.02′ W 108°09.21′		
▼ 8.3	SO	USFS Iron Springs Campground on left.
15.2 ▲	SO	USFS Iron Springs Campground on right.
▼ 8.5	BR	Old Highway 90 turns left.
15.0 ▲	BL	Intersection: Old Highway 90.
▼ 8.8	SO	FR 527 on right.
14.7 ▲	SO	FR 527 on left.
▼ 9.5	SO	Road on right is Transfer Road/FR 508 to Olathe.
14.0 ▲	SO	FR 508 on left.
▼ 10.9	SO	West Antone Spring on left.
12.7 ▲	SO	West Antone Spring on right.
▼ 11.9	SO	Road to Pool Creek on right.
11.6 ▲	SO	Road to Pool Creek on left.

▼ 13.7	SO	Pool Creek trailhead on right.
9.9 ▲	SO	Pool Creek trailhead on left.
▼ 14.0	SO	West Pool Creek on right.
9.5 ▲	SO	West Pool Creek on left.
▼ 15.2	SO	FR 546 on right.
8.3 ▲	SO	FR 546 on left.
▼ 16.3	SO	FR 545 on right.
7.3 ▲	SO	FR 545 on left.
▼ 17.5	SO	FR 520 on right to Long Creek.
6.0 ▲	SO	FR 520 on left to Long Creek.
▼ 18.2	SO	FR 506 on right to Payne Mesa.
5.4 ▲	SO	FR 506 on left to Payne Mesa.
▼ 18.7	SO	Cattleyards on left. FR 534 on right.
4.9 ▲	SO	FR 534 on left. Cattleyards on right.
▼ 19.7	SO	FR 531 to Moore Mesa on right.
3.9 ▲	SO	FR 531 to Moore Mesa on left.
▼ 21.2	SO	FR 505 on right.
2.4 ▲	SO	FR 505 on left.
▼ 22.8	SO	USFS Tabeguache scenic overlook on left.
0.7 ▲	SO	USFS Tabeguache scenic overlook on right.
▼ 23.6	BR	Columbine Pass. FR 503 and cattleyards are on left. Zero trip meter.
0.0 ▲		Continue on FR 402 to the left.
GPS: N 38°25.00' W 108°22.86'		
▼ 0.0		Continue on FR 402 to the right.
33.6 ▲	BL	Columbine Pass. FR 503 and cattleyards are on left. Zero trip meter.
▼ 0.3	SO	FR 533 to Monitor Mesa on the right.
33.2 ▲	SO	FR 533 to Monitor Mesa on the left.
▼ 0.7	SO	USFS Columbine Campground on left.
32.9 ▲	SO	USFS Columbine Campground on right.
▼ 0.9	TL	Cattle guard, then cross through creek to intersection. Follow FR 402 toward Windy Point. To the right is FR 503, Delta-Nucla Road.
32.7 ▲	TR	Intersection. FR 503 to Delta-Nucla is to the left. Turn right toward Columbine Pass. Cross creek, then cattle guard.
GPS: N 38°25.70' W 108°22.89'		
▼ 2.4	SO	Track on right.
31.1 ▲	SO	Track on left.
▼ 3.1	SO	FR 529 to Sawmill Mesa on right.
30.5 ▲	SO	FR 529 to Sawmill Mesa on left.
▼ 6.5	SO	FR 507, Lockhart on right.
27.1 ▲	SO	FR 507, Lockhart on left.
▼ 10.9	SO	FR 600 on left.
22.7 ▲	SO	FR 600 on right.
▼ 11.1	SO	Windy Point (great views!) on left.
22.5 ▲	SO	Windy Point (great views!) on right.
▼ 13.3	SO	FR 500 on right.
20.3 ▲	SO	FR 500 on left.
▼ 14.3	SO	Cattleyards on right.
19.3 ▲	SO	Cattleyards on left.
▼ 16.4	SO	Track on left.
17.2 ▲	SO	Track on right.
▼ 17.8	SO	Monument Hill on right.
15.7 ▲	SO	Monument Hill on left.
▼ 19.5	SO	Long Point and FR 421 on right.
14.0 ▲	SO	Long Point and FR 421 on left.
▼ 21.3	SO	FR 411 on left, then cattle guard.
12.3 ▲	SO	Cattle guard, then FR 411 on right.
▼ 21.6	SO	Short track on right.

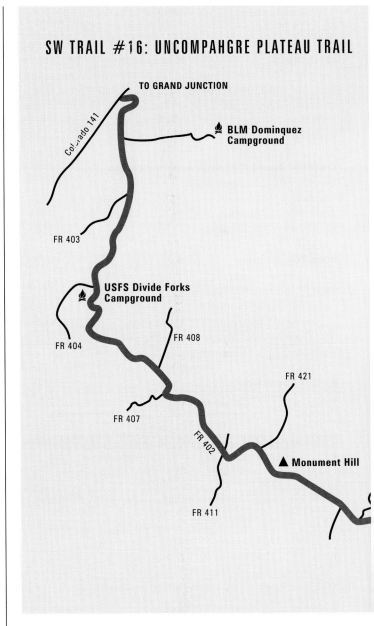

SW TRAIL #16: UNCOMPAHGRE PLATEAU TRAIL

12.0 ▲	SO	Short track on left.
▼ 23.0	SO	Uncompahgre Butte on right.
10.5 ▲	SO	Uncompahgre Butte on left.
▼ 24.2	SO	Track on right.
9.3 ▲	SO	Track on left.
▼ 25.0	SO	3 H on left.
8.6 ▲	SO	3 H on right.
▼ 25.8	SO	Mesa Creek FR 407 on left.
7.8 ▲	SO	Mesa Creek FR 407 on right.
▼ 27.3	SO	FR 408 on right.
6.3 ▲	SO	FR 408 on left.
▼ 28.2	SO	3 J on right dead-ends.
5.4 ▲	SO	3 J on left dead-ends.
▼ 29.2	SO	FR 410 on left dead-ends.
4.4 ▲	SO	FR 410 on right dead-ends.
▼ 29.4	SO	Track on right to USFS Cold Springs Work Center.
4.2 ▲	SO	Track on left to USFS Cold Springs Work Center.

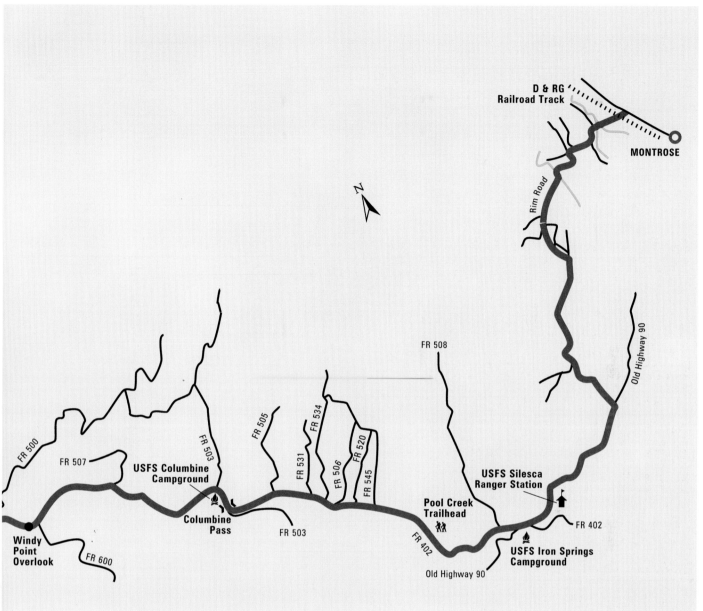

▼ 31.0	SO	Track and cattleyards on left.	
2.5 ▲	SO	Cattleyards and track on right.	
▼ 33.4	SO	USFS Divide Forks Campground on left.	
0.2 ▲	SO	USFS Divide Forks Campground on right.	
▼ 33.6	SO	FR 404 Uranium Road on left. Zero trip meter.	
0.0 ▲		Continue along FR 402.	

GPS: N 38°41.21' W 108°41.18'

▼ 0.0		Continue along FR 402.	
15.0 ▲	SO	FR 404 Uranium Road on right. Zero trip meter.	
▼ 2.9	SO	Cattle guard.	
12.1 ▲	SO	Cattle guard.	
▼ 5.4	SO	FR 403 to Big Creek Reservoir on left.	
9.6 ▲	SO	FR 403 to Big Creek Reservoir on right.	
▼ 7.0	SO	Cattle guard.	
8.0 ▲	SO	Cattle guard.	
▼ 8.8	SO	USFS Uncompahgre information board, seasonal closure gate and cattle guard.	
6.2 ▲	SO	Cattle guard. Seasonal closure gate and USFS Uncompahgre information board.	

▼ 9.2	SO	Dominquez State Wildlife area on right and road to Dominquez BLM campground.	
5.8 ▲	SO	Dominquez State Wildlife area on left and road to Dominquez BLM campground.	
▼ 12.9	SO	Cattle guard.	
2.1 ▲	SO	Cattle guard.	
▼ 15.0	SO	Cattle guard. End at intersection with Colorado 141.	
0.0 ▲		At intersection of County 90 and Colorado 141, zero trip meter and proceed along County 90. Cross cattle guard.	

GPS: N 38°50.26' W 108°34.45'

The South-Central Region

Trails in the South-Central Region

- **SC 1**   Old Monarch Pass Road
- **SC 2**   Black Sage Pass Road
- **SC 3**   Waunita Pass Road
- **SC 4**   Middle Quartz Creek Trail
- **SC 5**   Hancock Pass Trail
- **SC 6**   Tomichi Pass Trail
- **SC 7**   Cumberland Pass Trail
- **SC 8**   Alpine Tunnel Road
- **SC 9**   Tincup Pass Trail
- **SC 10** Mount Antero Trail
- **SC 11** Browns Lake Trail
- **SC 12** Baldwin Lakes Trail
- **SC 13** Boulder Mountain Trail
- **SC 14** Pomeroy Lakes and Mary Murphy Mine Trail
- **SC 15** Marshall Pass Poncha Creek Trail
- **SC 16** Marshall Pass Railway Grade Road
- **SC 17** Marshall Pass to Sargents
- **SC 18** Cochetopa Pass Road
- **SC 19** Taylor Canyon Trail
- **SC 20** Dome Lakes to Los Piños Pass Road
- **SC 21** Los Piños Pass Trail
- **SC 22** Schofield Pass and Devil's Punchbowl Trail
- **SC 23** Lead King Basin Trail
- **SC 24** Ohio Pass Road
- **SC 25** Kebler Pass Road
- **SC 26** Reno Divide Trail
- **SC 27** Taylor Pass Trail
- **SC 28** Hayden Pass Trail
- **SC 29** Medano Pass and Great Sand Dunes Trail
- **SC 30** Rampart Range Road

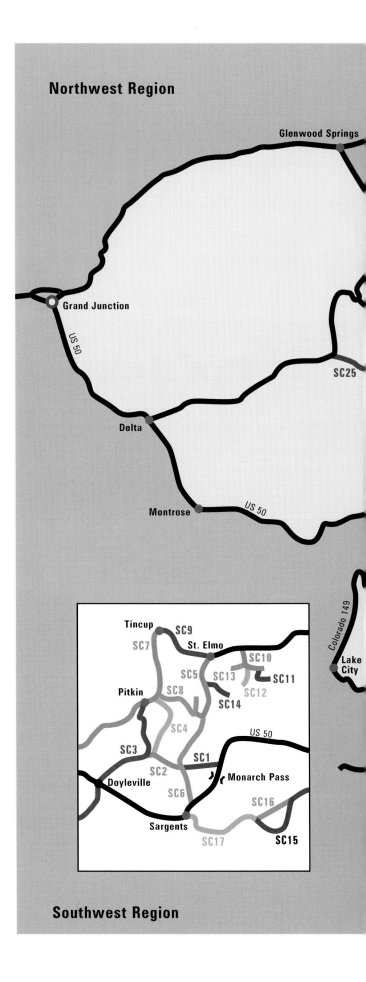

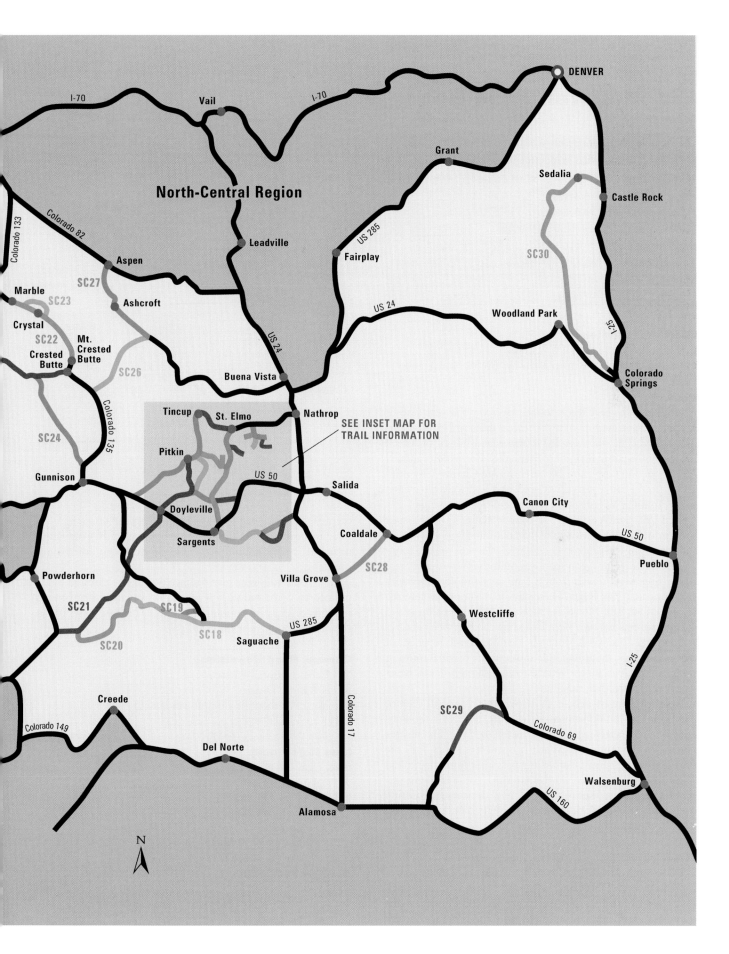

North-Central Region

DENVER

Vail

I-70

I-70

Grant

Sedalia

Castle Rock

Colorado 133

Colorado 82

US 285

SC30

I-25

Leadville

Fairplay

Aspen

SC27

Marble

SC23

Ashcroft

US 24

Woodland Park

Crystal

SC22

Mt. Crested Butte

Crested Butte

SC26

US 24

Colorado 135

Colorado Springs

Buena Vista

SC24

Tincup

St. Elmo

Nathrop

SEE INSET MAP FOR TRAIL INFORMATION

Pitkin

US 50

Gunnison

Salida

Canon City

Doyleville

Coaldale

US 50

Sargents

SC28

Pueblo

Powderhorn

Villa Grove

SC21

SC19

Westcliffe

SC18

SC20

Saguache

US 285

Creede

Colorado 17

SC29

Colorado 149

Colorado 69

Del Norte

I-25

Walsenburg

US 160

Alamosa

N

Old Monarch Pass Road

Starting Point:	**Intersection of US 50 and FR 237 (1 mile east of Monarch Pass)**
Finishing Point:	**Intersection of FR 237 and FR 888**
Total Mileage:	**10.3 miles**
Unpaved Mileage:	**10.3 miles**
Driving Time:	**1/2 hour**
Pass Elevation:	**11,375 feet**
Usually Open:	**Early June to November**
Difficulty Rating:	**1**
Scenic Rating:	**5**

Special Attractions

- Access to a network of 4WD trails.
- An alternative to the main highway, US 50.

History

In 1879, Nicholas Creede found silver on the east side of Monarch Pass; within months, three thousand prospectors had arrived. The discovery led to the establishment of several towns in the area, including Maysville, Garfield (originally called Junction City), and Monarch (called Chaffee City until 1884). In the same year, silver, gold, and lead were discovered in the Tomichi Valley on the west side of Monarch Pass.

In 1880, the Denver & Rio Grande Railroad built a spur line from Salida to Monarch that continued to operate in summer until 1982.

Also in 1880, a wagon road was built that served as a stage route. This route travels from the ski area and connects with Old Monarch Pass Road. These days it is sometimes referred to as the Old, Old Monarch Pass Road. It had been open as a 4WD road but has now been closed by the Forest Service.

In the 1920s, Old Monarch Pass Road was opened. It crossed the pass about one mile south of the original route. It was designed as a motor vehicle road, although it was never paved, and is still well maintained.

Following much debate about whether Marshall Pass or Monarch Pass should be used as the route for US 50, the present Monarch Pass Road was constructed in 1939. The ski area opened in the same year. When it opened, Charles Vail, the state highway engineer, named the pass after himself and had "Vail Pass" signs placed at the summit. Local residents expressed their objections to this unilateral decision by painting over the signs with black paint. Many years later, his wish was more permanently granted along I-70.

Description

Old Monarch Pass Road (FR 237) provides a good alternative route between US 50 from the east of Monarch Pass through to the 4WD roads in the Tomichi Valley. It commences one mile east of the present summit, and the entrance is well

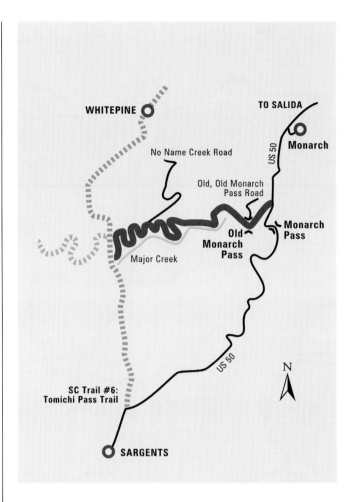

marked. The road is graded, wide, and easy for a passenger vehicle to negotiate. There are some sections with steep drop-offs, but in dry conditions, these do not pose any serious problems.

The route follows a high-voltage power line through dense pine forest with only a few stands of aspens and a limited number of expansive mountain views. The best views are at the highest point near the main pass.

Current Road Conditions

San Isabel National Forest
Salida Ranger District
325 West Rainbow Boulevard, Salida, CO 81201
(719) 539-3591

Map References

USFS San Isabel NF
Gunnison NF

USGS Chaffee County #3
Gunnison County #5

The Roads of Colorado, p. 102
Trails Illustrated, #130 (incomplete), #139

Route Directions

▼ 0.0	From US 50, turn onto Monarch Pass Road (FR 237). Zero trip meter and proceed west.
10.3 ▲	End at intersection with US 50.

	GPS: N 38°30.27′ W 106°19.65′		
▼ 0.2	SO	Road on right dead-ends in 0.3 miles.	
10.1 ▲	SO	Road on left dead-ends in 0.3 miles.	
▼ 1.1	SO	Track on right.	
9.2 ▲	SO	Track on left.	
▼ 1.3	SO	Monarch Pass summit. Vandals had removed the plaque from the summit marker when we were there.	
9.0 ▲	SO	Monarch Pass summit.	
	GPS: N 38°29.90′ W 106°20.25′		
▼ 2.8	SO	Campsites on left.	
7.5 ▲	SO	Campsites on right.	
▼ 3.3	SO	Campsites on left.	
7.0 ▲	SO	Campsites on right.	
▼ 4.6	SO	Track on left.	
5.7 ▲	SO	Track on right.	
▼ 7.6	SO	Track marked to Galena Gulch and No Name Creek on right. Note: This trail dead-ends due to locals putting a cable across the road about 3 miles in at GPS: N 38°30.84′ W 106°23.09′. There are ruins of an old mine where the track is blocked.	
2.7 ▲	SO	Track marked to Galena Gulch and No Name Creek on left.	
	GPS: N 38°29.88′ W 106°23.76′		
▼ 8.8	SO	Short track on left to campsites with attractive views.	
1.5 ▲	SO	Short track on right to campsites with attractive views.	
▼ 10.3		End at intersection with South-Central Trail #6: Tomichi Pass Trail (FR 888).	
0.0 ▲		At intersection of Tomichi Pass Road (FR 888) and FR 237, zero trip meter and proceed along FR 237 toward Old Monarch Pass.	
	GPS: N 38°29.16′ W 106°24.58′		

SOUTH-CENTRAL REGION TRAIL #2

Black Sage Pass Road

Starting Point:	**Intersection of FR 887 and FR 888**
Finishing Point:	**Intersection of FR 887 and FR 763**
Total Mileage:	**6.7 miles**
Unpaved Mileage:	**6.7 miles**
Driving Time:	**1/2 hour**
Pass Elevation:	**9,745 feet**
Usually Open:	**Early July to late October**
Difficulty Rating:	**1**
Scenic Rating:	**6**

Special Attractions

■ Easy road through gentle, attractive countryside.

■ Access to a network of 4WD trails.

History

The Hayden survey party traveled this route between Pitkin and Whitepine. When silver was discovered near Pitkin in the

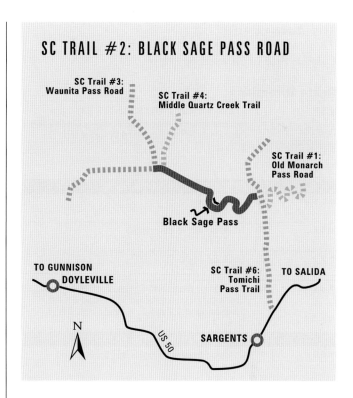

SC TRAIL #2: BLACK SAGE PASS ROAD

late 1870s, this route provided a lower, more undulating, albeit longer, entryway to the area. By 1880, a stagecoach and numerous freight wagons were using this road daily.

In 1882, the Denver, South Park & Pacific Railroad opened the line to Pitkin through the Alpine Tunnel. The route remained in use to deliver freight from Pitkin. By this time, the resort of Waunita Hot Springs was very popular and also needed stagecoaches and freight wagons to ferry tourists and supplies.

Subsequently, the pass was used principally for access between Whitepine and Gunnison. The stage way station at the summit of the pass continued to operate into the late 1890s.

Description

The road is accessible to passenger cars under dry conditions. It provides an easy drive through attractive ranch land and a gentle ascent to a forested summit before the scenery widens out into an open valley.

The route interconnects with a number of other routes in this book. To the east is Old Monarch Pass Road; and to the north are Tomichi Pass, Hancock Pass, and the Alpine Tunnel.

Current Road Conditions

Gunnison National Forest
Taylor River District
216 North Colorado, Gunnison, CO 81230
(970) 641-0471

Map References

USFS Gunnison NF
USGS Gunnison County #5

Trails Illustrated, #139
The Roads of Colorado, p. 101
Colorado Atlas & Gazetteer, pp. 59, 69

Route Directions

▼ 0.0		At intersection of FR 888 and FR 887, zero trip meter and proceed west along Black Sage Pass Road (FR 887) toward Waunita Hot Springs.
3.4 ▲		End at intersection with South-Central Trail #6: Tomichi Pass Trail (FR 888).

GPS: N 00°00.10' W 100°00.00'

▼ 1.1	SO	Cattle guard.
2.3 ▲	SO	Cattle guard.
▼ 1.4	SO	Track on left to campsites.
2.0 ▲	SO	Track on right to campsites.
▼ 2.1	SO	Track on right.
1.3 ▲	SO	Track on left.
▼ 3.4	SO	Summit of Black Sage Pass. Zero trip meter. Cross cattle guard. Short side-road on left dead-ends in 1.2 miles. Remain on FR 887.
0.0 ▲		Continue along FR 887.

GPS: N 38°29.46' W 106°27.11'

▼ 0.0		Continue toward Waunita Hot Springs and Pitkin.
3.3 ▲	SO	Track on right. Cross cattle guard. Summit of Black Sage Pass. Zero trip meter.
▼ 1.6	SO	Cattle guard.
1.7 ▲	SO	Cattle guard.
▼ 3.1	TL	Intersection. South-Central Trail #4: Middle Quartz Creek Trail is on the right.
0.2 ▲	TR	Intersection. South-Central Trail #4: Middle Quartz Creek Trail straight on. Remain on FR 887.

GPS: N 38°30.81' W 106°29.61'

▼ 3.3		End at intersection with South-Central Trail #3: Waunita Pass Road.
0.0 ▲		At intersection of FR 887 and FR 763, zero trip meter and proceed east on FR 887.

GPS: N38°30.82' W106°29.90'

SOUTH-CENTRAL REGION TRAIL #3

Waunita Pass Road

Starting Point:	**Pitkin**
Finishing Point:	**Intersection of County/FR 887 and US 50**
Total Mileage:	**18.7 miles**
Unpaved Mileage:	**18.7 miles**
Driving Time:	**1 hour**
Pass Elevation:	**10,303 feet**
Usually Open:	**All year**
Difficulty Rating:	**1**
Scenic Rating:	**6**

Special Attractions

- Easy road through gentle, attractive countryside.
- Access to a network of 4WD trails.

History

With the rich ore discoveries in the Monarch Pass area and on through the Tomichi Valley in 1878, stages and freight operations made regular journeys between Salida and Pitkin across Monarch, Black Sage, and Waunita Passes.

In 1880, the Denver & Rio Grande Railroad built a spur line from Salida to Monarch; and in 1882, the Alpine Tunnel railroad was opened, providing a railroad through to Pitkin. Waunita Pass Road continued to be used for freight to the Tomichi Valley silver mining area. The route also provided access between Pitkin and the resort facilities at Waunita Hot Springs. However, the road was in decline from the time of the railroad.

Description

The route is generally accessible to passenger vehicles, passing through gentle valley scenery along Hot Springs Creek, then through pine and aspen forest before reaching the pass and dropping down into Pitkin.

The road passes the site of Bowerman where J. C. Bowerman struck gold at the Independent Mine. While the strike was heavily promoted by newspapers at the time, little ore was ever shipped out of the mine. The town site is on private property.

Current Road Conditions

Gunnison National Forest
Taylor River District
216 North Colorado, Gunnison, CO 81230
(970) 641-0471

Map References

USFS Gunnison NF
USGS Gunnison County #5
Trails Illustrated, #139
The Roads of Colorado, p. 101
Colorado Atlas & Gazetteer, pp. 59, 69

Route Directions

▼ 0.0		From the Pitkin City Hall building at Main and 4th Streets in Pitkin, zero trip meter and proceed southwest.
10.4 ▲		End at the Pitkin City Hall building at Main and 4th Streets in Pitkin.

GPS: N 38°36.48' W 106°31.15'

▼ 0.1	TL	Onto 2nd Street.
10.3 ▲	TR	Onto Main Street.
▼ 0.2	TR	Onto State Street.
10.2 ▲	TL	Onto 2nd Street.
▼ 0.3	TL	Onto 1st Street.
10.1 ▲	TR	Onto State Street.
▼ 0.4	BR	Signpost to FR 763.
10.0 ▲	BL	Onto 1st Street.
▼ 0.5	SO	Bridge over Quartz Creek.
9.9 ▲	SO	Bridge over Quartz Creek.
▼ 1.4	SO	Cattle guard, then Gunnison National Forest sign.
9.0 ▲	SO	Cattle guard.
▼ 3.3	SO	Track on right.
7.1 ▲	SO	Track on left.
▼ 3.7	SO	Track on left.
6.7 ▲	SO	Track on right.
▼ 4.6	SO	Summit of Waunita Pass. Road to Wiley Gulch

SC TRAIL #3: WAUNITA PASS ROAD

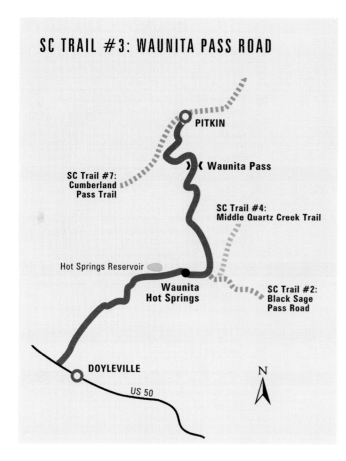

PITKIN

Waunita Pass

SC Trail #7:
Cumberland
Pass Trail

SC Trail #4:
Middle Quartz Creek Trail

Hot Springs Reservoir

Waunita
Hot Springs

SC Trail #2:
Black Sage
Pass Road

DOYLEVILLE

US 50

N

▼			
			on left and FR 698 on right.
	5.8 ▲	SO	FR 698 on left and Wiley Gulch road on right. Summit of Waunita Pass.

GPS: N 38°34.68' W 106°30.56'

▼ 6.4		SO	Two small tracks on left.
	4.0 ▲	SO	Two small tracks on right.
▼ 6.5		SO	Site of Bowerman (private property).
	3.8 ▲	SO	Site of Bowerman (private property).

GPS: N 38°33.75' W 106°30.69'

▼ 8.4		SO	Wiley Gulch on left.
	2.0 ▲	SO	Wiley Gulch on right.
▼ 10.4		TR	Intersection. Track on the left is South-Central Trail #2: Black Sage Pass Road. Zero trip meter.
	0.0 ▲		Proceed toward Pitkin on FR 763.

GPS: N 38°30.82' W 106°29.90'.

▼ 0.0			Proceed toward Waunita Hot Springs on FR 887.
	8.3 ▲	TL	T-intersection. Straight on is South-Central Trail #2: Black Sage Pass Road. Zero trip meter.
▼ 0.2		SO	Cattle guard.
	8.1 ▲	SO	Cattle guard.
▼ 0.4		SO	Waunita Hot Springs Ranch Resort on right.
	7.9 ▲	SO	Waunita Hot Springs Ranch Resort on left.
▼ 2.3		SO	Track to Waunita Hot Springs Reservoir on right.
	6.0 ▲	SO	Track to Waunita Hot Springs Reservoir on left.
▼ 2.5		SO	Track on right.
	5.8 ▲	SO	Track on left.
▼ 2.6		SO	Great Horse Gulch track on right.
	5.7 ▲	SO	Great Horse Gulch track on left.
▼ 2.9		SO	Short track on left.
	5.4 ▲	SO	Short track on right.
▼ 3.5		SO	Bridge over Hot Springs Creek.
	4.8 ▲	SO	Bridge over Hot Springs Creek.

▼ 8.3			Cattle guard and end at intersection with US 50.
	0.0 ▲		At intersection of US 50 and County/FR 887, zero trip meter and proceed north on 887.

GPS: N 38°27.39' W 106°37.02'

SOUTH-CENTRAL REGION TRAIL #4

Middle Quartz Creek Trail

Starting Point:	Intersection of Black Sage Pass Road and FR 774
Finishing Point:	Intersection of FR 767 and FR 765
Total Mileage:	12.4 miles
Unpaved Mileage:	12.4 miles
Driving Time:	1 1/4 hours
Highest Elevation:	11,000 feet
Usually Open:	Mid-June to late November
Difficulty Rating:	3
Scenic Rating:	6

Special Attractions

■ 4WD alternative to Waunita Pass Road.
■ Access to a network of 4WD roads.
■ Good camping along Middle Quartz Creek.

Description

Middle Quartz Creek Road is part of the network of forest roads on the eastern side of Waunita Pass Road. It crosses the same minor ridge line separating the waters of Hot Springs Creek and Quartz Creek as Waunita Pass, which is about two miles to the west.

The route is a less-used alternative to Waunita Pass Road and warrants a 4WD vehicle. It is part of a network of 4WD roads that allow exploration deep into Gunnison National Forest in areas such as Stridiron Gulch, Wiley Gulch, Canyon Creek, and the south and middle forks of Quartz Creek.

While the track is rough in spots, it should cause little difficulty in dry conditions. It offers more solitude than the more heavily used Waunita Pass Road and travels though aspen and pine forest. The scenery is attractive but lacks the spectacular views of other trails.

The area around Middle Quartz Creek offers good backcountry camping and fishing. It is surrounded with areas that offer scenic and historic day trips: historic and attractive Pitkin nearby to the west, Cumberland Pass and Tincup to the north, Brittle Silver Basin and Alpine Tunnel to the east, and Black Sage and Old Monarch Passes to the south.

Current Road Conditions

Gunnison National Forest
Taylor River District
216 North Colorado, Gunnison, CO 81230
(970) 641-0471

SC TRAIL #4:
MIDDLE QUARTZ CREEK TRAIL

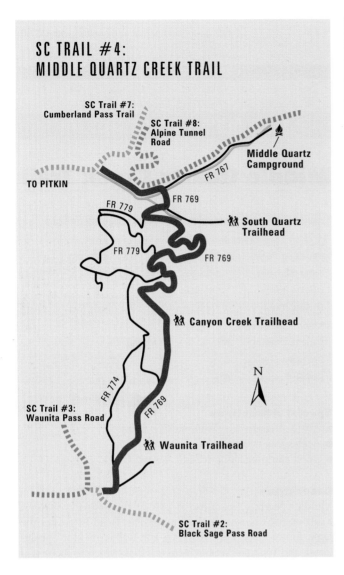

SC Trail #7:
Cumberland Pass Trail

SC Trail #8:
Alpine Tunnel Road

Middle Quartz Campground

FR 767

TO PITKIN

FR 769

FR 779

South Quartz Trailhead

FR 779

FR 769

Canyon Creek Trailhead

N

FR 774

FR 769

SC Trail #3:
Waunita Pass Road

Waunita Trailhead

SC Trail #2:
Black Sage Pass Road

Map References
USFS Gunnison NF
USGS Gunnison County #5
Trails Illustrated, #130
The Roads of Colorado, p. 101
Colorado Atlas & Gazetteer, p. 59

Route Directions

▼ 0.0   From T-intersection of Black Sage Pass Road (FR 887) and FR 774 to Middle Quartz Creek, zero trip meter and proceed east along FR 774. South-Central Trail #3: Waunita Pass Road is 0.2 miles west.

12.4 ▲   End at T-intersection with South-Central Trail #2: Black Sage Pass Road (FR 887). South-Central Trail #3: Waunita Pass Road is straight on 0.2 miles.

		GPS: N 38°30.81′ W 106°29.61′
▼ 0.3	BL	Track on right dead-ends.
12.1 ▲	BR	Track on left dead-ends.
▼ 0.7	BR	FR 774 on left. Follow FR 769.
11.7 ▲	BL	FR 774 on right. Follow FR 769.
▼ 1.3	SO	Waunita walking track on right.
11.1 ▲	SO	Waunita walking track on left.

		GPS: N 38°31.60′ W 106°28.88′
▼ 2.4	SO	Track on right.
10.0 ▲	SO	Track on left.
▼ 2.8	SO	Track on right (unmarked).
9.6 ▲	SO	Track on left (unmarked).
▼ 3.2	BR	Intersection. Sign on right points to Hicks Gulch behind and Buffalo Fork straight ahead. Sign on the left marks track to Stridiron Creek.
9.2 ▲	BL	Intersection. Hicks Gulch straight. Track to Stridiron Creek on right.

		GPS: N 38°32.80′ W 106°28.13′
▼ 3.3	SO	Trail on right.
9.1 ▲	SO	Trail on left.
▼ 4.8	BL	Fork in the road. Canyon Creek trailhead is to the right. Follow road left toward Middle Quartz Creek.
7.6 ▲	BR	Canyon Creek trailhead is to the left.

		GPS: N 38°34.06′ W 106°28.23′
▼ 6.4	SO	Track on right, then track on left. Remain on FR 769.
6.0 ▲	SO	Track on left, then track on right. Remain on FR 769.

		GPS: N 38°34.67′ W 106°27.86′
▼ 7.1	BR	Track on left.
5.3 ▲	BL	Track on right.

		GPS: N 38°34.80′ W 106°28.36′
▼ 7.6	TR	Fork in the road, FR 769 to the right; FR 779 to the left.
4.8 ▲	BL	Remain on FR 769. FR 779 on the right.

		GPS: N 38°35.22′ W 106°28.25′
▼ 9.7	TR	Intersection with FR 769 to the right; FR 779 to the left.
2.7 ▲	TL	Remain on FR 769. FR 779 on the right.

		GPS: N 38°35.71′ W 106°28.55′
▼ 10.3	SO	Cross over creek.
2.1 ▲	SO	Cross over creek.
▼ 10.4	SO	Track on right leads to South Quartz trailhead walking track.
2.0 ▲	SO	Track on left leads to South Quartz trailhead walking track.
▼ 10.7	TL	Cross over creek, then intersection with Middle Quartz Creek Road (FR 767). Middle Quartz Creek Campground to the right and Pitkin to the left.
1.7 ▲	TR	Intersection with FR 769.

		GPS: N 38°36.19′ W 106°28.07′
▼ 12.4		End at intersection with South-Central Trail #7 (FR 765). Pitkin is to the left and Tincup to the right.
0.0 ▲		At intersection of South-Central Trail #7 (FR 765) and FR 767, zero trip meter and proceed east along FR 767.

		GPS: N 38°36.72′ W 106°29.68′

Hancock Pass Trail

Starting Point:	St. Elmo
Finishing Point:	Alpine Tunnel Road at intersection of FR 888 and FR 839
Total Mileage:	9.3 miles
Unpaved Mileage:	9.3 miles
Driving Time:	1 1/4 hours
Pass Elevation:	12,140 feet
Usually Open:	Early July to October
Difficulty Rating:	4 (5 if traveling toward St. Elmo)
Scenic Rating:	9

Special Attractions

- St. Elmo township and the sites of Hancock and Romley.
- Spectacular summit views of Brittle Silver Basin.
- Hiking trail to the east portal of the Alpine Tunnel.
- Moderately difficult 4WD route.
- Access to a network of 4WD trails.

History

The history of the Hancock Pass crossing is poorly documented, perhaps because of the confusion between this pass and Williams Pass, which is located a couple of miles further north.

The Hancock Pass trail descending the west side of the pass

Hancock Pass was used as a mining route in the 1880s but has never been an important commercial route. It was not officially named until 1962.

Much of the route on the east side of the pass follows the old Denver, South Park & Pacific railway grade toward the Alpine Tunnel.

This trip originates at one of the most-photographed and best-preserved ghost towns in Colorado: St. Elmo. The town served as a supply center for the numerous mining camps in the area and provided Saturday night entertainment for the railroad workers putting in the Alpine Tunnel route for the Denver, South Park & Pacific Railroad.

The Allie Belle Mine building in 1950

The route also passes a number of other town sites. Romley was a mining camp for the nearby Mary Murphy Mine. In 1982, the mining company destroyed the buildings that remained in the deserted town. The Mary Murphy Mine, which provided the principal economic support for St. Elmo township from 1875 to 1926, is located on the road to Pomeroy Lakes (South-Central Trail #14).

Hancock was a construction town for the railroad workers building the Alpine Tunnel in 1880 to 1882. At Hancock, a 2.5-mile hiking trail continues along the old railroad grade to the site of the Atlantic Station at the east end of the old Alpine Tunnel.

Description

Romley is located about 2.5 miles from St. Elmo. Shortly past Romley is the turnoff for the road to Pomeroy Lakes, which goes past the Mary Murphy Mine.

At the 4.8-mile point is one of the most precarious-looking structures you are likely to see. The building, which looks as though it will slide into the middle of the road at any moment, once stored ore produced by the Allie Belle Mine while it was waiting to be loaded into rail trucks. Despite appearances, the building has been cantilevered this way for years and is presumably quite sound. A number of other mine buildings are located above this structure. A huge rock has rolled down the hill and crashed through the back wall of a miner's cabin—we hope not while he was in residence!

The precarious position of the Allie Belle Mine building today

Not far past the leaning storage shed lies the town site of Hancock. The last building remaining, a saloon, has also succumbed to the elements, but the collapsed timbers can still be seen.

Just past Hancock, there is a parking lot at the start of the hiking trail to the Atlantic railway station, which was located at the eastern end of the Alpine Tunnel. Before 1992, this road was open to vehicles, but a landslide blocked it in that year, leaving as the only access a 2.5-mile hike along the old railway grade.

Shortly after the parking lot, there is an intersection. Turn right, continue on the trail to Hancock Pass. Bear left to a 1.4-mile road to Hancock Lakes trailhead (GPS coordinates: N38°37.18' W106°21.29'). A half-mile walk along this trail leads to the Hancock Lakes.

Until this intersection, the route is an easy 2WD road and suitable for passenger vehicles. However, from this point on, the road becomes progressively tougher and is rated 4WD.

The summit of the pass provides a spectacular view of Brittle Silver Basin and the ridge of thirteen-thousand-foot peaks beyond. The Tomichi Pass shelf road is clearly visible, clinging to the southern ridge surrounding the basin.

From the summit, the remaining mile of road descends steeply into Brittle Silver Basin. For the last hundred yards, loose rocks can make getting traction a little difficult, especially if you are going uphill toward the pass.

Current Road Conditions

Gunnison National Forest
Taylor River District
216 North Colorado, Gunnison, CO 81230
(970) 641-0471

SC TRAIL #5: HANCOCK PASS TRAIL

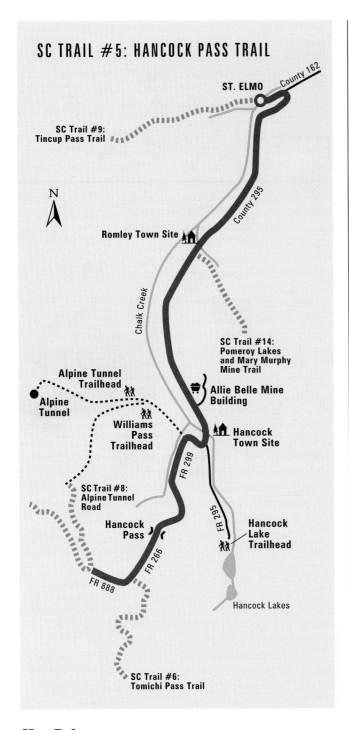

ST. ELMO

County 162

SC Trail #9:
Tincup Pass Trail

N

County 295

Romley Town Site 🏚️

Chalk Creek

SC Trail #14:
Pomeroy Lakes
and Mary Murphy
Mine Trail

Alpine Tunnel
Trailhead 🚶

Alpine
Tunnel ●

🛒 Allie Belle Mine
Building

Williams
Pass
Trailhead 🚶

🏚️ Hancock
Town Site

SC Trail #8:
Alpine Tunnel
Road

FR 299

FR 295

Hancock
Pass

Hancock
Lake
Trailhead 🚶

FR 266

FR 888

Hancock Lakes

SC Trail #6:
Tomichi Pass Trail

Map References

USFS Gunnison NF or San Isabel NF
USGS Chaffee County #2
   Chaffee County #3
   Gunnison County #5
Trails Illustrated, #130
The Roads of Colorado, p. 102
Colorado Atlas & Gazetteer, p. 59

Route Directions

▼ 0.0   At Miner's Exchange general store in St. Elmo, zero trip meter and proceed east out of St.

			Elmo on County 162.
5.7 ▲			End at Miner's Exchange general store in St. Elmo.

GPS: N 38°42.23' W 106°20.65'

▼ 0.3	TR		Onto County/FR 295 toward Hancock.
5.4 ▲	TL		Onto County 162 toward St. Elmo.
▼ 0.8	SO		San Isabel National Forest Service board sign on right.
4.9 ▲	SO		San Isabel National Forest Service board sign on left.
▼ 2.4	SO		Bridge over creek.
3.3 ▲	SO		Bridge over creek.
▼ 2.5	SO		Romley on right.
3.2 ▲	SO		Romley on left.
▼ 3.1	SO		South-Central Trail #14: Pomeroy Lakes and Mary Murphy Mine Trail is on left.
2.6 ▲	SO		Track on right to Pomeroy Lakes and Mary Murphy Mine.

GPS: N 38°40.40' W 106°21.98'

▼ 4.8	SO		Old ore storage house for the Allie Belle Mine on left, a precariously perched building overhanging the road.
0.9 ▲	SO		Ore storage house for the Allie Belle Mine on right.

GPS: N 38°39.08' W 106°22.07'

▼ 5.5	SO		Hancock town site.
0.2 ▲	SO		Hancock town site.

GPS: N 38°38.40' W 106°21.64'

▼ 5.6	BL		Cross over creek, then fork in road. Follow sign to Hancock Pass and Hancock Lakes. Track on right is parking for walking track to the Alpine Tunnel east portal.
0.1 ▲	BR		Left is parking area. Bear right toward Hancock, then cross over creek.
▼ 5.7	TR		Onto FR 299 toward Hancock Pass. (Left goes to Hancock Lakes trailhead.) Zero trip meter.
0.0 ▲			Proceed toward Hancock.

GPS: N 38°38.27' W 106°21.63'

▼ 0.0			Proceed along FR 299.
3.6 ▲	TL		Left goes to Hancock. Right goes to Hancock Lakes. Zero trip meter.
▼ 1.5	SO		Track on right to mine.
2.1 ▲	SO		Track on left to mine.
▼ 1.9-2.0	SO		Mine portals on right along the road.
1.6-1.7 ▲	SO		Mine portals on left along the road.
▼ 2.0	SO		Hancock Pass sign is slightly before the summit. After crest, road is now named FR 266.
1.6 ▲	SO		Hancock Pass sign is slightly past the summit. After crest, road is now named FR 299.

GPS: N 38°37.31' W 106°22.44'

▼ 2.9	SO		Rough and rocky shallow crossing through creek. Remains of old cabin on right.
0.7 ▲	SO		Remains of old cabin on left. Cross through creek.
▼ 3.0	TR		Intersection. Left to Tomichi Pass (FR 888) and right to Pitkin.
0.6 ▲	BL		Intersection. FR 888 continues to Tomichi Pass. Follow road to Hancock Pass (FR 266).

GPS: N 38°36.69' W 106°22.69'

▼ 3.6			End at intersection with South-Central Trail #8: Alpine Tunnel Road (FR 839).
0.0 ▲			At intersection of South-Central Trail #8: Alpine Tunnel Road (FR 839) and FR 888, zero trip meter and proceed along FR 888.

GPS: N 38°36.83' W 106°23.37'

Tomichi Pass Trail

Starting Point:	**Intersection of FR 888 and Hancock Pass Road (FR 266)**
Finishing Point:	**Intersection of FR 888 and US 50**
Total Mileage:	**15.9 miles**
Unpaved Mileage:	**12.1 miles**
Driving Time:	**2 hours**
Pass Elevation:	**11,979 feet**
Usually Open:	**Early July to October**
Difficulty Rating:	**5**
Scenic Rating:	**9**

Special Attractions

- A challenging 4WD trail.
- Wonderful summit views of Brittle Silver Basin and Hancock Pass Road.
- Town sites of Tomichi and Whitepine.
- Access to a network of 4WD trails.

History

"Tomichi" is the Ute word for hot water, a reference to the many hot springs in the area.

The main access to the mining areas of Tomichi and Whitepine was southeast to Monarch via Old Monarch Pass or west to Gunnison via Black Sage Pass. From the late 1870s this entire area was teeming with miners, and Tomichi Pass Road was built to provide access north from the mining settlements of Tomichi and Whitepine to the Denver, South Park & Pacific Railroad and the towns of Pitkin and, via Hancock Pass, St. Elmo. However, the route was too high and difficult to be developed much beyond a pack trail, although wagons did use it when road and weather conditions allowed.

Description

Tomichi Pass Trail remains one of the more difficult roads in the area. On the north side of the pass, the road crosses a plank bridge over boggy ground before climbing a very narrow shelf that can be blocked by talus slides. It may be necessary to clear the road in order to pass safely. The road is certainly better suited to a smaller 4WD vehicle; but we have

Tomichi Cemetery

traveled it both ways in a Suburban, so it is possible to safely negotiate it in a full-sized vehicle. The wrecked 4WD vehicle below the road serves as a cautionary billboard for the reckless.

The summit provides a wonderful view back to Hancock Pass Road.

A view of the Tomichi Pass 4WD trail from Hancock Pass

On the south side of the pass, the road begins a long, fairly gentle descent, with narrow sections where passing another vehicle is difficult. The road surface is rough but is mainly imbedded rock and provides a sound footing. People who are afraid of heights will be pleased to know that drop-offs along this road are mostly restricted to the immediate vicinity of the summit of the pass.

Once the road descends below timberline, it becomes smoother and easier. About three miles after the pass, the road goes through the old Tomichi cemetery. This heavily forested site is all that remains of the Tomichi township, which was finally destroyed by a snowslide in 1899. Though the population had fallen to just six, four of those were claimed by the snowslide.

From Whitepine, the road may be negotiated in a car.

Current Road Conditions

Gunnison National Forest
Taylor River District
216 North Colorado, Gunnison, CO 81230
(970) 641-0471

Map References

USFS Gunnison NF
USGS Gunnison County #5
Trails Illustrated, #130, #139
The Roads of Colorado, p. 102
Colorado Atlas & Gazetteer, pp. 59, 69

Route Directions

▼ 0.0		From intersection of FR 888 and FR 266, zero trip meter and proceed along FR 888 toward Tomichi.
15.9 ▲		End at intersection with South-Central Trail #5: Hancock Pass Trail (FR 266). Straight ahead leads to South-Central Trail #8: Alpine Tunnel Road.
GPS: N 38°36.69′ W 106°22.69′		
▼ 0.3	SO	Interesting mine with several old buildings, an old boiler and open portal.
15.6 ▲	SO	Interesting mine with several old buildings, an old boiler and open portal.
GPS: N 38°36.62′ W 106°22.46′		
▼ 0.8	SO	Plank bridge over boggy area.
15.1 ▲	SO	Plank bridge over boggy area.

SC TRAIL #6: TOMICHI PASS TRAIL

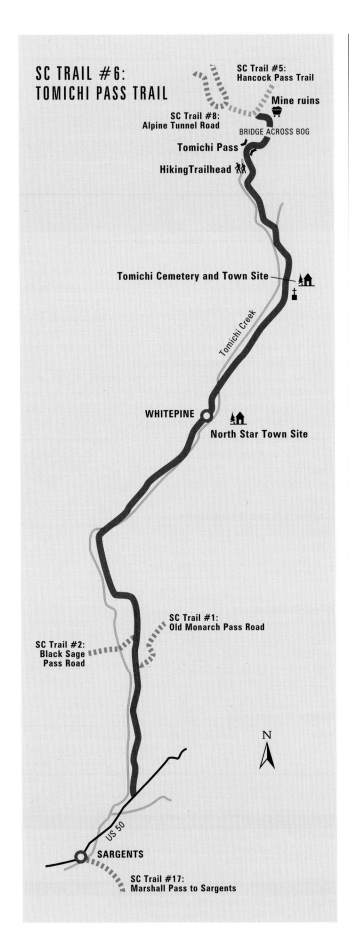

SC Trail #5: Hancock Pass Trail

Mine ruins

SC Trail #8: Alpine Tunnel Road

BRIDGE ACROSS BOG

Tomichi Pass

Hiking Trailhead

Tomichi Cemetery and Town Site

Tomichi Creek

WHITEPINE

North Star Town Site

SC Trail #1: Old Monarch Pass Road

SC Trail #2: Black Sage Pass Road

N

US 50

SARGENTS

SC Trail #17: Marshall Pass to Sargents

| ▼ 1.1 | SO | Summit of Tomichi Pass. |
| 14.8 ▲ | SO | Summit of Tomichi Pass. |

GPS: N 38°36.20' W 106°22.95'

| ▼ 1.3 | SO | Walking trail on right to Canyon Creek, South Quartz, Horseshoe Creek. |
| 14.6 ▲ | SO | Walking trail on left to Canyon Creek, South Quartz, Horseshoe Creek. |

| ▼ 1.9 | SO | Cross through creek. |
| 14.0 ▲ | SO | Cross through creek. |

| ▼ 2.0 | SO | Cross through creek. |
| 13.9 ▲ | SO | Cross through creek. |

| ▼ 2.4 | SO | Cross through creek. |
| 13.5 ▲ | SO | Cross through creek. |

| ▼ 2.6 | SO | Cross through creek. |
| 13.3 ▲ | SO | Cross through creek. |

| ▼ 2.9 | SO | Cross through creek. |
| 13.0 ▲ | SO | Cross through creek. |

| ▼ 3.4 | SO | Cross through creek. |
| 12.5 ▲ | SO | Cross through creek. |

| ▼ 4.0 | SO | Tomichi Cemetery on left. Bear right at intersection with 8881.C. |
| 11.9 ▲ | SO | Tomichi Cemetery on right. Bear left. |

GPS: N 38°34.26' W 106°22.19'

| ▼ 4.1 | SO | Cross through creek. |
| 11.8 ▲ | SO | Cross through creek. |

| ▼ 4.2 | SO | Track on left. |
| 11.7 ▲ | SO | Track on right. |

| ▼ 4.3 | SO | Track on left. |
| 11.6 ▲ | SO | Track on right. |

| ▼ 4.4 | TL | Track on right is a dead end. Turn toward Whitepine. |
| 11.5 ▲ | TR | Track on left is a dead end. Turn toward Tomichi Pass. |

GPS: N 38°34.06' W 106°22.44'

| ▼ 6.1 | SO | Bridge over Tomichi Creek. |
| 9.8 ▲ | SO | Bridge over Tomichi Creek. |

| ▼ 6.5 | SO | Town of Whitepine. |
| 9.4 ▲ | SO | Town of Whitepine. |

GPS: N 38°32.59' W 106°23.57'

| ▼ 6.8 | SO | Mine and mill on left. |
| 9.1 ▲ | SO | Mine and mill on right. |

| ▼ 8.4 | SO | USFS Snowblind Campground on left. |
| 7.5 ▲ | SO | USFS Snowblind Campground on right. |

| ▼ 10.0 | SO | Intersection with South-Central Trail #2: Black Sage Pass Road (FR 887) to the right. |
| 5.9 ▲ | SO | Intersection with South-Central Trail #2: Black Sage Pass Road (FR 887) to the left. |

GPS: N 38°30.11' W 106°25.25'

| ▼ 11.4 | SO | South-Central Trail #1: Old Monarch Pass Road on left. |
| 4.5 ▲ | SO | South-Central Trail #1: Old Monarch Pass Road on right. |

| ▼ 12.1 | SO | Paved road. |
| 3.8 ▲ | SO | Unpaved. |

| ▼ 15.9 | | End at intersection with US 50. |
| 0.0 ▲ | | At intersection of US 50 and FR 888, zero trip meter and proceed along FR 888 toward Whitepine. |

GPS: N 38°25.40 W 106°24.36'

Cumberland Pass Trail

Starting Point:	Tincup
Finishing Point:	Pitkin
Total Mileage:	15.6 miles
Unpaved Mileage:	15.2 miles
Driving Time:	1 1/2 hours
Pass Elevation:	12,015 feet
Usually Open:	Early July to late September
Difficulty Rating:	3
Scenic Rating:	10

Special Attractions

- The historic and attractive town of Tincup, one of the wildest towns of the old West.
- Tincup Cemetery.
- Access to a multitude of side roads near the summit.
- Spectacular, panoramic summit views.
- Bon Ton Mine, with its deserted cabins and mine buildings.

History

The main road over Cumberland Pass is one of the highest 2WD roads in the United States. This 4WD road takes an alternative, more direct, but slower route from Tincup to the north side of the pass.

The main road was built in 1882, upgrading an earlier pack trail. Until this time, Tincup, which was first settled in 1877, had received the majority of its supplies across the gentler slopes of Cottonwood Pass. However, when the Denver, South Park & Pacific Railroad reached Pitkin in 1882, it became necessary to have a good freight route to Tincup (which in its wild heyday was the second largest town in Gunnison County).

Description

The route leaves Tincup and travels past the old cemetery, complete with a Boot Hill and mounds for each religious group. Tincup's reputation as one of the wildest towns of the old West no doubt meant the cemetery had a continual supply of customers who made the one-way trip to Boot Hill.

The turnoff from the main Cumberland Pass road at the 0.3-mile point is unmarked.

The road then passes numerous abandoned mines, rusting mining machinery, and decaying cabins as it progresses through the pine forest toward the pass. Although it is narrow in sections and has some loose surfaces, the road provides no particular difficulty in dry conditions.

As the road ascends above timberline, magnificent panoramic views open up, and numerous 4WD trails crisscross the area. Staying on the correct trail can be tricky in this section; fortunately, the summit is visible, and most trails allow you to head in that direction. With the large number of people that use these roads, it is especially important to Tread Lightly! and remain on the trails open to 4WD vehicles.

At the summit, the high peaks of the Sawatch Range dominate the skyline to the east, the Elk Mountains in the distance to the west, and the Willow Creek Valley to the north, with the main 2WD road to Tincup visible as it descends into the valley.

The panoramic view from the northern approach to Cumberland Pass

The descent toward Pitkin is along a well-maintained 2WD road. It passes through the remains of the Bon Ton Mine, with its numerous cabins still standing. Five miles further is the turnoff for the Alpine Tunnel and Tomichi and Hancock passes.

Current Road Conditions

Gunnison National Forest
Taylor River District
216 North Colorado, Gunnison, CO 81230
(970) 641-0471

Map References

USFS Gunnison NF
USGS Gunnison County #5
Gunnison County #3
Trails Illustrated, #130
The Roads of Colorado, p. 101
Colorado Atlas & Gazetteer, p. 59

Route Directions

▼ 0.0			Start at intersection of Mirror Lake Road (FR 267) and Cumberland Pass Road (FR 765) in Tincup. Zero trip meter and proceed south.
	4.9 ▲		End at intersection with Mirror Lake Road (FR 267) or South-Central Trail #9: Tincup Pass Trail.
		GPS: N 38°45.27′ W 106°28.77′	
▼ 0.1		SO	Cross bridge.
	4.8 ▲	SO	Cross bridge.
▼ 0.2		SO	FR 765.2A to Tincup Cemetery on left.
	4.7 ▲	SO	FR 765.2A to Tincup Cemetery on right.
▼ 0.3		TL	Turn onto unmarked turnoff on left, FR 765.2B.
	4.6 ▲	TR	Turn onto FR 765 toward Tincup.
		GPS: N 38°44.98′ W 106°28.83′	
▼ 2.1		TL	Intersection.
	2.8 ▲	TR	Intersection.
		GPS: N 38°43.57′ W 106°28.73′	
▼ 2.3		SO	Private cottages on left.
	2.6 ▲	SO	Private cottages on right.
		GPS: N 38°43.37′ W 106°28.78′	
▼ 2.5		BL	Track on right.
	2.4 ▲	BR	Track on left.
		GPS: N 38°43.19′ W 106°28.70′	
▼ 2.6		SO	Mine on left, building ruins, and tailing dump.
	2.3 ▲	SO	Mine on right, building ruins, and tailing dump.

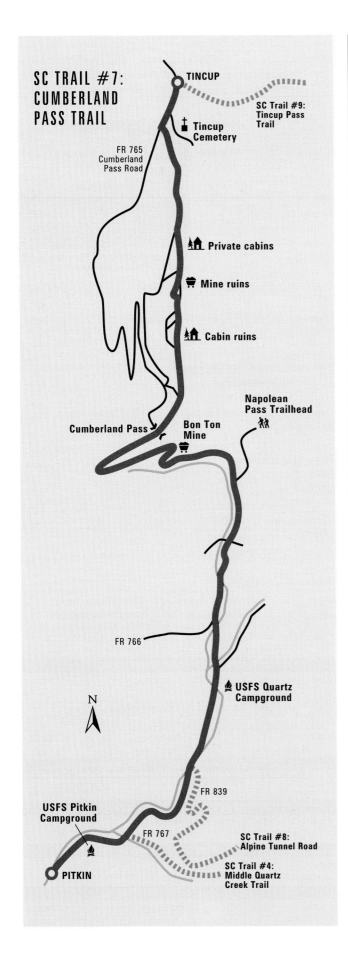

SC TRAIL #7: CUMBERLAND PASS TRAIL

▼ 2.6		BR	Track on left.
	2.3 ▲	BL	Track on right.
▼ 2.6		TL/TR	S-turn.
	2.2 ▲	TR/TL	S-turn.
		GPS: N 38°43.12' W 106°28.70'	
▼ 2.7		SO	Track on left. Abandoned mine machinery.
	2.1 ▲	SO	Track on right. Abandoned mine machinery.
		GPS: N 38°43.04' W 106°28.71'	
▼ 2.9		BL	Fork in road.
	2.0 ▲	BR	Track on left.
		GPS: N 38°42.87' W 106°28.68'	
▼ 3.0		BL	Fork in road.
	1.9 ▲	BR	Fork in road
▼ 3.1		SO/BR	Track on right to several cabin ruins. Then bear right at fork in road.
	1.8 ▲	BL/BR	Track on right. Track on left to cabin ruins.
		GPS: N 38°42.75' W 106°28.65'	
▼ 3.2		SO	Track on right. Track on left.
	1.7 ▲	SO	Track on left. Track on right.
▼ 3.4		BR	Fork in road.
	1.5 ▲	BL	Fork in road.
		GPS: N 38°42.47 W 106°28.70'	
▼ 3.4		SO	Track on right.
	1.4 ▲	SO	Track on left.
▼ 3.5		BL	Track on right.
	1.4 ▲	BR	Track on left.
▼ 4.1		BR	Fork in road.
	0.8 ▲	BL	Fork in road.
▼ 4.5		BR	Fork in road.
	30 yards ▲	BL	Fork in road.
▼ 30 yards		BL	Fork in road.
	0.4 ▲	BR	Fork in road.
▼ 4.9		TL	Cumberland Pass summit and intersection with Cumberland Pass Road. Zero trip meter at summit marker.
	0.0 ▲		Proceed along 765.2B.
		GPS: N 38°41.37' W 106°29.03'	
▼ 0.0			Continue south on FR 765 toward Pitkin.
	7.9 ▲	TR	Cumberland Pass summit. Zero trip meter at summit marker and shortly after turn right onto 4WD track (FR 765.2B).
▼ 0.6		SO	4WD track on right.
	7.3 ▲	SO	4WD track on left.
▼ 0.9		SO	4WD track on right.
	7.0 ▲	SO	4WD track on left.
▼ 1.0		UT	Track on right.
	6.9 ▲	UT	Track on left.
▼ 1.3		SO	4WD track on left.
	6.6 ▲	SO	4WD track on right.
▼ 2.8		SO	Bon Ton Mine on left and cluster of old mine buildings.
	5.0 ▲	SO	Bon Ton Mine on right and cluster of old mine buildings.
		GPS: N 38°40.97' W 106°28.80'	
▼ 4.0		SO	Track on left leads to Napoleon Pass trailhead.
	3.8 ▲	SO	Track on right leads to Napoleon Pass trailhead.
▼ 4.9		SO	Tracks on right and left.
	2.9 ▲	SO	Tracks on left and right.
▼ 5.3		SO	Cross North Quartz Creek.
	2.5 ▲	SO	Cross North Quartz Creek.
▼ 5.5		SO	Track on right.
	2.3 ▲	SO	Track on left.
▼ 5.9		SO	FR 766 to Hall's Gulch on right.

1.9 ▲	SO	FR 766 to Hall's Gulch on left.	

GPS: N 38°39.07' W 106°28.15'

▼ 6.6	SO	Track on left to Mosquito Creek.	
1.3 ▲	SO	Track on right to Mosquito Creek.	
▼ 6.9	SO	USFS Quartz Campground on left.	
1.0 ▲	SO	USFS Quartz Campground on right.	
▼ 7.9	SO	Town site of Quartz. South-Central Trail #8: Alpine Tunnel Road (FR 839) on left. Zero trip meter.	
0.0 ▲		Proceed along FR 765 toward Cumberland Pass.	

GPS: N 38°37.49' W 106°28.52'

▼ 0.0		Proceed along FR 765 toward Pitkin.	
2.9 ▲	SO	Town site of Quartz. South-Central Trail #8: Alpine Tunnel Road (FR 839) on right. Zero trip meter.	
▼ 1.5	SO	South-Central Trail #4: Middle Quartz Creek Trail (FR 767) on left.	
1.4 ▲	SO	South-Central Trail #4: Middle Quartz Creek Trail (FR 767) on right.	
▼ 1.9	SO	Seasonal gate, then USFS Pitkin Campground on left.	
1.0 ▲	SO	USFS Pitkin Campground on right, then seasonal gate.	
▼ 2.4	TR	Stop sign at intersection of State and 9th Streets in Pitkin. Silver Plume General Store.	
0.5 ▲	TL	Onto FR 765.	
▼ 2.5	TL	Onto Main Street.	
0.4 ▲	TR	Onto 9th Street.	
▼ 2.9		End at Pitkin City Hall at intersection of Main Street (County 76) and 4th Street.	
0.0 ▲		In front of the Pitkin City Hall at the intersection of Main Street (County 76) and 4th Street, zero trip meter and proceed northeast along Main Street.	

GPS: N 38°36.50' W 106°31.14'

SOUTH-CENTRAL REGION TRAIL #8

Alpine Tunnel Road

Starting Point:	**Intersection of Alpine Tunnel Road (FR 839) and Cumberland Pass Road (FR 765) at Quartz town site**
Finishing Point:	**Alpine Station**
Total Mileage:	**9.5 miles**
Unpaved Mileage:	**9.5 miles**
Driving Time:	**3/4 hour (one-way)**
Alpine Sta. Elev.:	**11,460 feet**
Usually Open:	**Early July to September**
Difficulty Rating:	**1**
Scenic Rating:	**10**

Special Attractions

- The restored Alpine Station.
- The Palisades section of the old railroad grade.
- Railroad water tanks.
- Town sites of Quartz and Woodstock and the site of the Sherrod Loop.

Steamtrain Water Tanks

Depending on the grade and the load, water tanks were typically required at intervals of about thirty miles along a railroad line. They were used to replenish the water carried by the tender—the small car pulled immediately behind the locomotive. The tenders carried coal and about 2,200 gallons of water.

Because of the steep, mountain grades between Quartz and the Alpine Tunnel, three tanks were positioned along the tracks. These were originally located at Midway, Woodstock, and Alpine Station.

Tanks were positioned below streams or springs and were gravity-fed. The tank's spout, hinged at the base and upright in its resting position, was lowered onto the tender, and a "flap valve" was opened to fill the tender's tank. The whole operation took about five minutes.

Tunnel Gulch water tank

Description

This historic route is an easy 2WD road that is popular with tourists and has plenty of pull-offs to enable passing where the road is narrow. The only caution is that it has very steep drop-offs in some sections.

This route starts at the town site of Quartz, approximately three miles northeast of Pitkin on Cumberland Pass Road (FR 765) at the Alpine Tunnel Road turnoff (FR 839). The town was originally founded in 1879 as a mining camp, but it was the arrival of the Denver, South Park & Pacific Railroad in 1882 that spurred its development. It was a major service depot for the railroad.

The remnants of the Midway water tank lie nearly three miles along the route. The tank was so named because it is at the halfway point between Pitkin and the Alpine Tunnel. The tank, which collapsed and has been removed from the base structure, used to hold 47,500 gallons.

A little more than two miles further is the Tunnel Gulch water tank, which has been restored by the Mile High Jeep Club. This 30,000-gallon tank replaced the Woodstock tank.

The route continues past the town site of Woodstock, which

Alpine Station

was completely destroyed by a snowslide on March 10, 1884, killing thirteen residents. The town was not rebuilt, but the stone base of the old Woodstock railway water tank remains.

The Sherrod Loop is marked by an information board. The loop was a horseshoe section of track that enabled the trains to turn 228 degrees to remain on the sunnier, south side of the valley. The snow on the north slope was ten to twenty feet deep and typically did not melt until the summer.

One of the most striking features is a man-made terrace, known as the Palisades, which was built to enable the train to travel along a spectacular cliff face. The ledge is supported by hand-cut stones that were laid without mortar into a

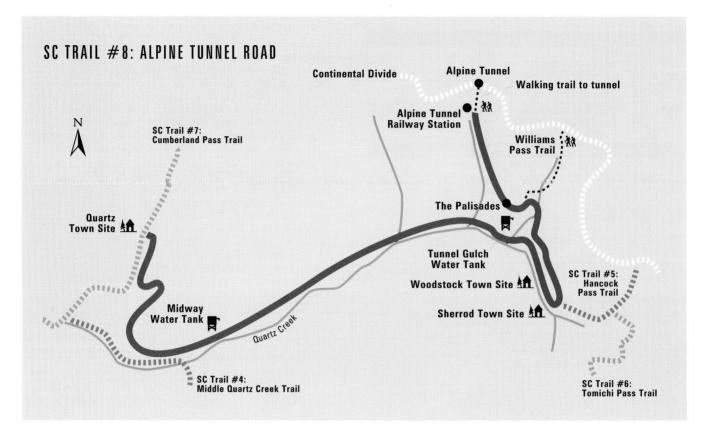

wall 33 feet high and 425 feet long.

The Alpine Station was constructed in 1881 to provide the main support for the imminent Alpine Tunnel railway operations. It consisted of two stone structures: a massive engine house that included an enclosed water tank, a coal bunker, a turntable, and a locomotive service area; and a section house that included a kitchen, a dining room, a pantry, and several bedrooms.

The section house was abandoned in 1896, while the engine house was destroyed by fire in 1906. The remains of both stone buildings lie in ruin across from the restored telegraph office.

Current Road Conditions

Gunnison National Forest
Taylor River District
216 North Colorado, Gunnison, CO 81230
(970) 641-0471

Map References

USFS Gunnison NF
USGS Chaffee County #2
Chaffee County #3
Gunnison County #5
Trails Illustrated, #130
The Roads of Colorado, p. 102
Colorado Atlas & Gazetteer, p. 59

Route Directions

▼ 0.0		From the T-intersection of Alpine Tunnel Road (FR 839) and South-Central Trail #7: Cumberland Pass Trail (FR 765) at the site of Quartz, zero trip meter and proceed east toward the Alpine Tunnel.
7.3 ▲		End at intersection with South-Central Trail #7: Cumberland Pass Trail.

GPS: N 38°37.47' W 106°28.52'

▼ 3.2	SO	Remains of Midway water tank on left. Only base is left standing.
4.1 ▲	SO	Remains of Midway water tank on right.
▼ 6.4	SO	Tunnel Gulch water tank on left.
0.9 ▲	SO	Tunnel Gulch water tank on right.
▼ 7.0	SO	Town site of Woodstock on right.
0.3 ▲	SO	Town site of Woodstock on left.
▼ 7.2	SO	Town site of Sherrod and Sherrod Loop on right.
0.1 ▲	SO	Town site of Sherrod and Sherrod Loop on left.
▼ 7.3	TL	Intersection with FR 888 (South-Central Trail #5: Hancock Pass Trail). Zero trip meter.
0.0 ▲		Continue on FR 839 toward Quartz and Pitkin.

GPS: N 38°36.83' W 106°23.36'

▼ 0.0		Continue on FR 839 toward Alpine Station.
0.0 ▲	TR	Intersection with FR 888 (South-Central Trail #5: Hancock Pass Trail). Zero trip meter.
▼ 0.1	SO	South Park Railroad marker on right and Gunnison National Forest.
▼ 0.2	SO	Track on left to private cabin.
▼ 0.9	SO	Williams Pass Road sign on right.
▼ 1.3	SO	"Palisades" marker on left. Elevation 11,300 feet.
▼ 2.2		Public toilets, picnic tables and gate. It is a short walk to the Alpine Station buildings beyond the gate.

GPS: N 38°38.29' W 106°24.45'

Tincup Pass Trail

Starting Point:	**St. Elmo**
Finishing Point:	**Tincup**
Total Mileage:	**12.4 miles**
Unpaved Mileage:	**12.4 miles**
Driving Time:	**1 1/4 hours**
Pass Elevation:	**12,154 feet**
Usually Open:	**Early July to October**
Difficulty Rating:	**3**
Scenic Rating:	**8**

Special Attractions

- The historic and attractive towns of St. Elmo and Tincup.
- Very attractive scenery, including the summit views and Mirror Lake.
- Access to a network of 4WD trails.
- Excellent backcountry campsites.

History

Tincup Pass was first used by the Indians and then as a pack trail. A wagon road was built following the flood of silver prospectors into the area in 1879. By 1880, the pass was an established freight route, with wagon service run by Witowski and Dunbar's Hack Line. In 1881, it was developed further and became a toll road; soon, three stage lines were running daily stages over the pass. The route was surveyed for a number of railroads, and a tunnel was even started under the pass; but the project was soon abandoned.

The pass road was used during World War I to train the cavalry. In 1954, prison laborers upgraded the road.

Description

The route starts from the western edge of St. Elmo, a famous ghost town that looks as if it were created by Hollywood, and

Mirror Lake

immediately starts the climb toward the pass. Initially, the road follows the North Fork of Chalk Creek, passing numerous backcountry campsites.

The road is reasonably wide but quite rough, although the surface is sound. As the road progresses, it becomes even rockier; but the rocks are imbedded, so the surface remains solid. The road travels through pine and spruce forest.

The summit offers beautiful views of the Arkansas River Valley and the Taylor Park area. Mirror Lake can be glimpsed in the foreground looking west toward Tincup.

About three miles west of the summit, the road travels along the edge of Mirror Lake, a popular fishing spot. Nearby, there is a U.S. Forest Service campground. There are also numerous, very good backcountry campsites between Mirror Lake and Tincup.

From Mirror Lake, the road is easily negotiated by a car.

Current Road Conditions

Gunnison National Forest
Taylor River District
216 North Colorado, Gunnison, CO 81230
(970) 641-0471

Map References

USFS San Isabel NF or Gunnison NF
USGS Chaffee County #2
        Gunnison County #5
        Gunnison County #3
Trails Illustrated, #129, #130
The Roads of Colorado, p. 101
Colorado Atlas & Gazetteer, p. 59

Route Directions

▼ 0.0		In front of the Miner's Exchange in St. Elmo, zero trip meter and proceed west.
9.3 ▲		End in front of the Miner's Exchange in St. Elmo.
GPS: N 38°42.23' W 106°20.65'		
▼ 0.1	**TR**	At Tincup sign; then cross bridge over North Fork of Chalk Creek.
9.2 ▲	TL	Onto St. Elmo's main street.
▼ 0.2	**BR**	Fork in road.
9.1 ▲	BL	Track on right.
▼ 0.4	**SO**	Poplar Gulch trailhead on right.
8.9 ▲	SO	Poplar Gulch trailhead on left.
▼ 0.8	**SO**	Cattle guard.
8.5 ▲	SO	Cattle guard.
▼ 1.8	**SO**	Cross over creek.
7.5 ▲	SO	Cross over creek.
▼ 3.0	**SO**	Track on right.
6.3 ▲	SO	Track on left.
▼ 3.9	**SO**	Tunnel Lake walking trail on left.
5.4 ▲	SO	Tunnel Lake walking trail on right.
GPS: N 38°41.54' W 106°24.80'		
▼ 4.6	**SO**	Cross through creek.
4.7 ▲	SO	Cross through creek.
▼ 6.1	**SO**	Tincup Pass summit. Enter Gunnison National Forest.
3.2 ▲	SO	Tincup Pass summit. Enter San Isabel National Forest.

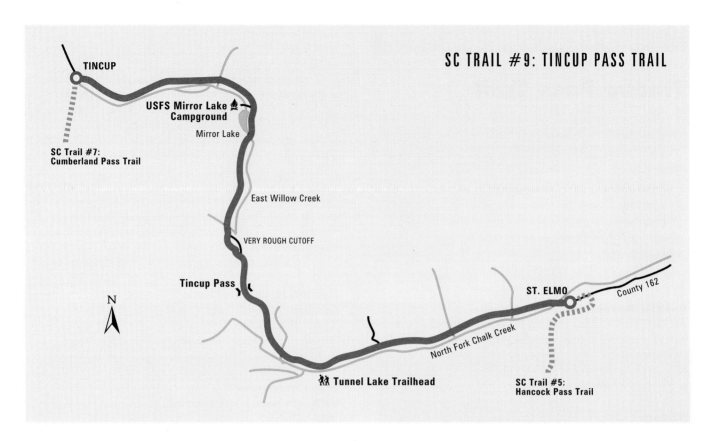

		GPS: N 38°42.57' W 106°26.00'
▼ 6.1	SO	Cattle guard.
3.2 ▲	SO	Cattle guard.
▼ 6.7	BL	Old alternative route is straight ahead.
2.6 ▲	BR	More difficult alternative route rejoins on left.
▼ 7.5	SO	More difficult alternative route rejoins on right.
1.8 ▲	BR	More difficult alternate route on left.
▼ 8.8	SO	Cross through creek at head of Mirror Lake.
0.5 ▲	SO	Cross through creek at head of Mirror Lake.
▼ 9.3	SO	Tincup side of Mirror Lake and angler parking on left. Zero trip meter.
0.0 ▲	BL	Follow track around the left side of Mirror Lake toward Tincup Pass.
		GPS: N 38°44.78' W 106°25.81'
▼ 0.0		Proceed along Mirror Lake Road (FR 267).
3.1 ▲	BL	Mirror Lake and angler parking on right. Zero trip meter.
▼ 0.1	SO	Track to USFS Mirror Lake Campground on left.
3.0 ▲	SO	Track to USFS Mirror Lake Campground on right.
▼ 0.4	SO	Timberline trailhead on right.
2.7 ▲	SO	Timberline trailhead on left.
▼ 0.9	SO	Cross over East Willow Creek.
2.2 ▲	SO	Cross over East Willow Creek.
▼ 2.9	BL	Fork in road. Entering Tincup.
0.2 ▲	BR	Leaving Tincup.
▼ 3.1		End at intersection with Cumberland Pass Road (FR 765) at stop sign. This is the start of South-Central Trail #7.
0.0 ▲		At intersection of Mirror Lake Road (FR 267) and Cumberland Pass Road (FR 765) in Tincup, zero trip meter and proceed toward Mirror Lake.
		GPS: N 38°45.27' W 106°28.77'

Mount Antero Trail

Starting Point:	**Intersection of County 162 and Baldwin Creek Road (FR 277)**
Finishing Point:	**Mount Antero**
Total Mileage:	**Approximately 6.5 miles**
Unpaved Mileage:	**Approximately 6.5 miles**
Driving Time:	**1 3/4 hours (one-way)**
Summit Elevation:	**14,269 feet**
Usually Open:	**Mid-June to late September**
Difficulty Rating:	**5**
Scenic Rating:	**9**

Special Attractions
- A very challenging and famous 4WD trail.
- Wonderful alpine scenery.
- Access to a network of 4WD trails.

History
Mount Antero is named for Chief "Graceful Walker" Antero of the Uintah band of the Ute Indians. Antero was one of the signatories to the Washington Treaty of 1880, which revised the terms of the Brunot Treaty signed seven years earlier and led to the Ute losing nearly all their land. Antero was a force for peace during the period of very problematic relations be-

tween the Ute and the whites in the late 1860s and 1870s. In 1869, John Wesley Powell spent the winter with Antero and Chief Douglas (who was later held responsible for the Meeker Massacre) and learned to speak the Ute language.

While Mount Antero was doubtless examined by prospectors in the late 1870s as silver was being discovered all around, it proved to have little silver to offer. In fact, not a single claim was staked. What the prospectors did not notice, or failed to appreciate, was that Mount Antero offered a fortune in gemstones.

Baldwin Creek crossing

In 1884, a prospector named Nathaniel D. Wanemaker discovered a number of blue aquamarines in the area. He constructed a small stone cabin high on the south side of the mountain. It is said that he discovered six hundred dollars' worth of gems in his first summer and continued to prospect for gems for many years.

Mount Antero has proved extraordinarily rich in aquamarines, topaz, and clear and smoky quartz crystals. The aquamarines have ranged in color from pale blue-green to deep blue. Some of the clear crystals from Mount Antero have been huge, such as a seven-inch specimen on display at the Harvard Mineralogical Museum and another that was cut into a six-inch-diameter sphere and displayed at the 1893 Colombian Exposition. The more common smoky quartz crystals have weighed as much as fifty pounds.

The most recent mining on Mount Antero has been for beryllium, a lightweight, corrosion-resistant, rigid, steel-gray metallic element that melts only at extremely high temperatures. Beryllium is prized as an aerospace structural material, as a moderator and reflector in nuclear reactors, and in a copper alloy used for springs, electrical contacts, and non-sparking tools. In the 1950s, the access road on the mountain's south shoulder was constructed by the beryllium mining company.

Description

The Mount Antero route starts at the intersection of the road between Nathrop and St. Elmo (County 162) and FR 277. The turnoff is 12 miles west of US 285 along County 162 and 3.3 miles east of St. Elmo.

FR 277 ascends steeply right from the point of departure from County 162. It's a rough, rocky shelf road through the pine and aspen forest but offers some very good views back into the valley and the township of Alpine. The track is narrow and has some very steep drop-offs. Pull-offs for passing other vehicles are only just adequate in some sections. High clearance is definitely required, but if you carefully select your line, the rocks are not so large as to cause vehicle damage.

Some good news: Once you have completed the first two miles, you are past the most difficult section of the route.

At the 2.7-mile point, you cross through Baldwin Creek,

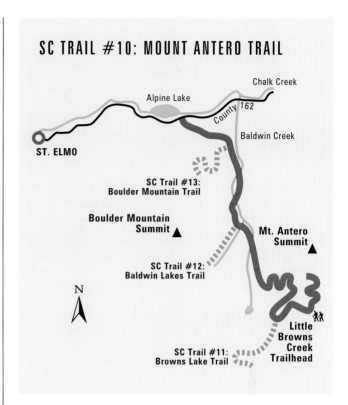

SC TRAIL #10: MOUNT ANTERO TRAIL

which has a firm base and is usually only about a foot deep. From the creek crossing, the road again commences to climb a couple of loose talus slopes before emerging above timberline. The road then commences a series of narrow switchbacks before winding around the south face and continuing up the east face. Passing opportunities are limited in this section, so it pays to watch for oncoming vehicles and plan ahead.

At the 3.8-mile point, there is an intersection. The track on the right leads to a dead end. This is the last chance to turn around before the end of the road, and the next section is more difficult than anything encountered until this point.

A view of the switchbacks before the road winds around the south face of Mount Antero

(Note: The difficulty rating for this route is based on stopping here.) We recommend that if you wish to see the last half mile of the road, you walk it.

Current Road Conditions
San Isabel National Forest
Salida Ranger District
325 West Rainbow Boulevard, Salida, CO 81201
(719) 539-3591

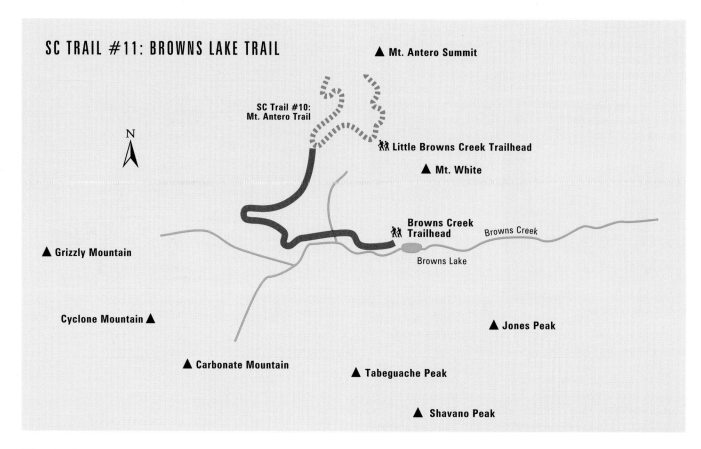

SC TRAIL #11: BROWNS LAKE TRAIL

▲ Mt. Antero Summit

SC Trail #10: Mt. Antero Trail

N

👫 Little Browns Creek Trailhead

▲ Mt. White

Browns Creek Trailhead 👫

Browns Creek

▲ Grizzly Mountain

Browns Lake

Cyclone Mountain ▲

▲ Jones Peak

▲ Carbonate Mountain

▲ Tabeguache Peak

▲ Shavano Peak

Map References

USFS San Isabel NF
USGS Chaffee County #2
            Chaffee County #3
Trails Illustrated, #130
The Roads of Colorado, p. 102
Colorado Atlas & Gazetteer, pp. 59-60

Route Directions

▼ 0.0		From County 162 (3.3 miles east of St. Elmo), turn onto Baldwin Creek Road (FR 277) toward Mt. Antero and zero trip meter.
		GPS: N 38°42.60' W 106°17.46'
▼ 1.1	SO	Track on right is South-Central Trail #13: Boulder Mountain Trail.
▼ 2.7	TL	South-Central Trail #12: Baldwin Lakes Trail is straight ahead (FR 277.2). Zero trip meter.
		GPS: N 38°40.99' W 106°16.32'
▼ 0.0		Cross through Baldwin Creek and continue on FR 278 toward Mt. Antero.
▼ 0.2	SO	Cross through creek.
▼ 0.3	SO	Track on left.
▼ 1.5	SO	Cross through creek.
▼ 3.3	BL	South-Central Trail #11: Browns Lake Trail (278.2) on right. Remain on 278.A.
		GPS: N 38°39.70' W 106°15.43'
▼ 3.4	SO	Intersection with 278.B on right, which climbs Mt. White 1.3 miles, providing spectacular views all around, especially looking back at Mt. Antero and into the valley to the south.
▼ 3.8	BL	Track on right. Park and walk remaining section.
		GPS: N 38°39.74' W 106°14.94'

Browns Lake Trail

Starting Point:	Intersection of FR 278.2 and the road to Mount Antero (FR 278A)
Finishing Point:	Browns Creek Trailhead
Total Mileage:	3.3 miles
Unpaved Mileage:	3.3 miles
Driving Time:	3/4 hour (one-way)
Highest Elevation:	12,800 feet
Usually Open:	Mid-June to late September
Difficulty Rating:	4
Scenic Rating:	10

Special Attractions

- The extremely scenic Browns Lake.
- Part of a network of 4WD trails near the summit of Mount Antero.

Description

Browns Lake 4WD trail is a side road from the Mount Antero road and sees much less traffic than the more-famous Mount Antero road.

After turning off the Mount Antero road, you cross an alpine meadow before commencing the rocky descent down into Browns Creek Valley. The road enters the timberline and wends its way through the pine forest with rather tight clearance between the trees.

The trail proceeds past the remains of a mining camp, including the ruins of a miner's cabin. As you proceed toward the trailhead and the end of the 4WD road, you'll enjoy picture-postcard views of Browns Lake, located in the valley at an altitude of 11,286 feet.

The road is moderately difficult, with sections of narrow switchbacks, loose surface rock, and some tight clearances; but the solitude and the scenery make it all worthwhile.

Current Road Conditions

San Isabel National Forest
Salida Ranger District
325 West Rainbow Boulevard, Salida, CO 81201
(719) 539-3591

Map References

USFS San Isabel NF
USGS Chaffee County #3
Trails Illustrated, #130
The Roads of Colorado, p. 102
Colorado Atlas & Gazetteer, pp. 59-60

Route Directions

▼ 0.0		At intersection of Mt. Antero Road (FR 278.A) and trail to Browns Lake (FR 278.2), zero trip meter and proceed along FR 278.2 down into the valley.
		GPS: N 38°39.70′ W 106°15.43′
▼ 1.9	SO	Cabin ruins on right.
▼ 2.0	SO	Cabin ruins on left.
▼ 2.5	SO	Cross through creek.
▼ 3.3		Track ends at Browns Creek trailhead.
		GPS: N 38°38.63′ W 106°14.70′

SOUTH-CENTRAL REGION TRAIL #12

Baldwin Lakes Trail

Starting Point:	Intersection of Baldwin Creek Road (FR 277) and the Mount Antero road (FR 278)
Finishing Point:	Parking area at Baldwin Lakes
Total Mileage:	2.9 miles
Unpaved Mileage:	2.9 miles
Driving Time:	1 hour (one-way)
Elevation:	12,200 feet
Usually Open:	Mid-June to late September
Difficulty Rating:	5
Scenic Rating:	7

Special Attractions

■ Challenging 4WD trail.
■ Scenic views of Baldwin Lakes.

Description

The Baldwin Lakes route is a very rough and rocky side road to the Mount Antero road. The talus roadbed is slippery, and sharp rocks make a flat tire a continual threat.

Baldwin Lakes

The first section of road travels along the creek, past open meadows and many backcountry camping spots. As it continues up to the first lake, you travel though the pine forest, emerging to cross huge talus rockslides and then reentering the forest. About two miles along the road, the surface rock becomes mostly imbedded in the soil and more stable. There is a fairly steep section where the melting snow drains across the trail, making it boggy and somewhat slippery when going uphill. The last section of the road has large imbedded rocks to negotiate before you reach the small parking area.

Views of Baldwin Creek Valley, the high alpine bowl encircled by steep valley walls, and the lakes cradled in its base combine to make the journey very scenic.

Current Road Conditions

San Isabel National Forest
Salida Ranger District
325 West Rainbow Boulevard, Salida, CO 81201
(719) 539-3591

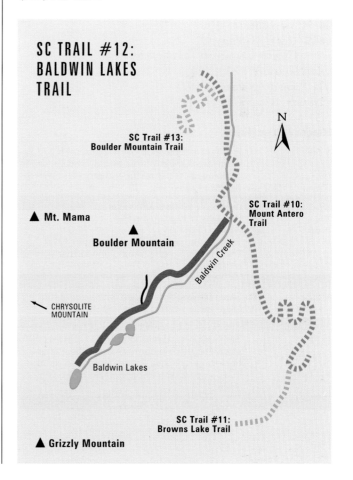

SC TRAIL #12: BALDWIN LAKES TRAIL

SC Trail #13: Boulder Mountain Trail

N

SC Trail #10: Mount Antero Trail

▲ Mt. Mama

▲ Boulder Mountain

Baldwin Creek

CHRYSOLITE MOUNTAIN

Baldwin Lakes

SC Trail #11: Browns Lake Trail

▲ Grizzly Mountain

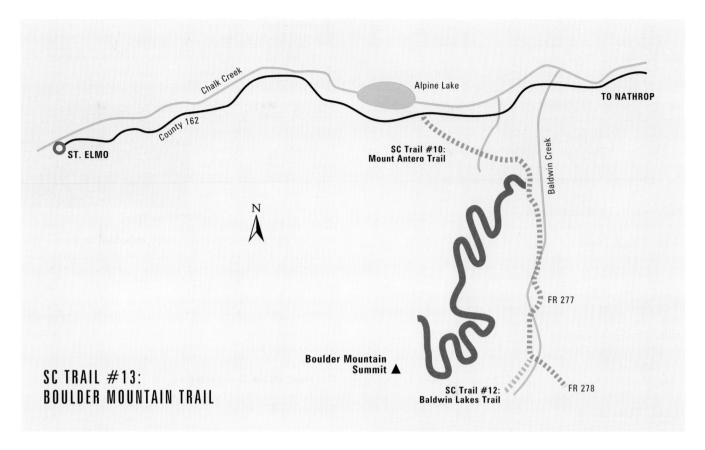

SC TRAIL #13:
BOULDER MOUNTAIN TRAIL

Map References

USFS San Isabel NF
USGS Chaffee County #2
  Chaffee County #3 (incomplete)
Trails Illustrated, #130
The Roads of Colorado, p. 102
Colorado Atlas & Gazetteer, p. 59

Route Directions

▼ **0.0** From the intersection of FR 278 and FR 277.2, at the small parking area beside Baldwin Creek crossing, zero trip meter and proceed toward Baldwin Lakes.

GPS: N 38°40.97' W 106°16.34'

▼ **0.2** **SO** Remains of log cabin ruins.
▼ **0.9** **BR** Fork in road.
▼ **1.5** **BL** Fork in road. Follow lower track (FR 277). Track on right goes to old mine farther up the mountain.

GPS: N 38°40.14' W 106°17.45'

▼ **2.2** **BR** Small parking area on left with view of the lakes and a walking track.

GPS: N 38°39.69' W 106°18.10'

▼ **2.9** Small parking/turn-around area. From this point, the track becomes more difficult than our rating indicates. Large, imbedded rocks make impact with the underside of the vehicle likely.

GPS: N 38°39.95' W 106°18.36'

Boulder Mountain Trail

Starting Point:	**Intersection of Baldwin Creek Road (FR 277) and Boulder Mountain Road**
Finishing Point:	**Mine shaft and cabin ruins near the top of the mountain**
Total Mileage:	**4.8 miles**
Unpaved Mileage:	**4.8 miles**
Driving Time:	**1 1/4 hours (one-way)**
Elevation:	**Approximately 12,800 feet**
Usually Open:	**Mid-June to late September**
Difficulty Rating:	**5**
Scenic Rating:	**8**

Special Attractions

■ Challenging 4WD trail.
■ Spectacular alpine views.

Description

This route, another side road to the Mount Antero Trail, is also rough and rocky but less so than the Mount Antero road. The challenge of this road is that it is narrow with very high drop-offs. To make matters more interesting, especially if you have a full-sized vehicle, small pine trees grow on the inside edge of the track, pushing you perilously close to the edge. If that is not enough, sections of the road are significantly off-camber!

The road carries less traffic than other roads in the area. You'll be glad of this, because there are sections where the only way to get around an oncoming vehicle is for one vehicle to reverse a good distance. Remember that the vehicle going uphill has the right of way, but common sense should always prevail. The steep talus slopes can mean that you often have to stop and clear rubble off the road.

On the way up, the route affords some

A relatively easy section of the Boulder Mountain 4WD trail

wonderful, panoramic views across to the Mount Antero road and the adjoining mountain peaks; but when you reach the mine at the top, the view is truly spectacular—across the Chalk Creek Valley, Alpine Lake, and the township of Alpine.

At the end of the trail are the windswept ruins of an old mine cabin and an open mine portal set into the bare, talus slope.

Current Road Conditions

San Isabel National Forest
Salida Ranger District
325 West Rainbow Boulevard, Salida, CO 81201
(719) 539-3591

Map References

USFS San Isabel NF
USGS Chaffee County #2
Trails Illustrated, #130
The Roads of Colorado, p. 102
Colorado Atlas & Gazetteer, p. 59

Route Directions

▼ 0.0		From the 1.1-mile mark on Mt. Antero Trail (Baldwin Creek Road), zero trip meter and make a sharp right turn onto an unmarked, rocky, track.
		GPS: N 38°42.21′ W 106°16.47′
▼ 0.9	SO	Campsites off to the left and right. Then cabin ruins and track on left.
▼ 4.8		Top of track. Mine shaft and ruins.
		GPS: N 38°41.20′ W 106°17.32′

Pomeroy Lakes and Mary Murphy Mine Trail

Starting Point:	Intersection of Hancock Road (FR 295) and FR 297.1
Finishing Point:	Parking area at Pomeroy Lakes
Total Mileage:	2.7 miles
Unpaved Mileage:	2.7 miles
Driving Time:	1 hour (one-way)
Lake Elevation:	12,035 feet
Usually Open:	Mid-June to late September
Difficulty Rating:	5
Scenic Rating:	7

Special Attractions

■ Remains of the Mary Murphy Mine.
■ A varied, challenging, short 4WD trail.
■ Pomeroy Lakes in their barren, scenic, alpine setting.

History

According to legend, Dr. A. E. Wright, who discovered the Mary Murphy Mine in the mid-1870s, named it after a nurse who cared for him when he was taken to the hospital in Denver. If Mary was a nurse with whom Wright was smitten, it is not clear how the adjoining Pat Murphy Mine was named. One thing is certain: The Mary Murphy Mine was enormously successful and was the main engine of the local economy. It supported the towns of St. Elmo, Romley, and Hancock. When the mine closed in 1926, it spelled the end for these

Mine ruins

towns and also for the remaining section of the old Alpine Tunnel railroad. The tracks were torn up within the year.

Description

This route starts along the road to Hancock that follows the Alpine Tunnel railroad grade.

After turning onto FR 297, the road passes many remains of the Mary Murphy Mine, located high above the road on the mountainside. Towers used by the tramway, which extended over two miles into Pomeroy Gulch from the railway grade, are still clearly evident as you drive along the initial section of the road. There are also a number of buildings where the tramway deposited the ore that it carried down from the top of the mountain.

Until this point the road is suitable for 2WD vehicles, but as the route proceeds along FR 297.2, the road becomes high-clearance 4WD only.

SC TRAIL #14: POMEROY LAKES AND MARY MURPHY MINE TRAIL

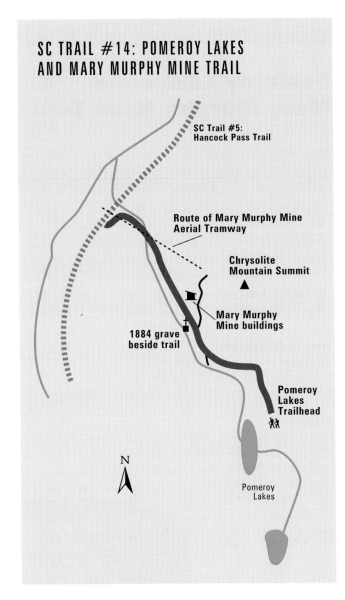

SC Trail #5: Hancock Pass Trail

Route of Mary Murphy Mine Aerial Tramway

Chrysolite Mountain Summit ▲

Mary Murphy Mine buildings

1884 grave beside trail

Pomeroy Lakes Trailhead

N

Pomeroy Lakes

Route Directions

▼ 0.0   At the intersection of Hancock Road with sign to Mary Murphy Mine and Pomeroy Lakes, zero trip meter and proceed along FR 297.1.

GPS: N 38°40.38' W 106°21.95'

▼ 0.1	SO	Track on left, then mine ruins on right.
▼ 0.3	SO	Cabin on left. Cross over creek.
▼ 0.6	SO	Track on left.
▼ 0.7	SO	Mine building ruins—Mary Murphy Mine headquarters.
▼ 0.8	SO	Tracks on left.
▼ 0.9	SO	Track on left goes to Mary Murphy Mine ruins. Zero trip meter.

GPS: N 38°39.95' W 106°21.34'

▼ 0.0	BR	Continue on FR 297.2 to Pomeroy Lakes.
▼ 0.1	SO	Track to camping.
▼ 0.2	SO	Track on right.
▼ 0.5	SO	Short track on left to mine ruins up the hill. Cross through creek.
▼ 0.7	SO	Grave on right (date: 1857-1884).
▼ 0.8	SO	Track on left.
▼ 1.0	TL	Track on right and straight ahead to campsites.
▼ 1.2	SO	Cross through creek.
▼ 1.8		End at Pomeroy Lakes and parking area.

GPS: N 38°38.90' W 106°20.34'

Continuing toward the lake, you pass a number of good backcountry camping sites and a grave on the side of the road that dates back to 1884.

The road gets progressively rockier and more rutted and eroded before reaching the parking area near the lakes, merely 2.7 miles from the start.

Current Road Conditions

San Isabel National Forest
Salida Ranger District
325 West Rainbow Boulevard, Salida, CO 81201
(719) 539-3591

Map References

USFS   San Isabel NF
USGS   Chaffee County #2
        Chaffee County #3
Trails Illustrated, #130
The Roads of Colorado, p. 102
Colorado Atlas & Gazetteer, p. 59

Marshall Pass Poncha Creek Trail

Starting Point:	**Mears Junction at US 285 and FR 200,**
	5 miles south of Poncha Springs
Finishing Point:	**Marshall Pass**
Total Mileage:	**11.2 miles**
Unpaved Mileage:	**11.2 miles**
Driving Time:	**1 1/4 hours**
Pass Elevation:	**10,846 feet**
Usually Open:	**Mid-June to late September**
Difficulty Rating:	**3**
Scenic Rating:	**8**

Special Attractions

■ 4WD alternative to the railroad grade route to Marshall Pass.
■ Very good views, especially as the summit is approached.
■ Access to good backcountry campsites, fishing, and many hiking trails.

Description

This route is narrower, rougher, and scenically more varied than the main road to Marshall Pass, which follows the old railroad grade (South-Central Trail #16). However, while not suitable for passenger vehicles, it offers little difficulty to a 4WD vehicle.

The trail starts at Mears Junction, which is the intersection of US 285 and County/FR 200. This was the junction of two

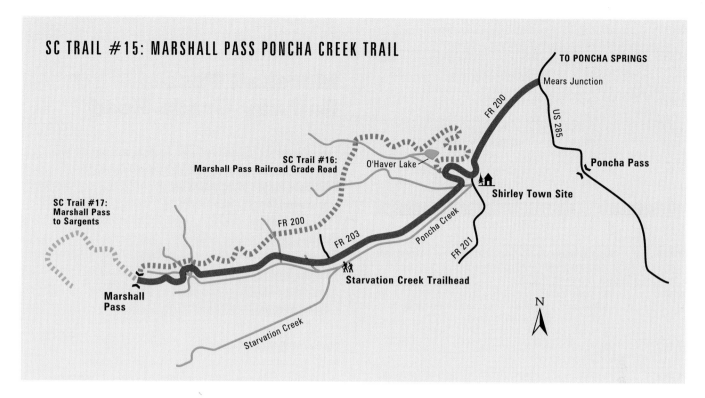

SC TRAIL #15: MARSHALL PASS PONCHA CREEK TRAIL

of Otto Mears's toll roads and is about 5 miles south of Poncha Springs and 2.4 miles north of Poncha Pass.

From the turnoff onto FR 203, the track gets progressively narrower and rougher, though it remains suitable for passenger vehicles in dry conditions. After Starvation Creek, creek crossings and the rougher road make a high-clearance vehicle necessary.

FR 203 offers numerous undeveloped campsites beside Poncha Creek for the first six miles after its intersection with County/FR 200. From this point, the trail starts its ascent toward the pass, and camping possibilities become scarce. Eventually, the road departs from the creek to make the final climb through a series of alpine meadows, offering spectacular views before reaching the pass.

There are some very good backcountry campsites and numerous fishing spots beside Poncha Creek. For those who prefer more of the comforts of home, the particularly scenic O'Haver Lake offers a developed U.S. Forest Service campground with access for RVs and camper trailers. A number of hiking trails run through the area, including the Colorado Trail and the Continental Divide Trail.

Old railroad bridge over Poncha Creek

Current Road Conditions
San Isabel National Forest
Salida Ranger District
325 West Rainbow Boulevard, Salida, CO 81201
(719) 539-3591

Map References
USFS Gunnison NF
       San Isabel NF
USGS Chaffee County #3
       Saguache County #2
Trails Illustrated, #139
The Roads of Colorado, p. 102
Colorado Atlas & Gazetteer, pp. 69-70

Route Directions

▼ 0.0		At Mears Junction, zero trip meter and turn from US 285 onto County/FR 200 and proceed west across cattle guard.
11.2 ▲		Cross cattle guard and end at intersection with US 285.

GPS: N 38°26.89' W 106°06.40'

▼ 1.8	SO	Railway bridge ruins on left.
9.4 ▲	SO	Railway bridge ruins on right.
▼ 2.2	TR	Shirley town site on left. Turn onto FR 202.
9.0 ▲	TL	Onto County 200.
▼ 2.6	SO	Camping on right and left.
8.6 ▲	SO	Camping on right and left.
▼ 3.1	TL	Toward Poncha Creek on FR 200. O'Haver Lake is 0.5 miles straight ahead on FR 202, with fishing access and developed camping. South-Central Trail #16: Marshall Pass Railroad Grade Road (FR 200) is to the right.
8.1 ▲	TR	Onto FR 202.

GPS: N 38°25.37' W 106°08.45'

▼ 3.9	SO	Track on right. Beaver Creek sign.
7.3 ▲	SO	Track on left. Beaver Creek sign.
▼ 4.1	BR	Intersection. Signpost reads "Via Poncha Creek 7 - FR 203." Numerous good backcountry camping spots are all along Poncha Creek.
7.1 ▲	BL	Intersection.

GPS: N 38°24.92' W 106°08.31'

▼ 6.5		SO	Trailhead for Starvation Creek walking trail.
	4.7 ▲	SO	Trailhead for Starvation Creek walking trail.
▼ 6.7		SO	Track on right is 0.25 miles in length with additional camping spots.
	4.5 ▲	SO	Track on left.
▼ 7.7		SO	Cross over Tent Creek.
	3.5 ▲	SO	Cross over Tent Creek.
▼ 8.2		SO	Track on left down to Poncha Creek and numerous campsites down below the road.
	3.0 ▲	SO	Track on right.
▼ 8.6		SO	Cross over creek. Slightly further, there's a short track on the right and four campsites.
	2.6 ▲	SO	Track on left, then cross over creek.

GPS: N 38°23.70′ W106°12.50

▼ 9.9		SO	Cross over Ouray Creek
	1.3 ▲	SO	Cross over Ouray Creek.
▼ 10.0		SO	Camping on right and left in grassy areas, then cross through Poncha Creek.
	1.2 ▲	SO	Cross through Poncha Creek.
▼ 10.1		SO	Open meadow on left with scenic views of valley and Sangre de Cristo mountain range to the east. No vehicle access.
	1.1 ▲	SO	Open meadow on right with scenic views.
▼ 10.2		SO	Track on left to campsite.
	1.0 ▲	SO	Track on right to campsite.
▼ 10.6		SO	4WD track on left (203.1A) to Starvation Creek walking trail. This side trip leads 1.6 miles to TR 1408, which loops back to Marshall Pass after 6.6 miles. At the 1.8 mile point there is a scenic overlook. GPS: N 38°22.96′ W 106°13.19′.
	0.6 ▲	SO	Track on right to scenic overlooks.

GPS: N 38°23.53′ W 106°14.22′

▼ 11.1		TL	Intersection with FR 200 (South-Central Trail #16: Marshall Pass Railroad Grade Road). Track on left is the Colorado Trail.
	0.1 ▲	TR	FR 200 continues straight ahead.

GPS: N 38°23.50′ W 106°14.75′

▼ 11.2			Summit of Marshall Pass. Zero trip meter. South-Central Trail #17: Marshall Pass to Sargents continues to Sargents.
	0.0 ▲		Summit of Marshall Pass. Zero trip meter.

GPS: N 38°23.50′ W 106°14.85′

Marshall Pass Railway Grade Road

Starting Point:	**Mears Junction at US 285 and FR 200,**
	5 miles south of Poncha Springs
Finishing Point:	**Marshall Pass**
Total Mileage:	**13.4**
Unpaved Mileage:	**13.4**
Driving Time:	**1/2 hour**
Pass Elevation:	**10,842 feet**
Usually Open:	**Late May to mid-October**
Difficulty Rating:	**1**
Scenic Rating:	**7**

Special Attractions

■ Easy, scenic road along a historic railroad grade.

■ Developed campground and good fishing at picturesque O'Haver Lake.

■ Provides a loop route between Marshall Pass and Mears Junction, when combined with South-Central #15: Marshall Pass Poncha Creek Trail.

History

This pass is named for Lieutenant William L. Marshall, who discovered it while on the Wheeler survey expedition in 1873. Reportedly, he was suffering from a toothache and sought a quicker route back to Denver and relief from a dentist!

In 1877, Otto Mears constructed a wagon road to Gunnison across the pass from his Poncha Pass toll road. It served as

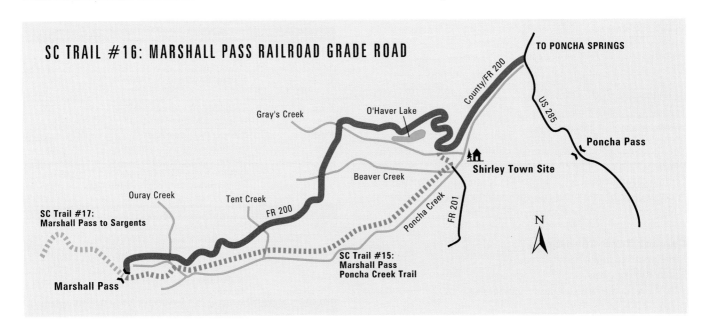

SC TRAIL #16: MARSHALL PASS RAILROAD GRADE ROAD

a stagecoach route until the opening of the railroad and was used by President Grant in 1880.

Mears sold the road to the Denver & Rio Grande Railroad. The Denver & Rio Grande was embroiled in a classic railroad battle during the early 1880s in its race to be first to link the Arkansas Valley and the Gunnison Basin area. The Denver, South Park & Pacific Railroad chose a route that necessitated the construction of the famous Alpine Tunnel (South-Central Trail #8).

With the aid of twenty-three snowsheds to protect it from the elements, a Denver & Rio Grande narrow-gauge railway won the battle by using the Marshall Pass route and commenced operations in 1881. It continued in operation until 1953; the tracks were dismantled in 1955. A post office was located at the station at the top of the pass, which continued to operate until 1952. President Taft was probably the most famous passenger to cross the pass by train.

Description

This route follows the old railroad grade and is easier than the alternative route via Poncha Creek (South-Central Trail #15). The route is unpaved but wide and well graded. It is suitable for RVs and trailers making their way to the campground at O'Haver Lake or across Marshall Pass on County 200.

The trail starts at Mears Junction, which is the intersection of US 285 and County/FR 200. Once the junction of two of Otto Mears's toll roads, the intersection is located about 5 miles south of Poncha Springs and 2.4 miles north of Poncha Pass.

O'Haver Lake offers good fishing and a developed U.S. Forest Service campground with access for RVs and camper trailers. A number of hiking trails run through the area, including the Colorado Trail and the Continental Divide Trail.

Current Road Conditions

San Isabel National Forest
Salida Ranger District
325 West Rainbow Boulevard, Salida, CO 81201
(719) 539-3591

Map References

USFS Gunnison NF
San Isabel NF
USGS Chaffee County #3
Saguache County #2
Trails Illustrated, #139
The Roads of Colorado, p. 102
Colorado Atlas & Gazetteer, pp. 69-70

Route Directions

▼ 0.0   At Mears Junction zero trip meter and turn from US 285 onto County/FR 200 heading west across cattle guard.

Marshall Pass summit

13.4 ▲		Cross cattle guard and end at intersection with US 285.
GPS: N 38°26.89' W 106°06.40'		
▼ 2.2	TR	Shirley town site. Public toilets on left. Turn right onto FR 202.
11.2 ▲	TL	Turn left onto County/FR 200. Shirley town site and public toilets on right.
▼ 3.1	TR	Intersection with County/FR 200. O'Haver Lake is straight ahead, with fishing access and developed camping. South-Central #15: Marshall Pass Poncha Creek Trail is to the left.
10.3 ▲	TL	Intersection with FR 202. O'Haver Lake is to the right. South-Central #15: Marshall Pass Poncha Creek Trail is straight ahead.
GPS: N 38°25.37' W 106°08.45'		
▼ 4.8	SO	Seasonal closure gate. Track on right is County 204.
8.6 ▲	SO	Track on left is County 204. Seasonal closure gate.
▼ 5.5	SO	O'Haver Lake on left below road.
7.9 ▲	SO	O'Haver Lake on right below road.
▼ 7.0	SO	Cross over Gray's Creek.
6.4 ▲	SO	Cross over Gray's Creek.
▼ 9.9	SO	Cross over Tent Creek.
3.5 ▲	SO	Cross over Tent Creek.
▼ 10.3	SO	Track on right.
3.1 ▲	SO	Track on left.
▼ 12.1	SO	Old railway embankment across Ouray Creek.
1.3 ▲	SO	Old railway embankment across Ouray Creek.
▼ 13.0	SO	Hiking trail on right to South Fooses Creek and Monarch Pass.
0.4 ▲	SO	Hiking trail on left to South Fooses Creek and Monarch Pass.
▼ 13.1	SO	Marshall Pass trailhead sign and public toilets on left.
0.3 ▲	SO	Marshall Pass trailhead sign and public toilets on right.
▼ 13.3	SO	Road on left is South-Central Trail #15: Marshall Pass Poncha Creek Trail. Track on left is the Colorado Trail.
0.1 ▲	BL	Track on right is the Colorado Trail. Then, South-Central Trail #15: Marshall Pass Poncha Creek Trail is on right.
▼ 13.4		Summit of Marshall Pass. Zero trip meter. South-Central Trail #17: Marshall Pass to Sargents continues to Sargents.
0.0 ▲		Marshall Pass summit. Zero trip meter.
GPS: N 38°23.50' W 106°14.85'		

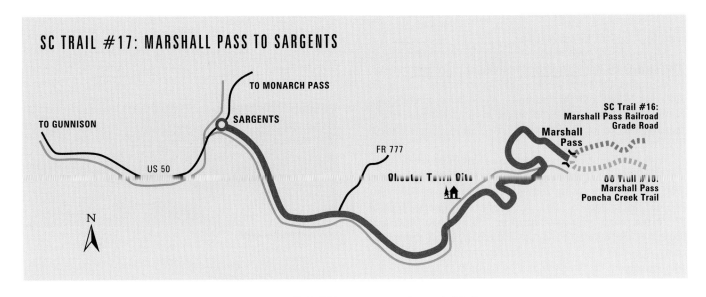

Marshall Pass to Sargents

Starting Point:	Marshall Pass
Finishing Point:	Sargents
Total Mileage:	16.3 miles
Unpaved Mileage:	16.3 miles
Driving Time:	3/4 hour
Pass Elevation:	10,846 feet
Usually Open:	Late May to late October
Difficulty Rating:	1
Scenic Rating:	5

Special Attractions

■ Northern access to Marshall Pass.
■ Steamtrain water tank in Sargents.

Description

The two routes between Mears Junction and Marshall Pass join at the summit. FR 243 continues along the old railroad grade into Sargents. This section of the journey runs through gentle, rolling countryside and ranch land with many stands of aspens adding color in the fall.

At Sargents, there is an old wooden water tank that used to service the steam locomotives that chugged up Marshall Pass from 1881 to 1953.

Current Road Conditions

San Isabel National Forest
Salida Ranger District
325 West Rainbow Boulevard, Salida, CO 81201
(719) 539-3591

Map References

USFS Gunnison NF

USGS San Isabel NF
Saguache County #1
Saguache County #2

Trails Illustrated, #139
The Roads of Colorado, p. 102
Colorado Atlas & Gazetteer, p. 69

Route Directions

▼ 0.0	SO	From the summit of Marshall Pass, zero trip meter and proceed west across cattle guard. FR 243 sign. Track on right.
16.3 ▲	SO	Track on left, then San Isabel National Forest sign and cattle guard. Summit of Marshall Pass. (To continue, refer to South-Central Trail #15 or #16.)

GPS: N 38°23.50' W 106°14.85'

▼ 0.1	SO	Seasonal gate.
16.2 ▲	SO	Seasonal gate.
▼ 0.9	SO	Track on left.
15.4 ▲	SO	Track on right.
▼ 1.2	SO	Track on left.
15.1 ▲	SO	Track on right.
▼ 3.8	SO	Track on left for hiking, horses, and snowmobiles.
12.5 ▲	SO	Track on right for non-motorized vehicles.
▼ 4.2	SO	Cattle guard.
12.0 ▲	SO	Cattle guard.
▼ 5.9	SO	Cross Millswitch Creek. Two tracks (closed) on left.
10.4 ▲	SO	Two tracks (closed) on right. Cross Millswitch Creek.
▼ 8.1	SO	Track on right to site of Chester
8.1 ▲	SO	Track on left to site of Chester.

GPS: N 38°22.28' W 106°18.45'

▼ 10.9	TL	Seasonal gate. Intersection with road on right.
5.4 ▲	TR	Intersection and seasonal gate. Take FR 243 toward Marshall Pass.

GPS: N 38°22.20' W 106°20.62'

▼ 11.4	SO	Cattle guard.
4.9 ▲	SO	Cattle guard. Entering National Forest sign.
▼ 11.9	SO	Sign: "Indian Creek." Road on right is County 35W. (You are on County XX32.)
4.4 ▲	SO	County 35W on left goes to a network of 4WD tracks and the Pinnacle Mine.
▼ 16.3	SO	End at intersection with US 50 in Sargents.

0.0 ▲   At intersection of US 50 and County XX32 (FR 243) in Sargents, zero trip meter and proceed along the county road toward Marshall Pass.

GPS: N 38°24.46' W 106°24.90'

Cochetopa Pass Road

Starting Point:	**Saguache Junction at the intersection of US 285 and Colorado 114**
Finishing Point:	**Los Piños Pass Road at the intersection of NN 14 and 15 GG**
Total Mileage:	**39.6 miles**
Unpaved Mileage:	**18.9 miles**
Driving Time:	**1 1/4 hours**
Pass Elevation:	**10,032 feet**
Usually Open:	**Always open**
Difficulty Rating:	**1**
Scenic Rating:	**5**

Special Attractions

■ Easy, historic pass road.

■ Access to a network of 4WD trails.

History

"Cochetopa" is the Ute word for "pass or gate of the buffalo." The Utes used the pass for centuries before the first documented crossing by the Spanish in 1779. It was frequently used by traders, trappers, and early explorers before the days of white settlement.

Cochetopa Pass's relatively gentle grades made it suitable for wagons; the first vehicles to cross the Continental Divide in Colorado were the wagons of Antoine Robidoux in 1825. Subsequently, parties exploring the area frequently used the pass. The gentle grades of the area allowed for a variety of routes across the Divide. In 1853, the expeditions of Frémont, Gunnison, and

A section of trail typical of the Cochetopa Pass route

Beale each traveled a different route. Use of the pass increased as miners and settlers moved through the area.

John Lawrence built a road over the pass in 1869, and from that time, the route carried a regular stagecoach mail run. Otto Mears further improved it as a toll road in 1875, providing access to Silverton and Gunnison from his Poncha Pass toll road.

Description

The pass road remains an easy journey on a well-maintained road. The east side of the pass offers better scenery, with a varied environment of rock formations, pine forest, and open fields. On the west side of the pass, there is a broad view across Cochetopa Park to the rugged San Juan Mountains rising above Lake City.

This area has an extensive network of side roads (including South-Central Trail #19) that covers a large expanse of national forest, offering the curious four-wheeler plenty of exploring along little-used tracks through mainly gentle, rolling countryside.

Current Road Conditions

Gunnison National Forest
Taylor River District
216 North Colorado, Gunnison, CO 81230
(970) 641-0471

Map References

USFS Rio Grande NF
        Gunnison NF
USGS Saguache County #1
Trails Illustrated, #139
The Roads of Colorado, pp. 117-118
Colorado Atlas & Gazetteer, pp. 69-70

Route Directions

▼ 0.0			From Saguache, at the junction of US 285 and Colorado 114, zero trip meter and proceed west on Colorado 114.
	20.7 ▲		End at intersection of US 285 and Colorado 114.
GPS: N 38°05.33' W 106°08.50'			
▼ 1.2		SO	Ute Pass turnoff on right.
	19.5 ▲	SO	Ute Pass turnoff on left.
▼ 10.4		SO	Stay on Colorado 114. Sargents turnoff on right.
	10.3 ▲	SO	Road to Sargents on left.
▼ 20.0		SO	Squaw Creek (30 CC) sign on left.
	0.7 ▲	SO	Squaw Creek (30 CC) sign on right.
▼ 20.7		TL	Turn onto County NN14. Signs to Luders Creek CG, Cochetopa Pass, and Dome Lakes. Zero trip meter.
	0.0 ▲		Continue toward Saguache.
GPS: N 38°07.94' W 106°27.73'			
▼ 0.0			Continue straight ahead on NN 14 toward Cochetopa Pass. Unpaved.
	5.4 ▲	TR	Turn onto Colorado 114. Paved.
▼ 1.6		SO	Cattle guard. Travel through Rabbit Canyon.
	3.8 ▲	SO	Cattle guard. Travel through Rabbit Canyon.
▼ 5.4		BL	South-Central Trail #19: Taylor Canyon Trail (FR 768) on right. Zero trip meter.
	0.0 ▲		Proceed straight ahead on NN-14.
GPS: N 38°09.55' W 106°32.70'			
▼ 0.0			Proceed straight ahead on NN 14 toward Cochetopa Pass.
	4.8 ▲	BR	South-Central Trail #19: Taylor Canyon Trail (FR 768) on left. Zero trip meter.

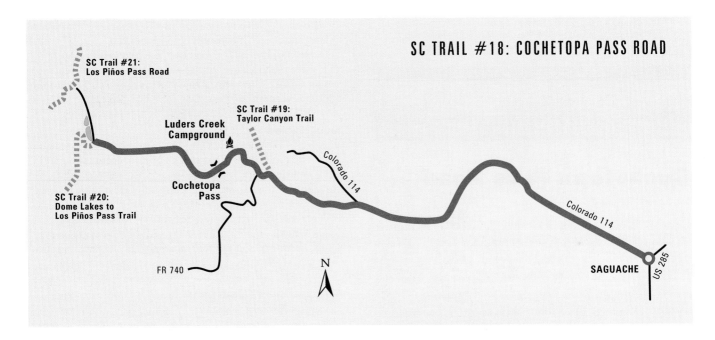

▼ 0.6		TR	Intersection with FR 740 to Windy Point.
	4.2 ▲	TL	Intersection with FR 740 to Windy Point.
▼ 2.9		SO	FR 768 on right is an alternative way to Taylor Canyon.
	1.9 ▲	SO	FR 768 on left is an alternative way to Taylor Canyon.
▼ 3.0		SO	Luders Creek Campground on right.
	1.8 ▲	SO	Luders Creek Campground on left.
▼ 4.4		SO	Firewood collection area on left.
	0.4 ▲	SO	Firewood collection area on right.
▼ 4.8		SO	Track on left. Cattle guard. Then Cochetopa Pass marker. Zero trip meter.
	0.0 ▲		Continue along track.

GPS: N 38°09.77′ W 106°35.99′

▼ 0.0			Proceed along track.
	8.7 ▲	SO	Cochetopa Pass marker, then cattle guard and track on left. Zero trip meter.
▼ 1.5		SO	4WD track on left.
	7.2 ▲	SO	4WD track on right.
▼ 1.7		SO	4WD track on left.
	7.0 ▲	SO	4WD track on right.
▼ 2.3		SO	Cattle guard.
	6.4 ▲	SO	Cattle guard.
▼ 3.2		SO	Track on right.
	5.5 ▲	SO	Track on left.
▼ 4.6		SO	Cattle guard.
	4.1 ▲	SO	Cattle guard.
▼ 5.2		SO	Cattle guard.
	3.5 ▲	SO	Cattle guard.
▼ 6.1		SO	17 FF (FR 787) on left.
	2.6 ▲	SO	17 FF (FR 787) on right.

GPS: N 38°10.76′ W 106°41.05′

▼ 7.2		SO	17 GG (FR 804) on right.
	1.5 ▲	SO	17 GG (FR 804) on left.
▼ 8.7			End at intersection with 15 GG on left (South-Central Trail #20: Dome Lakes to Los Piños Pass Trail).
	0.0 ▲		At intersection of NN 14 and 15 GG near Dome Lakes, zero trip meter and proceed southeast toward Cochetopa Pass.

GPS: N 38°11.29′ W 106°43.54′

Taylor Canyon Trail

Starting Point:	**Intersection of Cochetopa Pass Road (County NN 14) and FR 768**
Finishing Point:	**Intersection of Colorado 114 and County 31 CC**
Total Mileage:	**9.8 miles**
Unpaved Mileage:	**9.8 miles**
Driving Time:	**1 hour**
Highest Elevation:	**10,180 feet**
Usually Open:	**Late June to early November**
Difficulty Rating:	**2**
Scenic Rating:	**8**

Special Attractions
- Little-used, varied 4WD trail in a scenic setting.
- Good backcountry camping.
- Spring wildflowers.

Description
Taylor Canyon is a little-used side road from Cochetopa Pass Road. It offers an endless selection of good backcountry camping spots.

The route commences at the intersection of FR 770 and Cochetopa Pass Road and stretches through rolling grasslands and pine and aspen forest before traveling through the very scenic rock formations of the canyon. The area is carpeted with wildflowers in late spring and early summer.

Current Road Conditions
Rio Grande National Forest

Saguache Ranger District
46525 State Hwy 114, Saguache, CO 81149
(719) 655-2547

Map References
USFS Rio Grande NF
USGS Saguache County #1
Trails Illustrated, #139
The Roads of Colorado, p. 117
Colorado Atlas & Gazetteer, p. 69

Route Directions

▼ 0.0		From Cochetopa Pass Road, turn onto FR 768. Zero trip meter and proceed toward Taylor Canyon.
GPS: N 38°09.55' W 106°32.70'		
▼ 0.3	SO	FR 750.2B on the right. Stay on FR 768.
▼ 1.6	SO	Through gated fence (leave it as you found it).
▼ 2.1	TR	T-intersection. Turn onto FR 770. (FR 768 goes to the left and winds around to rejoin NN 14 closer to Luders Creek Campground. Right goes through Taylor Canyon and eventually back to 114.)
GPS: N 38°11.12' W 106°33.12'		
▼ 2.2	SO	Another track on the left.
▼ 3.6	UT	Another track straight ahead along canyon rim. U-turn to the right down into the canyon.
GPS: N 38°11.02' W 106°31.86'		
▼ 5.4	BR	Very faint track joins in on left.
▼ 6.5	SO	Fence and gate (leave it as you found it). Rio Grande National Forest sign.
GPS: N 38°10.08' W 106°29.49'		
▼ 7.3	SO	Corral in good condition on right, then horse trough.
GPS: N 38°09.80' W 106°28.76'		
▼ 8.0	SO	Colorado 114 underpass.
GPS: N 38°09.48' W 106°28.21'		
▼ 8.1	SO	Colorado 114. Track on left rejoins Colorado 114.

Rock formations in Taylor Canyon

▼ 8.9	TR	T-intersection.
GPS: N 38°08.98' W 106°27.73'		
▼ 9.1	TR	Three-way intersection.
▼ 9.8		Cattle guard. Stop sign at Colorado 114.
GPS: N 38°08.87' W 106°28.01'		

SOUTH-CENTRAL REGION TRAIL #20

Dome Lakes to Los Piños Pass Trail

Starting Point:	**Intersection of Cochetopa Pass Road (NN 14) and County 15 GG**
Finishing Point:	**Intersection of FR 790 and FR 788, 1 mile east of Los Piños Pass**
Total Mileage:	**29.5 miles**
Unpaved Mileage:	**29.5 miles**
Driving Time:	**1 1/2 hours**
Pass Elevation:	**10,200 feet**
Usually Open:	**Early June to mid-November**
Difficulty Rating:	**2**
Scenic Rating:	**7**

Special Attractions
- Fairly easy 4WD trail through attractive countryside.
- Relatively light traffic.
- Historic old stagecoach route.
- Good backcountry camping.
- Can be combined with South-Central Trail #21 to form a loop.

Description
This trail provides the option of a loop tour by using Los Piños Pass Trail (South-Central Trail #21) to return from Los Piños Pass rather than proceeding through to Lake City or north toward Gunnison.

It is an easy drive and could be confidently undertaken in most passenger cars, so long as the road is dry. Navigation is not difficult, and the region has the decided advantage over many other trails in this book of being uncrowded, except in hunting season.

SC TRAIL #20: DOME LAKES TO LOS PINOS PASS TRAIL

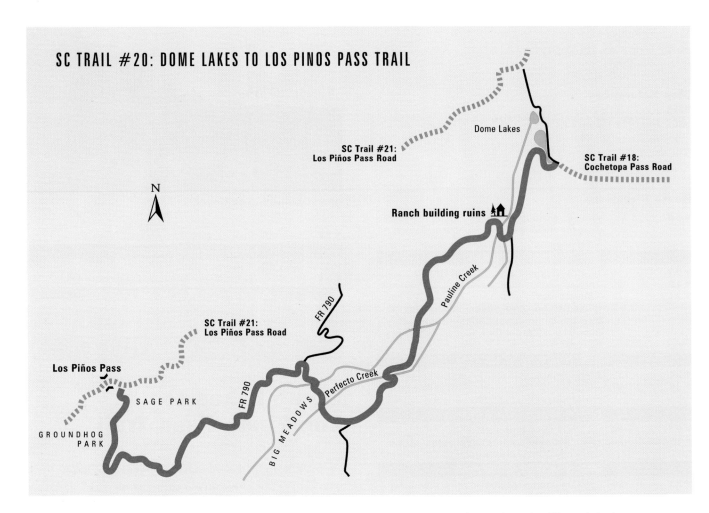

The route runs along a historic stagecoach route from Saguache to the San Juan Mountains. It travels through varied but mainly gentle, scenic countryside with broad open meadows interspersed with forest, including many stands of aspen that add to the beauty of the area in the fall.

Numerous backcountry campsites with plenty of space and good access to water and firewood are to be found along the route.

Current Road Conditions

Gunnison National Forest
Taylor River District
216 North Colorado, Gunnison, CO 81230
(970) 641-0471

Map References

USFS Gunnison NF
USGS Saguache County #1
Saguache County #3
Trails Illustrated, #139
The Roads of Colorado, pp. 116-117
Colorado Atlas & Gazetteer, p. 68

Route Directions

▼ 0.0		At intersection of 15 GG and NN 14, zero trip meter and proceed south on 15 GG

		(at southern tip of Dome Lakes).
15.9 ▲		End at intersection of 15 GG and NN 14. South-Central Trail #18: Cochetopa Pass Road commences to the right.
GPS: N 38°11.32′ W 106°43.58′		
▼ 0.8	SO	Track on right.
15.1 ▲	SO	Track on left.
▼ 0.9	SO	Access to Wild Trout Stream on right. Cattle guard.
15.0 ▲	SO	Cattle guard. Access to Wild Trout Stream on left.
▼ 2.6	SO	Cattleyards on right.
13.3 ▲	SO	Cattleyards on left.
▼ 4.0	BR	Cattle guard. Road on left is 14 DD.
11.9 ▲	BL	Road on right is 14 DD. Cattle guard.
▼ 4.4	SO	Cross over two creeks. Seasonal gate. Three old buildings on right.
11.5 ▲	SO	Three old buildings on left, then seasonal gate and cross over two creeks.
GPS: N 38°09.20′ W 106°45.66′		
▼ 7.9	SO	Historic Stage Route sign on right. Road on right is 790.1F.
8.0 ▲	SO	Road on left is 790.1F. Historic Stage Route sign on left.
GPS: N 38°08.41′ W 106°48.28′		
▼ 8.3	BL	Track on right.
7.6 ▲	BR	Track on left.
▼ 11.0	SO	Cross over Pauline Creek.
4.9 ▲	SO	Cross over Pauline Creek.
▼ 13.4	SO	Cross over Perfecto Creek.

	2.5 ▲	SO	Cross over Perfecto Creek.
▼ 13.7		SO	Cattle guard. Corral on left off in distance (0.5 mile).
	2.2 ▲	SO	Cattle guard.
▼ 15.9		TR	Road splits. Sign. Zero trip meter.
	0.0 ▲		Continue along track.

GPS: N 38°03.66' W 106°51.28'

▼ 0.0			Continue along track.
	13.6 ▲	TL	Intersection. Zero trip meter.
▼ 0.9		BR	Track forks.
	12.7 ▲	BL	Intersection.
▼ 1.4		SO	Cross over Perfecto Creek.
	12.2 ▲	SO	Cross over Perfecto Creek.
▼ 1.9		BR	Track on left.
	11.7 ▲	BL	Track on right.
▼ 2.6		SO	Track on left. Entering Big Meadows.
	11.0 ▲	SO	Track on right. Leave Big Meadows.
▼ 3.0		SO	Cross over Pauline Creek.
	10.6 ▲	SO	Cross over Pauline Creek.
▼ 3.9		TL	Onto Big Meadows Road (FR 790).
	9.7 ▲	TR	Onto FR 794. Enter Big Meadows.

GPS: N 38°05.32' W 106°53.28'

▼ 5.2		SO	Tracks on left and right.
	8.4 ▲	SO	Tracks on left and right.
▼ 6.0		SO	Cattle guard.
	7.6 ▲	SO	Cattle guard.
▼ 6.2		SO	FR 7901M on right (timber harvest road closed and gated). Entering Willow Park.
	7.4 ▲	SO	Leaving Willow Park. FR 7901M on left.
▼ 6.7		SO	Leaving Willow Park.
	6.9 ▲	SO	Entering Willow Park.
▼ 7.7		SO	Cross over East Los Piños Creek. Cebolla trailhead on left.
	5.9 ▲	SO	Cebolla trailhead on right. Cross over East Los Piños Creek.

GPS: N 38°03.64' W 106°55.94'

▼ 9.0		SO	Cross over creek.
	4.6 ▲	SO	Cross over creek.
▼ 10.0		SO	Cattle guard.
	3.6 ▲	SO	Cattle guard.
▼ 11.4		SO	Track on left. Entering Groundhog Park.
	2.2 ▲	SO	Leaving Groundhog Park. Track on right.
▼ 11.5		SO	Leaving Groundhog Park.
	2.1 ▲	SO	Entering Groundhog Park.
▼ 12.0		SO	Tracks to left and right. Continue on FR 790.
	1.6 ▲	SO	Continue on FR 790. Tracks to left and right.
▼ 13.1		SO	Seasonal closure gate.
	0.5 ▲	SO	Seasonal closure gate.
▼ 13.6			T-Intersection with South-Central Trail #21: Los Piños Pass Road (FR 788).
	0.0 ▲		At intersection of South-Central Trail #21: Los Piños Pass Road (FR 788) and Big Meadows Road (FR 790), zero trip meter and proceed along FR 790.

GPS: N 38°06.27' W 106°57.34'

Los Piños Pass Road

Starting Point:	Cathedral Junction—intersection of FR 788 (Hinsdale County 15) and Hinsdale County 5
Finishing Point:	Doyleville
Total Mileage:	44.6 miles
Unpaved Mileage:	43.3 miles
Driving Time:	1 3/4 hours
Pass Elevation:	10,200 feet
Usually Open:	Early June to mid-November
Difficulty Rating:	1
Scenic Rating:	7

Special Attractions

- Easy, scenic route.
- Aspen viewing in the fall.
- Historic stagecoach route.
- Numerous backcountry campsites.
- Can be combined with South-Central Trail #20 to form a loop.

History

Los Piños is Spanish for "the pine trees." The pass was a well-used Ute Indian trail. In 1869 the Los Piños Indian Agency was established, after various bands of Ute were relocated to this area from the San Luis Valley. This agency is now a forest service work center located on this route.

The Hayden survey party crossed the pass in 1874 on its way to examine the Cebolla Creek area. Otto Mears built the

A view of Los Piño Pass Road

Saguache and San Juan toll road over the pass road the same year. Stagecoaches ran from Saguache along this road, branching north to the Gunnison River and across to Montrose and south to Lake City.

Description

This is a delightful, easy route through pine and aspen forest and open meadows. Backcountry campsites abound, and except in hunting season, the area is lightly used.

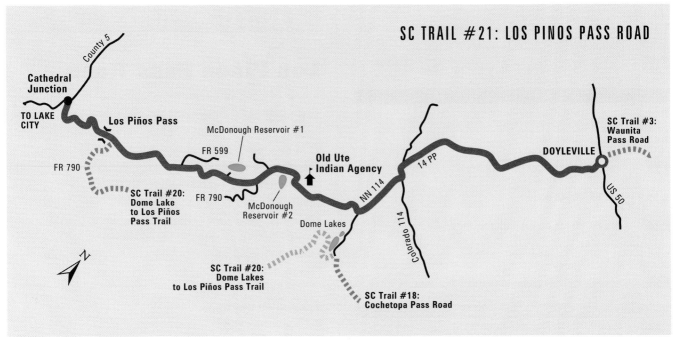

This easily navigated route starts at the intersection of Los Piños Pass Road (FR 788) and Hinsdale County 5 at Cathedral Junction. The pass is only six miles east from this point along an easy, 2WD road. Los Piños Pass is a gentle, wooded crossing.

One mile past the summit, FR 790 turns off to the right toward Dome Lakes (South-Central Trail #20). This route continues along FR 788 for another twelve miles to the old Los Piños Indian Agency before intersecting with Colorado 114. You travel north on 114 for only about a mile before turning right onto the well-maintained gravel road to Doyleville, an old Denver & Rio Grande railroad station and once small supply town on the route from Salida.

Current Road Conditions

Gunnison National Forest
Taylor River District
216 North Colorado, Gunnison, CO 81230
(970) 641-0471

Map References

USFS Gunnison NF
USGS Saguache County #1
Saguache County #3
Hinsdale County #1
Gunnison County #5
Trails Illustrated, #139
The Roads of Colorado, pp. 101, 116-117
Colorado Atlas & Gazetteer, pp. 68-69

Route Directions

▼ 0.0			At intersection of FR 788 and Hinsdale County 5 in Cathedral Junction, zero trip meter and proceed toward Los Piños Pass.
	5.7 ▲		End at intersection of FR 788 and County 5 in Cathedral Junction. Note: left goes to Lake City and right to Powderhorn and Gunnison.

GPS: N 38°05.74′ W 107°01.99′			
▼ 1.1		BL	Seasonal gate and intersection.
	4.6 ▲	BR	Seasonal gate and intersection.
GPS: N 38°05.09′ W 107°01.17′			
▼ 5.7		SO	Summit of Los Piños Pass. Zero trip meter.
	0.0 ▲		Proceed along FR 788.
GPS: N 38°06.26′ W 106°58.28′			
▼ 0.0			Proceed along FR 788.
	18.3 ▲	SO	Summit of Los Piños Pass. Zero trip meter.
▼ 0.5		SO	Track on left.
	17.8 ▲	SO	Track on right.
▼ 1.0		SO	South-Central Trail #20 (FR 790) on right.
	17.3 ▲	SO	South-Central Trail #20 (FR 790) on left.
GPS: N 38°06.27′ W 106°57.34′			
▼ 2.0		SO	Beaver pond on right. Road on right.
	16.3 ▲	SO	Road on left. Beaver pond on left.
▼ 2.6		SO	FR 599 on left.
	15.7 ▲	SO	FR 599 on right.
▼ 5.5		SO	Creek crossing.
	12.8 ▲	SO	Creek crossing.
▼ 7.2		SO	Seasonal closure gate.
	11.1 ▲	SO	Seasonal closure gate.
▼ 7.3		SO	McDonough Reservoir (0.5 mile) turnoff on left.
	11.0 ▲	SO	McDonough Reservoir (0.5 mile) turnoff on right.
▼ 7.5		SO	Track on left.
	10.8 ▲	SO	Track on right.
▼ 8.7		SO	Track on left.
	9.6 ▲	SO	Track on right.
▼ 9.5		SO	Road on right is FR 790/County Road 8 EE.
	8.8 ▲	SO	Road on left is FR 790/County Road 8 EE.
GPS: N 38°10.21′ W 106°51.18′			
▼ 11.0		SO	Historic Stage Route sign. FR 808 on left (gated-no access).
	7.3 ▲	SO	FR 808 on right. Historic Stage Route sign.
▼ 11.9		SO	Mine remains on left. Leaving National Forest sign.
	6.4 ▲	SO	Entering National Forest sign. Mine remains on right.

| ▼ 12.7 | SO | Old Agency Guard Station. Cattle guard. |
| 5.6 ▲ | SO | Cattle guard. Old Agency Guard Station. |

GPS: N 38°11.95' W 106°49.69'

| ▼ 18.3 | TL | T-Intersection with NN 14 and KK 14. Zero trip meter. |
| 0.0 ▲ | | Proceed along KK 14. |

GPS: N 38°13.99' W 106°44.80'

| ▼ 0.0 | | Proceed along NN 14. |
| 20.6 ▲ | TR | Onto KK 14. Zero trip meter. |

| ▼ 2.5 | SO | Moss Lake on left. |
| 18.1 ▲ | SO | Moss Lake on right. |

| ▼ 3.3 | TL | Cattle guard. T-Intersection with Colorado 114. |
| 17.3 ▲ | TR | Intersection with NN 14. |

GPS: N 38°16.63' W 106°44.10'

| ▼ 4.6 | TR | Onto 14 PP to Doyleville. |
| 16.0 ▲ | TL | Onto Colorado 114. |

| ▼ 13.9 | SO | Creek crossing and cattle guard. |
| 6.7 ▲ | SO | Cattle guard and creek crossing. |

| ▼ 14.4 | SO | 18 VV on left. |
| 6.2 ▲ | SO | 18 VV on right. |

| ▼ 18.1 | SO | 18 VV on left. Cattle guard. |
| 2.5 ▲ | SO | Cattle guard. 18 VV on right. |

| ▼ 20.6 | | Doyleville. End at T-Intersection with US 50. |
| 0.0 ▲ | | At intersection of US 50 and County 45 in Doyleville, zero trip meter and proceed south along County 45. |

GPS: N 38°27.14' W 106°36.48'

SOUTH-CENTRAL REGION TRAIL #22

Schofield Pass and Devil's Punchbowl Trail

Starting Point:	**Mount Crested Butte**
Finishing Point:	**Marble**
Total Mileage:	**21.2 miles**
Unpaved Mileage:	**20.1 miles**
Driving Time:	**3 1/2 hours**
Pass Elevation:	**10,707 feet**
Usually Open:	**Late July to mid-September**
Difficulty Rating:	**6**
Scenic Rating:	**10**

Special Attractions

■ Famous and dangerous 4WD trail along an old stagecoach route.

■ Historic mill on Crystal River.

■ Ghost towns of Gothic and Crystal and town site of Schofield.

■ Can be combined with South-Central Trail #25: Kebler Pass Road to form a loop.

History

Schofield Pass and the town of Schofield were named for Judge B. F. Schofield, who founded the town in the late 1870s.

The Ute Indians used the pass, and they led the first white men across it. Prospectors traveled the pass frequently during the 1870s, although the first big strikes in the area did not occur until around 1880. In the mid-1870s, the Hayden survey party crossed Schofield Pass and plotted it on their map.

By the early 1880s, the cities of Marble, Crystal, Schofield, and Gothic were all at their peak. The pass road was heavily used but was never improved beyond a rough, narrow wagon road. Nonetheless, a stage ran from Crested Butte to Crystal for a number of years.

This small road's political apogee came when it was traveled by President Ulysses S. Grant during his visit to many of the mining camps in the area, accompanied by John Routt, the last appointed governor of the territory and the first elected governor of the state.

Special Note on the Difficulty of this Road

The road through Crystal River Canyon down to the area known as the Devil's Punch Bowl is known as one of the most dangerous 4WD roads in Colorado. The road's reputation is well deserved, in light of the alarming number of fatalities that have occurred on it. The most tragic was in 1970, when seven members of one family perished when their Suburban plunged from the shelf road down a two-hundred-foot drop-off and into the river. Many accidents have taken additional lives in the years since. Seven vehicles slipped off the road in the summer of 1997, and at least one of these accidents resulted in fatalities.

It is hard to dispute statistics like these, but most experienced four-wheelers will be puzzled by such a record. Certainly the road is very narrow and drops off precipitously into the

Devil's Punchbowl

river; but the surface is sound, and the road is no narrower, nor the drop more frightening, than that of many other 4WD roads in the state. Undoubtedly most accidents here must be caused by a combination of factors: the driver's inexperience, the onset of fear when committed beyond the point of turning back, and perhaps even carelessness or a failure to appreciate the very small margin for error.

Another potential hazard is caused by having to cross the river immediately before starting down the canyon. Even in late summer, the water is likely to be bumper-deep and thoroughly soak your brakes. Therefore, follow the recommendation of the large sign erected by the Forest Service and check that your brakes are working properly before proceeding down the canyon. Also, do not be tempted to get out of your vehicle halfway down the canyon to take a photo and leave your vehicle reliant on the park gear position.

As is the case with all the more difficult roads in this book, you should not attempt this route until you have traveled many other less-difficult roads and are certain that you will not become flustered by the steep drop-off only a foot or so from your wheels. Less-experienced drivers are well advised not to attempt this route in a full-sized vehicle.

In spite of the risk it involves, this is a very rewarding trail. If you decide to give it a go, remember, take it very slowly and carefully.

Description

The route starts in the ski resort of Mount Crested Butte and follows a well-maintained gravel road to Gothic and on to the summit of Schofield Pass beyond Emerald Lake. The low, wooded summit does not offer the views that are associated with most pass summits. The road to the pass is suitable for a passenger car.

From that point on until about two miles out of Marble, stream crossings and rocky sections necessitate a high-clearance vehicle.

About 2.75 miles past the summit, you cross through a wide section of the South Fork of the Crystal River. In the later part

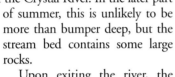

of summer, this is unlikely to be more than bumper deep, but the stream bed contains some large rocks.

Upon exiting the river, the road curves and immediately starts the narrow, steep descent down Crystal River Canyon. Shortly after commencing the downhill run, you are confronted with a large, imbedded rock in the center of the road. You have the choice of squeezing past on the side of the rock wall or on the side of the drop-off. The road suffers from snow and rock slides, and it is not unusual to find it impassable—or at least requiring some clearance work.

At the bottom of the canyon are the Devil's Punch Bowl and, less than two miles further, the township of Crystal.

One of the most-photographed sights in Colorado—the powerhouse overhanging the Crystal River (called the Dead Horse Mill or the Crystal Mill)—is about a quarter of a mile past Crystal on the left. The mill was built by G. C. Eaton and supplied power to the local mines. A water wheel turned an air compressor to supply air for drilling and power for a stamp mill and sawmill.

The road continues past the very scenic Beaver Lake and on into Marble.

While most years this road is open for about eight weeks, sometimes the snow does not melt and the road is closed all summer.

Current Road Conditions

White River National Forest
Sopris Ranger District
620 Main Street, Box 309, Carbondale, CO 81623
(970) 963-2266

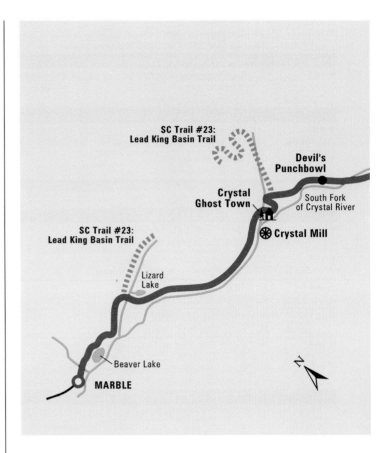

Map References

USFS Gunnison NF
USGS Gunnison County #1
　　　　 Gunnison County #2
Trails Illustrated, #128, #131, #133
The Roads of Colorado, p. 84
Colorado Atlas & Gazetteer, pp. 45-46, 58

Route Directions

▼ 0.0			In Mt. Crested Butte, where the Grand Butte Hotel walkway crosses over Gothic Road, zero trip meter and proceed north along Gothic Road.
	10.6 ▲		End in Mt. Crested Butte town center.
		GPS: N 38°53.97' W 106°57.97'	
▼ 1.1		SO	End of pavement. Follow main road.
	9.5 ▲	SO	Paved. Follow main road.
		GPS: N 38°54.77' W 106°57.74'	
▼ 1.7		SO	Cattle guard. Enter National Forest (FR 317) and proceed toward Gothic.
	8.9 ▲	SO	Leave National Forest and proceed toward Crested Butte. Cattle guard.
▼ 3.3		SO	Cattle guard.
	7.3 ▲	SO	Cattle guard.
▼ 4.7		SO	Bridge over East River.
	5.9 ▲	SO	Bridge over East River.
▼ 5.0		SO	Bridge.
	5.6 ▲	SO	Bridge.
▼ 5.1		SO	Gothic ghost town: general store and visitor center.
	5.4 ▲	SO	Gothic ghost town.
▼ 5.7		SO	Track on right to Judd Falls, Trailriders, and Cooper Creek trailheads.

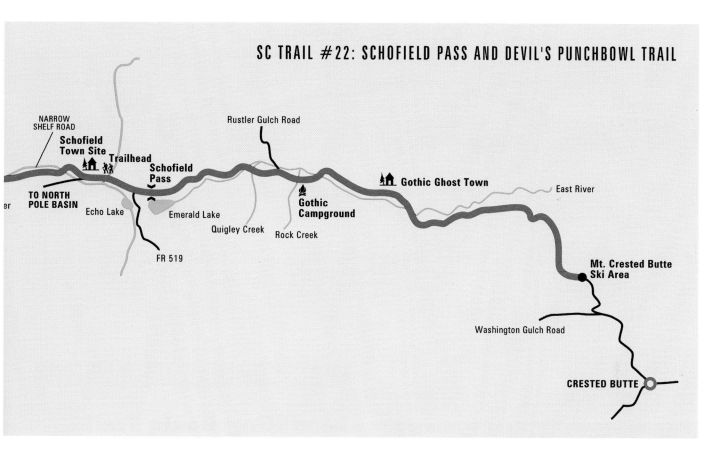

4.9 ▲	SO	Track on left to Judd Falls, Trailriders, and Cooper Creek trailheads.	
▼ 6.5	SO	Turnoff to USFS Avery Peak picnic grounds on right.	
4.1 ▲	SO	Turnoff to USFS Avery Peak picnic grounds on left.	
▼ 6.7	SO	Seasonal gate and bridge.	
3.9 ▲	SO	Bridge and seasonal gate.	
▼ 7.0	SO	USFS Gothic Campground on left. Then track to Wash Gulch on left.	
3.6 ▲	SO	Track to Wash Gulch, then USFS Gothic Campground on right.	
▼ 7.6	SO	Track to Rustler Gulch on right.	
3.0 ▲	SO	Track to Rustler Gulch on left.	
▼ 8.0	SO	Track on left.	
2.6 ▲	SO	Track on right.	
▼ 8.8	SO	Track on left.	
1.8 ▲	SO	Track on right.	
▼ 9.8	SO	Track on left to Emerald Lake.	
0.8 ▲	SO	Track on right to Emerald Lake.	
▼ 10.6	SO	Schofield Pass summit. Paradise Basin track on left, trailhead to Gothic on right. Zero trip meter.	
0.0 ▲		Continue on main road toward Gothic and Crested Butte. Leaving White River National Forest and entering Gunnison National Forest.	

GPS: N 39°00.93' W 107°02.80'

▼ 0.0		Continue straight ahead toward Marble. Leaving Gunnison National Forest and entering White River National Forest.	
4.4 ▲	SO	Schofield Pass summit. Paradise Basin track on right, trailhead to Gothic on left. Zero trip meter.	
▼ 0.7	SO	Baroni Mine portal on right. Then cross through creek.	
3.7 ▲	SO	Cross through creek. Baroni Mine portal on left.	

▼ 1.1	SO	Track on left to North Pole Basin.	
3.3 ▲	SO	Track on right to North Pole Basin.	
▼ 1.5	SO	Bridge over South Fork of Crystal River.	
2.9 ▲	SO	Bridge over South Fork of Crystal River.	
▼ 1.7	SO	Tracks on right.	
2.7 ▲	SO	Tracks on left.	
▼ 2.3	SO	Track on left to waterfall just off the road. Cross bridge with waterfall on right.	
2.1 ▲	SO	Waterfall on left, cross bridge. Track on right to waterfall just off the road.	
▼ 2.5	SO	Cross over creek.	
1.9 ▲	SO	Cross over creek.	
▼ 2.7	SO	Cross through river.	
1.7 ▲	SO	Cross through river.	

GPS: N 39°02.70' W 107°04.36'

▼ 2.8	SO	Tight squeeze past one large rock.	
1.6 ▲	SO	Tight squeeze past one large rock.	
▼ 2.8-3.2	SO	Very narrow and rocky descent.	
1.2-1.6 ▲	SO	Very narrow and rocky ascent.	
▼ 3.2	SO	Narrow bridge over Crystal River.	
1.2 ▲	SO	Narrow bridge over Crystal River.	

GPS: N 39°02.99' W 107°04.67'

▼ 4.4	BL	Intersection. Right goes to South-Central Trail #23: Lead King Basin Trail. Zero trip meter.	
0.0 ▲		Continue on main track toward Schofield Pass, Gothic, and Crested Butte.	

GPS: N 39°03.56' W 107°05.77'

▼ 0.0		Continue toward Crystal on FR 314.	
4.3 ▲	BR	Intersection. Left goes to South-Central Trail #23: Lead King Basin Trail. Zero trip meter.	
▼ 0.5	SO	Crystal township.	
3.8 ▲	SO	Crystal township.	

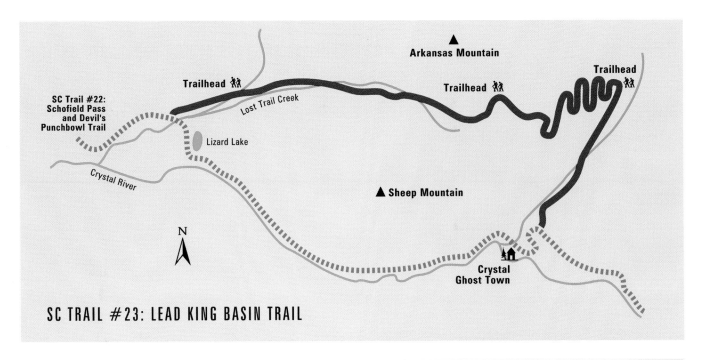

SC TRAIL #23: LEAD KING BASIN TRAIL

▼ 0.6	**SO**	Cross over Crystal River.
3.7 ▲	SO	Cross over Crystal River.
▼ 0.7	**SO**	Crystal Mill on left.
3.6 ▲	SO	Crystal Mill on right.
GPS: N 39°03.56' W 107°06.22'		
▼ 2.9	**SO**	Track on left.
1.5 ▲	SO	Track on right.
▼ 3.9	**SO**	Lizard Lake on right.
0.4 ▲	SO	Lizard Lake on left.
GPS: N 39°04.19' W 107°09.21'		
▼ 4.2	**SO**	Bridge over Lost Trail Creek.
0.1 ▲	SO	Bridge over Lost Trail Creek.
▼ 4.3	**BL**	Intersection. South-Central #23: Lead King Basin Trail (FR 315) on right. Left to Marble. Zero trip meter.
0.0 ▲		Continue along main road.
GPS: N 39°04.49' W 107°09.50'		
▼ 0.0		Proceed toward Marble.
1.9 ▲	BR	Intersection. South-Central #23: Lead King Basin Trail (FR 315) on left. Zero trip meter.
▼ 0.6	**SO**	Road on right.
1.3 ▲	SO	Road on left.
▼ 1.2	**SO**	Beaver Lake on left.
0.7 ▲	SO	Beaver Lake on right.
▼ 1.5	**TL**	Stop sign.
0.3 ▲	TR	Stop sign.
▼ 1.6	**TR**	Intersection.
0.3 ▲	TL	Intersection.
▼ 1.7	**SO**	Bridge.
0.1 ▲	SO	Bridge.
▼ 1.8	**TL/TR**	Onto 1st Street then right onto State Street.
0.1 ▲	TL/TR	Onto 1st Street then right onto Main Street (County 3/FR 315).
▼ 1.9		End at white Marble Community Church on State Street.
0.0 ▲		On State Street in Marble, go to the white Marble Community Church. Zero trip meter and proceed east.
GPS: N 39°04.25' W 107°11.30'		

Lead King Basin Trail

Starting Point:	Intersection of FR 314 and FR 315
Finishing Point:	Intersection of FR 315 and FR 314
Total Mileage:	7.7 miles
Unpaved Mileage:	7.7 miles
Driving Time:	1 3/4 hours
Elevation:	10,000 feet
Usually Open:	Late July to mid-September
Difficulty Rating:	5
Scenic Rating:	8

Special Attractions
- Abundant wildflowers in early summer.
- The challenging, narrow, and rocky section at the east end of the route.

Description
This road is a side road of Schofield Pass Road. It commences 3.7 miles west of Crystal township and 1.9 miles east of Marble and finishes 0.5 miles east of Crystal township.

Initially, FR 315 ascends from the road running alongside the Crystal River (FR 314) through pine and aspen forest. The road is bumpy with imbedded rock and drainage channels cut across it but is not difficult in dry conditions. Sections of black soil can become very boggy after rain.

A series of switchbacks is encountered in an uphill section; but the surface is firm, and the only difficulty is caused by wheel ruts worn by other vehicles.

At about the seven-mile point, the road gets more difficult as you follow the creek cascading down into the valley. The clearance between the trees and rocks is tight and a series of rock steps is challenging to negotiate. This section is more difficult if the trail is attempted from east to west.

The area is justly famous for the wildflowers that carpet the basin in July and August, and numerous aspen provide color later in the season.

Current Road Conditions

White River National Forest
Sopris Ranger District
620 Main Street, Box 309, Carbondale, CO 81623
(970) 963-2266

Map References

USFS Gunnison NF
USGS Gunnison County #1
Trails Illustrated, #128
The Roads of Colorado, p. 84
Colorado Atlas & Gazetteer, p. 46

Route Directions

▼ 0.0		At the intersection of FR 314 and FR 315 between Marble and Crystal, zero trip meter and follow sign toward Lead King Basin.
7.7 ▲		End at intersection of FR 315 and South-Central Trail #22 (FR 314) between Marble and Crystal.

GPS: N 39°04.49' W 107°09.50'

▼ 0.4	SO	Private track on left to Colorado Outward Bound School.
7.3 ▲	SO	Private track on right to Colorado Outward Bound School.
▼ 0.7	SO	North Lost Creek trailhead on left. Cross through North Lost Creek.
7.0 ▲	SO	Cross through North Lost Creek. North Lost Creek trailhead on right.
▼ 1.8	SO	Cross over creek.
5.9 ▲	SO	Cross over creek.
▼ 2.0	BL	Fork in road. Continue on FR 315.
5.7 ▲	BR	Fork in road. Continue on FR 315.

GPS: N 39°04.68' W 107°07.46'

▼ 2.3	SO	Cross through creek.
5.4 ▲	SO	Cross through creek.
▼ 3.7	BR	Track on left.
4.0 ▲	BL	Track on right.
▼ 4.0	SO	Cross through creek. Then track on left.
3.7 ▲	SO	Track on right. Cross through creek.
▼ 4.1	SO	Track on left.
3.6 ▲	SO	Track on right.
▼ 6.1	SO	Cross through creek.
1.6 ▲	SO	Cross through creek.
▼ 6.2	SO	Cross through creek.
1.5 ▲	SO	Cross through creek.
▼ 6.3	SO	Trailhead parking area on left.
1.4 ▲	SO	Trailhead parking area on right.
▼ 6.5	SO	Track on left crosses through creek.
1.2 ▲	SO	Track on right crosses through creek.
▼ 6.6	BR	Bridge over creek, then two intersections. Bear right at each.
1.1 ▲	BL	Bear left at each of two intersections. Cross bridge over creek.
▼ 6.7	SO	Cross through creek.
1.0 ▲	SO	Cross through creek.

▼ 7.7		End at intersection with FR 314. Marble and Crystal to the right. Schofield Pass, Crested Butte, and Gothic to the left.
0.0 ▲		At intersection of South-Central Trail #22 (FR 314) and FR 315, zero trip meter and proceed along FR 315.

GPS: N 39°03.56' W 107°05.77'

Ohio Pass Road

Starting Point:	**Intersection of Kebler Pass Road**
	(County 12) and Ohio Pass Road (FR 730)
Finishing Point:	**Gunnison**
Total Mileage:	**22.5 miles**
Unpaved Mileage:	**10.6 miles**
Driving Time:	**1 hour**
Pass Elevation:	**10,074 feet**
Usually Open:	**Early June to mid-November**
Difficulty Rating:	**1**
Scenic Rating:	**6**

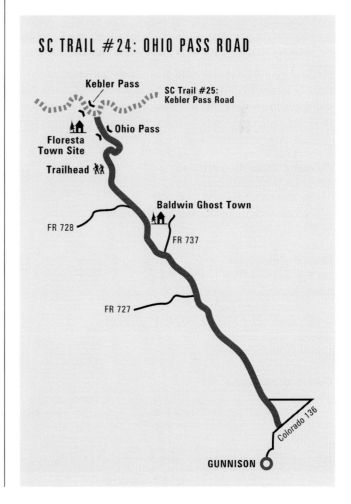

SC TRAIL #24: OHIO PASS ROAD

Special Attractions

■ Gentle, easy route that follows an old railway grade.
■ Wonderful aspen viewing in fall.
■ Town site of Baldwin.

History

A wagon road opened on this old Ute Indian route in 1880. In 1882, the Denver, South Park & Pacific Railroad started laying a spur line toward Ohio Pass. However, the ore ran out before construction was completed, and the tracks were never laid beyond Ohio Pass. The railway was used to haul coal from the area for many years and was purchased by the Denver & Rio Grande Railroad in 1937. By the mid-1940s the tracks were being torn up.

Description

Part of the route followed by FR 730 runs along the old railway grade. The route is an easy 2WD road that offers excellent views of the West Elk Mountains. The road trav-

One of the many wonderful stands of aspens along Ohio Pass Road

els through a forest thick with aspen, which turns into a sea of gold in the fall. After nearly 9 miles, the road passes the old town site of Baldwin just before becoming a paved surface. It follows the Ohio Creek into the valley before connecting to Colorado 135 about 3.5 miles from Gunnison.

Current Road Conditions

Gunnison National Forest
Taylor River District
216 North Colorado, Gunnison, CO 81230
(970) 641-0471

Map References

USFS Gunnison NF
USGS Gunnison County #2
Gunnison County #4
Trails Illustrated, #132, #133, #134
The Roads of Colorado, p. 100
Colorado Atlas & Gazetteer, p. 58

Route Directions

▼ 0.0		At intersection of County 12 (Kebler Pass Road) and FR 730 (Ohio Pass Road) zero trip meter and proceed south along FR 730 toward Gunnison.
10.6 ▲		End at intersection with County 12, which is also South-Central Trail #25: Kebler Pass Road.
GPS: N 38°51.16' W 107°05.81'		
▼ 4.0	SO	Beaver Ponds trailhead on right.

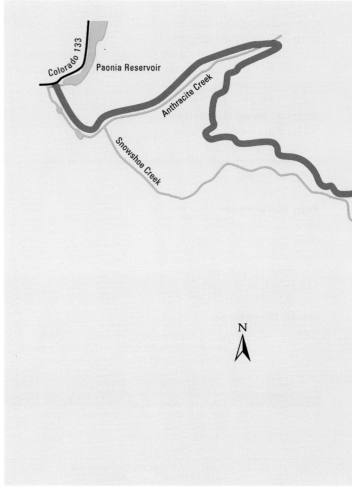

6.6 ▲	SO	Beaver Ponds trailhead on left.
▼ 7.9	SO	FR 728 on right.
2.7 ▲	SO	FR 728 on left.
▼ 8.7	SO	Town site of Baldwin on left.
1.9 ▲	SO	Town site of Baldwin on right.
▼ 10.6	SO	FR 737 on left to Carbon Creek and Squaw Gulch, which eventually dead-ends. Zero trip meter.
0.0 ▲		Continue on main road.
GPS: N 38°44.17' W 107°01.89'		
▼ 0.0		Continue south toward Gunnison.
11.9 ▲	SO	FR 737 on right to Carbon Creek and Squaw Gulch, which eventually dead-ends. Zero trip meter.
▼ 3.2	SO	Road on right to Mill Creek.
8.6 ▲	SO	Road on left to Mill Creek.
▼ 5.3	SO	County 7 on right.
6.6 ▲	SO	County 7 on left.
▼ 9.5	SO	County 818 on right.
2.4 ▲	SO	County 818 on left.
▼ 10.0	SO	County 8 on left.
1.8 ▲	SO	County 8 on right.
▼ 11.9		End at intersection with Colorado 135. Gunnison to the right, Crested Butte to the left.
0.0 ▲		At intersection of Colorado 135 and FR 730, zero trip meter and proceed north along Ohio Pass Road.
GPS: N 38°35.50' W 106°55.05'		

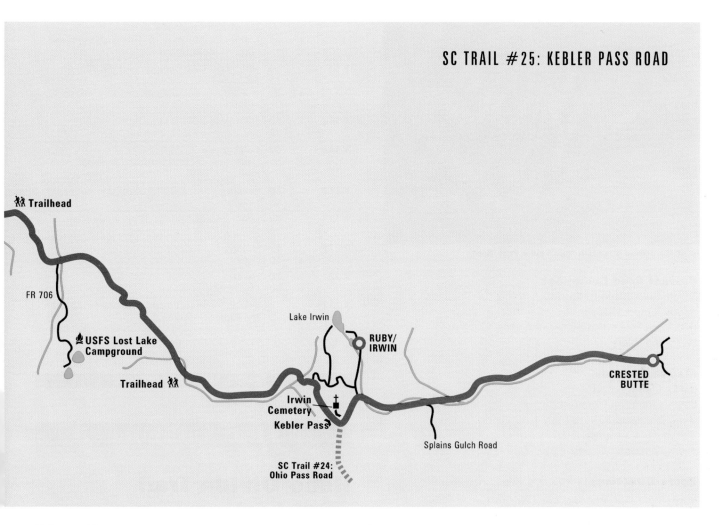

Kebler Pass Road

Starting Point:	**Crested Butte**
Finishing Point:	**Intersection of Colorado 133 and County**
	12 near the Paonia Reservoir
Total Mileage:	**29.9 miles**
Unpaved Mileage:	**27.9 miles**
Driving Time:	**1 1/4 hours**
Pass Elevation:	**9,980 feet**
Usually Open:	**Late May to early October**
Difficulty Rating:	**1**
Scenic Rating:	**6**

Special Attractions

■ Gentle, easy route that follows an old railway grade.

■ Wonderful aspen viewing in fall.

■ Irwin Cemetery.

■ Can be combined with South-Central Trail #22: Schofield Pass and Devil's Punchbowl Trail to form a loop.

History

Kebler Pass is named for John Kebler, president of the Colorado Fuel and Iron Corporation, which owned many properties in Colorado and mined coal in the area.

The pass was originally a Ute Indian trail. The Denver & Rio Grande Railroad ran a spur line from Crested Butte to the mining town of Irwin, which was booming in the early 1880s.

Description

Kebler Pass provides access to Crested Butte from either Grand Junction or Glenwood Springs, via Colorado 133. It also can form a loop tour from Crested Butte across Schofield Pass to Marble, then south to Paonia Reservoir, finally returning to Crested Butte over Kebler Pass. The road follows the old railway grade and is a wide, well-maintained road suitable for passenger cars.

The road offers excellent views of the Ruby Range to the north and the surrounding West Elk Mountains. In the fall, enormous stands of bright yellow aspen bring the scenery to life. The pass runs through a wooded area and does not offer the expansive views to be seen along the road.

Just east of the pass is the old Irwin cemetery, which has about fifty graves and a commemorative marker explaining the rise and fall of the town.

View of Marcellina Mountain from Kebler Pass Road

Current Road Conditions
White River National Forest
Sopris Ranger District
620 Main Street, Box 309, Carbondale, CO 81623
(970) 963-2266

Map References
USFS Gunnison NF
USGS Gunnison County #2
Trails Illustrated, #131, #133
The Roads of Colorado, p. 84
Colorado Atlas & Gazetteer, pp. 57-58

Route Directions

▼ 0.0		At bridge over Coal Creek on Whiterock Avenue (County 12) in Crested Butte, zero trip meter and proceed west out of town.
6.7 ▲		End in Crested Butte.
GPS: N 38°52.11′ W 106°59.35′		
▼ 1.0	SO	Unpaved.
5.7 ▲	SO	Paved.
▼ 4.8	SO	Splains Gulch turnoff on left.
1.8 ▲	SO	Splains Gulch turnoff on right.
▼ 6.1	SO	FR 826 on right toward Lake Irwin Campground.
0.6 ▲	SO	FR 826 on left toward Lake Irwin Campground.
GPS: N 38°51.48′ W 107°05.68′		
▼ 6.5	SO	South-Central Trail #24: Ohio Pass Road (FR 730) on left toward Gunnison.
0.2 ▲	SO	South-Central Trail #24: Ohio Pass Road (FR 730) turnoff on right toward Gunnison.
▼ 6.7	SO	Summit of Kebler Pass. Old Irwin Cemetery on right. Zero trip meter.
0.0 ▲		Continue toward Crested Butte.
GPS: N 38°50.97′ W 107°05.99′		
▼ 0.0		Continue along main road.
23.2 ▲	SO	Old Irwin Cemetery on left. Summit of Kebler Pass. Zero trip meter.
▼ 1.5	SO	Bridge over Ruby Anthracite Creek.
21.7 ▲	SO	Bridge over Ruby Anthracite Creek.
▼ 4.3	SO	Dark Canyon Trail on right and Horse Ranch Park.
18.9 ▲	SO	Dark Canyon Trail on left and Horse Ranch Park.
▼ 4.5	SO	Cross Ruby Anthracite Creek, then cattle

		guard. Cliff Creek trail on left.
18.7 ▲	SO	Cliff Creek trail on right. Then cattle grid and cross Ruby Anthracite Creek.
▼ 8.6	SO	USFS Lost Lake Campground (FR 706) on left.
14.6 ▲	SO	USFS Lost Lake Campground (FR 706) on right.
▼ 10.2	SO	Ruby Anthracite Trail on right.
13.0 ▲	SO	Ruby Anthracite Trail on left.
▼ 14.4	SO	Cattle guard.
8.8 ▲	SO	Cattle guard. Enter Gunnison National Forest.
▼ 17.2	SO	Paved.
6.0 ▲	SO	Unpaved.
▼ 17.5	SO	USFS Ericson Springs picnic area on left.
5.7 ▲	SO	USFS Ericson Springs picnic area on right.
▼ 17.7	SO	Unpaved.
5.5 ▲	SO	Paved.
▼ 22.7	SO	Paved.
0.5 ▲	SO	Unpaved.
▼ 23.2		End at T-intersection with Colorado 133 near the Paonia Reservoir.
0.0 ▲		At intersection of Colorado 133 and Kebler Pass Road (County 12) near the Paonia Reservoir, zero trip meter and proceed east toward Kebler Pass.
GPS: N 38°56.47′ W 107°21.70′		

SOUTH-CENTRAL REGION TRAIL #26

Reno Divide Trail

Starting Point:	Intersection of Colorado 135 and Cement Creek Road (FR 740)
Finishing Point:	Intersection of Taylor River Road (County/ FR 742) and Italian Creek Road (FR 759)
Total Mileage:	26.3 miles
Unpaved Mileage:	25.8 miles
Driving Time:	4 hours
Divide Elevation:	11,146 feet
Usually Open:	Mid-June to mid-October
Difficulty Rating:	4
Scenic Rating:	8

Special Attractions
■ Very scenic, varied, and moderately difficult 4WD trail.
■ Access from Crested Butte to Taylor Pass.
■ Good backcountry camping sites.

History
In 1879, prospectors crossed Pearl Pass into the Roaring Fork Valley and discovered ore near Ashcroft. In the following year, more rich ore was discovered near Aspen. By this time, the area was teeming with miners.

In 1880, a company was formed to build a road over Independence Pass from Leadville to Aspen, in order to pro-

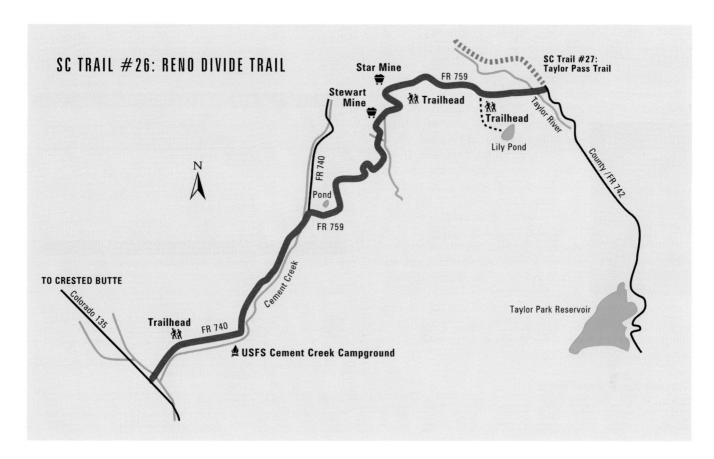

SC TRAIL #26: RENO DIVIDE TRAIL

Star Mine

Stewart Mine

Trailhead

Trailhead

FR 759

SC Trail #27:
Taylor Pass Trail

Taylor River

Lily Pond

County / FR 742

FR 740

Pond

FR 759

N

TO CRESTED BUTTE

Colorado 135

Cement Creek

Trailhead

FR 740

Taylor Park Reservoir

USFS Cement Creek Campground

vide access to Leadville's railhead and smelters. At the same time, the pack trail over Taylor Pass, which had been used by prospectors since the previous year, was upgraded to a wagon road to provide access from Taylor Park and Buena Vista.

The opening of Taylor Pass Road spurred the desire of those in Crested Butte to gain access to the new mining area. The road over Reno Divide was built to forge a stage route connection to Taylor Pass Road.

Creek crossing near Stewart Mine

The Denver & Rio Grande Railroad spur reached Crested Butte from Gunnison in 1881. By that time, Aspen was the center of a silver boom, following the first rich ore discoveries in the Roaring Fork Valley in 1879 and the further major discoveries the following year. Crested Butte was only twenty-four miles from Aspen and sixteen miles from Ashcroft, and the railroad was determined to expand access to its new railhead from the Roaring Fork Valley. This prompted the development of Pearl Pass Road in 1882. Though more direct, this was an extremely difficult route, requiring wagons to be snubbed over the pass (that is, taken apart and hauled over in pieces). Pearl Pass Road operated for only three years.

The toll road over Independence Pass from Leadville opened in 1881 and proved to be far more successful than either of the southern routes.

With the arrival in Aspen of the Denver & Rio Grande Railroad in 1887 and the Colorado Midland Railroad in 1888, the two southern roads became obsolete.

Description

This route provides access from Crested Butte to Taylor Pass Road, which leads across the Continental Divide into Aspen. It provides an alternative 4WD route to the more difficult Pearl Pass.

The route starts at the intersection of Colorado 135 and Cement Creek Road (FR 740), about seven miles south of Crested Butte. For the first nine miles of the route, Cement Creek Road travels alongside the creek in a very picturesque setting. The valley alternates between very wide sections and very narrow sections: the walls close in to form a canyon just wide enough for the creek and the road to squeeze through and then open up to panoramic views. The road through this section is easily traveled by a 2WD vehicle.

Immediately after the turn onto FR 759, the road starts to climb. While there are some sections of shelf road, they are lined with trees and are not intimidating. The surface of the road is sound and is maintained by the Gunnison 4-Wheelers Club.

After passing through the gate at the 3.6-mile point on FR 759, the road begins to deteriorate. For about the next four miles, the road is rough and can be very muddy after rain. Even under normal conditions, the road has muddy sections scarred with potholes, but it should not present too great an obstacle for a 4WD vehicle. This is the most difficult part of the journey.

Shortly after passing above timberline, you will encounter a steep-sided but narrow, small creek crossing along an off-camber section of the track. Having negotiated this crossing in

a Suburban, we can attest to it being passable in a full-sized 4WD vehicle.

The road flattens out and travels along an open alpine ridge past the Stewart and Star mines. The views of the Italian Creek Valley and the Taylor River Valley are spectacular.

As the road descends, it is a bit rough, rocky, and muddy in sections; but the surface is generally sound and should not pose any problems under normal conditions.

From the gate just after the Lilly Pond Trailhead, the road (in dry conditions) is easily navigable in a car. However, after rain it can be very muddy. There are numerous backcountry camping spots along this section.

Current Road Conditions

Gunnison National Forest
Taylor River District
216 North Colorado, Gunnison, CO 81230
(970) 641-0471

Map References

USFS Gunnison NF
USGS Gunnison County #3
Trails Illustrated, #131
The Roads of Colorado, pp. 85, 101
Colorado Atlas & Gazetteer, pp. 58-59

Route Directions

▼ 0.0		At intersection of Colorado 135 and FR 740 (Cement Creek Road), zero trip meter and proceed east.
8.8 ▲		End at intersection with Colorado 135.
	GPS: N 38°48.27' W 106°53.39'	
▼ 0.2	SO	Cross bridge.
8.6 ▲	SO	Cross bridge.
▼ 0.5	SO	Unpaved.
8.3 ▲	SO	Paved.
▼ 1.7	SO	Farris Creek trailhead on left.
7.1 ▲	SO	Farris Creek trailhead on right.
▼ 3.2	SO	Track to USFS Summer Home Group on right.
5.6 ▲	SO	Track to USFS Summer Home Group on left.
▼ 3.5	SO	USFS Cement Creek Campground.
5.3 ▲	SO	USFS Cement Creek Campground.
▼ 4.5	SO	Seasonal closure gate.
4.3 ▲	SO	Seasonal closure gate.
▼ 7.7	SO	Bridge.
1.1 ▲	SO	Bridge.
▼ 7.9	SO	Cross over Cement Creek.
0.9 ▲	SO	Cross over Cement Creek.
▼ 8.6	SO	Cross through small creek.
0.2 ▲	SO	Cross through small creek.

▼ 8.8	BR	Intersection on right with FR 759 (Italian Creek Road) toward Reno Divide. Cement Creek Road continues straight ahead. Zero trip meter.
0.0 ▲		Proceed south along Cement Creek Road.
	GPS: N 38°53.07' W 106°47.42'	
▼ 0.0		Proceed along FR 759.
9.2 ▲	TL	Intersection. Italian Creek Road and Cement Creek Road.
▼ 1.3	SO	Cabin ruins on left.
7.9 ▲	SO	Cabin ruins on right.
▼ 3.6	SO	Track on right. Gate. Track on left. Proceed through gate (leaving it as you found it). Follow FR 759.
5.6 ▲	SO	Track on right. Proceed through gate (leaving it as you found it). Follow FR 759. Track on left.
	GPS: N 38°54.46' W 106°45.76'	
▼ 5.4	SO	Cross through small, muddy creek.
3.8 ▲	SO	Cross through small, muddy creek.
▼ 5.7	SO	Cross through small creek.
3.5 ▲	SO	Cross through small creek.
▼ 6.5	SO	Pond on left and track on right (closed to motorized vehicles).
2.7 ▲	SO	Track on left (closed to motorized vehicles). Pond on right.
▼ 6.9	SO	Cross through creek.
2.3 ▲	SO	Cross through creek.
▼ 7.5	BR	Track on left.
1.6 ▲	BL	Track on the right is a difficult alternative track that rejoins the road at the gate at mileage point 5.6 ahead.
	GPS: N 38°55.97' W 106°44.36'	
▼ 7.7	SO	Cross through creek with steep sides.
1.5 ▲	SO	Cross through creek with steep sides.
▼ 7.8	SO	Cross through small creek.
1.3 ▲	SO	Cross through small creek.
▼ 8.1	SO	Stewart Mine and track to it on left.
1.1 ▲	SO	Stewart Mine and track to it on right.
▼ 8.4	SO	Stewart Mine cabin ruins on right.
0.8 ▲	SO	Stewart Mine cabin ruins on left.
▼ 8.8	BL	Track on right.
0.4 ▲	BR	Track on left.
	GPS: N 38°56.54' W 106°43.59'	
▼ 8.9	BL	Fork in road. Right fork leads to overlook and returns to main road in short distance.
0.3 ▲	BR	Fork in road. Left fork leads to overlook and returns to main road in short distance.
▼ 9.2	BL	Fork in road. Star trailhead on the right. Zero trip meter at sign.
0.0 ▲		Continue along main track.
	GPS: N 38°56.87' W 106°43.41'	
▼ 0.0		Proceed toward Taylor Road.
8.3 ▲	BR	Fork in road. Star trailhead on the left. Zero trip meter at sign.
▼ 0.8	SO	Track on right.
7.4 ▲	SO	Track on left.
▼ 1.0	SO/BL	Cabin ruins on left. Cross through small creek; then bear left past a track on the right.
7.3 ▲	BR/SO	Track on the left. Cross through a small creek; then cabin ruins on right.
▼ 1.1	SO	Cross through two small creeks.
7.2 ▲	SO	Cross through two small creeks.
▼ 1.2	BL	Mine ruins on right on private property. Follow sign toward Taylor Park.
7.1 ▲	BR	Mine ruins on left. Follow sign to Cement Creek.

▼ 1.4		TR	Intersection. Private road on the left.
	6.9 ▲	TL	Private road is straight ahead.
▼ 2.0		SO	Track on right. Follow sign to Taylor Park.
	6.2 ▲	SO	Follow sign to Cement Creek.
▼ 2.7		SO	Cross through creek.
	5.5 ▲	SO	Cross through creek.
▼ 4.6		SO	Cross through creek.
	3.7 ▲	SO	Cross through creek.
▼ 5.3		SO	Dorchester walking trail on left.
	3.0 ▲	SO	Dorchester walking trail on right.
▼ 5.5		SO	Lilly Pond walking trail on right.
	2.8 ▲	SO	Lilly Pond walking trail on left.
	GPS: N 38°57.20′ W 106°40.17′		
▼ 5.6		SO	Gate.
	2.6 ▲	SO	Gate.
▼ 7.8		SO	Cross bridge over Taylor River.
	0.4 ▲	SO	Cross bridge over Taylor River.
▼ 8.3			End at intersection with Taylor River Road (County/FR 742). Taylor Reservoir is to the right. Taylor Pass is to the left.
	0.0 ▲		At intersection of Taylor River Road (County/FR 742) and Italian Creek Road (FR 759), zero trip meter and proceed west. along Italian Creek Road.
	GPS: N 38°57.24′ W 106°37.26′		

SOUTH-CENTRAL REGION TRAIL #27

Taylor Pass Trail

Starting Point:	**Intersection of Taylor River Road (County/ FR 742) and Italian Creek Road (FR 759)**
Finishing Point:	**Aspen**
Total Mileage:	**25.3 miles**
Unpaved Mileage:	**15 miles**
Driving Time:	**2 1/2 hours**
Pass Elevation:	**11,928 feet**
Usually Open:	**Early July to late September**
Difficulty Rating:	**6**
Scenic Rating:	**9**

Special Attractions
- Very challenging 4WD trail.
- Taylor Lake, an attractive alpine lake near the summit.
- A challenging creek crossing.
- Spectacular summit views.
- Aspen viewing in the fall.

History
Taylor Pass was officially named in 1940 for mining pioneer Jim Taylor, who prospected the area as early as 1860. The pass road was instrumental in making Ashcroft, where the first ore discoveries in the Roaring Fork Valley had been made in 1879, a major, early supply center for mining in the area.

The road is one of three formed in the wake of the major ore discoveries in the inaccessible Roaring Fork Valley in 1879 and 1880, as interests in Buena Vista, Crested Butte, and Leadville vied for access to the new area.

In 1880, Taylor Pass Road was built by Stevens and Company, owned by H. B. Gillespie, to haul freight into the area from Taylor Park and Buena Vista. Subsequently, the same company ran stagecoaches along the route. In 1881, a telegraph line was run over the pass.

Although the Taylor Pass route to Crested Butte was easier than the Pearl Pass route, which opened in 1882, neither were satisfactory routes, as freight wagons had to be "snubbed" (that is, taken apart and hauled over in pieces) to cross the pass.

When rich ore was discovered in Aspen in 1880, it became apparent that Aspen was

Taylor Lake

likely to eclipse Ashcroft as the center of the mining activity in the valley. Local business interests were quick to organize the Twin Lakes and Roaring Fork Toll Company to construct a road over what is now known as Independence Pass to the smelters and railhead at Leadville. This road opened in 1881 and proved by far the most successful of the three.

The need for all of the roads passed in 1887, when the Denver & Rio Grande Railroad reached Aspen, followed by the Colorado Midland Railroad the following year.

Description
The start of this 4WD route can be reached either from Crested Butte by way of the Reno Divide (South-Central Trail #26)

Rocky section of the Taylor Pass 4WD trail

or from Tincup or Buena Vista by connecting with Taylor River Road (County 742) at Taylor Park Reservoir.

The route commences heading west on County 742, a well-maintained passenger vehicle road. The turnoff to Taylor Pass (FR 761) is a little more than two miles after the town site of Dorchester. From this point, the road is 4WD, although initially it is just a bumpy road through the forest.

At the 1.6-mile point in from County 742, the trail formerly traveled along right in the creek for about a hundred yards, requiring negotiation of the rocky stream bed in water up to bumper-deep. However, in the summer of 1997, the forest service rerouted the creek and leveled the road somewhat. This section had been the most difficult part of the road, particularly when the water obscured large boulders. It is unclear how rough and challenging the road will be after the renovations are finished and have had time to settle.

A couple of miles further on, after reaching the timberline, the road splits into a number of alternative routes past Taylor Lake and up the final ascent to the summit. The one detailed in the directions below is the easiest and most scenic. It proceeds around the southern and western sides of Taylor Lake.

From the summit of the pass, you enter the White River National Forest. Two roads lead down to Aspen: Express Creek Road and Richmond Hill Road (FR 123). The directions follow the quicker and easier Express Creek Road via the ghost town of Ashcroft.

The initial descent is a very steep, narrow shelf road, and the gravel road surface can be loose and slippery. We recommend that you engage first or second gear in low-range, to avoid locking the brakes, and proceed slowly. The steep descent, in two stages, lasts for about half a mile.

The views from the summit and during the descent along Express Creek are magnificent. At the timberline, the road enters a dense aspen forest as it continues its descent to Castle Creek Road, about one-quarter of a mile north of the ghost town of Ashcroft. From this point, the road is paved all the way into Aspen.

Current Road Conditions

Gunnison National Forest
Taylor River District
216 North Colorado, Gunnison, CO 81230
(970) 641-0471

Map References

USFS Gunnison NF or White River NF
USGS Gunnison County #3
Pitkin County #2
Trails Illustrated, #127, #131
The Roads of Colorado, p. 85
Colorado Atlas & Gazetteer, pp. 46, 59

Route Directions

▼ 0.0		At intersection of Taylor River Road (County/FR 742) and Italian Creek Road (FR 759), zero trip meter and proceed northwest. This intersection is 11 miles north of Taylor Park Reservoir. Note: sign here reads "Dead end."
5.6 ▲		End at intersection with South-Central Trail #26: Reno Divide Trail (FR 759).
		GPS: N 38°57.24' W 106°37.26'
▼ 1.8	SO	Tellurium Creek Road on right.
3.8 ▲	SO	Tellurium Creek Road on left.
▼ 2.4	SO	Track on left to Old Dorchester Guard Station.
3.2 ▲	SO	Track on right to Old Dorchester Guard Station.
▼ 2.6	SO	USFS Dorchester Campground turnoff on left.
3.0 ▲	SO	USFS Dorchester Campground turnoff on right.
▼ 2.9	SO	Fishing Access Road on left.
2.7 ▲	SO	Fishing Access Road on right.
▼ 5.5	SO	Cattle guard.
0.1 ▲	SO	Cattle guard.

SC TRAIL #27: TAYLOR PASS TRAIL

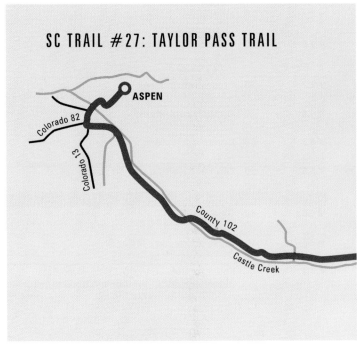

▼ 5.6	TR	Onto Taylor Pass Road (FR 761). Zero trip meter.
0.0 ▲		Proceed on FR 742.
		GPS: N 38°59.73' W 106°42.17'
▼ 0.0		Proceed onto FR 761.
3.4 ▲	TL	Intersection: FR 761 and Taylor River Road (FR 742). Zero trip meter.
▼ 1.4	SO	Cross through creek.
2.0 ▲	SO	Cross through creek.
▼ 1.5	BR	Fork in road.
1.9 ▲	BL	Fork in road.
▼ 1.6	SO	Road follows the path of the old creek bed. Note: In the summer of 1997, the creek was diverted from this section to the east side of the road.
1.8 ▲	SO	Road follows the path of the old creek bed.
▼ 2.9	SO	Cross through creek.
0.5 ▲	SO	Cross through creek.
▼ 3.4	TL	Fork in road with sign to Taylor Pass Divide Road. 761.1A on left; 761.1 to the right. Zero trip meter.
0.0 ▲		Proceed on FR 761.
		GPS: N 39°01.04' W 106°44.92'
▼ 0.0		Proceed along 761.1A.
1.4 ▲	TR	Fork in road. Zero trip meter.
▼ 0.1	SO	Taylor Lake on right.
1.3 ▲	SO	Taylor Lake on left.
▼ 0.6	SO	Ponds on left.
0.9 ▲	SO	Ponds on right.
▼ 0.6	BR	Fork in road. Follow sign to Taylor Pass.
0.8 ▲	SO	Follow sign to "Taylor Pass Road #761, 1 mile."
		GPS: N 39°00.71' W 106°45.42'
▼ 0.7	SO	Cross through creek.
0.7 ▲	SO	Cross through creek.
▼ 1.4	BL	Taylor Pass. Zero trip meter.
0.0 ▲	BR	Proceed from summit on the track to the southwest, which descends from the left-hand side of the "Taylor Pass" sign, entering Gunnison National Forest.

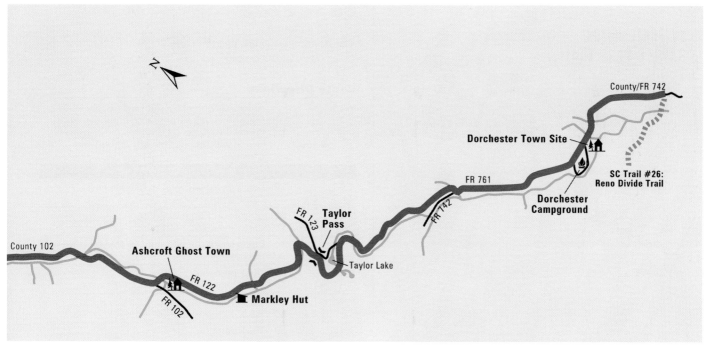

		GPS: N 39°01.21' W 106°45.32'
▼ 0.0	BL	Proceed on the track (FR 122) that descends from the right hand side of the "Taylor Pass" sign, entering White River National Forest. Follow Express Creek Road (FR 122) toward Ashcroft.
4.6 ▲	BR	Taylor Pass. Zero trip meter.
▼ 0.6	SO	Bridge over Express Creek.
4.0 ▲	SO	Bridge over Express Creek.
▼ 2.2	SO	Cross through creek.
2.4 ▲	SO	Cross through creek.
▼ 2.7	SO	Track on left to Markley Hut.
1.8 ▲	SO	Track on right to Markley Hut.
		GPS: N 39°02.21' W 106°47.26'
▼ 4.0	SO	Cross through creek.
0.6 ▲	SO	Cross through creek.
▼ 4.2	SO	Private track on left.
0.4 ▲	SO	Private track on right.
▼ 4.4	SO	Bridge over Castle Creek.
0.2 ▲	SO	Bridge over Castle Creek.
▼ 4.6	TR	Intersection with Castle Creek Road (FR 102). The restored ghost town of Ashcroft is just to the left. Zero trip meter.
0.0 ▲		Proceed toward Taylor Pass on Express Creek Road.
		GPS: N 39°03.63' W 106°48.03'
▼ 0.0		Proceed north along Castle Creek Road toward Aspen.
10.3 ▲	TL	Intersection: Castle Creek Road (FR 102) and Express Creek Road (County 15C). The restored ghost town of Ashcroft is 0.4 miles south. Zero trip meter.
▼ 10.3	TR	Intersection with County 13. Then almost immediately is the intersection with Colorado 82. Aspen is to the right. End of trail.
0.0 ▲		At the intersection of Colorado 82 and County 13 in Aspen, zero trip meter and proceed southwest. Almost immediately turn left onto Castle Creek Road.
		GPS: N 39°11.74' W 106°50.39'

Hayden Pass Trail

Starting Point:	Villa Grove
Finishing Point:	Intersection of Hayden Creek Road (County 6) and US 50
Total Mileage:	15.8 miles
Unpaved Mileage:	14.4 miles
Driving Time:	1 1/2 hours
Pass Elevation:	10,709 feet
Usually Open:	Early July to mid-October
Difficulty Rating:	3
Scenic Rating:	7

Special Attractions

- One of the few 4WD trails in the Sangre de Cristo Range.
- Varied 4WD route with good views, particularly of the San Luis Valley.
- Can be combined with South-Central Trail #29 across Medano Pass to form a loop.

History

This pass was another used by the Ute Indians to cross between the San Luis Valley and the Arkansas River to the northeast. In 1874, a wagon road was built across the pass, and Ferdinand Hayden noted this road when his survey party crossed it in 1875.

By the late 1870s, Hayden Pass was a popular route to Villa Grove—an important supply center at that time, to the mining area of Bonanza, and to the main route west via Co-

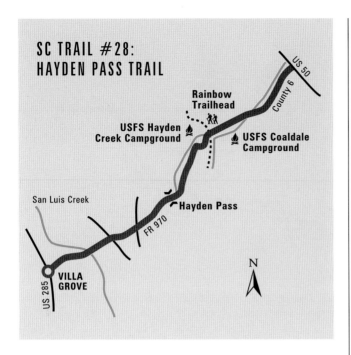

SC TRAIL #28: HAYDEN PASS TRAIL

chetopa Pass. It connected to the network of toll roads built by Otto Mears over the Cochetopa, Los Piños, and Poncha passes and between Villa Grove and Bonanza.

The pass is officially named for an early settler of the Wet Mountain Valley, Lewis Hayden.

Description

The route heads east from Villa Grove, but the turnoff is unmarked except for a "Villa Grove Common" sign. The road

A section of easy shelf road on the east side of Hayden Pass

initially travels through the ranch land of the San Luis Valley before starting its ascent toward the pass.

The route is easy to navigate but has a few sections, mainly on the east side, that are steep and quite rough and require high clearance. It travels through pine forest most of the way but provides some good views along the route, particularly the sweeping views back down across the San Luis Valley.

The route passes the Rainbow Trail, a 55-mile hiking trail, and two U.S. Forest Service campgrounds before reaching US 50 at Coaldale, 4.1 miles west of Cotopaxi and 20 miles south of Salida.

Current Road Conditions

San Isabel National Forest
Salida Ranger District
325 West Rainbow Boulevard, Salida, CO 81201
(719) 539-3591

Map References

USFS Rio Grande NF
San Isabel NF

USGS Saguache #2
Fremont #1
The Roads of Colorado, p. 119
Colorado Atlas & Gazetteer, pp. 70-71

Route Directions

▼ 0.0		At intersection of US 285 and County LL 57 (FR 970) in Villa Grove, zero trip meter and proceed east along LL 57.
6.9 ▲		End at intersection with US 285 in Villa Grove.

GPS: N 38°14.96′ W 105°56.92′

▼ 0.1	SO	Cattle guard and sign to Hayden Pass.
6.8 ▲	SO	Cattle guard.
▼ 1.6	SO	Cross over San Luis Creek.
5.3 ▲	SO	Cross over San Luis Creek.
▼ 2.7	SO	Cattle guard, then County 60 MM on left.
4.2 ▲	SO	County 60 MM on right, then cattle guard.
▼ 2.8	SO	Track on right.
4.1 ▲	SO	Track on left.
▼ 4.1	SO	Track on left.
2.8 ▲	SO	Track on right.
▼ 4.2	SO	Track on right.
2.7 ▲	SO	Track on left.
▼ 4.6	SO	Enter Rio Grande National Forest.
2.3 ▲	SO	Leave Rio Grande National Forest.

GPS: N 38°16.84′ W 105°52.30′

▼ 6.9	SO	Summit of Hayden Pass. Zero trip meter.
0.0 ▲		Continue. Enter Rio Grande National Forest. Name of road changes to FR 970.

GPS: N 38°17.60′ W 105°50.95′

▼ 0.0		Continue. Enter San Isabel National Forest. Name of road changes to FR 64.
8.9 ▲	SO	Summit of Hayden Pass. Zero trip meter.
▼ 1.1	SO	Track on left.
7.8 ▲	SO	Track on right.
▼ 1.5	SO	Cabin on right.
7.4 ▲	SO	Cabin on left.
▼ 1.9	SO	Track on left.
7.0 ▲	SO	Track on right.
▼ 2.0	SO	Track on left.
6.9 ▲	SO	Track on right.
▼ 2.8	SO	Track on left.
6.1 ▲	SO	Track on right.
▼ 4.1	TR	Intersection. San Isabel National Forest Campground entrance and Rainbow Trail walking track straight ahead. Turn onto County 6 (FR 006) toward Coaldale.
4.8 ▲	TL	Intersection. San Isabel National Forest Campground entrance and Rainbow Trail walking track. Turn onto FR 64.

GPS: N 38°19.79′ W 105°49.36′

▼ 5.4	SO	USFS Coaldale Campground on right.
3.5 ▲	SO	USFS Coaldale Campground on left.
▼ 8.6	SO	Paved road on left.
0.3 ▲	SO	Paved road on right.
▼ 8.9		End at intersection with US 50.
0.0 ▲		Intersection: US 50 and County 6, at Coaldale. Sign: "NF Access Hayden Creek." Zero trip meter and proceed south along County 6 (FR 006), also called Hayden Creek Road.

GPS: N 38°22.06′ W 105°45.11′

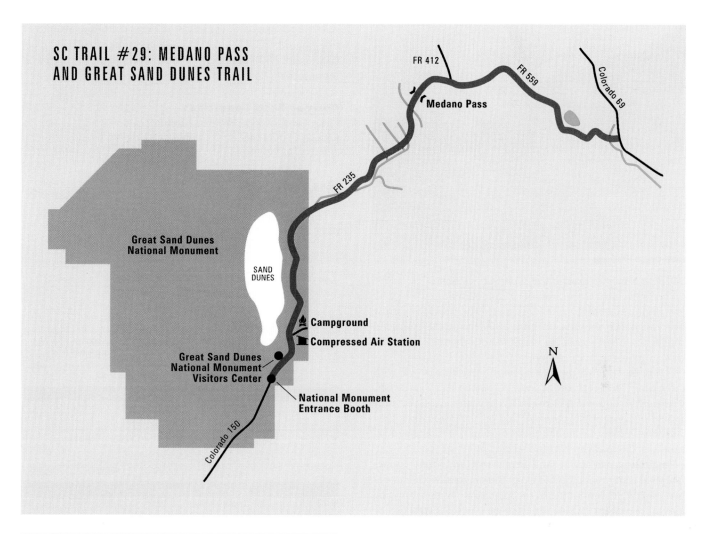

SC TRAIL #29: MEDANO PASS
AND GREAT SAND DUNES TRAIL

Medano Pass and Great Sand Dunes Trail

Starting Point:	**Intersection of Colorado 69 and FR 559**
Finishing Point:	**Tollbooth for Great Sand Dunes National**
	Monument on Colorado 150
Total Mileage:	**21.6 miles**
Unpaved Mileage:	**20.1 miles**
Driving Time:	**2 hours**
Pass Elevation:	**9,940 feet**
Usually Open:	**Late May to late October**
Difficulty Rating:	**4**
Scenic Rating:	**10**

Special Attractions

■ The spectacular Great Sand Dunes National Monument with much more scenic access than the paved roads.

■ Sand four-wheel driving and numerous creek crossings.
■ Historic pass route that can be combined with South-Central Trail #28 across Hayden Pass to form a loop.

History

Medano means "sand hill" in Spanish. In 1807, Zebulon Pike crossed the pass after his famous attempt to climb the fourteen-thousand-foot peak that bears his name. By the 1850s, the pass was much used by fur traders and the mountain men heading for the San Juan region of Colorado. Captain John Gunnison even considered using it as a railroad route as early as 1853. In that same year, the Frémont expedition party also crossed the pass but viewed the sand as too great an obstacle for the pass to be developed as a successful wagon route.

In 1866, Ute Indians attacked and killed settlers near La Veta, a small settlement thirty-five miles southeast of Medano Pass. They retreated back over the pass but were captured by Kit Carson and Chief Ouray.

The route has never been developed for use by wagons or as a railroad and remains much as it has always been.

Description

This route commences at the intersection of Colorado 69 and FR 559, twenty-three miles south of Westcliffe and nine miles west of Gardener. For nearly the first seven miles, the road is

Medano Creek crossing

2WD as it travels through the Wolf Springs Ranch.

From the intersection with FR 412, it becomes a 4WD road and begins to switchback its way toward the pass. It is narrow and rough but presents no great problem as the surface is sound. The forest service has cut numerous channels across the road to protect it from erosion.

From the summit, the scenery on the descent changes, with interesting rock formations and numerous creek crossings. These are shallow enough (twelve to eighteen inches) that they should not pose any problem for a 4WD vehicle; rather, they add some variety to the trail. Use caution if it has rained recently, as the road can become boggy.

Increasing patches of sand herald the Great Sand Dunes National Monument, one of Colorado's natural wonders. Before entering the monument, the main route is intersected by a number of side roads, along many of which the sand can be a greater obstacle than it is on this section of the main road.

A section of road that travels along-side the towering sand dunes

After entering the Great Sand Dunes National Monument, the road travels beside the towering sand dunes, providing a much better view of them than that from the paved roads most visitors use. In places, the sand dunes are as few as seventy-five yards from the trail. There are a number of pull-offs, but be careful as the sand can be treacherous. It is a short walk to the creek and across to the face of the dunes.

As the road travels deeper into the monument, the sand gets progressively worse and may require you to deflate your tires to about twenty pounds. You may reinflate your tires at an air compressor station, which is open during the peak season months. At other times, or if it is not available, inquire at the Visitor Center for assistance.

Signs warn you of the most difficult section, where the sand

is deep and loose and requires steady momentum to avoid getting bogged. Shortly after this, you encounter the paved road (Colorado 150) that carries most visitors to the national monument.

Current Road Conditions
Great Sand Dunes National Monument
Mosca, CO 81146
(719) 378-2312

Map References
USFS Rio Grande NF
San Isabel NF
USGS Huerfano #1
Saguache #5
Alamosa
The Roads of Colorado, pp. 135-136
Colorado Atlas & Gazetteer, p. 81

Route Directions

▼ 0.0			At the intersection of Colorado 69 and FR 559, zero trip meter and turn onto FR 559 at sign marked National Forest Access, Medano Pass.
	9.3 ▲		End at intersection with Colorado 69.
		GPS: N 37°50.19' W 105°18.44'	
▼ 0.3		**SO**	Cross over Muddy Creek.
	9.0 ▲	**SO**	Cross over Muddy Creek.
▼ 6.8		**SO**	Cattle guard. Enter San Isabel National Forest.
	2.5 ▲	**SO**	Cattle guard. Leave San Isabel National Forest.
		GPS: N 37°51.66' W 105°24.09'	
▼ 7.2		**SO**	Track on left.
	2.1 ▲	**SO**	Track on right.
▼ 7.3		**SO**	Track on right.
	2.0 ▲	**SO**	Track on left.
▼ 7.4		**SO**	FR 412 on right to South Muddy Creek.
	1.9 ▲	**SO**	FR 412 on left to South Muddy Creek.
▼ 9.3		**SO**	Medano Pass. Track on right, then gate. Zero trip meter.
	0.0 ▲	**SO**	Continue along trail, which is now called FR 559.
		GPS: N 37°51.37' W 105°25.91'	
▼ 0.0		**SO**	Continue along trail, which is now called FR 235.
	6.0 ▲	**SO**	Gate, track on left, then Medano Pass. Zero trip meter.
▼ 0.2		**SO**	Bridge over creek.
	5.8 ▲	**SO**	Bridge over creek.
▼ 0.5		**BL**	Fork in track. Remain on 235. Turning right leads to some attractive backcountry campsites.
	5.5 ▲	**BR**	Fork in track. Remain on 235. Turning left leads to some attractive backcountry campsites.
▼ 1.4		**SO**	Cross through creek.
	4.6 ▲	**SO**	Cross through creek.
▼ 1.6		**SO**	Cross through creek.
	4.4 ▲	**SO**	Cross through creek.
▼ 1.9		**SO**	Track on right to cabin ruins. Then cross through creek.
	4.1 ▲	**SO**	Cross through creek. Track on left to cabin ruins.
▼ 2.2		**SO**	Cluster of old cabin ruins.
	3.8 ▲	**SO**	Cluster of old cabin ruins.

GPS: N 37°49.85' W 105°26.76'		
▼ 2.6	SO	Cross through creek.
3.4 ▲	SO	Cross through creek.
▼ 3.3	SO	Cross through creek.
2.7 ▲	SO	Cross through creek.
▼ 3.6	SO	Small track on right.
2.4 ▲	BR	Small track on left.
▼ 3.7	SO	Cross through creek twice.
2.3 ▲	SO	Cross through creek twice.
▼ 4.4	SO	Cross through creek.
1.6 ▲	SO	Cross through creek.
▼ 4.9	SO	Cross through creek.
1.1 ▲	SO	Cross through creek.
▼ 5.1	SO	Ruins (chimney) of old building.
0.9 ▲	SO	Ruins (chimney) of old building.
GPS: N 37°48.47' W 105°28.99'		
▼ 5.2	SO	Cross through creek.
0.8 ▲	SO	Cross through creek.
▼ 5.6	SO	Cross through large creek.
0.4 ▲	SO	Cross through large creek.
▼ 5.8-5.9	SO	Tracks on left.
0.1-0.2 ▲	SO	Tracks on right.
▼ 6.0	SO	Leaving Rio Grande National Forest, entering Great Sand Dunes National Monument. Zero trip meter.
0.0 ▲	SO	Cross through gate and proceed along FR 235.
GPS: N 37°48.10' W 105°29.85'		
▼ 0.0	SO	Cross through gate and proceed along FR 235.
4.8 ▲	SO	Leaving Great Sand Dunes National, entering Rio Grande National Forest. Zero trip meter.
▼ 0.1	SO	Sand Creek trail on right. Little Medano trail on left.
4.7 ▲	SO	Little Medano trail on right. Sand Creek trail on left.
▼ 0.6	SO	Cross through creek. Then picnic area, parking, and cabins.
4.2 ▲	SO	Cabins. Parking and picnic areas, then cross through creek.
▼ 2.4	SO	Gate and picnic spots.
2.4 ▲	SO	Picnic spots and gate.
▼ 4.8	TR	Pavement. Intersection with Colorado 150. (Note: compressed air is available across the road.) Zero trip meter.
0.0 ▲		Proceed on Medano Pass Road (FR 235), sign reads "Medano Pass Primitive Road."
GPS: N 37°44.66' W 105°30.39'		
▼ 0.0		Proceed along Colorado 150.
1.5 ▲	TL	Opposite the National Parks building marked "private residence" and tire air station on right. Zero trip meter.
▼ 0.5	SO	Road on right to sand dunes and picnic area.
1.0 ▲	SO	Road on left to sand dunes and picnic area.
▼ 0.7	SO	Nature trail on left.
0.8 ▲	SO	Nature trail on right.
▼ 0.9	SO	Intersection. Visitor Center on the right.
0.6 ▲	SO	Visitor Center on the left. Intersection.
▼ 1.5		End at the tollbooth for Sand Dunes National Monument.
0.0 ▲		At the tollbooth for Sand Dunes National Monument, zero trip meter and proceed toward the dunes.
GPS: N 37°43.50' W 105°31.12'		

Rampart Range Road

Starting Point:	Sedalia
Finishing Point:	Garden of the Gods, Colorado Springs
Total Mileage:	65.1 miles
Unpaved Mileage:	55.4 miles
Driving Time:	3 1/2 hours
Highest Elevation:	9,420 feet
Usually Open:	Early April to December
Difficulty Rating:	1
Scenic Rating:	6

Special Attractions

- Access to a network of 4WD trails.
- Easy access from Denver and Colorado Springs.
- Red rock formations and the Garden of the Gods.
- Access to numerous trail-bike and hiking trails.
- Numerous picnic spots.

Description

This is a wide, normally well-maintained, unpaved 2WD road. The road may be corrugated and suffer some erosion, but it can be safely traversed by a normal passenger car in good conditions. However, a number of more-difficult side roads make this a good spot to gain 4WD experience.

A rock formation along Rampart Range Road

The route travels through pine forest with occasional aspen groves and past many interesting, large rock formations. Near the end of the route, the rocks turn to red as you approach the Garden of the Gods, with its 250-million-year-old sedimentary formations.

This route commences in Sedalia and heads southwest on Colorado 67 toward Deckers before turning south onto Rampart Range Road at the 9.7-mile point.

About thirteen miles after turning on to Rampart Range

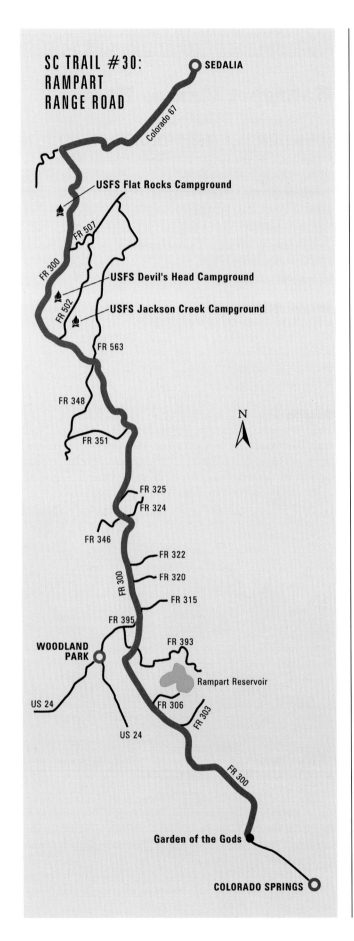

SC TRAIL #30:
RAMPART
RANGE ROAD

SEDALIA

Colorado 67

USFS Flat Rocks Campground

FR 507

FR 300

USFS Devil's Head Campground

FR 502

USFS Jackson Creek Campground

FR 563

FR 348

FR 351

N

FR 325

FR 324

FR 346

FR 322

FR 320

FR 300

FR 315

FR 395

WOODLAND
PARK

FR 393

Rampart Reservoir

US 24

FR 306

FR 303

US 24

FR 300

Garden of the Gods

COLORADO SPRINGS

Road, FR 502 intersects the route on the left. This road goes to the Jackson Creek campground. It also provides an optional side road that loops back to Rampart Range Road and has sections that are more challenging than the Rampart Range route; the more difficult sections would be rated 3. To take this loop, turn left off Rampart Range Road onto FR 502. Follow this road to the intersection with FR 563 (Dakan Mountain Road) in four miles (GPS coordinates are: N39°16.91' and W105°03.48'). Turn right onto FR 563 and head south for 1.9 miles to an intersection. Stay left and continue south reconnecting with Rampart Range Road in 5.4 miles. At this point, you will be 2.6 miles farther along Rampart Range Road than when you turned onto FR 502.

If you stayed on the main route, FR 348 intersects to the right with Rampart Range Road 0.1 miles before FR 563 enters on the left (the side-road loop discussed above). This road provides another side-road opportunity that also loops back to Rampart Range Road. To take this loop, turn right from Rampart Range Road, heading south on FR 348. At the five-mile point, FR 351 intersects from the left (GPS coordinates: N39°09.71' and W105°05.01'). Turn left onto FR 351, reconnecting with Rampart Range Road in 3.7 miles, at a point 4 miles further on than when you turned off onto FR 348.

As you approach Colorado Springs, the road starts to switchback as it descends from Rampart Range, and there are some excellent views across to the plains of eastern Colorado. The road ends at the Garden of the Gods.

If you are beginning this trail from the Garden of the Gods, finding the start of Rampart Range Road can be a little tricky. From I-25 take exit 146 and zero your trip meter. Proceed west on Garden of the Gods Road. After 2.2 miles, turn left onto 30th Street following the sign to Garden of the Gods. At the 3.5-mile point, the Garden of the Gods Visitor Center is on the left and at the 3.6-mile point turn right into the Garden of the Gods park. At the 4.1-mile point turn right onto Juniper Way Loop. There are three intersections along this road before you reach Rampart Range Road. At the intersection at 5.0 miles, bear right; at 5.7 miles, bear right; and at 5.9 miles, bear left. At the 6.2-mile point, turn right on to Rampart Range Road. This is where the trail starts.

Current Road Conditions
Pike National Forest
Pikes Peak Ranger District
601 South Weber Street, Colorado Springs, CO 80903
(719) 636-1602

Map References
USFS Pike NF
USGS Douglas #1
　　　　　 Douglas #2
　　　　　 El Paso #1
Trails Illustrated, #135, #137
The Roads of Colorado, pp. 72-73, 88-89
Colorado Atlas & Gazetteer, pp. 50, 62

Route Directions

▼ 0.0		In Sedalia, at the intersection of US 85 (Santa Fe) and Colorado 67, zero trip meter and proceed southwest toward Deckers.
9.7 ▲		End at intersection with US 85 in Sedalia.

GPS: N 39°26.34′ W 104°57.68′

▼ 9.7	TL	Onto Rampart Range Road (FR 300). There are various information boards at the entrance. Zero trip meter.
0.0 ▲		Continue on Colorado 67 toward Sedalia.

GPS: N 39°22.67′ W 105°05.60′

▼ 0.0		Continue along Rampart Range Road toward Devil's Head.
8.7 ▲	TR	Onto Colorado 67. Zero trip meter.
▼ 0.1	SO	Seasonal gate.
8.6 ▲	SO	Seasonal gate.
▼ 4.5	SO	USFS Flat Rocks Campground on right.
4.2 ▲	SO	USFS Flat Rocks Campground on left.
▼ 4.6	SO	Flat Rocks scenic overlook on left.
4.1 ▲	SO	Flat Rocks scenic overlook on right.
▼ 6.2	SO	FR 507 on left toward Jackson Creek Road. Telephone box.
2.5 ▲	SO	FR 507 on right toward Jackson Creek Road. Telephone box.

GPS: N 39°18.23′ W 105°05.26′

▼ 6.9	SO	FR 681 forks off to the left.
1.8 ▲	SO	FR 681 forks off to the right.
▼ 8.3	SO	USFS Cabin Ridge picnic ground turnoff on right (0.2 miles in from FR 300).
0.4 ▲	SO	USFS Cabin Ridge picnic ground turnoff on left.

GPS: N 39°16.77′ W 105°06.30′

▼ 8.7	BR	Intersection: Devil's Head Campground straight ahead (0.5 miles in from FR 300). Zero trip meter.
0.0 ▲		Continue on Rampart Range Road.

GPS: N 39°16.54′ W 105°06.43′

▼ 0.0		Continue on Rampart Range Road.
22.4 ▲	BL	Intersection: Devil's Head Campground on right. Zero trip meter.
▼ 2.0	SO	USFS Topaz Point picnic area on right.
20.4 ▲	SO	USFS Topaz Point picnic area on left.
▼ 4.6	SO	FR 502 on left to Jackson Creek Campground.
17.8 ▲	SO	FR 502 on right to Jackson Creek Campground.

GPS: N 39°14.01′ W 105°05.73′

▼ 7.1	SO	FR 348 to Fern Creek, Colorado 67, Woodland Park, Colorado Springs on right.
15.3 ▲	SO	FR 348 to Fern Creek, Colorado 67, Woodland Park, Colorado Springs on left.

GPS: N 39°13.15′ W 105°03.85′

▼ 7.2	SO	FR 563 to Dakan Mountain on left.
15.2 ▲	SO	FR 563 to Dakan Mountain on right.

GPS: N 39°13.19′ W 105°03.68′

▼ 11.8	SO	Gate. Track on right goes to radio towers.
10.6 ▲	SO	Track on left goes to radio towers. Gate.
▼ 12.1	SO	FR 351 (Fern Creek Road) on right. FR 327 on left.
10.3 ▲	SO	FR 327 on right. FR 351 (Fern Creek Road) on left.

GPS: N 39°10.40′ W 105°01.50′

▼ 16.7	SO	Saylor Park. FR 325 on left.
5.7 ▲	SO	Saylor Park. FR 325 on right.

GPS: N 39°06.97′ W 105°02.04′

▼ 18.1	SO	FR 346 (Hotel Gulch Road) on right toward Mt. Deception.
4.3 ▲	SO	FR 346 (Hotel Gulch Road) on left.
▼ 18.4	SO	FR 324 (Ice Cave Creek Road) on left.
4.0 ▲	SO	FR 324 (Ice Cave Creek Road) on right.
▼ 19.0	SO	FR 323 (Winding Stairs Road) on left.
3.4 ▲	SO	FR 323 (Winding Stairs Road) on right.
▼ 21.4	SO	FR 322 (Balanced Rock Road) on left.
1.0 ▲	SO	FR 322 (Balanced Rock Road) on right.
▼ 22.4	BR	FR 320 (Mt. Herman Road) on left goes to Monument. Zero trip meter.
0.0 ▲		Continue on FR 300.

GPS: N 39°03.36′ W 105°01.06′

▼ 0.0		Continue on FR 300.
18.7 ▲	BL	FR 320 (Mt. Herman Road) on right goes to Monument. Zero trip meter.
▼ 1.9	SO	FR 315 (Beaver Creek Road) on left (rejoins FR 320).
16.8 ▲	SO	FR 315 (Beaver Creek Road) on right (rejoins FR 320).
▼ 2.3	SO	FR 312 (Ensign Gulch Road) to Carrol Lakes on left.
16.4 ▲	SO	FR 312 (Ensign Gulch Road) to Carrol Lakes on right.
▼ 2.5	BL	Intersection with FR 393 toward Woodland Park on right. Proceed toward Rampart Reservoir.
16.2 ▲	BR	Intersection with FR 393 toward Woodland Park on left.

GPS: N 39°01.48′ W 105°00.70′

▼ 3.8	SO	Leaving National Forest sign.
14.9 ▲	SO	Entering Pike National Forest.
▼ 4.0	SO	Stop sign. Intersection with Shubarth Road to the left. Woodland Park and Loy Gulch to the right. Follow sign to Rampart Road. Sign prohibits target shooting for next 17.5 miles.
14.7 ▲	SO	Intersection with Shubarth Road to the right. Woodland Park and Loy Gulch to the left.
▼ 4.8	SO	USFS Springdale Campground on left.
13.9 ▲	SO	USFS Springdale Campground on right.
▼ 6.4	SO	Rainbow Gulch trailhead (to reservoir area) on left.
12.3 ▲	SO	Rainbow Gulch trailhead (to reservoir area) on right.
▼ 7.8	SO	FR 306 on left to Rampart Reservoir.
10.9 ▲	SO	FR 306 on right to Rampart Reservoir.

GPS: N 38°57.70′ W 104°59.72′

▼ 9.9	BR	FR 303 (Northfield Road) on left.
8.8 ▲	SO	FR 303 (Northfield Road) on right.
▼ 12.9	SO	Ridge Crest Scenic Overlook on right.
5.8 ▲	SO	Ridge Crest Scenic Overlook on left.
▼ 18.7	SO	USFS Rampart Shooting Range on right. Zero trip meter.
0.0 ▲		Proceed on Rampart Range Road.

GPS: N 38°53.86′ W 104°54.68′

▼ 0.0		Proceed on Rampart Range Road.
5.6 ▲	SO	USFS Rampart Shooting Range on left. Zero trip meter.
▼ 4.1	SO	Track on right.
1.5 ▲	SO	Track on left.
▼ 5.3	SO	Rock formations-part of Garden of the Gods.
0.1 ▲	SO	Rock formations-part of Garden of the Gods.
▼ 5.6		Intersection. End at Garden of the Gods.
0.0 ▲		At Garden of the Gods, exit onto Rampart Range Road (FR 300) and zero trip meter.

GPS: N 38°51.97′ W 104°53.79′

The North-Central Region

Trails in the North-Central Region

- NC 1   Webster Pass Trail
- NC 2   Handcart Gulch Trail
- NC 3   Red Cone Peak Trail
- NC 4   Radical Hill Trail
- NC 5   Deer Creek Road
- NC 6   Saints John and Glacier Mountain Trail
- NC 7   Santa Fe Peak Trail
- NC 8   Middle Fork of the Swan Trail
- NC 9   Georgia Pass Trail
- NC 10   Boreas Pass Road
- NC 11   Guanella Pass Trail
- NC 12   Shrine Pass Road
- NC 13   Ptarmigan Pass and McAllister Gulch Loop
- NC 14   Breakneck Pass and Browns Pass Trail
- NC 15   Mosquito Pass Trail
- NC 16   Hagerman Pass Road
- NC 17   Weston Pass Road
- NC 18   Mount Bross Trail
- NC 19   Brush Creek Road to Crooked Creek Pass
- NC 20   Cottonwood Pass Road

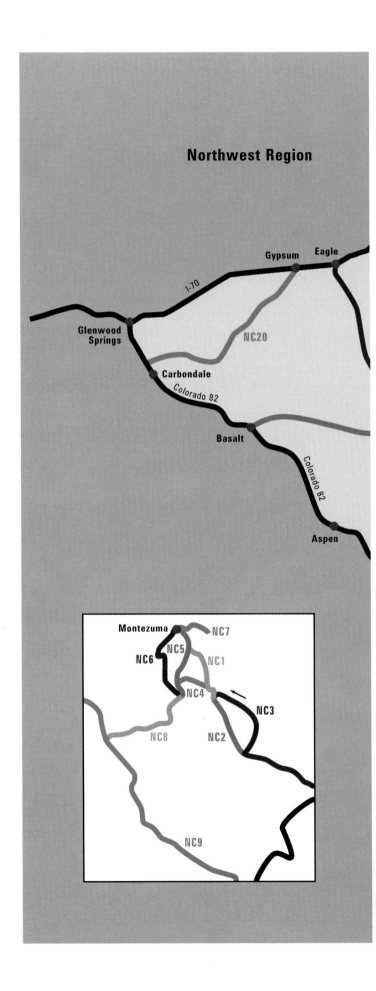

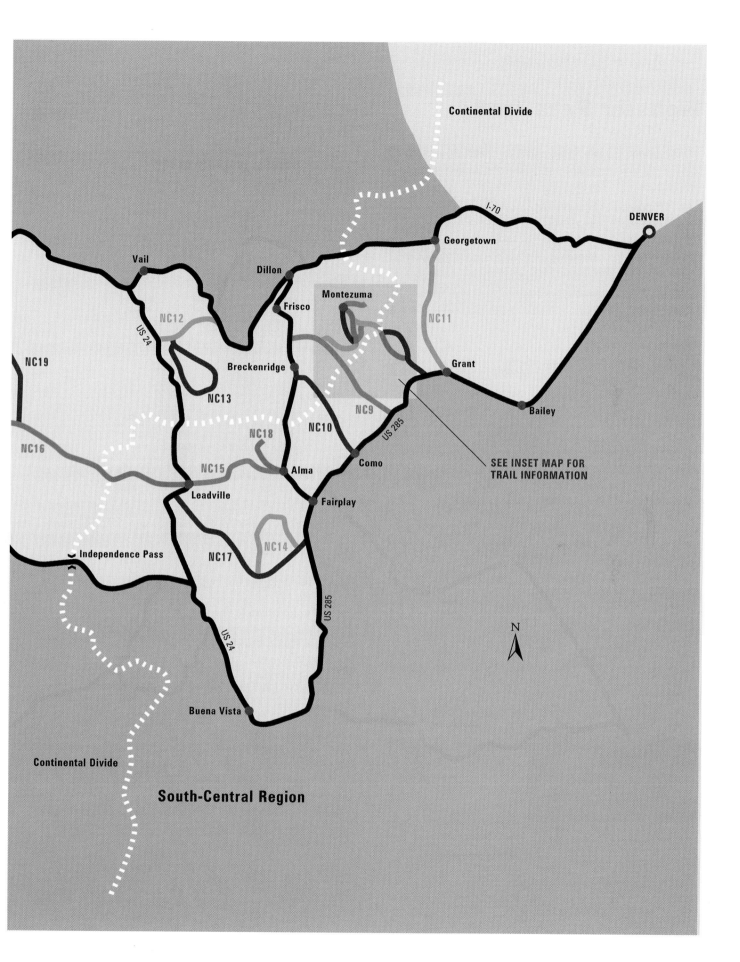

Continental Divide

DENVER

I-70

Georgetown

Vail

Dillon

Frisco

Montezuma

NC11

NC12

US 24

NC19

Breckenridge

Grant

NC13

Bailey

NC16

NC18

NC10

NC9

US 285

SEE INSET MAP FOR
TRAIL INFORMATION

NC15

Alma

Como

Leadville

Fairplay

Independence Pass

NC17

NC14

US 285

N

US 24

Continental Divide

South-Central Region

Buena Vista

Webster Pass Trail

Starting Point:	Intersection of FR 285 with Handcart Gulch Road (FR 121) and Red Cone Peak Trail
Finishing Point:	Montezuma
Total Mileage:	4.9 miles
Unpaved Mileage:	4.9 miles
Driving Time:	1/2 hour
Pass Elevation:	12,096 feet
Usually Open:	Early July to late September
Difficulty Rating:	3
Scenic Rating:	8

Special Attractions

- Views from the summit.
- Access to an extensive network of 4WD trails.
- Attractive Snake River Valley.

History

American Indians used Webster Pass for many years before the arrival of the white man. Prospectors first traveled the pass in the 1860s. In 1878, the Webster brothers built a wagon road over the crossing. The route was a popular crossing at that time and was used by the itinerant Father Dyer in his far-flung ministry.

In the early 1890s, David Moffat, the president of the Denver & Rio Grande Railroad, surveyed the crossing at Webster Pass as a possible rail route.

The road fell into disuse and was reopened in 1971 through the efforts of 4WD clubs.

Description

This route takes you from Webster Pass, where it intersects the road over Red Cone Peak and Handcart Gulch Road, down the Snake River Valley and into the township of Montezuma.

A view of Webster Pass from Red Cone showing the Webster Pass Trail descending on the right and the Handcart Gulch 4WD Trail descending on the left

From the pass, there is a magnificent view of the Handcart Gulch area to the southeast and the Snake River Valley to the northwest. The road up Red Cone Peak is one way and cannot be entered from Webster Pass. A snowdrift usually blocks the alternative road into Handcart Gulch until late in summer.

The route remains above timberline as it switchbacks down from Webster Pass on a reasonably wide road that has a sound surface. Passing other vehicles is easy at the switchbacks. As you reach the valley floor, you will cross the headwaters of the

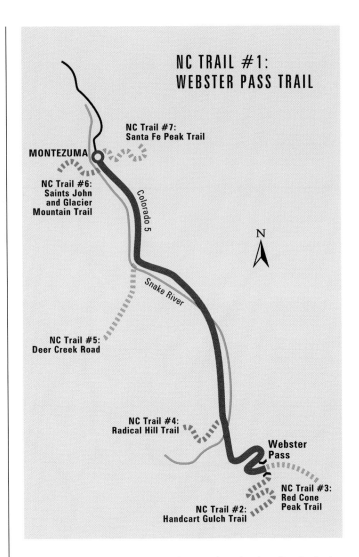

NC TRAIL #1:
WEBSTER PASS TRAIL

NC Trail #7:
Santa Fe Peak Trail

MONTEZUMA

NC Trail #6:
Saints John and Glacier Mountain Trail

Colorado 5

Snake River

N

NC Trail #5:
Deer Creek Road

NC Trail #4:
Radical Hill Trail

Webster Pass

NC Trail #3:
Red Cone Peak Trail

NC Trail #2:
Handcart Gulch Trail

Snake River and pass the road toward Radical Hill, which departs to the left.

This route is simple to navigate.

Current Road Conditions

Pike National Forest
South Platte Ranger District
19316 Goddard Ranch Court, Morrison, CO 80465
(303) 275-5610

Map References

USFS White River NF
USGS Summit County #2
Park County #1
Trails Illustrated, #104
The Roads of Colorado, p. 71 (Webster Pass Road incorrectly shown as FR 215)
Colorado Atlas & Gazetteer, p. 38

Route Directions

▼ **0.0** From the summit of Webster Pass, zero trip meter and proceed down FR 285.

3.9 ▲ End at intersection with North-Central #3: Red Cone Peak Trail straight ahead (a one-way

GPS: N 39°31.90′ W 105°49.92′			
▼ 1.4	SO	Cross Snake River. Track to the left is North-Central Trail #4: Radical Hill Trail.	
2.5 ▲	SO	Track to the right is North-Central Trail #4: Radical Hill Trail. Cross Snake River.	
GPS: N 39°32.27′ W 105°50.44′			
▼ 2.6	SO	Cross through creek, then intersection. Campsites on right. Remnants of old building. Track on left closed off.	
1.3 ▲	SO	Track on right closed off. Remnants of old building. Campsites on left. Intersection. Then cross through creek.	
▼ 3.2	SO	Seasonal closure gate.	
0.7 ▲	SO	Seasonal closure gate.	
▼ 3.3-3.8	SO	Tracks on right and left.	
0.1-0.6 ▲	SO	Tracks on right and left.	
▼ 3.9	TR	Intersection of Webster Pass Road and North-Central Trail #5: Deer Creek Road (County 5/FR 5). Zero trip meter.	
0.0 ▲		Proceed along Webster Pass Road (FR 285).	
GPS: N 39°34.10′ W 105°51.57′			
▼ 0.0		Proceed north along County 5.	
1.0 ▲	TL	Intersection of North-Central Trail #5: Deer Creek Road (County 5/FR 5) and Webster Pass Road. Zero trip meter.	
▼ 0.3	SO	Ruins of mine and log buildings.	
0.7 ▲	SO	Ruins of mine and log buildings.	
▼ 1.0		End at Montezuma Snake River Fire Station.	
0.0 ▲		From the Montezuma Snake River Fire Station, zero trip meter and proceed south on County 5 (FR 5).	
GPS: N 39°34.85′ W 105°52.04′			

NORTH-CENTRAL REGION TRAIL #2

Handcart Gulch Trail

Starting Point:	**Intersection of US 285 and Park County 60 (FR 120), at the town site of Webster**
Finishing Point:	**Webster Pass**
Total Mileage:	**9.6 miles**
Unpaved Mileage:	**9.6 miles**
Driving Time:	**1 3/4 hours**
Pass Elevation:	**12,096 feet**
Usually Open:	**Mid-August to late September**
Difficulty Rating:	**5**
Scenic Rating:	**9**

Special Attractions

■ Varied four-wheel driving challenges, including an extremely narrow shelf road.

■ Spectacular views, particularly of Red Cone Peak.

■ Access to an extensive network of 4WD trails.

The narrow shelf section of Handcart Gulch trail descending from Webster Pass before switchbacking into the valley

History

The area is named for two prospectors who in 1860 brought their handcart loaded with supplies up the valley and made the area's first gold discovery while panning the creek.

Description

The route starts at the town site of Webster (nothing remains of the town), at the intersection of US 285 and Park County 60 (FR 120), 3.2 miles west of Grant.

Initially, this is the same route that leads to Webster Pass by way of Red Cone Peak. The well-maintained 2WD road travels along Hall Valley beside headwaters of the North Fork of the South Platte River though pine and aspen groves.

After the intersection with Red Cone Peak Trail five miles along the route, the road quickly gets rougher and rockier. Large rocks in the road make selecting the correct line important.

A very muddy and wheel-rutted spot lies just in front of a log cabin, some 1.7 miles after the turnoff to Red Cone. With permission from the cabin's owner, you can bypass the muddy stretch by driving through the cabin's yard.

The road continues through two manageable creek crossings and then commences its final assault on the pass. This starts with a number of switchbacks and culminates in a long, very narrow, off-camber, rough shelf cut into the steep, talus mountainside. This stretch of road is frequently obstructed by rocks that you must clear in order to pass and is on-

$50,000 Waiting to Be Found

Jim Reynolds was one of the first settlers in Fairplay, but when the Civil War started, he left to join the Confederate Army. Toward the end of the war, he and eight other soldiers, including his brother, returned to Colorado to steal gold to help fund the war effort.

They held up a stage in South Park and raced along the South Platte River with a posse hot on their tails, eventually evading it by crossing Webster Pass and making camp on Deer Creek, having hidden the loot on the way.

The posse finally caught up with them. One of Reynolds's gang was killed in the shoot-out, but the rest got away. The posse displayed the head of the unfortunate robber in Fairplay.

Jim Reynolds was eventually captured and put on trial in Denver, along with four others in the gang. All five were convicted and sentenced to jail in Fort Leavenworth. While being transported there, they were all shot and killed.

Reynolds revealed the location of the gold he had hidden, but no one has been able to find it. It is supposed to be buried in Handcart Gulch. Its value today would be $50,000.

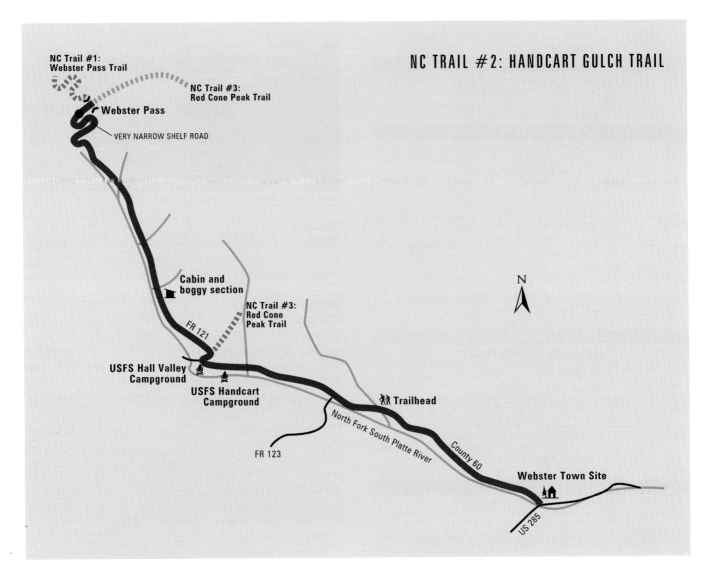

ly just wide enough for a full-sized vehicle to squeeze through. The last hundred feet are usually blocked by a snowdrift until late into summer.

The view from the pass is wonderful: To the east is the one-way (downhill only) road off Red Cone Peak, southeast is the west face of Red Cone, north is the Snake River Valley, and southwest is the shelf road you have just ascended.

Current Road Conditions

Pike National Forest
South Platte Ranger District
19316 Goddard Ranch Court, Morrison, CO 80465
(303) 275-5610

Map References

USFS Pike NF
USGS Summit County #2
    Park County #1
    Park County #2
Trails Illustrated, #104 (route incomplete)
The Roads of Colorado, p. 71
Colorado Atlas & Gazetteer, pp. 38, 48-49

Route Directions

▼ 0.0		From intersection of US 285 and Park County 60 (FR 120) at the site of Webster, zero trip meter. Proceed west on unpaved road marked with sign to Red Cone Road and Handcart Gulch.
5.0 ▲		End at intersection with US 285 at the site of Webster.
GPS: N 39°27.46' W 105°43.27'		
▼ 0.9	SO	Enter Pike National Forest.
4.1 ▲	SO	Leave Pike National Forest.
▼ 1.7	SO	Track on left with campsite. Cattle guard.
3.3 ▲	SO	Cattle guard. Track on right with campsite.
▼ 2.9	SO	Burning Bear walking trail on right.
2.1 ▲	SO	Burning Bear walking trail on left.
▼ 3.1	SO	Road on left to Beaver Creek (FR 123).
1.9 ▲	SO	Road on right to Beaver Creek (FR 123).
▼ 4.6	SO	USFS Handcart Campground.
0.3 ▲	SO	USFS Handcart Campground.
▼ 4.9	SO	Hall Valley Campground and Gibson Lake trailhead (120B) to the left.
0.1 ▲	SO	Hall Valley Campground and Gibson Lake trailhead (120B) to the right.
GPS: N 39°28.98' W 105°48.20'		
▼ 5.0	TL	T-intersection. Turn left onto Handcart Gulch

			Road (FR 121). Track on right is North-Central Trail #3: Red Cone Peak Trail, which also leads to Webster Pass. Zero trip meter.
0.0 ▲			Proceed along Handcart Gulch Road.
GPS: N 39°29.02' W 105°48.27'			
▼ 0.0			Proceed along Handcart Gulch Road.
4.6 ▲	BR		Intersection. Left goes to North-Central Trail #3: Red Cone Peak and loops back to Webster Pass. Right leads to US 285. Zero trip meter.
▼ 0.1	SO		Track on right.
4.5 ▲	BR		Track on left.
▼ 0.4	BL		Intersection. FR 5652 on right.
4.1 ▲	BR		Intersection. FR 5652 on left.
▼ 0.5	SO		Track on right to walking trail.
4.0 ▲	SO		Track on left to walking trail.
▼ 1.7	SO		Building on right. Potentially very boggy and rutted section of the track.
2.9 ▲	SO		Building on left. Potentially very boggy and rutted section of the track.
▼ 2.8	SO		Cross through creek.
1.8 ▲	SO		Cross through creek.
▼ 3.1	SO		Cross through creek.
1.5 ▲	SO		Cross through creek.
GPS: N 39°31.31' W 105°49.89'			
▼ 4.2-4.6	SO		Travel along a very narrow shelf.
0.0-0.4 ▲	SO		Travel along a very narrow shelf.
▼ 4.6			End at Webster Pass.
0.0 ▲			From the summit of Webster Pass, zero trip meter and proceed south on Handcart Gulch Road (FR 120) along a narrow shelf.
GPS: N 39°31.86' W 105°49.92'			

NORTH-CENTRAL REGION TRAIL #3

Red Cone Peak Trail

Starting Point:	**Intersection of US 285 and Park County 60 (FR 120), at the town site of Webster**
Finishing Point:	**Webster Pass**
Total Mileage:	**11.2 miles**
Unpaved Mileage:	**11.2 miles**
Driving Time:	**2 hours**
Route Elevation:	**12,600 feet**
Usually Open:	**Early July to late September**
Difficulty Rating:	**7**
Scenic Rating:	**10**

Special Attractions

■ Spectacular alpine views.
■ The adventure of tackling a very challenging 4WD trail.
■ Access to an extensive network of 4WD trails.

Special Note on the Difficulty Rating of this Road

This trail is the most difficult included in this book. We have limited the scope of this book primarily to trails with difficul-

ty ratings up to a maximum of 5. So why include one rated 7? First, the views are fabulous. Second, it provides a route for those four-wheelers who want to test their skills on a truly demanding road.

However, please be warned, some experienced four-wheelers consider this the most dangerous 4WD trail in the state.

The route offers a range of challenges. Clearance is very tight between the trees in the early part of the trail. There are also a number of very tight switchbacks, severely eroded sections, and quite large (and not always imbedded) rocks. However, these obstacles by themselves would warrant a difficulty rating of only 5.

By far the most challenging and potentially dangerous obstacle is the very steep downhill section of loose talus at the end of the trail. It is because of this section that the U.S. Forest Service has banned travel on this road from the Webster Pass direction, making the road one-way only.

Heading down the steep section of Red Cone Peak Trail

If you do not handle your vehicle properly when descending the talus slope, the rear of the vehicle is likely to swing around, causing the vehicle to roll. The floor of Handcart Gulch is about 1,500 feet below—and that is where you will stop!

However, there is a safe way to make the descent: Select first gear in low range, and go down slowly. You must exercise particular care if you use the brakes, because if the wheels lock up, the rear of the vehicle will swing around. If the back of the vehicle starts to come around, the only way to straighten it is to accelerate. Many drivers will find this the opposite of their instincts in the heat of crisis. If you need to employ this technique, be careful not to overdo it. This steeply descending section of the road is bumpy, with broad corrugations caused by vehicles sliding on the talus; so if you have to accelerate, be prepared to bounce all over the place.

Description

This trail commences at the intersection of North-Central Trail #2: Handcart Gulch Trail, five miles from US 285. Navigating this trail is easy, as there are no other side roads.

The start of Red Cone Road is quite rocky. The road travels through pine and aspen forest that becomes just pine as the road ascends. The clearance between the trees is just wide enough for a full-sized vehicle.

The road crosses through a creek bed that is often heavily eroded. Along the way, you will also encounter your share of switchbacks and rocks. A couple of uphill sections are quite challenging. Though short, they have large rocks and a loose, eroded surface.

After emerging from the timberline, the road travels along

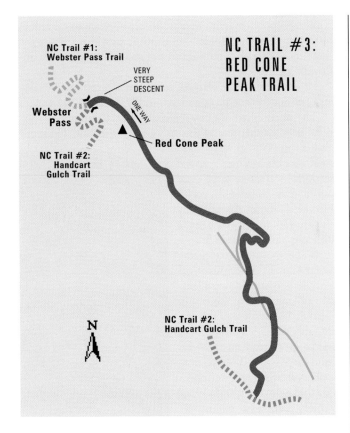

NC TRAIL #3: RED CONE PEAK TRAIL

NC Trail #1: Webster Pass Trail

VERY STEEP DESCENT

ONE WAY

Webster Pass

Red Cone Peak

NC Trail #2: Handcart Gulch Trail

NC Trail #2: Handcart Gulch Trail

N

▼ 2.9	SO	Burning Bear walking trail on right.
▼ 3.1	SO	Road on left to Beaver Creek (FR 123).
▼ 4.6	SO	USFS Handcart Campground.
▼ 4.9	SO	Hall Valley Campground and Gibson Lake trailhead (120B) to the left.

GPS: N 39°28.98′ W 105°48.20′

▼ 5.0	TR	T-intersection. Road on left is North-Central Trail #2: Handcart Gulch Trail (FR 121), which also leads to Webster Pass. Zero trip meter and proceed along Red Cone Road (FR 565).

GPS: N 39°29.02′ W 105°48.27′

▼ 0.1	TR	Sign for Webster Pass. Red Cone to the right.
▼ 1.0	SO	Cross through creek.
▼ 3.6	BL	Fork in road.
▼ 5.5	SO	First steep descent.
▼ 6.2		End at Webster Pass crossing.

GPS: N 39°31.90′ W 105°49.92′

NORTH-CENTRAL REGION TRAIL #4

Radical Hill Trail

Starting Point:	**Deer Creek Road**
Finishing Point:	**Webster Pass Trail (FR 285)**
Total Mileage:	**2.5 miles**
Unpaved Mileage:	**2.5 miles**
Driving Time:	**3/4 hour**
Route Elevation:	**12, 600 feet**
Usually Open:	**Mid-June to late September**
Difficulty Rating:	**6**
Scenic Rating:	**10**

Special Attractions

■ Very challenging 4WD trail.
■ Interconnects with a network of other 4WD trails.
■ Wonderful alpine scenery.

Description

This is a short, challenging road with a steep, loose, and very narrow shelf section. If you start at Deer Creek Road, the difficult section is downhill. This is the easier way of tackling it.

From Deer Creek Road, the route commences a gentle ascent through a broad expanse of alpine tundra across the top of Radical Hill and over to Teller Mountain. After only about the first mile of the route, from the top of Teller Mountain, there is a particularly good view down into the Snake River Valley.

The narrow section of shelf road

---

a lengthy, open tundra ridge before making its final, sharp ascent to a narrow perch above the steep, dangerous descent to Webster Pass. This is a good place to stop and admire one of the most breathtaking views in Colorado while gathering yourself for the last section, now in clear view.

The distance from the summit of Red Cone Peak to Webster Pass is about three-quarters of a mile and is broken into three short, steep sections, with the first being the hardest.

From Webster Pass, you get to look back on the slope you have just negotiated and across to the vivid red surface of Red Cone Peak.

Current Road Conditions

Pike National Forest
South Platte Ranger District
19316 Goddard Ranch Court, Morrison, CO 80465
(303) 275-5610

Map References

USFS Pike NF
Trails Illustrated, #104 (route incomplete)
Colorado Atlas & Gazetteer, pp. 38, 48

Route Directions

▼ 0.0		From intersection of US 285 and Park County 60 (FR 120) at the site of Webster, zero trip meter. Proceed northwest on unpaved road marked with sign to Red Cone Road and Handcart Gulch.

GPS: N 39°27.46′ W 105°43.27′

▼ 0.9	SO	Enter Pike National Forest.
▼ 1.7	SO	Track on left with campsite. Cattle guard.

NC TRAIL #4:
RADICAL HILL TRAIL

NC Trail #1:
Webster Pass Trail

Teller Mountain ▲

STEEP, NARROW SHELF ROAD

▲ Radical Hill

Snake River

Cashier
Mine

N

NC Trail #5:
Deer Creek Road

As you proceed from this point, the road turns and descends sharply. This road switchbacks onto a very narrow shelf cut into the face of the mountain. The road has significant erosion in spots as well as being off-camber and having a loose surface. As it curves around the mountain, it levels off and becomes wide enough to accommodate two vehicles when passing is necessary.

A rocky section of the Radical Hill 4WD trail

The balance of this short trail is a rough, rocky ride; but the worst is definitely over.

Current Road Conditions
White River National Forest
Dillon Ranger District
680 Blue River Parkway, Silverthorne, CO 80498
(970) 468-5400

Map References
USFS White River NF
Trails Illustrated, #104
The Roads of Colorado, p. 71 (route incomplete)
Colorado Atlas & Gazetteer, p. 38 (route incomplete)

Route Directions

▼ 0.0			From intersection of Deer Creek Road (FR 5) and Radical Hill Trail (FR 286), zero trip meter and turn onto FR 286.
	2.5 ▲		End at intersection with Deer Creek Road (FR 5).
		GPS: N 39°31.66′ W 105°51.91′	
▼ 0.1		SO	Track on right is alternative track to Deer Creek Road.
	2.4 ▲	BL	Track on left is alternative track to Deer Creek Road.

▼ 0.9		SO	Scenic overlook and start of steep, narrow descent.
	1.6 ▲	SO	Scenic overlook.
▼ 1.4		SO	Track on right to cabin.
	1.1 ▲	SO	Track on left to cabin.
		GPS: N 39°32.05′ W 105°51.18′	
▼ 2.5		BL	Track on right, then end at intersection with North-Central Trail #1: Webster Pass Trail.
	0.0 ▲		At intersection of North-Central Trail #1: Webster Pass Trail and Radical Hill road (FR 286), zero trip meter and proceed along FR 286.
		GPS: N 39°32.29′ W 105°50.46′	

NORTH-CENTRAL REGION TRAIL #5

Deer Creek Road

Starting Point:	Montezuma
Finishing Point:	Three-way intersection of Deer Creek Road
	with Middle Fork of the Swan road and
	North Fork of the Swan/Saints John road
Total Mileage:	4.9 miles
Unpaved Mileage:	4.9 miles
Driving Time:	1/2 hour
Pass Elevation:	12,400 feet
Usually Open:	Mid-June to late September
Difficulty Rating:	3
Scenic Rating:	7

Special Attractions
■ Provides access to an extensive network of 4WD trails.

Description
Deer Creek Road serves as the backbone for an extensive network of 4WD roads branching in all directions. Many of the roads are poorly marked, and navigation can be difficult. We strongly recommend that you use a copy of the *Trails Illustrated* map for the area. It is not entirely accurate but is much more up to date than any of the alternative maps.

Other than navigation, this route presents no major difficulties. The road is bumpy and includes some easy switchbacks, but the surface is sound.

Current Road Conditions
White River National Forest
Dillon Ranger District
680 Blue River Parkway, Silverthorne, CO 80498
(970) 468-5400

Map References
USFS White River NF
USGS Summit County #2 (incomplete)
Trails Illustrated, #104
The Roads of Colorado, p. 71
Colorado Atlas & Gazetteer, p. 38

NC TRAIL #5: DEER CREEK ROAD

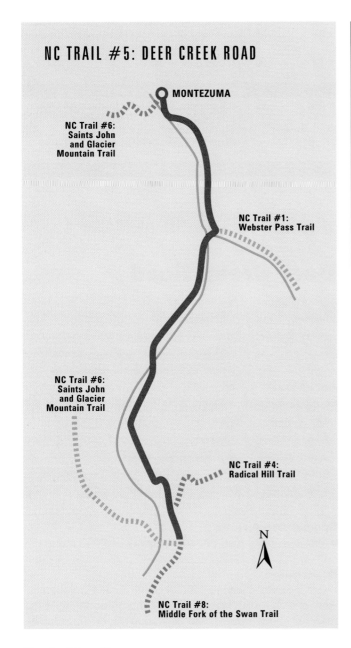

Route Directions

▼ 0.0   From the Montezuma Snake River Fire Station, zero trip meter and proceed south on County 5 (FR 5).

     1.0 ▲   End at the Montezuma Snake River Fire Station.

GPS: N 39°34.85' W 105°52.03'

▼ 0.7   SO   Ruins of mine and log buildings.

     0.3 ▲   SO   Ruins of mine and log buildings.

▼ 1.0   SO   Track on left is North-Central Trail #1: Webster Pass Trail. Zero trip meter.

     0.0 ▲   Continue along County 5/FR5.

GPS: N 39°34.08' W 105°51.57'

▼ 0.0   Continue on County 5/FR 5.

     3.9 ▲   SO   Track on right is North-Central Trail #1: Webster Pass Trail. Zero trip meter.

▼ 0.4   SO   Parking area. Cross over creek.

     3.6 ▲   SO   Cross over creek. Parking area.

▼ 0.9   SO   Track on right dead-ends at mines.

     3.1 ▲   SO   Track on left dead-ends at mines.

▼ 1.0   SO   Arapaho National Forest information board. Seasonal closure gate.

     2.9 ▲   SO   Seasonal closure gate. Arapaho National Forest information board.

▼ 1.5   SO   Track to the right goes to mines.

     2.4 ▲   SO   Track to the left goes to mines.

▼ 1.6   SO   Cross over Deer Creek. Track on the left.

     2.3 ▲   SO   Track on right. Cross over Deer Creek.

▼ 1.7   SO   Track on left goes to numerous mines.

     2.2 ▲   SO   Track on right goes to numerous mines.

▼ 2.0   SO   Short track to the right.

     1.9 ▲   SO   Short track to the left.

▼ 2.2   BL   Track on the right.

     1.7 ▲   BR   Track on the left.

▼ 3.4   BR   Track on left is first turnoff to North-Central Trail #4: Radical Hill Trail (FR 286).

     0.5 ▲   BL   Track on right is second turnoff to Radical Hill.

▼ 3.5   SO   Track on left is second turnoff to Radical Hill.

     0.4 ▲   SO   Track on right is first turnoff to North-Central Trail #4: Radical Hill Trail (FR 286).

▼ 3.9   End at three-way intersection signpost that points to the Middle Fork of the Swan to the south, Montezuma to the north, and the North Fork of the Swan and Saints John to the west.

     0.0 ▲   Begin at three-way intersection signpost that points to the Middle Fork of the Swan to the south, Montezuma to the north, and the North Fork of the Swan and Saints John to the west. Zero trip meter and take road toward Montezuma.

GPS: N 39°31.24' W 105°52.09'

NORTH-CENTRAL REGION TRAIL #6

Saints John and Glacier Mountain Trail

Starting Point:	**Montezuma**
Finishing Point:	**Three-way intersection of Deer Creek Road**
	with Middle Fork of the Swan road and
	North Fork of the Swan/Saints John road
Total Mileage:	**7.2 miles**
Unpaved Mileage:	**7.1 miles**
Driving Time:	**1 1/2 hours**
Route Elevation:	**12,200 feet**
Usually Open:	**Mid-July to late September**
Difficulty Rating:	**4**
Scenic Rating:	**8**

Special Attractions

■ Moderately challenging 4WD trail that offers a mix of historic sites, trail conditions, and excellent scenery.

■ Access to a network of 4WD trails.

Description

This route offers a variety of attractions: the historic mining town of Saints John, old mines, creek crossings, and stunning alpine views.

As the roads in the area are frequently unmarked, we recommend that you take a copy of the *Trails Illustrated* map listed below. It is not completely accurate but is much more up to date than any of the alternatives and will prove most helpful.

The road is rough in sections but sound. Some sections are steep but should prove well within the capability of a 4WD vehicle.

The road starts in Montezuma and ascends some switchbacks to the Saints John township. It passes by the Wild Irishman Mine before switchbacking a steep slope onto the exposed Glacier Mountain. It then winds along the narrow ridge past the General Teller Mine and ends at the three-way intersection with Deer Creek Road and the Middle Fork of the Swan River road.

Current Road Conditions

White River National Forest
Dillon Ranger District
680 Blue River Parkway, Silverthorne, CO 80498
(970) 468-5400

Map References

USFS White River NF
USGS Summit County #2 (incomplete)
Trails Illustrated, #104 (minor inaccuracies)
The Roads of Colorado, p. 71 (incomplete)
Colorado Atlas & Gazetteer, p. 38 (incomplete)

Route Directions

▼ 0.0		From the Montezuma Snake River Fire Station, zero trip meter and proceed south on County 5 (FR 5).
7.2 ▲		End at the Montezuma Snake River Fire Station.
GPS: N 39°34.85′ W 105°52.03′		
▼ 150 yds	TR	Onto County 275 toward Saints John. Unpaved.
7.2 ▲	TL	Onto County 5 toward Montezuma.
▼ 0.2	SO	Track on left goes to the Equity Mine with old buildings in 0.2 miles.
7.0 ▲	SO	Track on right goes to the Equity Mine with old buildings.
▼ 0.5	SO	Enter Arapaho National Forest.
6.7 ▲	SO	Leave Arapaho National Forest.
▼ 0.6	SO	Track on right crosses Saints John Creek and leads to Grizzly Gulch.
6.6 ▲	SO	Track on left crosses Saints John Creek and leads to Grizzly Gulch.
▼ 1.3	SO	Town site of Saints John.
5.9 ▲	SO	Town site of Saints John.
GPS: N 39°34.33′ W 105°52.85′		
▼ 1.4	TR	Follow Jeep trail sign. Cross Saints John Creek. Track on left.
5.8 ▲	TL	Track on right. Cross Saints John Creek.
▼ 1.8	SO	Cross Saints John Creek. Arapaho National Forest information board. Seasonal closure gate.
5.4 ▲	SO	Seasonal closure gate. Cross Saints John Creek.
GPS: N 39°34.00′ W 105°53.23′		
▼ 2.3	TL	T-Intersection. Right goes to camping possibilities. Cross creek.

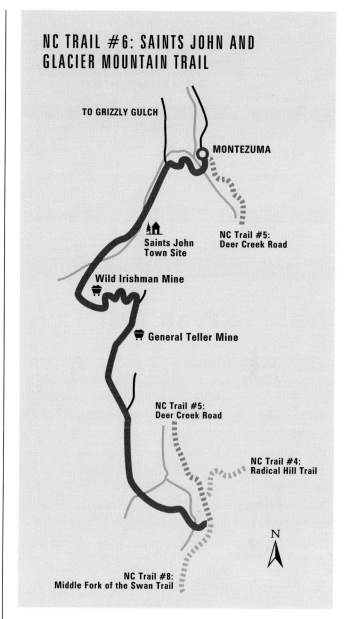

NC TRAIL #6: SAINTS JOHN AND GLACIER MOUNTAIN TRAIL

4.9 ▲	TR	Cross creek. Track on left goes to camping possibilities.
▼ 2.5	SO	Creek crossing.
4.7 ▲	SO	Creek crossing.
▼ 2.8	SO	Wild Irishman Mine is approximately 100 yards off the road on left.
4.4 ▲	SO	Wild Irishman Mine is approximately 100 yards off the road on right.
▼ 2.9	SO	Wild Irishman Mine tailings.
4.3 ▲	SO	Wild Irishman Mine tailings.
▼ 3.0	TR	Trail on left goes to Wild Irishman Mine.
4.2 ▲	TL	Trail on right goes to Wild Irishman Mine.
▼ 3.5	SO	Short trail on left.
3.7 ▲	SO	Short trail on right.
▼ 3.7	SO	Trail on left.
3.5 ▲	SO	Trail on right.
▼ 3.8	SO	General Teller Mine remains on left exposed on mountain ridge.
3.4 ▲	SO	General Teller Mine remains on right exposed on mountain ridge.

▼ 4.5		SO	Track on left dead-ends at old mine.
	2.7 ▲	SO	Track on right dead-ends at old mine.
▼ 6.5		TL	T-intersection. Signpost to Saints John. Track on right leads to North Fork of the Swan via Wise Mountain. Track on left goes to Deer Creek, Radical Hill, and Middle Fork of the Swan.
	0.7 ▲	TR	Intersection.

GPS: N 39°31.39' W 105°52.89'

▼ 7.2			End at T-intersection. Signpost to Montezuma left, Middle Fork of the Swan right.
	0.0 ▲		Begin at three-way intersection signpost that points to the Middle Fork of the Swan to the south, Montezuma to the north, and North Fork of the Swan and Saints John to the west. Zero trip meter and take road toward Saints John.

GPS: N 39°31.24' W 105°52.09'

NORTH-CENTRAL REGION TRAIL #7

Santa Fe Peak Trail

Starting Point:	**Montezuma**
Finishing Point:	**Santa Fe Peak, near the Silver Wave Mine,**
	at the end of a dead-end road (FR 264)
Total Mileage:	**5.2 miles**
Unpaved Mileage:	**5.2 miles**
Driving Time:	**1 1/2 hours (one-way)**
Route Elevation:	**12,800 feet**
Usually Open:	**Early June to early October**
Difficulty Rating:	**5**
Scenic Rating:	**9**

Special Attractions

■ Spectacular, panoramic alpine views.
■ Shelf road with some very challenging sections.
■ Many other 4WD trails in the vicinity.

Description

This route commences at the first intersection on the left as you drive into Montezuma from Keystone (or, coming from the fire station, the last intersection on the right). The unpaved route heads uphill through the homes within the town limits. At this point, there are a number of side roads, but stay on the main road and proceed up a series of mild switchbacks. As the road ascends from timberline, it begins a tighter series of switchbacks.

Once you are out of town, navigation becomes fairly straightforward. The road levels out as it travels

A narrow section of shelf road with the valley floor far below

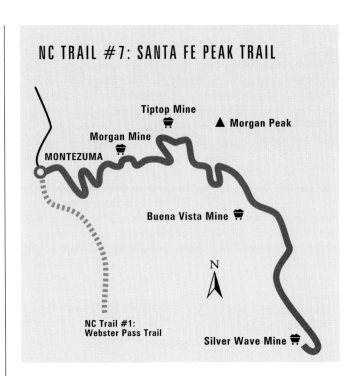

along an open ridge that provides some wonderful views. It then commences another series of short switchbacks before leveling off at an open, rocky meadow that offers spectacular 360-degree views.

As you leave this meadow, the road gets significantly more difficult—especially if you are in a full-sized vehicle. It narrows, becomes rougher, and has a looser surface. Proceeding, the road starts to descend gently around a rocky, narrow shelf with a steep drop-off along the west side of Santa Fe Peak. We recommend that from this point you park your vehicle in an out-of-the-way spot and walk down to the Silver Wave Mine, as there is nowhere to turn around at the mine. You may park along a ridge just under half a mile from the mine, or at the last switchback, about 150 yards before the mine. The ridge provides a great view of Geneva Creek Valley to the east, the Snake River Valley to the southwest, and Red Cone Peak and Webster Pass to the south.

Current Road Conditions

White River National Forest
Dillon Ranger District
680 Blue River Parkway, Silverthorne, CO 80498
(970) 468-5400

Map References

USFS White River NF
USGS Summit County #2
Clear Creek County
Trails Illustrated, #104
The Roads of Colorado, p. 71
Colorado Atlas & Gazetteer, p. 38

Route Directions

▼ 0.0	From the Montezuma Snake River Fire Station, zero trip meter and proceed north on County 5 (FR 5).

GPS: N 39°34.85' W 105°52.03'

▼ 0.1	TR	Intersection with Santa Fe Peak Road (FR 264).
▼ 0.2	SO	Enter National Forest.

GPS: N 39°34.96′ W 105°51.92′

▼ 0.9	SO	Track on left—closed.
▼ 1.3	SO	Mine ruins on right (private property).
▼ 1.4	SO	Track to cabin (private property) on right, then mine ruins on right.
▼ 1.7	SO	Track to mine on right (private property).
▼ 1.9	SO	Mine on right.
▼ 2.6	SO	Track on right. Stay on FR 264.
▼ 2.7	SO	Timberline.
▼ 3.0	SO	Quail Mine on right.

GPS: N 39°34.83′ W 105°50.72′

▼ 3.3	SO	View down onto Montezuma and Snake River Valley.
▼ 3.8	SO	Intersection. Track on right goes to Buena Vista Mine. Remain on FR 264.

GPS: N 39°34.67′ W 105°50.33′

▼ 4.1	SO	Enter large plateau with spectacular 360-degree views.
▼ 4.6	SO	Turn-around and parking opportunity prior to shelf road.
▼ 4.8	SO	Ridge. Full-sized vehicles should stop at this point. Last good spot for turning around.

GPS: N 39°34.09′ W 105°50.08′

▼ 5.1	BR	Last switchback.
▼ 5.2		Silver Wave Mine.

GPS: N 39°34.02′ W 105°50.11′

NORTH-CENTRAL REGION TRAIL #8

Middle Fork of the Swan Trail

Starting Point:	**Three-way intersection of Deer Creek Road with Middle Fork of the Swan Trail and North Fork of the Swan/Saints John road**
Finishing Point:	**Breckenridge at intersection of Colorado 9 and Tiger Road.**
Total Mileage:	**12.7 miles**
Unpaved Mileage:	**11.8 miles**
Driving Time:	**1 hour**
Route Elevation:	**12,200 feet**
Usually Open:	**Mid-June to early October**
Difficulty Rating:	**5**
Scenic Rating:	**8**

Special Attractions
- Beautiful, wooded valley.
- The trail follows the course of the Middle Fork of the Swan River.
- Challenging uphill section.
- Access to a network of 4WD trails.

Description
This route commences at the three-way intersection at the end of Deer Creek Road and travels along an alpine ridge

This benign-looking uphill section of Middle Fork of the Swan Trail can become impassable in wet conditions

toward the headwaters of the Middle Fork of the Swan River.

Shortly after, the road travels along the side of the mountain. The road is significantly off-camber for some distance before starting the steep descent down to the valley floor. The road surface during the descent is quite loose in sections and can be considerably looser if wet. Traveling uphill under such conditions in a stock vehicle can be nearly impossible. It is for this short section of road that the route warrants its difficulty rating; otherwise a rating of 3 would be more appropriate.

The road continues along the extremely attractive Middle Fork of the Swan River before intersecting with North-Central Trail #9: Georgia Pass Trail.

From this point, the road is easily accessible to 2WD vehicles as it threads a path through an almost continual line of huge tailings dumps from the dredge mining in the early 1900s. At the 3.6-mile point from the intersection with Georgia Pass Trail, in a pond among the tailings, lie the remains of the mining boat Tiger Dredge #1.

The route ends at the intersection of Colorado 9 and Tiger Road (at the Highlands at Breckenridge public golf course). This intersection was the location of the town sites of Delaware Flats and Braddocks, named for the Denver, South Park & Pacific Railroad station that was located there.

Current Road Conditions
White River National Forest
Dillon Ranger District
680 Blue River Parkway, Silverthorne, CO 80498
(970) 468-5400

Map References
USFS Arapaho NF-Dillon Ranger District (incomplete)
USGS Summit County #2 (incomplete)
Trails Illustrated, #104 (minor inaccuracies), #109
The Roads of Colorado, p. 71 (incomplete)
Colorado Atlas & Gazetteer, p. 38 (incomplete)

NC TRAIL #8: MIDDLE FORK OF THE SWAN TRAIL

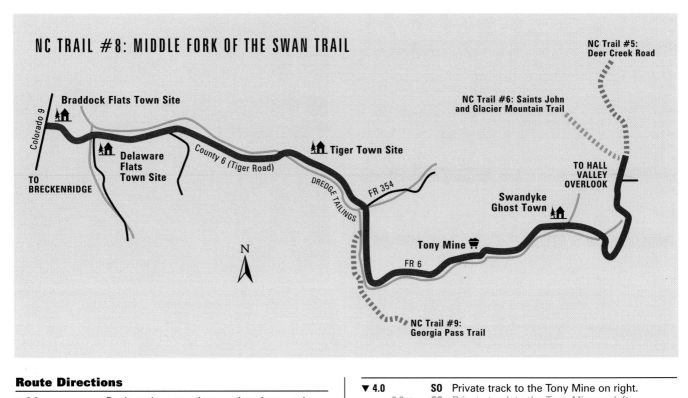

Route Directions

▼ 0.0		Begin at three-way intersection signpost that points to Middle Fork of the Swan to the south, Montezuma to the north, and North Fork of the Swan and Saints John to the west. Zero trip meter and take the road toward Middle Fork of the Swan.
6.6 ▲		End at three-way intersection signpost that points to Middle Fork of the Swan to the south, Montezuma to the north, and North Fork of the Swan and Saints John to the west.

GPS: N 39°31.24' W 105°52.09'

▼ 0.5	SO	Track on left.
6.1 ▲	SO	Track on right.
▼ 0.6	TR	Track on left, followed by an intersection. Sign to Hall Valley (this side road ends at a scenic overlook in 0.8 miles). Proceed toward Middle Fork of the Swan on FR 220.
6.0 ▲	TL	T-intersection. Hall Valley scenic overlook is to the right. Follow sign to Montezuma. Then pass a small track on right.

GPS: N 39°30.83' W 105°51.74'

▼ 1.5	SO	Track on left.
5.1 ▲	SO	Track on right.
▼ 1.8	SO	Log cabin ruins on right.
4.9 ▲	SO	Log cabin ruins on left.
▼ 2.2	SO	Cross through creek.
4.4 ▲	SO	Cross through creek.
▼ 2.4	SO	Track on right.
4.2 ▲	SO	Track on left.
▼ 2.7	SO	Deserted log cabin on right. Site of Swandyke.
3.9 ▲	SO	Deserted log cabin on left. Site of Swandyke.

GPS: N 39°30.49' W 105°53.50'

▼ 3.0	SO	Cross through creek, then track on right.
3.6 ▲	SO	Track on left, then cross through creek.
▼ 3.4	SO	Track on left.
3.2 ▲	SO	Track on right.
▼ 3.8	SO	Cabin ruins on right.
2.8 ▲	SO	Cabin ruins on left.

▼ 4.0	SO	Private track to the Tony Mine on right.
2.6 ▲	SO	Private track to the Tony Mine on left.

GPS: N 39°30.14' W 105°54.71'

▼ 4.1	SO	Track on left.
2.5 ▲	SO	Track on right.
▼ 4.8	SO	Track on left.
1.8 ▲	SO	Track on right.
▼ 5.9	SO	Seasonal gate.
0.7 ▲	SO	Seasonal gate.
▼ 6.6	SO	Road on left goes to North-Central Trail #9: Georgia Pass Trail. Zero trip meter.
0.0 ▲		Continue straight on.

GPS: N 39°30.39' W 105°56.71'

▼ 0.0		Continue straight ahead on County 6 (Tiger Road) toward Breckenridge.
6.1 ▲	SO	Road on right is North-Central Trail #9: Georgia Pass Trail. Signpost points to Middle Fork of the Swan straight ahead and South Fork (Georgia Pass) to the right. Zero trip meter.
▼ 0.5	BL	Cross bridge. Road on right to North Fork and Wise Mountain.
5.6 ▲	BR	Road on left to North Fork and Wise Mountain. Cross bridge.
▼ 3.6	SO	Parking area for viewing of historic dredge boat on right.
2.5 ▲	SO	Parking area for viewing historic dredge boat on left.
▼ 6.1		End at intersection with Colorado 9. Breckenridge is to the left.
0.0 ▲		At intersection of Route 9 and County 6 (Tiger Road), 3.2 miles north of Breckenridge Visitor Center, zero trip meter and proceed east along Tiger Road. This intersection is marked with a sign for the Breckenridge Public Golf Course.

GPS: N 39°31.95' W 106°02.58'

Georgia Pass Trail

Starting Point:	**Middle Fork of the Swan Trail**
Finishing Point:	**Jefferson**
Total Mileage:	**16.1 miles**
Unpaved Mileage:	**16.1 miles**
Driving Time:	**1 1/2 hours**
Pass Elevation:	**11,585 feet**
Usually Open:	**Mid-June to late September**
Difficulty Rating:	**4**
Scenic Rating:	**7**

Special Attractions

- Historic route and mining sites.
- Parkville Cemetery.
- Can form a loop route, returning over Webster Pass.

History

Until 1861 (before the establishment of the Colorado Territory), Georgia Pass traversed the boundary of the Utah and Kansas Territories.

Crossing over the Continental Divide, the pass was traveled heavily by both the Ute and, after their migration south from Montana and Wyoming in the early 1800s, the Arapaho. The Arapaho were the more hostile of the two tribes and caused many early prospectors and setters to avoid the pass when they were in the vicinity. John Frémont visited the area in 1844, but he chose to detour to Hoosier Pass due to the presence of the Arapaho.

Despite the threat of attack by the Arapaho, many early prospectors braved the route. It was heavily used in the 1859 gold rush to the Blue River diggings, which included the mining camps of Breckenridge, Lincoln City, and Frisco on the Blue River; Tiger and Parkville on the Swan River; and Montezuma, Saints John, and Argentine in the Snake River area.

Breckenridge produced Colorado's largest gold nugget, the fourteen-pound "Tom's Baby," which disappeared a few years after it was discovered and was presumed stolen to be broken down or melted. But in 1971, officials of the Denver Museum of Natural History found it in a box that was thought to contain dinosaur bones. The nugget is now on exhibit there.

The first recorded wagon crossing over Georgia Pass was in November 1861; later that year approval for a toll road was granted. A stagecoach service operated across the pass between Swandyke, on the Middle Fork of the Swan River, and Jefferson.

The huge, unsightly gravel mounds along Swan River are tailings dumped there by the four huge dredge boats that placer-mined the river for gold up until 1904. The remains of the last

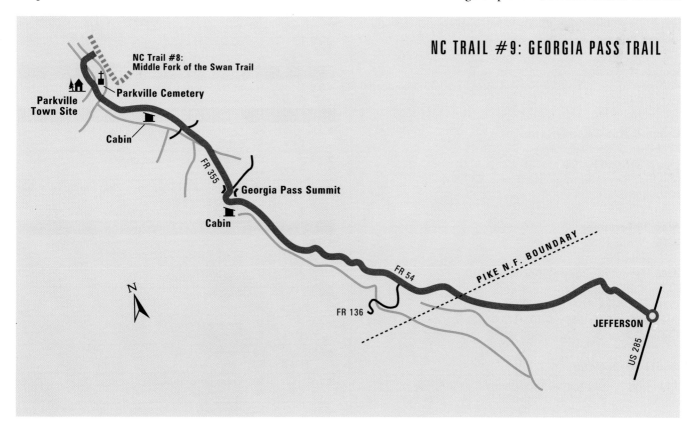

NC TRAIL #9: GEORGIA PASS TRAIL

NC Trail #8:
Middle Fork of the Swan Trail

Parkville Cemetery

Parkville Town Site

Cabin

FR 355

Georgia Pass Summit

Cabin

FR 54

FR 136

PIKE N.F. BOUNDARY

JEFFERSON

US 285

N

dredge boat are along the route, and better-preserved remains of another boat are located in French's Gulch. Workers assembled these boats on-site from two hundred tons of components that were freighted in from Milwaukee at around the turn of the century.

Description

The route commences at the intersection with North-Central Trail #8: Middle Fork of the Swan Trail. Initially, the road is easily accessible to 2WD vehicles but slowly becomes more difficult.

Soon after the start, the route passes the town site of Parkville, the main mining camp in Summit County during the gold rush of the 1860s. All that remains of the once bustling town of ten thousand is the cemetery, which can be reached via a short walking track.

The Georgia Pass Trail approaching the summit

After Parkville, the road forks. This route follows the left fork; the right fork turns toward Georgia Gulch and leads to Breckenridge via Georgia Gulch, American Gulch, French's Gulch, and the town site of Lincoln City.

From here to the summit, stay on the main road rather than following a number of intersecting roads—most are dead ends.

The summit is an open, grassy saddle with good views of Mount Guyot to the west.

The south side of the pass down to Jefferson is narrow initially, but much easier than the north side.

From Jefferson, it is 16 miles southwest to Fairplay, 23 miles east to Bailey, and 8.4 miles northeast to the turnoff for North-Central Trail #2: Handcart Gulch Trail.

Current Road Conditions

White River National Forest
Dillon Ranger District
680 Blue River Parkway, Silverthorne, CO 80498
(970) 468-5400

Map References

USFS   White River NF
         Pike NF
USGS   Summit County #2 (incomplete)
         Park County #1
Trails Illustrated, #104, #105, #108, #109
The Roads of Colorado, pp. 70-71
Colorado Atlas & Gazetteer, pp. 38, 48

Route Directions

▼	▲		
0.0			Begin at intersection of County 6/Tiger Road (North-Central Trail #8: Middle Fork of the Swan Trail) and FR 355. Zero trip meter and proceed toward Georgia Pass on FR 355.
	4.4 ▲		End at intersection of County 6 (Tiger Road). This is North-Central Trail #8: Middle Fork of the Swan Trail.
GPS: N 39°30.37' W 105°56.73'			
0.6		SO	Cross through creek bed. Town site of Parkville on right.
	3.8 ▲	SO	Cross through creek bed. Town site of Parkville on left.
0.7		SO	Walking track on left. Parkville Cemetery and Masonic marker are about 150 yards down the trail.
	3.7 ▲	SO	Walking track on right. Parkville Cemetery and Masonic marker are about 150 yards down the trail.
0.8		BL	Fork in the road. Track on right goes to Georgia Gulch. Cross bridge.
	3.5 ▲	BR	Cross bridge to intersection. Track on the left goes to Georgia Gulch.
GPS: N 39°27.70' W 105°56.82'			
1.5		SO	Log cabin on left.
	2.8 ▲	SO	Log cabin on right.
2.2		SO	White cabin (private property) on right.
	2.2 ▲	SO	White cabin (private property) on left.
2.7		BL	Follow FR 355. Track on right crosses through creek.
	1.7 ▲	BR	Track on left crosses through creek.
GPS: N 39°28.73' W 105°55.33'			
2.8		BL	Cross through creek.
	1.6 ▲	BR	Cross through creek.
2.9		BR	Fork in road. Take right fork and cross through creek.
	1.5 ▲	BL	Cross through creek. Track on right.
3.0		BR	Fork in road. Track on left.
	1.4 ▲	SO	Track on right.
3.1		BR	Track on left.
	1.2 ▲	BL	Track on right.
3.3		SO	Seasonal closure gate.
	1.1 ▲	SO	Seasonal closure gate.
GPS: N 39°28.31' W 105°55.08'			
3.5		TL	Intersection.
	0.9 ▲	TR	Intersection.
GPS: N 39°28.15' W 105°55.18'			
3.6		SO	Cross over creek.
	0.8 ▲	SO	Cross over creek.
4.3		SO	Intersection. Proceed up hill.
	0.1 ▲	SO	Intersection.
4.4		SO	Summit of Georgia Pass. Zero trip meter at the summit marker.
	0.0 ▲		Continue along Georgia Pass Road.
GPS: N 39°27.50' W 105°54.98'			
0.0			Continue toward Jefferson and Michigan Creek Campground on FR 54.
	11.7 ▲	SO	Summit of Georgia Pass. Zero trip meter at the summit marker.
0.2		SO	Track on right.
	11.5 ▲	BR	Track on left.
0.3		SO	Track on right.
	11.4 ▲	SO	Track on left.
0.5		SO	Cabin on right.
	11.2 ▲	SO	Cabin on left.
2.3		SO	Cross over creek.
	9.4 ▲	SO	Cross over creek.
3.6		SO	Numerous camping spots on left. Cross over creek.

8.1 ▲	SO	Cross over creek.
▼ 5.3	SO	FR 136 on right.
6.4 ▲	SO	FR 136 on left.
▼ 5.9	SO	USFS Michigan Creek Campground on right.
5.8 ▲	SO	USFS Michigan Creek Campground on left.
	GPS: N 39°24.68′ W 105°53.01′	
▼ 6.5	TR	Intersection.
5.2 ▲	TL	Intersection.
▼ 6.9	SO	Leave Pike National Forest.
4.8 ▲	SO	Enter Pike National Forest.
▼ 8.9	BL	Intersection.
2.8 ▲	BR	Intersection.
▼ 9.8	SO	Intersection. Jefferson Lake to the left.
1.9 ▲	SO	Intersection. Jefferson Lake to the right.
▼ 11.7		End at intersection of US 285 and County 35 in Jefferson.
0.0 ▲		At intersection of US 285 and County 35 in Jefferson, zero trip meter and proceed along County 35 toward Georgia Pass. This intersection is marked with a National Forest sign to Jefferson Lake Road and Michigan Creek Road.
	GPS: N 39°22.67′ W 105°48.01′	

NORTH-CENTRAL REGION TRAIL #10

Boreas Pass Road

Starting Point:	Breckenridge
Finishing Point:	Como
Total Mileage:	21.3 miles
Unpaved Mileage:	17.0 miles
Driving Time:	1 1/4 hours
Pass Elevation:	11,481 feet
Usually Open:	Late May to mid-October
Difficulty Rating:	1
Scenic Rating:	8

Special Attractions

■ Travel the route of a famous old narrow-gauge railway that in its time was the highest in the United States.

■ Narrow railway cuttings, fine views, and the sites of many old mining camps.

■ In fall, excellent views of the changing aspens.

History

This pass was called by many names—Ute, Hamilton, Tarryall, and Breckenridge—before receiving its present name in the late 1880s. Boreas, the Greek god of the north wind, is an appropriate namesake for this gusty mountain route.

The Ute Indians crossed the pass going south to spend their winters in warmer regions. In 1839, Thomas Farnham, a Vermont lawyer, traveled the pass on his trek across Colorado. In the late 1850s, prospectors poured over the pass from South Park to reach the gold discoveries in the Blue River district. At this time, the crossing was nothing more than a burro trail, but

miners braved the winter snow to walk the pass on snowshoes.

In the 1860s the road was upgraded, and a daily stage traveled across Boreas Pass. In 1881, the Denver, South Park & Pacific Railroad laid narrow-gauge tracks over the pass. For a time, the line was the highest in the United States and required over a

Rotary snowplow clearing the tracks in the winter of 1898

dozen snowsheds. Steep grades of more than 4 percent made the route difficult for trains pulling heavy loads. The grades were such a problem that when P. T. Barnum's circus came to Breckenridge, they had to unload their elephants to help pull the train the last three miles to the summit. The railroad continued to operate until 1937.

In 1952, the U.S. Army Corps of Engineers converted the old railroad grade for automobile use but bypassed the most dangerous section of the route, Windy Point.

Description

This scenic and extremely popular route is suitable for passenger vehicles, although it is unpaved and frequently scarred by numerous potholes.

The route starts in Breckenridge and joins Boreas Pass Road a short distance south of town. Windy Point, identifiable by a

large rock outcropping, lies about a half mile from the turnoff onto Boreas Pass Road. The route continues past the restored Bakers Tank (refer to the section on South-Central Trail #8 for further information about water tanks that serviced the steam engines).

The summit of Boreas Pass was the site of a Denver, South Park & Pacific Railroad station. The station house, which is being restored as an interpretative center, is only one of the buildings that used to be located at the site.

Bakers Tank

There was also a two-room telegraph house and a storehouse, as well as a wye in the tracks to allow the trains to turn around.

At Como, the stone roundhouse still stands, but the wooden portion of the roundhouse and the forty-three-room Pacific Hotel were destroyed by fire. The roundhouse is being restored.

Current Road Conditions

White River National Forest
Dillon Ranger District
680 Blue River Parkway, Silverthorne, CO 80498
(970) 468-5400

Map References

USFS White River NF
Pike NF

USGS Park County #1
Summit County #2
Trails Illustrated, #109
The Roads of Colorado, pp. 70-71, 87
Colorado Atlas & Gazetteer, p. 48

Route Directions

▼ 0.0		Outside Breckenridge Visitor Information Center at 309 North Main Street, zero trip meter and proceed south.
21.3 ▲		End at Breckenridge Visitor Information Center at 309 North Main Street.

GPS: N 39°29.12′ W 106°02.73′

▼ 0.8	TL	Onto Boreas Pass Road (County 33/FR 33).
20.5 ▲	TR	Onto Colorado 9.
▼ 4.3	SO	Unpaved.
17.0 ▲	SO	Paved.
▼ 4.4	SO	Cross through gate.
16.9 ▲	SO	Cross through gate.
▼ 5.8	SO	Walking track on left.
15.5 ▲	SO	Walking track on right.
▼ 7.3	SO	Bakers Tank on left with walking track behind it.
14.0 ▲	SO	Bakers Tank on right with walking track behind it.
▼ 7.9	SO	Track on left.
13.4 ▲	SO	Track on right.
▼ 8.2	SO	Track on left.
13.1 ▲	SO	Track on right.
▼ 9.1	SO	Site of Farnham Station, post office, and store on left. On right is a walking track to Dyersville site, about 0.5 miles from road.
12.2 ▲	SO	Site of Farnham Station, post office, and store on right. On left is a walking track to Dyersville site, about 0.5 miles from road.

GPS: N 39°25.50′ W 105°58.88′

▼ 10.6	SO	Summit of Boreas Pass and historic buildings.
10.7 ▲	SO	Summit of Boreas Pass and historic buildings.

GPS: N 39°24.64′ W 105°58.07′

▼ 13.2	SO	Cross over Selkirk Gulch Creek.
8.1 ▲	SO	Cross over Selkirk Gulch Creek.
▼ 14.4	SO	Track on right goes to Upper Tarryall Road and access to Selkirk Campground.
6.9 ▲	SO	Track on left goes to Upper Tarryall Road and access to Selkirk Campground.
▼ 15.2	SO	Cross over Halfway Gulch Creek.
6.1 ▲	SO	Cross over Halfway Gulch Creek.
▼ 17.5	SO	Seasonal gate.
3.8 ▲	SO	Seasonal gate.
▼ 17.7	SO	North Tarryall Creek Road on right.
3.6 ▲	SO	North Tarryall Creek Road on left.
▼ 18.4	SO	Site of Tarryall City mining camp.
2.9 ▲	SO	Site of Tarryall City mining camp.
▼ 18.8	SO	Cross Tarryall Creek. Mining ruins on right.
2.5 ▲	SO	Mining ruins on left. Cross Tarryall Creek.
▼ 20.0	SO	Site of Hamilton mining camp.
2.3 ▲	SO	Site of Hamilton mining camp.
▼ 20.4	SO	Cattle guard. Paved road returns.
0.9 ▲	SO	Paved road returns. Cattle guard.
▼ 20.5	SO	Town of Como.
0.8 ▲	SO	Leaving Como.
▼ 20.7	TL	Intersection.
0.6 ▲	TR	Intersection.
▼ 20.8	SO	Old stone roundhouse on left.
0.5 ▲	SO	Old stone roundhouse on right.

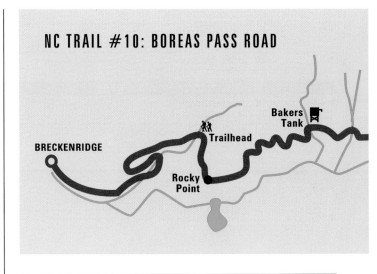

NC TRAIL #10: BOREAS PASS ROAD

▼ 21.3		Cattle guard. End at intersection with US 285.
0.0 ▲		At intersection of Boreas Pass Road (County 33/FR 33) and US 285 in Como, zero trip meter and proceed along County 33 toward Boreas Pass.

GPS: N 39°18.64′ W 105°53.15′

NORTH-CENTRAL REGION TRAIL #11

Guanella Pass Trail

Starting Point:	**Grant, at intersection of US 285 and County 62**
Finishing Point:	**Georgetown, at Old Georgetown Railway Station**
Total Mileage:	**23.4 miles**
Unpaved Mileage:	**11.7 miles**
Driving Time:	**1 hour**
Pass Elevation:	**11,669 feet**
Usually Open:	**Year-round**
Difficulty Rating:	**1**
Scenic Rating:	**4**

Special Attractions

- Attractive scenery with expansive views from the summit.
- An accessible backcountry route, which can be undertaken by passenger vehicles.
- Fall viewing of the aspens.

History

This pass is named for Byron Guanella, a Clear Creek commissioner who was a supporter of building a road over the pass.

Buffalo used to graze their way across this pass, and the Indians used the pass as they followed the migration of the buffalo herds. Early prospectors seeking to use the pass were always on guard against being attacked by the Indians.

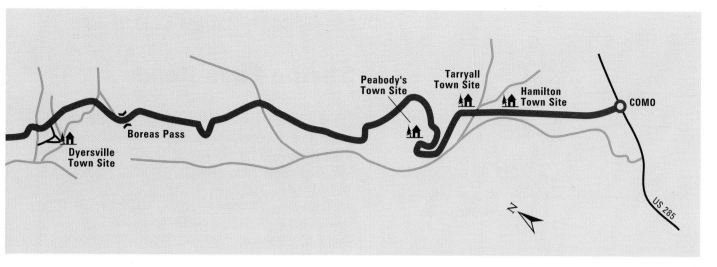

In 1861, Captain Edward Berthoud and Jim Bridger crossed the pass when surveying potential routes for a railroad west.

Description

Today, this very popular route is used year-round for picnics, camping, hunting, and cross-country skiing. The easy 2WD route is very scenic and provides good fall viewing of the aspens.

The route starts at the tiny township of Grant and heads north on FR 118 beside Geneva Creek, traveling through a wooded valley with scenic rock formations along the road. The roadside alternates between private property and national forest.

After about four miles, the road starts its climb toward the pass summit and leaves the creek behind. It continues above the timberline, with the scenery becoming considerably more rugged.

The summit offers expansive views of Mount Bierstadt, Mount Evans, and the Sawtooth Range to the east and the Continental Divide to the west.

The descent to Georgetown follows Clear Creek past a number of lakes and reservoirs, as well as the Cabin Creek hydroelectric plant.

The route offers access to four U.S. Forest Service campgrounds and numerous hiking trails.

Current Road Conditions

Georgetown Visitor Information Center
613 6th Street, Georgetown, CO 80444
(303) 569-2888

Map References

USFS Arapaho & Roosevelt NF
USGS Clear Creek County
        Park County #2
Trails Illustrated, #104 (most of the route)
The Roads of Colorado, p. 71
Colorado Atlas & Gazetteer, pp. 39, 49

Route Directions

▼ 0.0		At intersection of US 285 and County 62 in Grant, zero trip meter and turn onto Guanella Pass Road toward Georgetown.
12.7 ▲		End at intersection with US 285 in Grant.

GPS: N 39°27.61' W 105°39.75'		
▼ 0.5	SO	Unpaved.
12.2 ▲	SO	Paved.
▼ 1.3	SO	Enter National Forest.
11.4 ▲	SO	Leave National Forest.
▼ 1.6	SO	Geneva Creek Picnic Grounds.
11.1 ▲	SO	Geneva Creek Picnic Grounds.
▼ 2.3	SO	USFS Whiteside Campground.
10.4 ▲	SO	USFS Whiteside Campground.
▼ 2.7	SO	Driving through Geneva Creek Canyon.
10.0 ▲	SO	Driving through Geneva Creek Canyon.
▼ 5.0	SO	Cattle guard.
7.7 ▲	SO	Cattle guard.
▼ 5.1	SO	Geneva Park.
7.6 ▲	SO	Geneva Park.
▼ 5.2	SO	USFS Burning Bear Campground.
7.5 ▲	SO	USFS Burning Bear Campground.
▼ 6.0	SO	Track to Geneva City town site at Duck Creek Picnic Ground on left.
6.7 ▲	SO	Track to Geneva City town site at Duck Creek Picnic Ground on right.
▼ 6.7	SO	Track on left to Geneva Creek (FR 119).
6.0 ▲	SO	Track on right to Geneva Creek (FR 119).
▼ 9.2	SO	Unpaved.
3.5 ▲	SO	Paved.
▼ 12.7	SO	Summit of Guanella Pass. Zero trip meter.
0.0 ▲		Continue toward Grant.
GPS: N 39°35.72' W 105°42.61'		
▼ 0.0		Continue toward Georgetown.
10.7 ▲	SO	Summit of Guanella Pass. Zero trip meter.
▼ 1.8	SO	Silver Dollar Lake trail (1 mile) on left.
8.9 ▲	SO	Silver Dollar Lake trail (1 mile) on right.
▼ 1.9	SO	USFS Guanella Campground on left.
8.8 ▲	SO	USFS Guanella Campground on right.
▼ 3.7	SO	Cross over South Clear Creek.
7.0 ▲	SO	Cross over South Clear Creek.
▼ 4.7	SO	USFS Clear Lake Campground on left.
6.0 ▲	SO	USFS Clear Lake Campground on right.
▼ 4.8	SO	Paved.
5.9 ▲	SO	Unpaved.
▼ 6.0	SO	Clear Lake on right.
4.7 ▲	SO	Clear Lake on left.
▼ 6.5	SO	Green Lake on right.
4.2 ▲	SO	Green Lake on left.

NC TRAIL #11: GUANELLA PASS ROAD

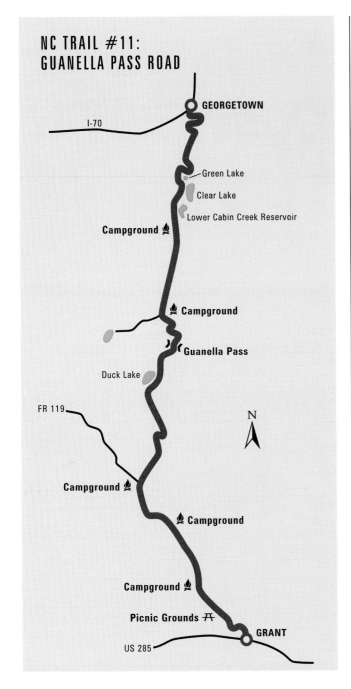

▼ 7.7	SO	Road on left to Waldorf and Argentine Pass.
3.0 ▲	SO	Road on right to Waldorf and Argentine Pass.
▼ 8.5	SO	Georgetown reservoir on right.
2.2 ▲	SO	Georgetown reservoir on left.
▼ 10.0	SO	Enter Georgetown, remaining on the paved road. As it comes into town, the name becomes Rose Street.
0.7 ▲	SO	Leave Georgetown on Rose Street toward Guanella Pass.
▼ 10.7		End at Georgetown Loop Railroad station on the corner of Rose and 11th Streets.
0.0 ▲		From the Georgetown Loop Railroad station at the corner of Rose and 11th Streets in Georgetown, zero trip meter and proceed south along Rose Street, which will become County 381.

GPS: N 39°42.69′ W 105°41.69′

Shrine Pass Road

Starting Point:	Redcliff
Finishing Point:	Interstate 70, at exit 190 near Vail Pass
Total Mileage:	10.8 miles
Unpaved Mileage:	10.7 miles
Driving Time:	3/4 hour
Pass Elevation:	11,089 feet
Usually Open:	Mid-June to late September
Difficulty Rating:	2
Scenic Rating:	8

Special Attractions

- Spectacular views of the Mount of the Holy Cross.
- Fall viewing of the aspens.
- Summer wildflowers.

History

Shrine Pass is so named because it overlooks and provides a wonderful view of the Mount of the Holy Cross, a famous fourteen-thousand-foot peak. The route was an old Indian trail. It rose to prominence in the 1920s when Orion W. Draggett, a Redcliff newspaper publisher, proposed a shrine be built there. His amazing plans included not only viewing facilities but also an airport and a golf course. In 1931, he opened the road that he intended to use for this project, attracting a crowd of hundreds to the event. The project was never undertaken, but proponents continued to raise it periodically for some years.

The Mount of the Holy Cross was declared a national monument by President Herbert Hoover; but it lost its status in 1950 due to the deterioration of the right arm of the cross.

Before 1940, the pass road served as the main route between Denver and Grand Junction.

Description

The route leaves Redcliff, and travels initially beside Turkey Creek through the narrow, wooded valley. As the route gains altitude, there are a number of viewing spots along the way that provide distant but spectacular views of the Mount of the Holy Cross to the southwest.

Closer to the broad, open pass, the alpine meadows are famous for their vivid wildflower displays in summer. The huge stands of aspens also attract many sightseers in the fall. In the winter, the area is very popular for cross-country skiing.

The road is easy and accessible to 2WD vehicles the entire distance.

Current Road Conditions

White River National Forest
Holy Cross Ranger District
24747 US Hwy 24, Minturn, CO 81645
(970) 827-5715

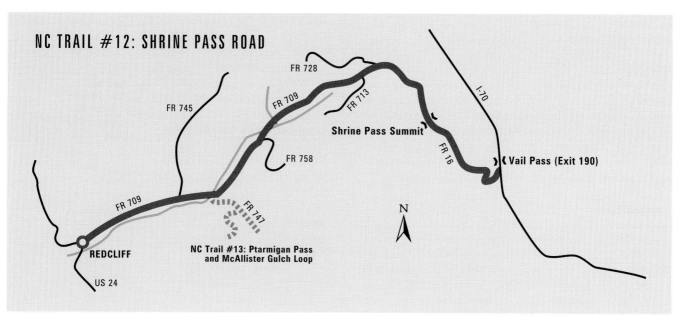

NC TRAIL #12: SHRINE PASS ROAD

Map References

USFS White River NF
USGS Summit County #2
    Eagle County #4
Trails Illustrated, #108
The Roads of Colorado, p. 70
Colorado Atlas & Gazetteer, pp. 37-38

Route Directions

▼ 0.0		At intersection of US 24 and FR 709 in Redcliff, zero trip meter and proceed east, following sign to Shrine Pass (FR 709).
2.4 ▲		End at intersection with US 24 in Redcliff.
GPS: N 39°30.78' W 106°22.03'		
▼ 0.1	SO	Unpaved.
2.3 ▲	SO	Paved.
▼ 1.9	SO	Seasonal gate. FR 745 on left.
0.5 ▲	SO	FR 745 on right. Seasonal gate.
▼ 2.4	SO	Track on right over bridge is North-Central Trail #13: Ptarmigan Pass and McAllister Gulch Loop. Zero trip meter.
0.0 ▲		Continue along FR 709 toward Redcliff.
GPS: N 39°31.39' W 106°19.49'		
▼ 0.0		Continue along FR 709 toward Shrine Pass.
8.4 ▲	SO	Track on left over bridge is North-Central Trail #13: Ptarmigan Pass and McAllister Gulch Loop. Zero trip meter.
▼ 0.6	SO	FR 258 on right. Cabins.
7.8 ▲	SO	Cabins. FR 258 on left.
▼ 1.7	SO	Cross over Turkey Creek.
6.7 ▲	SO	Cross over Turkey Creek.
▼ 3.2	SO	Cross over creek.
5.2 ▲	SO	Cross over creek.
▼ 3.4	SO	Track on right.
5.0 ▲	SO	Track on left.
▼ 4.0	TL	FR 713 on right.
4.4 ▲	TR	FR 713 on left.
GPS: N 39°33.41' W 106°16.07'		
▼ 4.7	BR	FR 728 on left.
3.7 ▲	BL	FR 728 on right.

▼ 5.3	SO	Track on right.
3.1 ▲	SO	Track on left.
▼ 6.2	SO	Summit of Shrine Pass. Track on right.
2.2 ▲	SO	Track on left. Summit of Shrine Pass.
GPS: N 39°32.72' W 106°14.45'		
▼ 8.4		Seasonal gate, then in 100 yards, a stop sign. Paved road. End at interstate 70.
0.0 ▲		The intersection for Shrine Pass is on I-70 at exit 190, approximately 1 mile east of Vail Pass summit. Zero trip meter where the side road goes from paved to unpaved.
GPS: N 39°31.74' W 106°13.06'		

NORTH-CENTRAL REGION TRAIL #13

Ptarmigan Pass and McAllister Gulch Loop

Starting Point:	**Intersection of Shrine Pass Road (FR 709)**
	and FR 747
Finishing Point:	**Intersection of Shrine Pass Road (FR 709)**
	and FR 747
Total Mileage:	**21.4 miles**
Unpaved Mileage:	**21.4 miles**
Driving Time:	**3 hours**
Pass Elevation:	**11,765 feet**
Usually Open:	**Mid-June to late September**
Difficulty Rating:	**4**
Scenic Rating:	**9**

Special Attractions

■ Panoramic views of the Mount of the Holy Cross, a fourteen-thousand-foot peak.

- Numerous creek crossings.
- Historic site of the Camp Hale Army Base.

History

During World War II, this area was used to train the Tenth Mountain Division of the U.S. Army, based at the now decommissioned Camp Hale Army Base. The base was the only facility that offered training in mountain and winter warfare. The division fought with distinction. After the war, a number of the veterans from the Tenth Mountain Division were instrumental in establishing Colorado's ski industry.

Description

This route is a side road of North-Central Trail #12: Shrine Pass Road. Initially, it travels through a very scenic, narrow canyon with barely enough room at its base for the road and Wearyman Creek. The road crosses through the shallow creek a number of times before reaching FR 708 in less than a mile.

FR 708 immediately starts to climb steeply and continues through the dense forest with numerous switchbacks, where passing oncoming vehicles is possible.

The road rises above timberline into a broad alpine meadow and continues to the top of Hornsilver Mountain, from which point there is a spectacular, 360-degree view; to the southwest is the Holy Cross Wilderness Area and the Mount of the Holy Cross, a famous fourteen-thousand-foot peak. This mountain was declared a national monument by President Herbert Hoover; but it lost its status in 1950 due to the deterioration of the right arm of the cross.

The route continues across a fairly level ridge to Resolution Mountain. At around the six-mile point of the route, the road commences a steep descent that lasts for about half a mile.

As you turn onto FR 702 (Resolution Road), a right turn takes you to the old Camp Hale Army Base and US 24; a left turn heads toward Ptarmigan Pass. The road to the pass is wide and well maintained.

The descent from the pass via FR 747 (Wearyman Road)

A section of trail typical of this route

heads back below timberline and is rougher, narrower, and often boggy. There is also another short section of shelf road. You will have to cross the creek several times before returning to the intersection with Shrine Pass Road.

We highly recommend the *Trails Illustrated* maps listed below to assist with navigation of this route.

Current Road Conditions

White River National Forest
Holy Cross Ranger District
24747 US Hwy 24, Minturn, CO 81645
(970) 827-5715

Map References

USFS White River NF
USGS Eagle County #4
Summit County #2
Trails Illustrated, #108, #109
The Roads of Colorado, p. 70
Colorado Atlas & Gazetteer, pp. 37, 47

Route Directions

▼ 0.0		From intersection of Shrine Pass Road (FR 709) and FR 747, zero trip meter at Wearyman Creek bridge and proceed toward Ptarmigan Pass and McAllister Gulch.
0.7 ▲		Cross bridge and end at Shrine Pass Road (FR 709).
GPS: N 39°31.39′ W 106°19.49′		
▼ 0.2	SO	Cross through creek, then 100 yards farther, cross through creek again.
0.5 ▲	SO	Cross through creek, then 100 yards farther, cross through creek again.
▼ 0.3	SO	Cross through creek.
0.4 ▲	SO	Cross through creek.
▼ 0.4	SO	Cross through creek.
0.3 ▲	SO	Cross through creek.
▼ 0.7	TR	Cross through creek. Intersection with McAllister Gulch Road (FR 708). Zero trip meter.
0.0 ▲		Proceed along FR 747.
GPS: N 39°31.20′ W 106°18.87′		
▼ 0.0		Proceed along FR 708.
10.0 ▲	TL	Intersection with Wearyman Road (FR 747) Cross through creek. Zero trip meter.
▼ 1.1	BR	Fork in road.
8.9 ▲	BL	Fork in road.
▼ 2.1	BL	Track on right.
7.9 ▲	BR	Track on left.
▼ 2.2	BL	Track on right.
7.8 ▲	BR	Track on left.
▼ 2.9	BL	Intersection. Spot on right with broad, panoramic views of Eagle River Valley to the southwest and northwest.
7.0 ▲	BR	Intersection. Spot on left with broad, panoramic views of Eagle River Valley to the southwest and northwest.
GPS: N 39°29.98′ W 106°19.88′		
▼ 3.6	SO	Meadow at top of Hornsilver Mountain with 360-degree views.
6.4 ▲	SO	Meadow at top of Hornsilver Mountain with 360-degree views.
GPS: N 39°29.86′ W 106°19.41′		
▼ 4.3	BR	Intersection.
5.6 ▲	BL	Intersection.

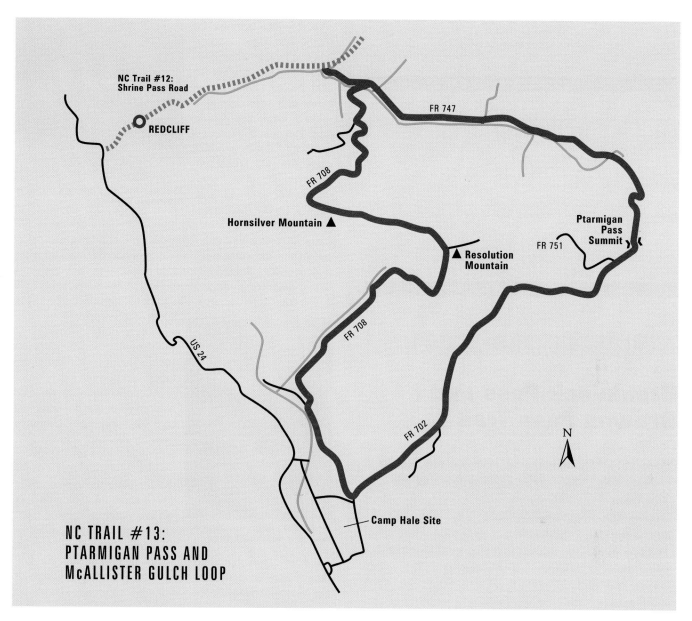

NC TRAIL #13:
PTARMIGAN PASS AND
McALLISTER GULCH LOOP

		GPS: N 39°29.27' W 106°17.82'
▼ 8.4	SO	Private cabin on right. National Forest boundary.
1.6 ▲	SO	National Forest boundary. Private cabin on left.
▼ 8.8	TL	Intersection. Track on right dead-ends.
1.2 ▲	TR	Intersection. Sign to McAllister Gulch. Dead end is straight ahead.
		GPS: N 39°27.76' W 106°19.76'
▼ 9.2	TL	Intersection. Follow Ptarmigan Pass sign to the left.
0.8 ▲	TR	Intersection.
▼ 10.0	TL	Intersection with Resolution Road (FR 702). Road on right connects with US 24 in 1.1 miles and site of old Camp Hale U.S. Army Base. Zero trip meter.
0.0 ▲		Continue along FR 708.
		GPS: N 39°26.90' W 106°19.12'
▼ 0.0		Continue along FR 702.
5.3 ▲	TR	Onto FR 708. Zero trip meter
▼ 0.2	SO	Seasonal gate.
5.1 ▲	SO	Seasonal gate.

▼ 1.3	SO	Track on right dead-ends. Remain on Resolution Road (FR 702).
4.0 ▲	SO	Track on left dead-ends.
▼ 4.8	TR	Intersection with FR 751.
0.5 ▲	TL	Intersection with Resolution Road (FR 702)
▼ 5.3	SO	Summit of Ptarmigan Pass. Road becomes FR 747. Zero trip meter.
0.0 ▲		Continue along FR 702.
		GPS: N 39°29.59' W 106°15.14'
▼ 0.0		Continue along FR 747.
5.4 ▲	SO	Summit of Ptarmigan Pass. Road becomes FR 702. Zero trip meter.
▼ 1.4	SO	Cross through creek.
4.0 ▲	SO	Cross through creek.
▼ 2.1	SO	Cross through creek.
3.2 ▲	SO	Cross through creek.
▼ 3.1	SO	Cross through creek.
2.3 ▲	SO	Cross through creek.
▼ 4.6	SO	Cross through creek.
0.8 ▲	SO	Cross through creek.

▼ 4.7		SO	Intersection with FR 708 to McAllister Gulch on left. Cross through creek.
	0.7 ▲	SO	Cross through creek. Intersection with FR 708 to McAllister Gulch on right.

GPS: N 39°31.20' W 106°18.87'

▼ 5.0		SO	Cross through creek.
	0.4 ▲	SO	Cross through creek.
▼ 5.1		SO	Cross through creek.
	0.3 ▲	SO	Cross through creek.
▼ 5.2		SO	Cross through creek.
	0.2 ▲	SO	Cross through creek.
▼ 5.3		SO	Cross through creek.
	0.1 ▲	SO	Cross through creek.
▼ 5.4			Cross bridge and end at Shrine Pass Road (FR 709).
	0.0 ▲		From intersection of Shrine Pass Road (FR 709) and FR 747, zero trip meter at Wearyman Creek bridge and proceed toward Ptarmigan Pass and McAllister Gulch.

GPS: N 39°31.39' W 106°19.49'

NORTH-CENTRAL REGION TRAIL #14

Breakneck Pass and Browns Pass Trail

Starting Point:	**Intersection of US 285 and Park County 5**
Finishing Point:	**Intersection of County 20 and US 285**
Total Mileage:	**13.9 miles**
Unpaved Mileage:	**11.8 miles**
Driving Time:	**1 1/2 hours**
Pass Elevation:	**Breakneck-10,910 feet; Browns-11,372 feet**
Usually Open:	**Early June to early October**
Difficulty Rating:	**3**
Scenic Rating:	**7**

Special Attractions
- Access to a network of 4WD trails.
- Fairly easy 4WD trail that travels under the canopy of the dense forest.
- Aspen viewing in the fall.

History
Little is known about the history of these two pass roads; but it is likely that they were built, or at least improved, in the early 1900s to open access to the mines in the Sheep Park area.

Description
The route commences at the intersection of US 285 and North-Central Trail #17: Weston Pass Road (County 5) about 4.5 miles south of Fairplay and travels through attractive ranch land for 1.6 miles before turning onto Breakneck Pass Road (FR 175).

Proceeding from the intersection, the road is fairly steep and rocky in sections. It might also be boggy if rain has fallen recently.

The remains of a miner's cabin near Breakneck Pass

The clearance between the trees is tight in spots, especially if you have a full-sized vehicle. Nonetheless, while the road becomes rougher and narrower, it is not difficult.

The unmarked Breakneck Pass is at the intersection with FR 426, at which point the main road proceeds straight on, the road on the left is closed, and FR 426 (to the right) takes you on an alternative loop past ruins of a mine and a cabin. FR 426 is a more interesting route than FR 175 from this point and rejoins the main road at the start of Sheep Park. The route directions for FR 426 are provided below.

As you travel through Sheep Park, Browns Pass Road (FR 176) turns off to the right. The track climbs uphill steeply for about three-tenths of a mile and can be quite difficult if it is wet (under which circumstances the road's difficulty rating would be higher than 3).

A stand of aspens envelops the road near Breakneck Pass

After this initial ascent, the road levels out and is easy except for some tight clearance between the trees. Browns Pass is marked with a rough sign.

This little-used route lacks the dramatic scenery of many 4WD roads in Colorado but offers a variety of scenery, from the tranquil meadows of Sheep Park to dense forests with thick stands of aspen that cover the road in gold during the fall. Some higher sections of the route also provide good views of the Mosquito Range to the west.

Current Road Conditions
Pike National Forest
South Park Ranger District
320 Hwy 285, Fairplay, CO 80440
(719) 836-2031

Map References
USFS Pike NF
USGS Park County #1
Park County #3
Trails Illustrated, #110
The Roads of Colorado, p. 86
Colorado Atlas & Gazetteer, p. 48

Route Directions

▼ 0.0	At intersection of US 285 and Park County 5, zero trip meter and proceed west on Weston Pass Road, County 5. Cross cattle grid and follow sign to Weston Pass.

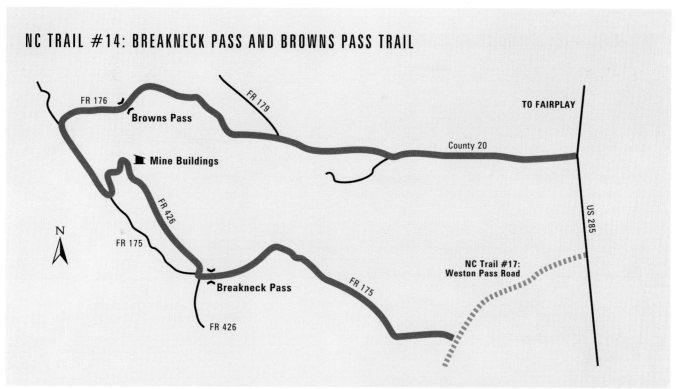

5.0 ▲			End at intersection with US 285.
GPS: N 39°09.20′ W 105°59.93′			
▼ 1.6		**TR**	Cross cattle guard. Turn onto Breakneck Pass Road (FR 175).
3.4 ▲		TL	Turn onto County 5. Cross cattle guard.
GPS: N 39°08.39′ W 106°01.42′			
▼ 3.2		**SO**	Cattle guard. Enter Pike National Forest.
1.8 ▲		SO	Leave Pike National Forest. Cattle guard.
▼ 3.5		**SO**	Track on left to camping.
1.5 ▲		SO	Track on right to camping.
▼ 5.0		**TR**	Intersection with Round Hill Road (FR 426) on right. To the left, 426 is closed a little farther on. Zero trip meter.
0.0 ▲			Continue along FR 175.
GPS: N 39°08.91′ W 106°04.65′			
▼ 0.0			Proceed along FR 426.
2.8 ▲		TL	Intersection with Breakneck Pass Road (FR 175). Zero trip meter.
▼ 1.4		**BL**	Track on right. Cabin ruins and mine.
1.4 ▲		BR	Track on left. Cabin ruins and mine.
▼ 1.6		**SO**	Cabin ruins on right.
1.2 ▲		SO	Cabin ruins on left.
▼ 2.0		**TR**	Intersection to rejoin FR 175.
0.8 ▲		TL	Intersection with FR 426, a faint trail to the left near the end of Sheep Park.
▼ 2.8		**BR**	Onto Browns Pass Road (FR 176). Zero trip meter.
0.0 ▲			Proceed along FR 175.
GPS: N 39°10.35′ W 106°06.42′			
▼ 0.0			Proceed along FR 176.
6.1 ▲		BL	Onto FR 175. Zero trip meter.
▼ 0.5		**SO**	Several miners' cabin ruins on right.
5.6 ▲		SO	Several miners' cabin ruins on left.
▼ 0.6		**SO**	Summit of Browns Pass. FR 1761 track on the left.
5.5 ▲		SO	Summit of Browns Pass. FR 1761 track on the right.

GPS: N 39°10.47′ W 106°05.77′			
▼ 1.1		**SO**	Cabin ruins on right.
5.0 ▲		SO	Cabin ruins on left.
▼ 1.4		**BR**	Track on left.
4.7 ▲		BL	Track on right.
▼ 2.8		**SO**	Cross through creek.
3.3 ▲		SO	Cross through creek.
▼ 2.9		**BR**	Track on left (FR 179). Remain on FR 176.
3.2 ▲		BL	Track on right (FR 179). Remain on FR 176.
GPS: N 39°10.17′ W 106°03.53′			
▼ 3.2		**SO**	FR 178 on left.
2.9 ▲		SO	FR 178 on right.
▼ 3.4		**SO**	Leaving Pike National Forest. Gate (leave it as you find it).
2.7 ▲		SO	Gate (leave it as you find it). Entering Pike National Forest.
▼ 3.6		**SO**	Gravel road.
2.5 ▲		SO	Gravel road.
▼ 4.0		**TL**	Intersection with County 20.
2.1 ▲		TR	Turn from County 20 onto FR 176. Signs read: "Browns Pass, Fourmile Road, National Forest Access."
GPS: N 39°09.99′ W 106°02.45′			
▼ 4.5		**SO**	Cattle guard.
1.6 ▲		SO	Cattle guard.
▼ 6.1			Cattle guard. End at intersection with US 285.
0.0 ▲			At intersection of County 20 and US 285 (there is a sign for National Forest access and Browns Pass), zero trip meter and proceed along County 20.
GPS: N 39°10.14′ W 106°00.06′			

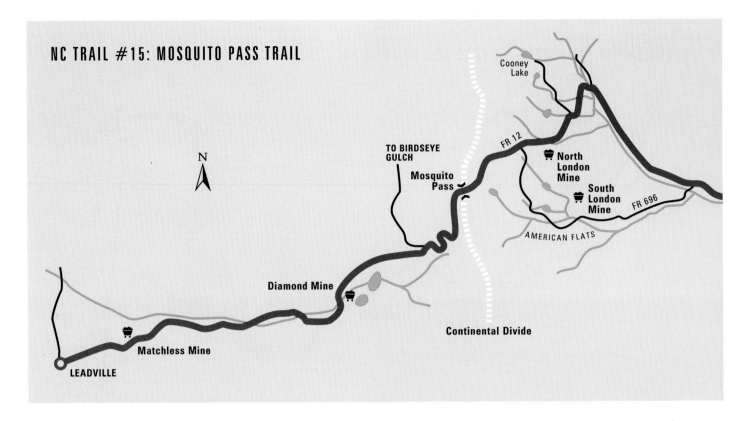

Mosquito Pass Trail

Starting Point:	**Colorado 9 and Mosquito Pass Road (Park County 12)**
Finishing Point:	**Leadville**
Total Mileage:	**16.7 miles**
Unpaved Mileage:	**15.2 miles**
Driving Time:	**2 hours**
Pass Elevation:	**13,186 feet**
Usually Open:	**Early August to mid-September**
Difficulty Rating:	**4**
Scenic Rating:	**9**

Special Attractions
- The highest pass road in America.
- High historic significance.
- Wonderful alpine views.

History
According to legend, this pass got its name in 1861 at a meeting of local residents who gathered to try to choose one of the many names proposed at their previous, inconclusive meeting. When they opened the minutes from that meeting, they found that a mosquito had been squashed in the middle of their list of proposed names. The new name was approved by acclamation!

The Indians used the pass, but the first white men recorded to have crossed it were Thomas Farnham and his party in their exploratory journey across Colorado in 1839. In 1861, the Mosquito gold-mining camp was established to the east of the pass.

From 1864, the pass was used by the itinerant Methodist preacher Father Dyer, who carried the mail across the pass for pay of eighteen dollars per week. In winter, he traveled on snowshoes at night, when the surface of the snow was harder. A small memorial to him stands at the summit of the pass.

Horace A. W. Tabor crossed the pass with Augusta, his wife, on horseback in 1870 but noted that a road barely existed. In 1873, Hayden's survey team crossed the pass and noted only a well-used burro trail.

Western Union built a telegraph line over the pass in 1878. Later that year, Horace Tabor and other investors formed the Mosquito Pass Wagon Road Company to construct a toll road over the pass. This wagon road was completed the following year, when freight wagons and stagecoaches were among the 150 vehicles crossing the pass each day. The pass became known as the "highway of frozen death" because of the many travelers who froze to death while walking across the pass road in winter to avoid paying the stagecoach fare.

In 1882, both the Denver, South Park & Pacific Railroad and the Denver & Rio Grande Railroad reached town, ringing the death knell for the pass road.

The road fell into disuse and was closed from 1910 until 1949, when local residents restored it to hold the first Get Your Ass Over the Pass burro race. The race is now a well-established event each July.

Description
The route commences at Alma Junction, the intersection of Colorado 9 and Mosquito Pass Road (County 12), which was

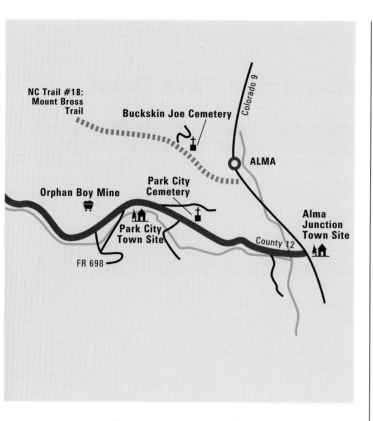

the junction of the railway spur to the London Mill and the main line.

The easy 2WD road continues past the town of Park City, an old stagecoach stop, and then past the Orphan Boy Mine, which operated well into the twentieth century, at the 3.3-mile point. At the 4.4-mile point, the route continues past the intersection of FR 696 on the left, which travels around the south of London Mountain and reconnects with the pass road but is usually closed to through traffic.

A couple of miles further, FR 12 turns left, crosses Mosquito Creek, and commences the ascent toward the pass, providing scenic views of the valley.

The road to Cooney Lake has several creek crossings and passes through the water at the bottom tip of the lake. The water at these crossings can be over eighteen inches deep, and the road can be very rutted and boggy in places. It is an interesting side road, but considerably more challenging than the main pass road.

At the summit, the view is spectacular: South Park spreads out to the east, and to the west is Leadville, Turquoise Lake, and the massive Sawatch Range with its fifteen fourteeners, including the three highest peaks in the Rockies.

The road descending toward Leadville, though it begins steeply, is generally easier than the road on the east side.

About 1.5 miles from the summit, the Birdseye Gulch road intersects on the right. This road heads north toward Colorado 91 but has some extremely boggy sections at about the 1.5-mile point. To avoid damage to the terrain, do not attempt this trail without a winch (and a long winch extension strap to reach the sometimes-distant winching points).

The main road from this point affords a straightforward drive into Leadville, past Horace Tabor's Matchless Mine.

Current Road Conditions
Pike National Forest
Leadville Ranger District
2015 N. Poplar, Leadville, CO 80461
(719) 486-0749

Map References
USFS Pike NF
San Isabel NF
USGS Lake County
Park County #1
Trails Illustrated, #109
The Roads of Colorado, p. 86
Colorado Atlas & Gazetteer, pp. 47-48

Route Directions

▼ 0.0		Start at Alma Junction, which is the intersection of Colorado 9 and County 12 (FR 12), 1.3 miles south of Alma. Turn onto County 12, zero trip meter, and proceed west along Mosquito Pass Road. Sign points toward Mosquito Gulch.
7.8 ▲		End at intersection with Colorado 9.

GPS: N 39°16.23′ W 106°02.83′

▼ 0.1	SO	Site of cabins and other buildings that were part of Alma Junction. Grade of old railroad wye is visible between the river and the highway.
7.7 ▲	SO	Site of cabins and other buildings that were part of Alma Junction. Grade of old railroad wye is visible between the river and the highway.
▼ 2.4	SO	Road on right to Park City Cemetery.
5.4 ▲	SO	Road on left to Park City Cemetery.
▼ 2.5	SO	Site of Park City, a stage stop that grew into a town.
5.3 ▲	SO	Site of Park City, a stage stop that grew into a town.
▼ 3.3	SO	Orphan Boy Mine.
4.5 ▲	SO	Orphan Boy Mine.
▼ 4.4	SO	Intersection. Remain on FR 12. South London Mine ruins are to the left along FR 696.
3.4 ▲	SO	Intersection. Remain on FR 12. South London Mine ruins are to the right along FR 696.

GPS: N 39°16.72′ W 106°07.29′

▼ 5.4	SO	View of wooden tram towers in trees on slope to the left.
2.4 ▲	SO	View of wooden tram towers in trees on slope to the right.
▼ 6.2	SO	Track on left to North London Mill and tailings dump.
1.6 ▲	SO	Track on right to North London Mill and tailings dump.
▼ 6.7	TL	Intersection. Turn left, remaining on FR 12. On the right is FR 856. Then cross creek.
1.1 ▲	TR	Cross creek. Intersection. On the left is FR 856.
▼ 6.8	SO	Mosquito Pass sign and Mosquito Pass Historic Stage Route marker.
1.0 ▲	SO	Mosquito Pass Historic Stage Route marker.

GPS: N 39°17.97′ W 106°09.28′

▼ 7.4	SO	Track on right to Champaign Mine.
0.4 ▲	SO	Track on left to Champaign Mine.
▼ 7.5	SO	Cross through creek.
0.3 ▲	SO	Cross through creek.
▼ 7.8	TL	Intersection. Road on right goes to Cooney Lake. Zero trip meter.
0.0 ▲		Continue along FR 12.

	GPS: N 39°17.46' W 106°09.67'		
▼ 0.0			Continue along FR 12.
	1.7 ▲	BR	Intersection. Side road to Cooney Lake. Zero trip meter.
▼ 0.1		SO	North London Mine on left.
	1.6 ▲	SO	North London Mine on right.
▼ 0.2		SO	Track on right and mining machinery on left.
	1.5 ▲	SO	Mining machinery on right and track on left.
▼ 0.7		SO	Track on the left with sign indicating locked gates ahead is FR 696.
	1.0 ▲	SO	Track on right.
▼ 1.7		SO	Tracks on the left and right. Then summit of Mosquito Pass. Zero trip meter.
	0.0 ▲		Proceed toward Leadville. Mosquito Pass Road changes to FR 12 on this side.
	GPS: N 39°16.86' W 106°11.12'		
▼ 0.0			Proceed toward Leadville. Mosquito Pass Road changes to FR 438 on this side.
	7.2 ▲	SO	Summit of Mosquito Pass. Tracks on the left and right. Zero trip meter.
▼ 0.3		BL	Bypass trail on right is one-way downhill and rejoins at 0.8 miles.
	6.9 ▲	SO	Track from 6.4-mile point rejoins on left.
▼ 0.4		SO	Track on left.
	6.8 ▲	SO	Track on right.
▼ 0.8		SO	Track from 0.3-mile point rejoins on right.
	6.4 ▲	BR	Track on left (no entry—one way).
▼ 1.4		SO	Track to Birdseye Gulch on right. Stay on main road toward Leadville.
	5.8 ▲	SO	Track on left to Birdseye Gulch. Stay on main road toward Mosquito Pass.
	GPS: N 39°16.15' W 106°11.74'		
▼ 2.8		TL	Road forks. Stay to the left.
	4.4 ▲	BR	Road forks. Stay to the right.
	GPS: N 39°15.69' W 106°13.15'		
▼ 3.0		SO	Cross over creek. Then gate to Diamond Mine on left. Follow main road.
	4.2 ▲	SO	Gate to Diamond Mine on right. Cross over creek.
	GPS: N 39°15.57' W 106°13.06'		
▼ 3.2		TR	Intersection.
	4.0 ▲	TL	Intersection.
▼ 3.3		SO	Mine structure on right.
	3.9 ▲	SO	Mine structure on left.
▼ 3.6		SO	Cross over creek.
	3.6 ▲	SO	Cross over creek.
▼ 3.8		SO	Mine on right and left.
	3.4 ▲	SO	Mine on right and left.
▼ 4.6		SO	Road on left.
	2.6 ▲	SO	Road on right.
▼ 5.4		SO	Intersection. Road on right.
	1.8 ▲	SO	Intersection. Road on left.
▼ 5.6		SO	Road on left.
	1.6 ▲	SO	Road on right.
▼ 6.0		SO	Matchless Mine on right.
	1.2 ▲	SO	Matchless Mine on left.
▼ 6.9		SO	Leadville, Colorado & Southern Railway station on right.
	0.3 ▲	SO	Leadville, Colorado & Southern Railway station on left.
▼ 7.2			End at intersection of 7th Street and Harrison (main) Avenue in Leadville.
	0.0 ▲		In Leadville, at the intersection of Harrison (main) Avenue and 7th Street, zero trip meter and proceed east along 7th Street.
	GPS: N 39°14.99' W 106°17.47'		

Hagerman Pass Road

Starting Point:	Leadville
Finishing Point:	Basalt
Total Mileage:	62.1 miles
Unpaved Mileage:	21.7 miles
Driving Time:	3 hours
Pass Elevation:	11,982 feet
Usually Open:	Mid-July to late September
Difficulty Rating:	3
Scenic Rating:	7

Special Attractions

■ Historic railroad route.
■ Network of 4WD trails.

History

Hagerman Pass Road is the product of one of the great railroad stories of the 1880s, the golden period of railroad expansion in Colorado. The pass was named for James J. Hagerman, the president of the Colorado Midland Railroad. Previously it had been known as Cooke Pass, and before that, the Hayden survey party had called it the Frying Pan Pass in 1873.

In 1885, the Colorado Midland Railway began construction on a railway running from Aspen to Leadville. The railway was remarkable at that time because it was a standard-gauge track rather than the prevalent narrow-gauge.

To cross the Continental Divide, the company commenced construction of the Hagerman Tunnel in 1885, completing the project the following year. It was 2,164 feet long and located only 450 feet from the pass's summit at 11,528 feet, the highest standard-gauge railroad in the United States at the time. To reach the tunnel, the tracks made three horseshoe turns at a grade of 1.5 percent. One of the turns was made with the help of an enormous 1,084-foot curved trestle bridge.

On the east side of the tunnel was Douglass City, a notorious mining camp that boasted six saloons and one brothel. The camp was home to the railroad construction workers as well as to miners.

The railroad opened in 1887 but faced financial difficulties right from the start. The operating costs were prohibitive. Six locomotives had to operate full-time to clear the rails in the winter, embank-

The famous railroad trestle bridge near Hagerman Tunnel

ments collapsed from water damage, and the trestle bridge required constant upkeep.

In 1893, the rail line was closed, and the train was rerouted

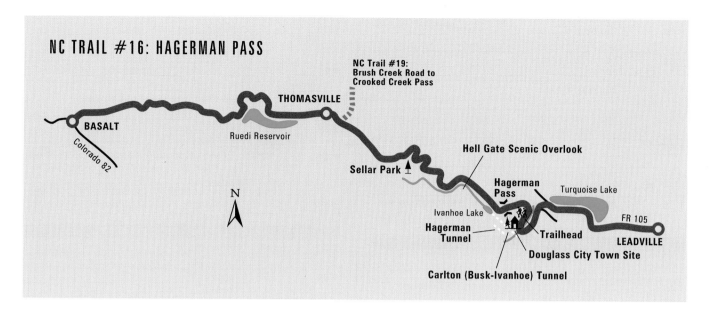

NC TRAIL #16: HAGERMAN PASS

to the new Busk-Ivanhoe Tunnel that had been constructed six hundred feet lower. The new tunnel had proved much more difficult to build than anticipated because of liquid mud flooding in. When completed, it was over 1.75 miles long, 15 feet wide, and 21 feet high. Construction had taken three years, claimed twenty lives, and cost three times the budgeted price of $1 million.

In 1897, after suffering continuous financial troubles since its formation, the Colorado Midland Railway was sold at a foreclosure. The new owners initially reverted to using the Hagerman Tunnel but went back to the Busk-Ivanhoe Tunnel in 1899.

From 1922 until 1943, after the tracks had been torn up, the Busk-Ivanhoe Tunnel was known as the Carlton Tunnel and used as State Highway 104. As it was only wide enough for a single lane of motor vehicles, an alternating system of traffic control was used.

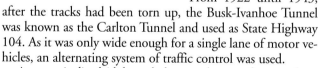

An old railroad grade cutting

A water pipeline laid through the tunnel to transfer water from the western slope of the Rockies to the east is still in use today.

In the 1960s, a new tunnel was built to divert additional water to the eastern slope as part of the multimillion-dollar Fryingpan-Arkansas Project, which provides electricity to many Front Range cities. This lower, four-mile tunnel is known as the Charles H. Bousted Tunnel.

Description

The Hagerman Pass turnoff is 2.2 miles past the Turquoise Lake dam wall. The road is not difficult, but high clearance is recommended. In the narrower sections, adequate pull-offs facilitate passing. Below timberline, the road travels through pine and aspen forest.

The east entrance to the Carlton (Busk-Ivanhoe) Tunnel is about 3.5 miles along Hagerman Pass Road. A mile farther on is a hiking trail that leads to the remains of Douglass City, the

site of the trestle bridge, Hagerman Lake, and the east entrance of the Hagerman Tunnel. It is an easy walk along the old railway grade that takes about two hours and thirty minutes.

The road continues through the pine forest that opens before the summit to an impressive view. Also evident is the high-voltage line between Denver and Grand Junction; the Hagerman Pass Road was used in the construction of the line.

On the west side of the pass, a turnoff provides an opportunity to visit Ivanhoe Lake and the west side of the Carlton (Busk-Ivanhoe) Tunnel. Hell Gate gauging station is further along on the left, a scenic stop on the Colorado Midland Railroad.

The road, which continues past the open expanse of Sellar Park, becomes an easy 2WD road before returning to pavement about fourteen miles from the summit.

Current Road Conditions

San Isabel National Forest
Leadville Ranger District
2015 N. Poplar, Leadville, CO 80461
(719) 486-0749

Map References

USFS   San Isabel NF
        White River NF
USGS   Lake County
        Pitkin County #2
        Eagle County #3
Trails Illustrated, #109, #110, #126, #127
The Roads of Colorado, pp. 68-69, 85-86
Colorado Atlas & Gazetteer, pp. 46-47

Route Directions

▼ 0.0	In Leadville, from the intersection of West 6th Street and Harrison (main) Avenue, zero trip meter and proceed west from the traffic light toward Turquoise Lake.
7.5 ▲	End at intersection with Harrison (main) Avenue in Leadville.

GPS: N 39°14.93' W 106°17.49'

▼ 0.8	TR	Stop sign.
6.7 ▲	TL	Stop sign.

▼ 3.0	SO	Cross railway line.
4.5 ▲	SO	Cross railway line.

▼ 3.4	BR	Fork in road.
4.1 ▲	BL	Road on right.

▼ 4.1	SO	Road on right.
3.4 ▲	SO	Road on left.

▼ 4.3	SO	Dam wall—Turquoise Lake.
3.2 ▲	SO	Dam wall—Turquoise Lake.

▼ 5.6	SO	Road on right.
1.9 ▲	SO	Road on left.

▼ 7.5	BL	Onto Hagerman Pass Road (FR 105). Zero trip meter.
0.0 ▲		Proceed along Turquoise Lake Road.

GPS: N 39°16.12′ W 106°25.00′

▼ 0.0		Proceed along FR 105.
7.6 ▲	TR	Onto Turquoise Lake Road. Zero trip meter.

▼ 1.7	SO	Track on left is Sugarloaf Mountain Road (FR 105.1A).
5.9 ▲	SO	Track on right is Sugarloaf Mountain Road (FR 105.1A).

▼ 3.4	SO	Cross over Busk Creek.
4.2 ▲	SO	Cross over Busk Creek.

▼ 3.5	BR	East entrance (sealed) of the Carlton (Busk-Ivanhoe) Tunnel on left.
4.1 ▲	BL	East entrance (sealed) of the Carlton (Busk-Ivanhoe) Tunnel on right.

▼ 4.5	SO	Colorado Midland Centennial Trail marker on left. Walking trail to trestle, tunnel, and Hagerman Lake via TR 1491.
3.1 ▲	SO	Colorado Midland Centennial Trail marker on right. Walking trail to trestle, tunnel, and Hagerman Lake via TR 1491.

GPS: N 39°15.56′ W 106°27.51′

▼ 6.4	SO	Track on right to Skinner Hut.
1.2 ▲	SO	Track on left to Skinner Hut.

▼ 7.1	SO	Seasonal closure gate.
0.5 ▲	SO	Seasonal closure gate.

▼ 7.6	SO	Hagerman Pass summit. Zero trip meter.
0.0 ▲		Continue along FR 105.

GPS: N 39°15.80′ W 106°28.83′

▼ 0.0		Continue along FR 105.
14.0 ▲	SO	Hagerman Pass summit. Zero trip meter.

▼ 3.6	SO	Seasonal gate.
10.4 ▲	SO	Seasonal gate.

▼ 3.7	SO	Intersection with FR 532 on the right and FR 527 (to Ivanhoe Lake) on the left. Remain on FR 105 and follow sign to Ruedi Reservoir.
10.3 ▲	SO	Remain on 105 and follow sign to Hagerman Pass.

▼ 4.9	SO	Track on right.
9.1 ▲	SO	Track on left.

▼ 5.3	SO	Hell Gate scenic overlook and gauging station in the valley on left among trees.
8.7 ▲	SO	Hell Gate scenic overlook and gauging station in the valley on right among trees.

▼ 10.9	SO	Sellar Park on left. Track on right goes to Diemer Lake and up to North Fork Road.
3.1 ▲	SO	Sellar Park on right. Track on left goes to Diemer Lake and up to North Fork Road.

GPS: N 39°19.21′ W 106°36.63′

▼ 14.0	BR	Intersection with road on left. Proceed onto paved Fryingpan Road. Zero trip meter.
0.0 ▲		Continue along main road.

GPS: N 39°17.89′ W 106°35.21′

▼ 0.0		Continue along main road.
33.0 ▲	BL	Intersection. Continue toward Hagerman Pass on unpaved FR 105. Zero trip meter.

▼ 0.1	SO	Road on left to Fryingpan Lakes trailhead.
32.9 ▲	SO	Road on right to Fryingpan Lakes trailhead.

▼ 3.4	SO	USFS Chapman Dam Campground.
29.6 ▲	SO	USFS Chapman Dam Campground.

▼ 3.7	SO	USFS Chapman Dam Campground.
29.3 ▲	SO	USFS Chapman Dam Campground.

▼ 6.9	SO	Road on right is North-Central Trail #19: Brush Creek Road to Crooked Creek Pass. It goes to Eagle.
26.1 ▲	SO	Road on left is North-Central Trail #19: Brush Creek Road to Crooked Creek Pass. It goes to Eagle.

GPS: N 39°21.10′ W 106°41.30′

▼ 8.2	SO	Thomasville.
24.8 ▲	SO	Thomasville.

▼ 9.6	SO	Meredith.
23.6 ▲	SO	Meredith.

▼ 10.0	SO	Ruedi Reservoir on left.
23.0 ▲	SO	Ruedi Reservoir on right.

▼ 30.7	SO	Basalt.
2.3 ▲	SO	Leaving Basalt.

▼ 30.9	TR	Intersection with Midland and Two Rivers Road (Business Route 82).
2.1 ▲	TL	Intersection with Fryingpan Road.

▼ 33.0		End at intersection with Colorado 82 in Basalt.
0.0 ▲		From traffic light at intersection of Colorado 82 and Business Route 82 (Two Rivers Road), zero trip meter and proceed along Business Route 82 toward Basalt.

GPS: N 39°22.27′ W 107°04.23′

Weston Pass Road

Starting Point:	Intersection of US 24 and County 7, 5 miles south of Leadville Airport
Finishing Point:	Intersection of Park County 5 and US 285
Total Mileage:	25.7 miles
Unpaved Mileage:	23.4 miles
Driving Time:	1 1/2 hours
Pass Elevation:	11,921 feet
Usually Open:	Late June to late September
Difficulty Rating:	2
Scenic Rating:	7

Special Attractions

■ Attractive scenery along an easy 4WD trail.
■ Access to a network of 4WD trails.

History

Like so many passes in the Colorado Rockies, Weston Pass was an old Ute Indian trail before being developed as a wagon

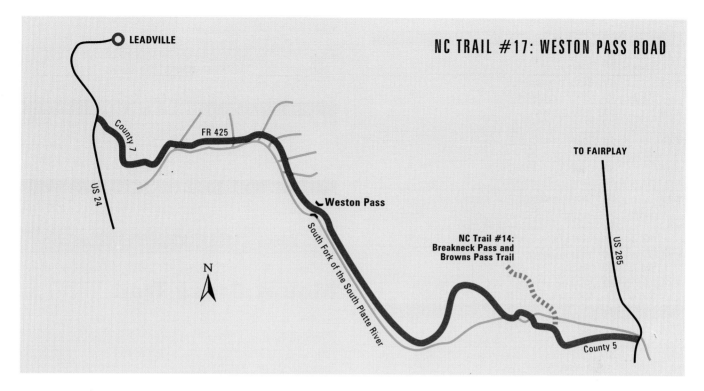

road. In 1860, during the first gold boom in the Leadville area, the new wagon road was known as the Ute Trail. The stagecoach way station on the eastern side of the pass grew into the town of Weston.

Father Dyer made early use of the pass and in 1861 was caught in a blizzard and nearly perished here.

A view of one of the stands of aspens along the Weston Pass route

Four freight and passenger service companies sprang up to meet the enormous demand. One, the Wall & Witter Stage Company, maintained four hundred horses, eleven freight wagons, and seven stagecoaches to service its operations.

In 1873, the Hayden survey party found a good wagon road over Weston Pass, at a time when there was barely a burro trail over Mosquito Pass.

The Denver, South Park & Pacific Railroad reached Weston in 1879, adding new impetus to the town's growth. In that year, the Wall & Witter Stage Company collected $1.5 million in fares; on just one day in September, 225 teams were counted as they crossed the pass, pulling either wagons or stagecoaches. As proof that traveling the pass road was thirsty work, Park County issued no fewer than eight new liquor licenses in 1879 to establishments between the town and the top of the pass.

However, in 1881, the railroad made it into Leadville, sending Weston Pass into rapid decline.

In the 1950s, the pass road was renovated and has been well maintained ever since as a recreational road.

Description

The route commences at the intersection of US 24 and County 7, 5.1 miles south of the Leadville Airport entrance on the left as you leave Leadville.

Navigation along the Weston Pass route is a simple matter, and the road is suitable for cars—except for a couple of miles on the west side of the summit, where high clearance is preferable.

The road travels beside Union Creek on the west side and along the South Fork of the South Platte River on the east side. Both offer numerous, good backcountry camping sites. Additionally, on the west side there is a U.S. Forest Service campground.

Current Road Conditions

Pike National Forest
Leadville Ranger District
2015 N. Poplar, Leadville, CO 80461
(719) 486-0749

Map References

USFS Pike NF
San Isabel NF
USGS Park County #3
Lake County
Trails Illustrated, #110
The Roads of Colorado, p. 86
Colorado Atlas & Gazetteer, pp. 47-48

Route Directions

▼ 0.0   At intersection of US 24 and County 7, zero trip meter and proceed southeast along County 7 (FR 425) toward Weston Pass. There is a sign for Massive Lakes.

10.5 ▲		End at intersection with US 24.

GPS: N 39°10.58′ W 106°19.27′

▼ 3.0	SO	Cattle guard.
7.5 ▲	SO	Cattle guard.
▼ 7.1	SO	Cross over creek.
3.4 ▲	SO	Cross over creek.
▼ 7.5	SO	Track on left.
3.0 ▲	SO	Track on right.
▼ 8.4	SO	Track on left.
2.1 ▲	SO	Track on right.
▼ 8.7	SO	Cabin ruins on right.
1.8 ▲	SO	Cabin ruins on left.
▼ 8.8	SO	Track on left.
1.7 ▲	SO	Track on right.
▼ 9.3	SO	Cabin ruins below shelf road.
1.2 ▲	SO	Cabin ruins below shelf road.
▼ 10.4	SO	Track on right.
0.1 ▲	SO	Track on left.
▼ 10.5	SO	Summit of Weston Pass. Zero trip meter.
0.0 ▲		Continue along FR 425.

GPS: N 39°07.88′ W 106°10.88′

▼ 0.0		Continue along FR 425.
8.4 ▲	SO	Summit of Weston Pass. Zero trip meter.
▼ 0.1	SO	Cabin ruins on the left and right. Track on left to small lake.
8.3 ▲	SO	Track on left to small lake. Cabin ruins on the left and right.
▼ 0.2	SO	Site of the Ruby Mine.
8.2 ▲	SO	Site of the Ruby Mine.
▼ 0.8	SO	Track on left.
7.6 ▲	SO	Track on right.
▼ 1.7	SO	Track on left.
6.7 ▲	SO	Track on right.
▼ 1.9	SO	Site of Park Place roadside restaurant on left.
6.5 ▲	SO	Site of Park Place roadside restaurant on right.
▼ 4.5	SO	Road on right to USFS Weston Pass Campground.
3.9 ▲	SO	Road on left to USFS Weston Pass Campground.

GPS: N 39°04.63′ W 106°07.99′

▼ 5.6	SO	Rich Creek trailhead on right and cattle guard. Leave the National Forest.
2.8 ▲	SO	Leave the National Forest. Cattle guard, then Rich Creek trailhead on left.
▼ 6.8	BL	Road on right goes to a private ranch.
1.6 ▲	CR	Road on left goes to a private ranch.
▼ 7.5	SO	Cattle guard.
0.9 ▲	SO	Cattle guard.
▼ 7.9	SO	Road on left.
0.5 ▲	SO	Road on right.
▼ 8.4	TL	FR 425 ends at fork in the road. Left fork goes to US 285 via County 5. Right fork goes to US 285 via County 22. Both alternatives reach the highway in seven miles. Zero trip meter.
0.0 ▲		Proceed along FR 425.

GPS: N 39°05.85′ W 106°05.28′

▼ 0.0		Proceed along County 5.
6.8 ▲	BR	Onto FR 425. Zero trip meter.
▼ 1.6	SO	Cattle guard.
5.2 ▲	SO	Cattle guard.
▼ 1.9	BR	Road on left.
4.9 ▲	BL	Road on right.
▼ 2.2	SO	Cattle guard.
4.6 ▲	SO	Cattle guard.

▼ 3.6	SO	Cattle guard.
3.2 ▲	SO	Cattle guard.
▼ 5.2	SO	North-Central Trail #14: Breakneck Pass on left. Cattle guard.
1.6 ▲	SO	Cattle guard. North-Central Trail #14: Breakneck Pass on right.

GPS: N 39°08.39′ W 106°01.42′

▼ 6.8		Cattle guard, then end at intersection with US 285.
0.0 ▲		At intersection of US 285 and Park County 5, zero trip meter and proceed west on Weston Pass Road, County 5. Cross cattle grid and follow sign to Weston Pass.

GPS: N 39°09.20′ W 105°59.93′

NORTH-CENTRAL REGION TRAIL #18

Mount Bross Trail

Starting Point:	**Alma**
Finishing Point:	**Summit of Mount Bross**
Total Mileage:	**10.4 miles**
Unpaved Mileage:	**10.4 miles**
Driving Time:	**1 1/2 hours (one-way)**
Elevation:	**14,172 feet**
Usually Open:	**Late June to late September**
Difficulty Rating:	**5**
Scenic Rating:	**10**

Special Attractions

- One of the highest roads in the United States.
- Stunning, panoramic views.
- Challenging shelf road.
- Numerous old mines and side trails.

History

Mount Bross has the broadest, roundest summit of any of Colorado's fifty-four fourteen-thousand-foot peaks. It was named for William Bross, a local miner and former lieutenant governor of Illinois. Bross climbed Mount Lincoln, the peak closely adjoining Mount Bross, with Father Dyer in 1876. He talked so much of the view from the summit that the local miners began calling the peak to the south Mount Bross.

Mining in the area commenced with gold strikes in the 1860s. By 1861, Quartzville, located on the northeastern slope of Mount Bross on the creek between it and Mount Lincoln, had fifty cabins. With the second mining boom in the 1880s, this time based on silver, the town population peaked at two thousand; but the ore was not as good as hoped, and the town could not survive the silver crash of 1893.

Description

This route starts in the township of Alma. Initially, the road is a graded dirt road. Depending on how long it has been since the road has been graded, it may have some large potholes! It passes the Buckskin Joe Cemetery and town site.

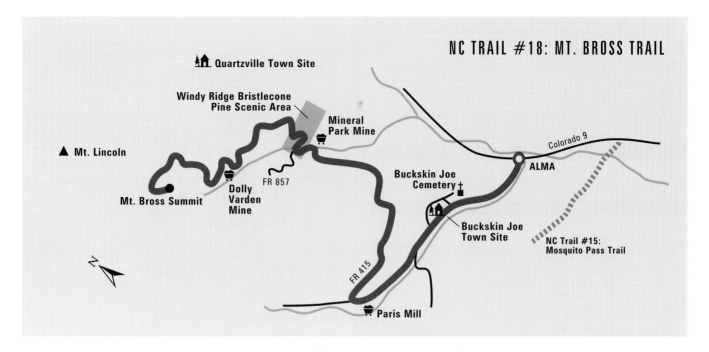

After about 5.5 miles, near the Mineral Park Mine, the road narrows down to a 4WD road as it starts to ascend Mount Bross and rises above timberline.

Shortly after the Mineral Park Mine, you'll pass the Windy Ridge Bristlecone Pine Scenic Area, where information boards tell about these ancient trees.

Upon passing timberline, the road gains altitude quickly. Though the surface of the road is a bit loose, it is in good condi-

A miner's cabin with a million-dollar view

tion, and you should have no problems with traction. As you progress up the mountain, there are numerous tracks and navigation can be difficult, although many of the tracks rejoin the main road farther on. At around seven miles, the road proceeds along a shelf that drops off steeply. At this point, the road becomes narrow, making passing difficult in some sections.

As you continue up Mount Bross, you'll see remains of the Dolly Varden Mine and numerous open mine shafts. Continuing, you pass a miner's cabin with one of the best living-room views in Colorado!

The road continues right to the summit. At 14,172 feet, it is one of the highest roads in the country—higher than either the road up Pikes Peak or the end of the roadway on Mount Evans.

Note that at times, near the summit, there are so many tracks, in such close succession, that it was impossible to include them all in the route directions below. Follow the main road, which switchbacks its way right to the summit.

In its upper reaches, this road is prone to rock slides and erosion that may make it necessary to divert onto one of the alter-

native routes to the summit. At times erosion can also make the trail dangerously narrow and unstable. Exercise caution.

From the summit, it looks as though a road traverses the ridge to Mount Lincoln. However, it does not go through and turning around is difficult. The road that used to ascend Mount Lincoln is now closed.

Current Road Conditions
Park County Tourism Office
P.O. Box 220, Fairplay, CO 80440
(719) 836-4279

Map References
USFS Pike NF
USGS Park County #1
Trails Illustrated, #109
The Roads of Colorado, p. 86
Colorado Atlas & Gazetteer, p. 48

Route Directions

0.0		In Alma, at the intersection of Colorado 9 and County 8, zero trip meter and proceed west along County 8 (Buckskin Road). Cross next intersection and continue on Buckskin Road toward Kite Lake.
	GPS: N 39°17.04' W 106°03.74'	
▼ 1.1	SO	Track on right.
▼ 1.4	SO	Site of Buckskin Joe mining town. Track on right to Buckskin Joe Cemetery (now Alma Cemetery).
▼ 1.6	SO	Track on left to Buckskin Joe Mine.
▼ 2.6	SO	Paris Mill on left.
▼ 2.7	TR	Intersection. Make sharp turn toward Windy Ridge on County 787 (FR 415).
	GPS: N 39°17.79' W 106°06.46'	
▼ 3.2	SO	Paris Mine on left.
▼ 3.3	SO	Cabin on right.
▼ 4.2	SO	Track on right to cabin and Sweet Home Mine.
▼ 5.5	SO	Mineral Park Mine.

		GPS: N 39°19.03' W 106°05.03'
▼ 5.7	BR	Fork in road. FR 857 goes to the left. Shortly after, cross through creek.
▼ 6.2	SO	Windy Ridge Bristlecone Pine scenic area on right.
▼ 6.4	BL	Fork in road. Mine building on right.
▼ 6.7	SO	Two tracks join on right (one closed).
▼ 7.4	BL	Fork in road. FR 415 goes to the right and is an alternative way to reach the summit. Zero trip meter.
		GPS: N 39°19.53' W 106°05.66'
▼ 0.0		Continue along track.
▼ 0.3	BR	Fork in road. Track to the Dolly Varden Mine is to the left.
		GPS: N 39°19.56' W 106°05.91'
▼ 1.3	SO	Track on right. (Turning here goes back down the mountain.)
▼ 1.4	SO	Cabin ruin on right and mine with a great view!
▼ 1.6	SO	Track on left and open mine portals along road on left.
▼ 1.7	SO	Track enters on right.
▼ 1.9	BL	Track enters on right.
▼ 2.0	SO	Track enters on right.
▼ 2.1	SO	Series of open mine portals on left.
		GPS: N 39°20.21' W 106°06.12'
▼ 2.2	SO	Track on left.
▼ 2.4	SO	Track on left.
▼ 2.8	BL/BR	Track on right. Then track on left.
▼ 2.8	BR	Track on left. Continue toward summit.
▼ 3.0		Mt. Bross marker. 100 yards farther is the summit.
		GPS: N 39°20.15' W 106°06.42'

NORTH-CENTRAL REGION TRAIL #19

Brush Creek Road to Crooked Creek Pass

Starting Point:	**Eagle**
Finishing Point:	**Intersection of FR 400 and Fryingpan Road**
	(County 104), 0.5 miles east of Thomasville
Total Mileage:	**30.8 miles**
Unpaved Mileage:	**20.6 miles**
Driving Time:	**1 1/2 hours**
Pass Elevation:	**9,995 feet**
Usually Open:	**Early June to early November**
Difficulty Rating:	**2**
Scenic Rating:	**7**

Special Attractions

- Varied forest scenery along an easy 4WD trail.
- Access to a network of 4WD trails.

Description

This route starts in Eagle and follows the Brush Creek Valley through attractive ranch land, remaining on paved road for the first ten miles before the road forks. The route follows the

right-hand fork toward Sylvan Lake.

After Sylvan Lake the road narrows but remains an easy 2WD road to Crooked Creek Pass. While there are sections of shelf road with high drop-offs from the edge of the road, the road remains relatively wide and does not rank as a scary Colorado shelf road.

From the gentle pass, the road descends through similar countryside, traveling through Crooked Creek Park and then beside Crooked Creek Reservoir, taking several sharp bends before reaching Fryingpan Road approximately half a mile east of the town site of Thomasville, an old railroad station along the Colorado Midland Railway line.

Current Road Conditions

White River National Forest
Eagle Ranger District
125 West 5th Street, Eagle, CO 81631
(970) 328-6388

Map References

USFS White River NF
USGS Eagle County #1
Eagle County #3
Pitkin County #2
Trails Illustrated, #121, #126
The Roads of Colorado, p. 69
Colorado Atlas & Gazetteer, pp. 36, 46-47

Route Directions

▼ 0.0		At the intersection of Grand Avenue and Broadway in Eagle, zero trip meter and proceed south along Broadway toward Sylvan Lake.
10.2 ▲		End at intersection of Grand Avenue and Broadway in Eagle.
		GPS: N 39°39.35' W 106°49.65'
▼ 0.2	TL	Stop sign. Turn onto 5th.
10.0 ▲	TR	Onto Broadway.
▼ 0.3	TR	Onto Capitol (will become Brush Creek Road and County 307).
9.9 ▲	TL	Onto 5th.
▼ 4.1	SO	Cross over bridge.
6.1 ▲	SO	Cross over bridge.
▼ 6.1	SO	Cross over bridge.
4.1 ▲	SO	Cross over bridge.
▼ 9.5	SO	Enter White River National Forest. Road becomes FR 400.
0.7 ▲	SO	Leave White River National Forest. Road becomes County 307.
▼ 10.2	BR	Road forks. Left goes to Yeoman Park and Fulford.
0.0 ▲		Continue on FR 400.
		GPS: N 39°32.35' W 106°45.14'
▼ 0.0		Proceed along FR 400 toward Sylvan Lake and Fryingpan River.
9.7 ▲	BL	Intersection.
▼ 1.2	SO	Cross over creek.
8.4 ▲	SO	Cross over creek.
▼ 2.3	SO	Walking trail on right to McKenzie Gulch.
7.4 ▲	SO	Walking trail on left to McKenzie Gulch.
▼ 4.5	SO	Sylvan Lake entrance.

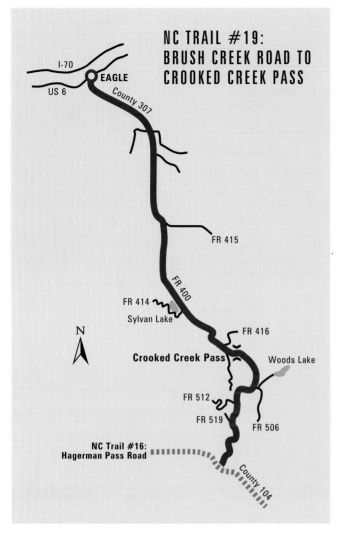

**NC TRAIL #19:
BRUSH CREEK ROAD TO
CROOKED CREEK PASS**

▼ 5.0	SO	FR 512 on right.
5.9 ▲	SO	FR 512 on left.

GPS: N 39°24.18' W 106°40.53'

▼ 7.0	SO	FR 519 on right. Then cattle guard.
3.8 ▲	SO	Cattle guard. FR 519 on right.
▼ 8.3	SO	Seasonal gate.
2.5 ▲	SO	Seasonal gate.
▼ 8.5	SO	Cross over creek.
2.3 ▲	SO	Cross over creek.
▼ 10.1	SO	Bridge over creek.
0.8 ▲	SO	Bridge over creek.
▼ 10.9		End at intersection with Fryingpan Road, about 0.5 miles east of Thomasville. This is the western portion of North-Central Trail #16: Hagerman Pass Road.
0.0 ▲		At intersection of Fryingpan Road (County 104) and FR 400, zero trip meter and proceed north on FR 400. This intersection is about 0.5 miles east of Thomasville.

GPS: N 39°21.10' W 106°41.30'

NORTH-CENTRAL REGION TRAIL #20

Cottonwood Pass Road

Starting Point:	**Gypsum**
Finishing Point:	**Intersection of Colorado 82 and Garfield County 113**
Total Mileage:	**26.5 miles**
Unpaved Mileage:	**16.1 miles**
Driving Time:	**1 1/4 hours**
Pass Elevation:	**8,280 feet**
Usually Open:	**Early July to early November**
Difficulty Rating:	**2**
Scenic Rating:	**7**

Special Attractions

■ Easy, scenic, historic 4WD trail.
■ Access to a network of 4WD trails.

History

This pass is some sixty miles northwest of the other, better-known Cottonwood Pass that links Buena Vista with Taylor Park.

This pass was in use from 1873 and was upgraded to a wagon road in 1883 to provide access from Gypsum into the north end of the booming Roaring Fork Valley. Until World War II, Cottonwood Pass was one of the major pass routes in Colorado and was a primary route between Denver and Grand Junction. Later, a major highway route was constructed through Glenwood Canyon.

Description

From Gypsum to the pass, the road travels through land owned by the Bureau of Land Management, which is used for ranching. The route passes through gentle, rolling hills and a broad valley before climbing through the corner of the White River National Forest to the pass.

5.2 ▲	SO	Sylvan Lake entrance.
▼ 5.5	SO	FR 414 on right to Gypsum Creek and LEDE Reservoir. Then seasonal gate.
4.2 ▲	SO	Seasonal gate. Track on left to Gypsum Creek and reservoir.

GPS: N 39°28.28' W 106°43.64'

▼ 7.2	SO	Track on right to FR 431.
2.4 ▲	SO	Track on left to FR 431.
▼ 9.6	SO	Track on right to Red Table Mountain.
0.1 ▲	SO	Track on left to Red Table Mountain.
▼ 9.7	SO	Track on left. Cattle guard. Crooked Creek Pass. Zero trip meter.
0.0 ▲		Continue on FR 400 toward Eagle.

GPS: N 39°26.49' W 106°41.08'

▼ 0.0		Continue on FR 400.
10.9 ▲	SO	Crooked Creek Pass. Cattle guard. Track on left. Zero trip meter.
▼ 0.7	SO	Cross over creek.
10.2 ▲	SO	Cross over creek.
▼ 2.0	SO	Cross over creek.
8.8 ▲	SO	Cross over creek.
▼ 2.3	SO	Crooked Creek Reservoir on left.
8.6 ▲	SO	Crooked Creek Reservoir on right.
▼ 3.1	SO	FR 506 on left to Woods Lake. Cross over creek.
7.8 ▲	SO	Cross over creek. FR 506 on right to Woods Lake.

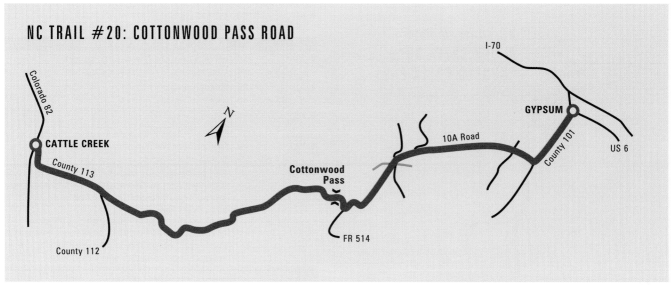

NC TRAIL #20: COTTONWOOD PASS ROAD

From the pass, the road descends through similar country but provides views of several Elk Range fourteeners, including Snowmass Mountain and Mount Sopris. The road continues beside Cattle Creek before exiting on Colorado 82.

In dry conditions, the road is relatively easy—even for 2WD vehicles—but it can become impassable after rain, especially on the north side of the pass.

Current Road Conditions

White River National Forest
Eagle Ranger District
125 West 5th Street, Eagle, CO 81631
(970) 328-6388

Map References

USFS White River NF
USGS Eagle County #3
          Garfield County #5
The Roads of Colorado, pp. 68-69
Colorado Atlas & Gazetteer, pp. 36, 45-46

Route Directions

▼ 0.0		At intersection of Valley Road and US 6 in Gypsum, zero trip meter and proceed south along Valley Road.
11.1 ▲		End at T-intersection with US 6 in Gypsum.
GPS: N 39°38.69′ W 106°56.90′		
▼ 1.9	TR	Follow Cottonwood Pass sign.
9.2 ▲	TL	T-intersection with Valley Road (County 101).
GPS: N 39°36.99′ W 106°56.90′		
▼ 2.7	SO	Cross bridge.
8.4 ▲	SO	Cross bridge.
▼ 3.3	TR	Follow Cottonwood Pass sign.
7.8 ▲	TL	T-intersection and stop sign.
GPS: N 39°36.53′ W 106°58.04′		
▼ 3.5	SO	Cattle guard.
7.6 ▲	SO	Cattle guard.
▼ 4.1	SO	Road on right. Cattle guard.
7.0 ▲	SO	Cattle guard. Road on left.

▼ 4.8	SO	Track on left.
6.2 ▲	SO	Track on right.
▼ 6.4	SO	Track on left.
4.6 ▲	SO	Track on right.
▼ 7.4	SO	Track on right.
3.7 ▲	SO	Track on left.
▼ 8.2	SO	Track on right.
2.9 ▲	SO	Track on left.
▼ 8.3	SO	Track on left. Cross over creek.
2.8 ▲	SO	Cross over creek. Track on right.
▼ 11.1	SO	Red Table Road (FR 514) on left. Zero trip meter.
0.0 ▲		Continue along 10A.
GPS: N 39°31.80′ W 107°02.78′		
▼ 0.0		Continue along main road.
15.4 ▲	SO	Red Table Road (FR 514) on right. Zero trip meter.
▼ 0.8	SO	Cottonwood Pass (unmarked).
14.5 ▲	SO	Cottonwood Pass (unmarked).
GPS: N 39°31.83′ W 107°03.49′		
▼ 5.5	SO	Enter Garfield County. Name of road changes to 113.
9.8 ▲	SO	Road becomes 10A. Enter Eagle County.
▼ 7.0	BR	Stay on 113.
8.4 ▲	BL	Intersection. Stay on 113 toward Cottonwood Pass.
▼ 7.7	BL	Stay on 113.
7.6 ▲	BR	Fork in road. Follow County 113 toward Gypsum.
▼ 8.1	SO	Cross over creek.
7.3 ▲	SO	Cross over creek.
▼ 8.5	BR	Road on left. Pavement.
6.9 ▲	BL	Onto unpaved road. Road on right.
▼ 12.1	SO	County 112 on the left.
3.3 ▲	SO	County 112 on the right.
▼ 15.4		End at intersection with County 82 in Cattle Creek.
0.0 ▲		Begin in Cattle Creek, between Glenwood Springs and Carbondale on County 82. Zero trip meter at the intersection of County 82 and Cattle Creek Road (County 113) and proceed east along the paved road.
GPS: N 39°27.48′ W 107°15.68′		

The Northwest Region

Trails in the Northwest Region

- **NW 1** Baxter Pass Trail
- **NW 2** Ellis Jeep Trail
- **NW 3** Elkhorn Mountain and Stock Driveway
- **NW 4** Troublesome Pass Loop
- **NW 5** Red Dirt Creek and Derby Mesa Trail

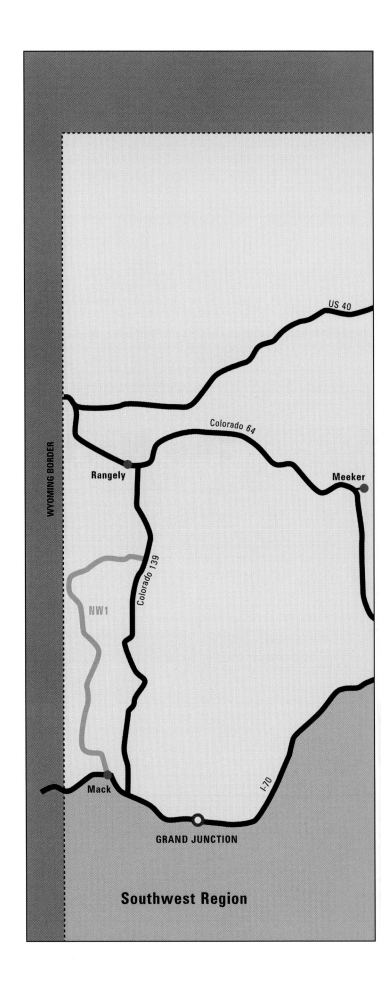

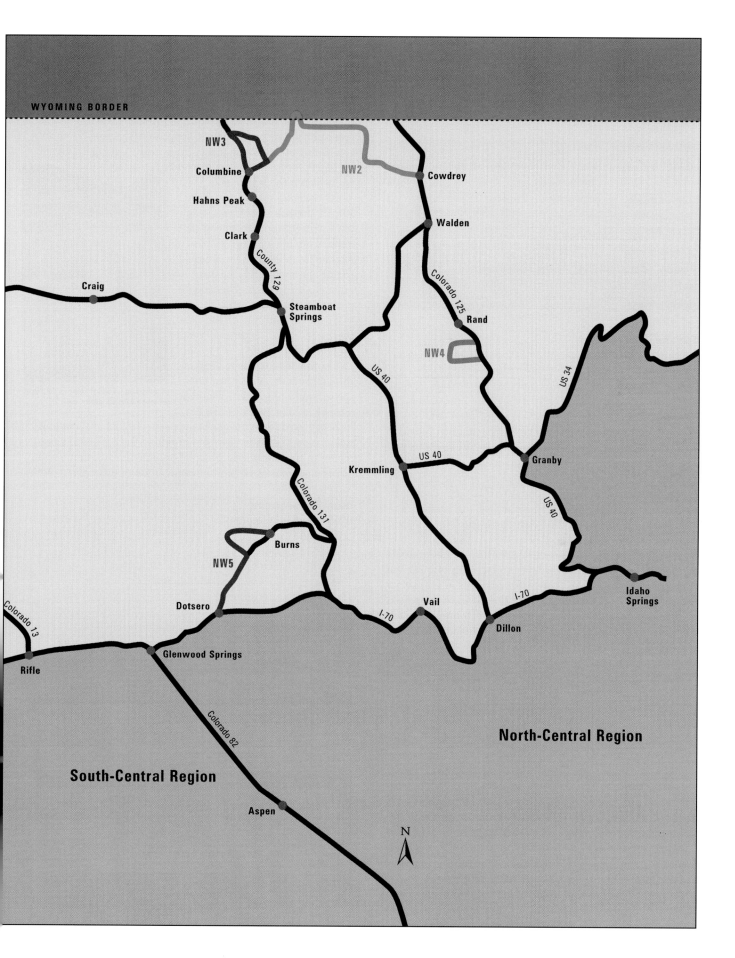

Baxter Pass Trail

Starting Point:	Mack
Finishing Point:	Intersection of County 116 and
	Colorado 139
Total Mileage:	80.2 miles
Unpaved Mileage:	72.2 miles
Driving Time:	4 hours
Pass Elevation:	8,422 feet
Usually Open:	Early June to mid-October
Difficulty Rating:	4
Scenic Rating:	8

Special Attractions

- Remote, scenic location.
- Landscape that is unique in Colorado.
- Access to a network of 4WD trails.

History

This pass was originally an old Ute Indian trail that provided access between the Gunnison area and the White River and Green River regions of western Colorado and eastern Utah.

Albert "Bert" Carlton, who had made a fortune in Cripple Creek, decided to shift his attention to copper mining in Utah. To transport the ore, he established the seventy-two-mile Uintah Railway in 1905, which traveled from Mack, Colorado, to Watson, Utah.

The route went up and over Baxter Pass, which created a huge obstacle with some of the hardest grades any railroad had attempted to climb. The route was dangerous and auxiliary steam engines were required to make the ascent to the pass.

The Watson area was found to be very rich in uintaite (also known as Gilsonite, a natural asphalt, petroleum-based resource). The Gilsonite mines, most of them near Dragon, Utah, were developed by the Barber Asphalt Company of St. Louis. Baxter Pass was actually named for C.O. Baxter of the Barber Asphalt Company.

The "Gilsonite Road" railway looped and turned to climb over Baxter Pass until 1939. The railway ceased operations when it became cheaper to pipe the Gilsonite over the pass to Mack.

Description

This route provides the opportunity to travel through some of the most remote county in Colorado with scenery much different than that along any of the other trails in this book.

Eight miles from exit 11 on I-70, on County 8, the pavement ends, but the road is still a wide, maintained, rural road suitable for 2WD vehicles. The road deteriorates slowly as you travel toward the pass and becomes quite rutted in spots as it traverses the barren sage plateau. After heavy rain, it is very boggy and can become impassable. In muddy conditions, the

difficulty rating for this road could increase to 5 or higher.

There are numerous side roads, many of which are used for natural gas mining operations and pipeline maintenance and are not open to the public. If they are open, nearly all are definitely dry-weather options. Proceed with caution, however, because nearly all of this backcountry is privately owned. The side roads provide an occasional challenge to navigation. Some are used nearly as frequently as the "main" road, making it difficult to discern which is the main road and which is the side road.

As the road approaches Baxter Pass, it alternates between a single track with turnouts and a two-lane track. The last mile to the pass is reasonably steep as it switchbacks to the summit, and the road is quite eroded in parts. The sections of shelf road are not intimidating.

From the summit of the pass, there are scenic, expansive views on both sides.

On the descent, the road travels through stands of aspens interspersed in the pine forest. There are a couple of short sections that may

A section of mud that is typical of conditions after rain

be boggy, even when the rest of the track is dry. After about four miles, there is a scenic view of McAndrews Lake. Further along the route, the road winds through beautiful canyon country and across numerous creek beds or washes (most of them dry).

Map References

USGS Garfield County #2
Rio Blanco #5
Mesa County #1
Rio Blanco County #1
The Roads of Colorado, pp. 48, 64, 80
Colorado Atlas & Gazetteer, pp. 32, 42

Route Directions

▼ 0.0		Take I-70 west of Grand Junction to exit 11 into the town of Mack. Zero trip meter at the stop sign and turn left.
35.3 ▲		End at junction to I-70.
GPS: N 39°13.36' W 108°51.74'		
▼ 2.3	TR	Onto County 8 (8 Road).
32.9 ▲	TL	Onto County 80 (US 6).
▼ 5.1	TL	Onto S Road, also County 4. Straight ahead will dead-end.
30.2 ▲	TR	Onto County 8 (8 Road).
GPS: N 39°16.97' W 108°54.05'		
▼ 8.0	SO	Cattle guard. Unpaved road.
27.3 ▲	SO	Paved. Cattle guard.
▼ 10.3	SO	Bridge over creek.
25.0 ▲	SO	Bridge over creek.
▼ 10.8	SO	Bridge over creek.
24.4 ▲	SO	Bridge over creek.
▼ 10.9	BR	Fork in the road. Left goes to Prairie Canyon. Follow County 4.
24.3 ▲	SO	Track on right goes to Prairie Canyon. Remain on County 4.

▼ 11.8	SO	Cattle guard.
23.4 ▲	SO	Cattle guard.
▼ 15.0	SO	Cattleyards on right. Approximately here, road name changes from Mesa County 4 to Garfield County 201.
20.2 ▲	SO	Cattleyards on left. Approximately here, road name changes from Garfield County 201 to Mesa County 4.
▼ 16.0	SO	Cattle guard.
19.3 ▲	SO	Cattle guard.
▼ 20.6	SO	Cattle guard.
14.6 ▲	SO	Cattle guard.
▼ 21.8	SO	Bridge.
13.5 ▲	SO	Bridge.
▼ 22.8	SO	Cattle guard and cattleyards on right.
12.4 ▲	SO	Cattleyards on right. Cattle guard.
▼ 23.1	SO	Track on left.
12.2 ▲	SO	Track on right.
▼ 24.3	SO	Track on right.
11.0 ▲	SO	Track on left.
▼ 24.4	SO	Track on left.
10.9 ▲	SO	Track on right.
▼ 25.4	SO	Track on left into West Canyon.
9.9 ▲	SO	Track on right into West Canyon.
▼ 25.5	SO	Cattle guard.
9.8 ▲	SO	Cattle guard.
▼ 27.6	BL	Fork in road.
7.7 ▲	SO	Fork in road.

GPS: N 39°32.19' W 108°55.30'

▼ 27.7	SO	Cattle guard.
7.5 ▲	SO	Cattle guard.
▼ 29.6	SO	Fork in road. Old town site of Atchee on right with one remaining building.
5.7 ▲	SO	Old town site of Atchee on left with one remaining building.

GPS: N 39°33.81' W 108°54.74'

▼ 30.8	SO	Cattle guard.
4.5 ▲	SO	Cattle guard.
▼ 31.1	SO	Bridge over creek.
4.2 ▲	SO	Bridge over creek.
▼ 33.2	BL	Track on right.
2.0 ▲	BR	Track on left.
▼ 33.6	SO	Track on right.
1.7 ▲	SO	Track on left.
▼ 35.3	SO	Cattle guard and Baxter Pass. Tracks on left and right are jeep trails. Zero trip meter.
0.0 ▲		Continue on County 201.

GPS: N 39°34.96' W 108°57.14'

▼ 0.0		Continue on County 201.
15.8 ▲	SO	Baxter Pass. Cattle guard. Tracks on the left and right are jeep trails. Zero trip meter.
▼ 3.1	SO	Shack on left.
12.7 ▲	SO	Shack on right.
▼ 4.5	SO	Old shack on left and McAndrews Lake.
11.3 ▲	SO	Old shack on right and McAndrews Lake.
▼ 6.0	SO	Gate—leave it as you find it.
9.8 ▲	SO	Gate—leave it as you find it.
▼ 6.6	SO	Gate. Ranch on right.
9.2 ▲	SO	Ranch on left. Gate.
▼ 8.3	SO	Cattle guard. Approximately here, road name changes from Garfield County 201 to Rio Blanco County 25.
7.5 ▲	SO	Cattle guard. Approximately here, road name

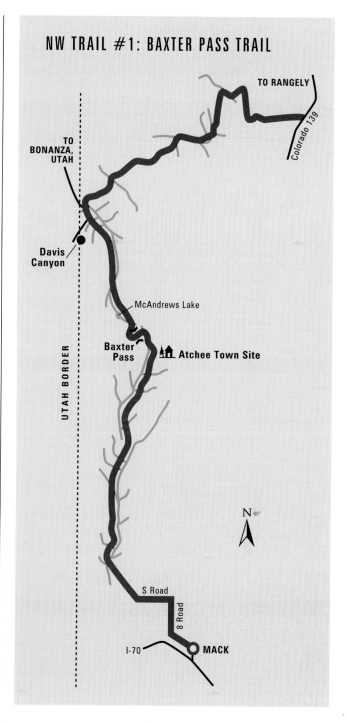

NW TRAIL #1: BAXTER PASS TRAIL

changes from Rio Blanco County 25 to Garfield County 201.

▼ 9.0	SO	Cattle guard.
6.8 ▲	SO	Cattle guard.
▼ 10.2	SO	Cabin ruins on left.
5.6 ▲	SO	Cabin ruins on right.
▼ 10.4	SO	Gate and cattleyard. Cross creek.
5.4 ▲	SO	Cross creek. Cattleyard and gate.
▼ 12.1	SO	Cross over creek.
3.7 ▲	SO	Cross over creek.
▼ 13.4	SO	Road on left to Whiskey Creek and Gentry Ranch.
2.4 ▲	SO	Road on right to Whiskey Creek and Gentry Ranch.

GPS: N 39°43.12' W 109°01.44'

▼ 14.6	SO	Track on left to Davis Canyon.
1.2 ▲	SO	Track on right to Davis Canyon.
▼ 15.8	TR	Intersection. You are almost on the Utah border. Bearing left leads toward Bonanza, Utah. Turn right to Rangely, Colorado. Zero trip meter.
0.0 ▲		Proceed toward Baxter Pass on County 25.

GPS: N 39°44.83' W 109°02.92'

▼ 0.0		Proceed toward Rangely on County 109.
4.6 ▲	TL	Intersection. You are almost on the Utah border. Zero trip meter.
▼ 0.1	SO	Cross through Evacuation Creek.
4.4 ▲	SO	Cross through Evacuation Creek.
▼ 2.1	BR	Track on left.
2.4 ▲	BL	Track on right.
▼ 2.6	BL	Track on right to network of trails.
1.9 ▲	BR	Track on left to network of trails.
▼ 3.0	SO	Private mining track on right.
1.5 ▲	SO	Private mining track on left.
▼ 3.7	SO	Cross through wash.
0.9 ▲	SO	Cross through wash.
▼ 4.4	BL	Track on right. Then cross through wash.
0.2 ▲	BR	Cross through wash. Road forks.
▼ 4.6	BR	Fork in road. Old cabin on left. Zero trip meter.
0.0 ▲		Continue on County 109.

GPS: N 39°46.90' W 108°59.67'

▼ 0.0		Continue on County 109.
24.5 ▲	BL	Old cabin on right. Road forks. Zero trip meter.
▼ 4.1	SO	Cross through wash.
20.4 ▲	SO	Cross through wash.
▼ 4.3	SO	Cross through wash.
20.2 ▲	SO	Cross through wash.
▼ 5.5	SO	Cross through wash.
19.0 ▲	SO	Cross through wash.
▼ 7.0	BL	Track on right.
17.5 ▲	BR	Fork in road.
▼ 7.9	SO	Track on left.
16.6 ▲	SO	Track on right.
▼ 8.0	SO	Track on right.
16.5 ▲	SO	Track on left.
▼ 8.8	TL	T-intersection. To the right dead-ends.
15.7 ▲	TR	Intersection. Straight on dead-ends.

GPS: N 39°50.62' W 108°53.71'

▼ 9.2	SO	Intersection. Tracks on left and right.
15.3 ▲	SO	Intersection. Tracks on left and right.
▼ 9.4	BL	Fork in the road. Follow County 109.
15.1 ▲	BR	Road on left.
▼ 9.8	SO	Oil well on left.
14.7 ▲	SO	Oil well on right.
▼ 10.1	SO	Track on right.
14.4 ▲	SO	Track on left.
▼ 10.3	SO	Track on left.
14.2 ▲	SO	Track on right.
▼ 10.6	SO	Track on left.
13.9 ▲	SO	Track on right.
▼ 11.0	TR	T-intersection.
13.5 ▲	TL	Road on left.

GPS: N 39°51.79' W 108°54.30'

▼ 12.9	BL	County 111 on right.
11.6 ▲	BR	County 111 on left.
▼ 13.3	SO	County 113 on left.
11.2 ▲	SO	County 113 on right.
▼ 15.2	SO	County 107 on left.
9.3 ▲	SO	County 107 on right.
▼ 20.0	SO	Track on right.
4.5 ▲	BL	Fork in road. Follow Little Horse Draw.
▼ 21.0	SO	Conoco Natural Gas plant on right.
3.5 ▲	SO	Conoco Natural Gas plant on left.
▼ 22.1	SO	Conoco Natural Gas plant.
2.4 ▲	SO	Conoco Natural Gas plant.
▼ 24.5		End at intersection of County 116 with Colorado 139.
0.0 ▲		At intersection of Colorado 139 and County 116 (also signposted as "Little Horse Draw"), zero trip meter and proceed west along County 116.

GPS: N 39°49.91' W 108°44.62'

NORTHWEST REGION TRAIL #2

Ellis Jeep Trail

Starting Point:	Intersection of FR 550 and FR 500
Finishing Point:	Cowdrey
Total Mileage:	50.6 miles
Unpaved Mileage:	45.6 miles
Driving Time:	3 1/2 hours
Elevation:	9,370 feet at the Continental Divide
Usually Open:	Mid-June to mid-September
Difficulty Rating:	6
Scenic Rating:	9

Special Attractions

■ Challenging, remote 4WD trail.

■ Elk viewing.

■ Forms a 4WD loop route when combined with Northwest Trail #3: Elkhorn Mountain and Stock Driveway.

History

Jack Ellis, an Elk River cattleman, built the Ellis Jeep Trail in 1888, to supply lumbermen in the Hog Park area with beef and supplies. The trail ran from the Elk River to Hahns Peak and Hog Park and on to the Encampment River. It was the main supply route between the towns of Hahns Peak and Commissary on the Colorado/Wyoming border just north of the Hog Park guard station. The supply wagons and sleds were pulled by as many as eight, and seldom less than four, horses.

Description

You will definitely need a 4WD vehicle to cross the extremely boggy sections of this trail in the meadows along the South Fork of Hog Park Creek. The difficulty rating for this trail is based on its state under the driest conditions; in other conditions, the route is impassable and many vehicles get bogged each year.

Crossing these meadows requires careful investigation on foot to locate the driest route. As this is a very remote area of Colorado, you will be wise to take the trail in more than one vehicle or bring a winch (and extension straps) if you do not want to risk a long

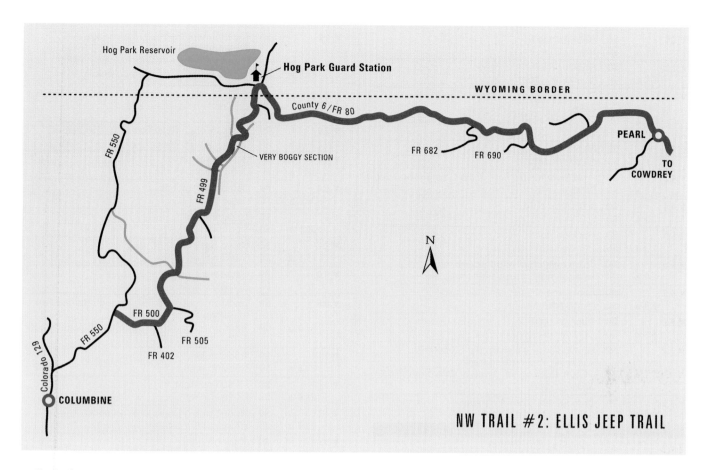

NW TRAIL #2: ELLIS JEEP TRAIL

walk. Such precautions will also help avoid damage to the trail.

The route involves several creek crossings, some of which have narrow clearance between the trees and deep wheel ruts and potholes. Some lower-clearance 4WD vehicles and those fitted with sidesteps may have difficulties at these crossings.

The route travels through lodgepole pine forest interspersed with open meadows. Elk and mule deer are frequently viewed in the early morning or late afternoon.

The route starts at the intersection of FR 550 and FR 500, 3.6 miles after turning off County 129 and some 34 miles north of Steamboat Springs. The boggiest section of the trail is encountered at the 9.5-mile point.

Before crossing the creek it is advisable to walk ahead for the next mile or so to check conditions. The creek crossing can itself be boggy, but the more difficult sections come after it. Shortly after crossing the creek, the trail turns right and descends down an open meadow. It then turns left into the trees, crosses the creek again, and emerges into another meadow. This is the boggiest section of the trail; if you cannot get through, you will have a very hard time getting back out.

From this point, there are a few tricky creek crossings where the surrounding area can be rutted and boggy, and clearance between the trees tight. But if you've made it this far, these crossings should seem easy!

The route continues uneventfully to Hog Park guard station and the Wyoming border, then continues east to Cowdrey on a well-maintained, unpaved road; but you may also choose to loop around to the west and then south back to Steamboat Springs, by way of either Elkhorn Mountain and Stock Drive-

way (Northwest Trail #3) or the well-maintained FR 550. From Hog Park USFS picnic ground to the intersection of FR 550 and FR 508 (to connect with Northwest Trail #3) is 8.6 miles.

Backcountry campsites are plentiful along the trail, and water is readily available.

Current Road Conditions
Routt National Forest
Hahns Peak Ranger District
925 Weiss Drive, Steamboat Springs, CO 80487
(970) 879-1870

Map References
USFS Routt NF
USGS Routt County #2
　　　　　Jackson County #1
　　　　　Jackson County #2
Trails Illustrated, #113, #116
The Roads of Colorado, pp. 20-22
Colorado Atlas & Gazetteer, pp. 16-17

Route Directions

▼ 0.0		At intersection of FR 550 and FR 500, zero trip meter and proceed east along FR 500 toward Big Red Park.
7.5 ▲		End at intersection with FR 550.
		GPS: N 40°53.46' W 106°54.93'
▼ 0.1	SO	FR 506 on left.
7.4 ▲	SO	FR 506 on right.

▼ 1.0	SO	500.1D on left.	
6.5 ▲	SO	500.1D on right.	
▼ 1.1	SO	FR 509 on left.	
6.4 ▲	SO	FR 509 on right.	
▼ 1.6	SO	FR 402 on right. Cross over King Solomon Creek.	
5.9 ▲	SO	Cross over King Solomon Creek. FR 402 on left.	
▼ 2.4	SO	FR 505 on right.	
5.1 ▲	SO	FR 505 on left.	
▼ 4.2	SO	Cross over Middle Fork of the Little Snake River.	
3.3 ▲	SO	Cross over Middle Fork of the Little Snake River.	
▼ 4.6	SO	500.1A on right.	
2.9 ▲	SO	500.1A on left.	
▼ 5.1	SO	Track on right.	
2.3 ▲	SO	Track on left.	
▼ 5.5	SO	Cross over creek and track on left.	
2.0 ▲	SO	Track on right. Cross over creek.	
▼ 6.6	SO	Faint track on left.	
0.9 ▲	SO	Faint track on right.	
▼ 7.2	SO	Track on right.	
0.3 ▲	SO	Track on left.	
▼ 7.3	SO	FR 499 south is a sharp right (becomes Wyoming Trail walking track).	
0.1 ▲	SO	FR 499 south on left (becomes Wyoming Trail walking track).	
▼ 7.5	TR	Onto FR 499. Zero trip meter.	
0.0 ▲	SO	Continue along FR 500.	
		GPS: N 40°56.59' W 106°51.70'	
▼ 0.0		Continue along FR 499.	
2.6 ▲	TL	Onto FR 500. Zero trip meter.	
▼ 0.2	SO	Cabin ruins on right.	
2.4 ▲	SO	Cabin ruins on left.	
▼ 2.0	SO	Cross through the South Fork of Hog Park Creek.	
0.6 ▲	SO	Cross through the South Fork of Hog Park Creek.	
		GPS: N 40°57.77' W 106°50.89'	
▼ 2.1	BR	Descend down a boggy meadow.	
0.5 ▲	BL	Ascend another boggy meadow, then bear left.	
▼ 2.3	BL	Cross through creek and enter second meadow with some potentially very boggy sections.	
0.3 ▲	BR	Cross boggy meadow. Cross through creek, then bear right.	
▼ 2.6	SO	Creek crossing. Zero trip meter.	
0.0 ▲		Continue along FR 499.	
		GPS: N 40°58.34' W 106°50.22'	
▼ 0.0		Continue along FR 499.	
3.3 ▲	SO	Creek crossing. Zero trip meter.	
▼ 1.0	BL	Intersection of FR 499 and FR 82. Proceed along FR 82.	
2.3 ▲	BR	Intersection of FR 499 and FR 82. Proceed along FR 499.	
		GPS: N 40°58.96' W 106°49.61'	
▼ 2.9	BL	Proceed through gate, then intersection with FR 82.1A. Remain on FR 82.	
0.4 ▲	BR	Intersection with FR 82.1A, then gate. Remain on FR 82.	
		GPS: N 41°00.00' W 106°49.23'	
▼ 3.3	TR	Intersection with County 6B (also posted as FR 496, but the FR label will change to FR 80 shortly). Zero trip meter.	
0.0 ▲		Proceed along County 6B west.	
		GPS: N 41°00.27' W 106°49.04'	
▼ 0.0		Proceed along County 6B east.	
37.2 ▲	TL	Intersection with County 6B. Zero trip meter.	

▼ 0.2	SO	Encampment trailhead, then bridge over Encampment River. Road on left (FR 496) to Encampment, Wyoming. Remain on FR 80 east.	
37.0 ▲	SO	FR 496 on right to Encampment, Wyoming. Bridge over Encampment River.	
▼ 2.0	SO	Gated track on left.	
35.2 ▲	SO	Gated track on right.	
▼ 2.4	SO	Cross through Ryan Park.	
34.8 ▲	SO	Cross through Ryan Park.	
▼ 4.1	SO	Gated track on left.	
33.1 ▲	SO	Gated track on right.	
▼ 4.4	SO	Gated track on left.	
32.8 ▲	SO	Gated track on right.	
▼ 6.7	SO	Track on right.	
30.5 ▲	SO	Track on left.	
▼ 8.7	SO	Gated track on right.	
28.5 ▲	SO	Gated track on left.	
▼ 9.0	SO	Gated track on left.	
28.2 ▲	SO	Gated track on right.	
▼ 9.6	SO	Track on right is FR 682, through Buffalo Park to Buffalo Ridge trailhead.	
27.6 ▲	SO	Track on left is FR 682, through Buffalo Park to Buffalo Ridge trailhead.	
▼ 10.4	SO	Track on left.	
26.8 ▲	SO	Track on right.	
▼ 13.2	SO	FR 690 on right.	
24.0 ▲	SO	FR 690 on left.	
▼ 13.5	SO	FR 681 to Big Creek Lake on right.	
23.7 ▲	SO	FR 681 to Big Creek Lake on left.	
▼ 15.6	SO	Track on right.	
21.6 ▲	SO	Track on left.	
▼ 15.7	SO	FR 691 on left.	
21.5 ▲	SO	FR 691 on right.	
▼ 16.0	SO	Cattle guard. Entering private land.	
21.2 ▲	SO	Cattle guard.	
▼ 17.4	BR	Road on left.	
19.8 ▲	BL	Road on right.	
		GPS: N 40°59.76' W 106°33.81'	
▼ 19.0	SO	Town of Pearl. Bear Creek Road (FR 600) on right.	
18.2 ▲	SO	Bear Creek Road (FR 600) on left. Town of Pearl.	
▼ 19.5	SO	Bridge over South Fork of Big Creek.	
17.7 ▲	SO	Bridge over South Fork of Big Creek.	
▼ 22.1	SO	FR 609 on right.	
15.1 ▲	SO	FR 609 on left.	
▼ 29.4	SO	County 7 on right.	
7.8 ▲	SO	County 7 on left.	
▼ 30.6	SO	Road on right.	
6.6 ▲	SO	Road on left.	
▼ 32.1	SO	County 35 on left.	
5.1 ▲	SO	County 35 on right.	
▼ 32.2	SO	Paved.	
5.0 ▲	SO	Unpaved.	
▼ 35.2	SO	Bridge over North Platte River.	
2.0 ▲	SO	Bridge over North Platte River.	
▼ 36.0	SO	Cross over bridge.	
1.2 ▲	SO	Cross over bridge.	
▼ 37.2		End at intersection of County 6W and County 125 beside Cowdry General Store.	
0.0 ▲		In Cowdry at intersection of 6W and County 125 (beside Cowdry General Store), zero trip meter and proceed west on County 6W.	
		GPS: N 40°51.58' W 106°18.76'	

Elkhorn Mountain and Stock Driveway

Starting Point:	**Intersection of County 129 and FR 550**
Finishing Point:	**Intersection of County 129 and FR 550**
Total Mileage:	**33.5 miles**
Unpaved Mileage:	**33.5 miles**
Driving Time:	**2 1/2 hours**
Highest Elevation:	**9,400 feet**
Usually Open:	**Mid-June to late September**
Difficulty Rating:	**4**
Scenic Rating:	**8**

Special Attractions

- Remote 4WD trail.
- Varied scenery, with wonderful aspen viewing in the fall.
- Forms a 4WD loop route when combined with Northwest Trail #2: Ellis Jeep Trail.

History

Basque shepherds developed this route in the late 1800s. The carvings on the aspens date from that time.

Description

This route commences along FR 550, a well-maintained gravel road that intersects with County 129 about thirty miles north of Steamboat Springs.

About two miles after the turnoff onto FR 508, the road becomes 4WD. Shortly after passing the Elkhorn Mine, the road starts the first of two rather steep sections as it ascends Elkhorn Mountain. After leveling off for about half a mile, the road descends the west side of Elkhorn Mountain. The track is rocky and eroded in places, but in dry conditions should not pose any problems other than a bumpy ride.

An old water trough along the stock driveway

The road travels through some magnificent stands of aspen, with the clearance between the trees being a squeeze for a full-sized vehicle. In fall, the aspen leaves radiate a yellow glow that casts a luminous effect over the entire area.

The route continues through a couple of areas that are likely to be boggy and rutted after rain. The base is reasonably firm, so these sections should not pose too much of an obstacle if you have high clearance and maintain a steady momentum.

At County 129, the road returns to well-maintained 2WD conditions and proceeds south to rejoin FR 550, where this route commenced.

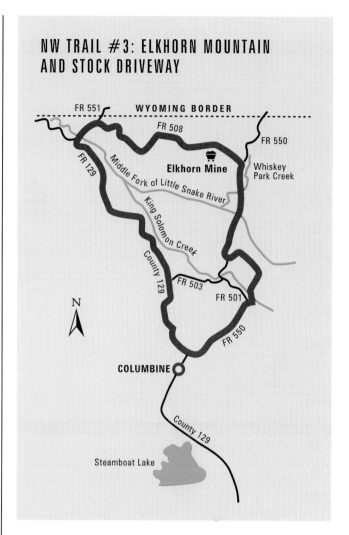

NW TRAIL #3: ELKHORN MOUNTAIN AND STOCK DRIVEWAY

Current Road Conditions

Routt National Forest
Hahns Peak Ranger District
925 Weiss Drive, Steamboat Springs, CO 80487
(970) 879-1870

Map References

USFS Routt NF
USGS Routt County #1
Routt County #2
Trails Illustrated, #116
The Roads of Colorado, pp. 20-21
Colorado Atlas & Gazetteer, p. 16

Route Directions

▼ 0.0		At intersection of County 129 and FR 550, just north of Columbine, zero trip meter, turn onto Whiskey Park Road (FR 550), and proceed northeast.
11.5 ▲		End at intersection of County 129 and FR 550.
	GPS: N 40°51.65′ W 106°57.63′	
▼ 0.1	SO	Seasonal gate.
11.4 ▲	SO	Seasonal gate.
▼ 3.6	SO	Road on right to Big Red Park is FR 500, turnoff for Northwest Trail #2: Ellis Jeep Trail.

▼ 7.9 ▲	SO	Road on left to Big Red Park is FR 500, turnoff for Northwest Trail #2: Ellis Jeep Trail.	

GPS: N 40°53.46' W 106°54.93'

▼ 3.6	SO	FR 501 on left.	
7.8 ▲	SO	FR 501 on right.	
▼ 4.2	SO	Cross over King Solomon Creek.	
7.3 ▲	SO	Cross over King Solomon Creek.	
▼ 6.1	SO	Duncan Road (FR 504) on right.	
5.4 ▲	SO	Duncan Road (FR 504) on left.	
▼ 7.5	SO	FR 503 on left to King Solomon Creek and Slater. Then cattle guard.	
3.9 ▲	SO	Cattle guard. FR 503 on right to King Solomon Creek and Slater.	
▼ 8.4	SO	Cross over Middle Fork of the Little Snake River.	
3.1 ▲	SO	Cross over Middle Fork of the Little Snake River.	
▼ 9.2	SO	FR 502.1A on left. FR 553 on right.	
2.3 ▲	SO	FR 553 on right. FR 502.1A on left.	
▼ 9.5	SO	Cross over Middle Fork of Snake River.	
2.0 ▲	SO	Cross over Middle Fork of Snake River.	
▼ 9.8	SO	FR 511 on right.	
1.7 ▲	SO	FR 511 on left.	
▼ 10.5	SO	Enter Whiskey Park.	
0.9 ▲	SO	Leave Whiskey Park.	
▼ 10.7	SO	Cross over Whiskey Park Creek.	
0.8 ▲	SO	Cross over Whiskey Park Creek.	
▼ 11.4	SO	Leave Whiskey Park.	
0.1 ▲	SO	Enter Whiskey Park.	
▼ 11.5	TL	Onto Elkhorn Mountain Road (FR 508).	
0.0 ▲		Continue along FR 550. Zero trip meter.	

GPS: N 40°58.36' W 106°54.95'

▼ 0.0		Proceed along FR 508.	
8.8 ▲	TR	Onto FR 550. Zero trip meter.	
▼ 0.6	SO	FR 508B on left.	
8.2 ▲	SO	FR 508B on right.	
▼ 1.1	SO	Track on right.	
7.7 ▲	SO	Track on left.	
▼ 1.2	BR	Fork in the road. Follow FR 508.	
7.6 ▲	BL	Fork in the road. Follow FR 508.	
▼ 1.6	SO	Whiskey Park trailhead. Cross over creek.	
7.2 ▲	SO	Cross over creek. Whiskey Park trailhead.	
▼ 2.4	SO	Elkhorn Mine building ruins on left.	
6.4 ▲	SO	Elkhorn Mine building ruins on right.	
▼ 2.5	SO	Track to Elkhorn Mine on left.	
6.3 ▲	SO	Track to Elkhorn Mine on right.	
▼ 2.6	BR	Fork in the road. Follow FR 508. 508F is straight ahead.	
6.2 ▲	BL	Follow FR 508.	
▼ 2.7	BR	Fork in the road. Follow FR 508.	
6.1 ▲	BL	Track on right.	
▼ 4.0	BR	Walking track 1149 on left.	
4.8 ▲	SO	Walking track 1149 on right.	
▼ 4.7	BL	Fork in the road. FR 1149 on right.	
4.0 ▲	BR	Fork in the road. FR 1149 on left.	

GPS: N 40°59.45' W 106°59.02'

▼ 5.1	SO	Stock trough on right.	
3.6 ▲	SO	Stock trough on left.	

GPS: N 40°59.23' W 106°59.33'

▼ 5.3	SO	Cross through small creek.	
3.4 ▲	SO	Cross through small creek.	
▼ 5.5	SO	508H on left.	
3.2 ▲	SO	508H on right.	
▼ 5.6	SO	Track on left.	
3.2 ▲	SO	Track on right.	

▼ 7.6	SO	Cross over creek.	
1.1 ▲	SO	Cross over creek.	
▼ 8.7	SO	Cattle guard. Leaving Routt National Forest; entering Three Forks Ranch.	
0.1 ▲	SO	Leaving Three Forks Ranch; entering Routt National Forest. Cattle guard.	

GPS: N 40°59.98' W 107°01.84'

▼ 8.8	TL	T-intersection with FR 551. Zero trip meter.	
0.0 ▲		Continue on FR 508.	

GPS: N 40°59.95' W 107°01.96'

▼ 0.0		Continue on FR 551.	
13.2 ▲	TR	Intersection with FR 508. Zero trip meter.	
▼ 0.8	SO	Cross bridge.	
12.4 ▲	SO	Cross bridge.	
▼ 1.1	TL	T-intersection. U-turn left onto FR 129.	
12.1 ▲	TR	Onto FR 551.	

GPS: N 40°59.38' W 107°02.91'

▼ 2.3	SO	Cattle guard. Three Forks Ranch entrance.	
10.9 ▲	SO	Three Forks Ranch entrance. Cattle guard.	
▼ 2.7	SO	Cattle guard.	
10.5 ▲	SO	Cattle guard.	
▼ 3.3	SO	FR 407 on left.	
9.9 ▲	SO	FR 407 on right.	
▼ 6.6	SO	Cattle guard.	
6.6 ▲	SO	Cattle guard.	
▼ 8.1	SO	Cattle guard.	
5.1 ▲	SO	Cattle guard.	
▼ 9.3	BR	FR 503 on left. Follow FR 129 toward Columbine.	
3.9 ▲	SO	FR 503 on right.	
▼ 11.9	SO	FR 129.1A on left.	
1.3 ▲	SO	FR 129.1A on right.	
▼ 13.2		End at intersection with FR 550.	
0.0 ▲		At intersection of FR 550 and FR 129 above Columbine, zero trip meter and proceed along FR 129.	

GPS: N 40°51.65' W 106°57.63'

NORTHWEST REGION TRAIL #4

Troublesome Pass Loop

Starting Point:	**Intersection of Colorado 125 and FR 106**
Finishing Point:	**Intersection of FR 730 and Colorado 125**
Total Mileage:	**26.7 miles**
Unpaved Mileage:	**26.7 miles**
Driving Time:	**2 hours**
Pass Elevation:	**10,027 feet (the road's highest elevation is 9,698 feet)**
Usually Open:	**Late May to mid-October**
Difficulty Rating:	**2**
Scenic Rating:	**7**

Special Attractions

- Easy 4WD trail.
- Varied scenery and road conditions.
- Many side roads.

NW TRAIL #4: TROUBLESOME PASS LOOP

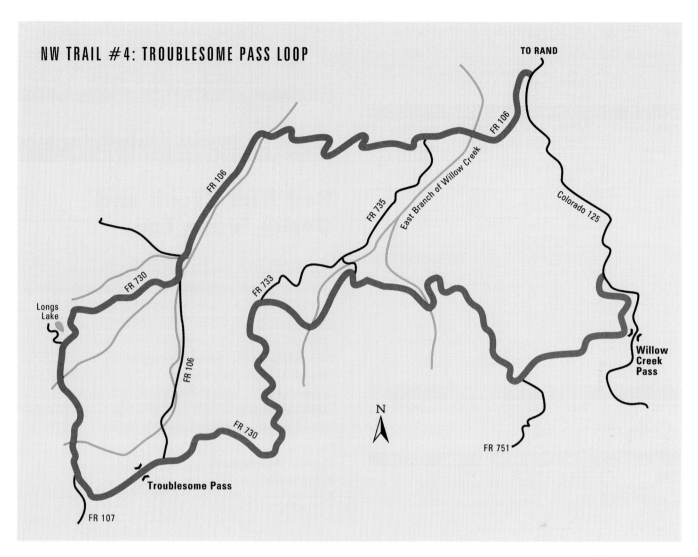

Description

This is a lightly used route (except in hunting season) that is not difficult but does involve a number of small creek crossings as it winds through a mature lodgepole pine forest interspersed with mountain meadows and small willow bottoms. Numerous channels are cut across the road to control erosion. Lengthy sections of shelf road are quite wide and have a sound surface.

The area has a network of side roads, many presumably used for logging as considerable reforestation is evident. Despite the number of side roads, navigation should not be a problem.

The route commences at the intersection of Colorado 125 and Willow Creek Road (FR 106) about five miles southeast of Rand. FR 106 is an easy, graded road, but after turning on to FR 730 it narrows somewhat and becomes rougher, with drainage channels cut across it to control erosion of the surface.

FR 730 continues through to rejoin Colorado 125 some 3.5 miles south of where the route started.

Current Road Conditions

Routt National Forest
Walden Ranger District
100 Main Street, Walden, CO 80480
(970) 723-8204

Map References

USFS Routt NF
USGS Jackson County #4
Trails Illustrated, #115
The Roads of Colorado, p. 38
Colorado Atlas & Gazetteer, p. 28

Route Directions

▼ 0.0		At intersection of Colorado 125 and Willow Creek Road (FR 106), zero trip meter and proceed along FR 106.
	7.1 ▲	End at intersection with Colorado 125.
	GPS: N 40°24.25′ W 106°06.97′	
▼ 1.1	**SO**	FR 190 on left.
	6.0 ▲	**SO** FR 190 on right.
▼ 1.3	**SO**	Cross over east branch of Willow Creek.
	5.8 ▲	**SO** Cross over east branch of Willow Creek.
▼ 2.0	**SO**	FR 735 on left (cuts across Troublesome Pass Loop to FR 730).
	5.1 ▲	**SO** FR 735 on right.
▼ 4.9	**SO**	Cross over Willow Creek, then cattle guard.
	2.2 ▲	**SO** Cattle guard. Cross over Willow Creek.
▼ 5.0	**SO**	FR 734 on right.
	2.1 ▲	**SO** FR 734 on left.

▼ 6.8	SO	FR 715 on right toward Rock Creek and Grassy Run.
0.3 ▲	SO	FR 715 on left.
▼ 7.1	TR	Onto FR 730. Straight cuts directly to Troublesome Pass. Zero trip meter.
0.0 ▲		Continue along FR 106.

GPS: N 40°22.07′ W 106°12.42′

▼ 0.0		Proceed along FR 730 toward Longs Lake and Poison Ridge. Zero trip meter.
19.6 ▲	TL	Intersection with FR 106. Zero trip meter.
▼ 0.2	SO	Gated track on left.
19.4 ▲	SO	Gated track on right.
▼ 0.9	SO	Track on right.
18.7 ▲	SO	Track on left.
▼ 1.7	BR	Track on left.
17.9 ▲	BL	Track on right.
▼ 2.3	BR	Track on left. Then cross through small creek.
17.3 ▲	BL	Cross through small creek. Then track on right.
▼ 3.9	SO	Cross through small creek.
15.7 ▲	SO	Cross through small creek.
▼ 4.1	SO	Cross through small creek.
15.5 ▲	SO	Cross through small creek.
▼ 4.6	BL	FR 107 on right to Poison Ridge. Remain on FR 730.
15.0 ▲	BR	FR 107 on left to Poison Ridge. Remain on FR 730.

GPS: N 40°19.74′ W 106°13.89′

▼ 5.6	SO	Track on right goes to Troublesome walking trail and Haystack Creek trail.
14.0 ▲	SO	Track on left goes to Troublesome walking trail and Haystack Creek trail.

GPS: N 40°19.90′ W 106°13.00′

▼ 5.9	SO	Willow Creek Road (FR 106) on left.
13.7 ▲	SO	Willow Creek Road (FR 106) on right.
▼ 6.0	SO	Seasonal gate. Cross through and leave it as you found it.
13.6 ▲	SO	Seasonal gate. Cross through and leave it as you found it.
▼ 10.7	SO	FR 733 on left.
8.9 ▲	SO	FR 733 on right.

GPS: N 40°21.76′ W 106°11.13′

▼ 11.6	SO	Cross over creek.
8.0 ▲	SO	Cross over creek.
▼ 11.6	SO	Track on right (closed a short distance up the hill).
7.9 ▲	SO	Track on left (closed a short distance up the hill).
▼ 12.5	SO	Intersection. FR 735 on left.
7.1 ▲	SO	Intersection. FR 735 on right.
▼ 13.6	SO	Cross through small creek.
5.9 ▲	SO	Cross through small creek.
▼ 14.0	SO	Cross through creek.
5.6 ▲	SO	Cross through creek.
▼ 15.3	SO	Road on left closed.
4.3 ▲	SO	Road on right closed.

GPS: N 40°21.90′ W 106°08.05′

▼ 16.6	SO	Track on right.
3.0 ▲	SO	Track on left.
▼ 16.9	BL	FR 751 on right.
2.7 ▲	BR	FR 751 on left.
▼ 18.7	SO	Track on left.
0.8 ▲	SO	Track on right.
▼ 19.4	SO/TR	Seasonal gate. Cross through and leave it as you found it. Then T-intersection.
0.2 ▲	TL/SO	Intersection. Then seasonal gate. Cross through and leave it as you found it.

▼ 19.6		End at intersection with Colorado 125 just north of Willow Creek Pass.
0.0 ▲		At intersection of Colorado 125 and FR 730 (just north of Willow Creek Pass) zero trip meter and proceed along FR 730.

GPS: N 40°21.83′ W 106°05.57′

Red Dirt Creek and Derby Mesa Tail

Starting Point:	**Dotsero**
Finishing Point:	**Derby Junction at the intersection of**
	County 39 and County 301
Total Mileage:	**31.7 miles**
Unpaved Mileage:	**16.8 miles**
Driving Time:	**2 1/4 hours**
Highest Elevation:	**9,600 feet**
Usually Open:	**Mid-June to late October**
Difficulty Rating:	**3**
Scenic Rating:	**8**

Special Attractions

■ Moderately easy 4WD route.

■ Varied scenery, including the red-walled canyon along Red Dirt Creek.

Description

The route begins at Dotsero and travels north on County 301, a scenic road traveling along the raging Colorado River. The first turnoff onto FR 611 is unmarked but is easy to find, im-mediately after a one-lane bridge over the Colorado River where the road re-turns to the west side of the river. Immediately after the intersection, FR 611 squeezes back between the river and the valley wall.

The start of a trail as it squeezes between the rock wall and the stream

The road follows the course of Red Dirt Creek along the scenic, red-walled, wooded canyon. The road is narrow but has adequate pull-offs for passing.

As the road departs the creek, the scenery changes to oak brush and sagebrush, and the ascent to Derby Mesa com-mences. About 2.4 miles after leaving the creek, there is a short, steep section with a large rock to be negotiated in the middle of the road.

The road continues though open country before the final, reasonably steep and narrow switchback onto the mesa.

NW TRAIL #5: RED DIRT CREEK AND DERBY MESA TRAIL

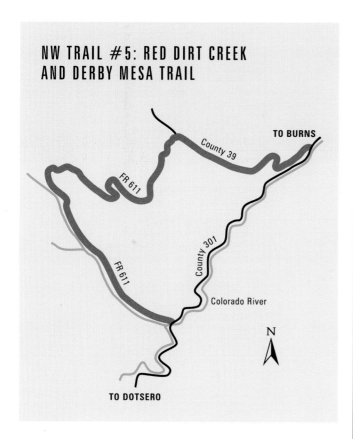

From the intersection with County 39, it is a straightforward, 5-mile journey to Derby Junction, 1 mile south of the Burns post office and 6.25 miles north of the intersection of FR 611, where the route initially turned off County 39.

Current Road Conditions

White River National Forest
Eagle Ranger District
125 West 5th Street, Eagle, CO 81631
(970) 328-6388

Map References

USFS White River NF
USGS Eagle County #1
Trails Illustrated, #120, #122
The Roads of Colorado, pp. 52-53, 68
Colorado Atlas & Gazetteer, p. 36

Route Directions

▼ 0.0			Take Exit 133 north from I-70 into Dotsero. Zero trip meter at the intersection of Frontage Road and County 301. Proceed north on County 301.
14.9 ▲			End at the intersection of Frontage Road and County 301 in Dotsero.

GPS: N 39°38.97' W 107°03.93'

▼ 14.9		TL	After a one-lane bridge, there is an unmarked track, County 39 (FR 611) on the left along the canyon wall. Zero trip meter.
0.0 ▲			Proceed south on County 301.

GPS: N 39°48.28' W 106°58.27'

▼ 0.0			Proceed along FR 611.
11.8 ▲		TR	Onto County 301. Zero trip meter.
▼ 0.1		BR/BR	Fork in road. Then track on left.
11.7 ▲		BL/BL	Track on right. Then fork in road.
▼ 0.4		SO	Track on left.
11.4 ▲		SO	Track on right.
▼ 0.6		SO	Fence and gate.
11.2 ▲		SO	Fence and gate.
▼ 1.5		SO	Fence and gate.
10.3 ▲		SO	Fence and gate.
▼ 2.1		BL	Private driveway on right.
9.7 ▲		BR	Private driveway on left.
▼ 2.7		BL	Two small tracks on right.
9.1 ▲		BR	Two small tracks on left.
▼ 2.8		SO	Small track on right at bend in the road.
9.0 ▲		SO	Small track on left at bend in the road.
▼ 3.1		SO	Old cabin on left. Then cattle guard and enter the National Forest.
8.7 ▲		SO	Cattle guard. Leave the National Forest. Old cabin on right.
▼ 4.8		SO	Cattle guard.
7.0 ▲		SO	Cattle guard.
▼ 5.2		TR	Fork in road. Straight will dead-end in a short distance.
6.6 ▲		BL	Track on right dead-ends.

GPS: N 39°51.24' W 107°02.06'

▼ 5.7		SO	Water trough on left.
6.1 ▲		SO	Water trough on right.
▼ 6.0		SO	Gate. Cross through and leave it as you found it.
5.8 ▲		SO	Gate. Cross through and leave it as you found it.
▼ 7.6		SO	Short, steep uphill section.
4.2 ▲		SO	Short, steep descent.
▼ 9.4		SO	Gate. Cross through and leave it as you found it.
2.4 ▲		SO	Gate. Cross through and leave it as you found it.
▼ 9.7		SO	Track on right.
2.1 ▲		SO	Track on left.
▼ 10.5		SO	Cross over creek.
1.3 ▲		SO	Cross over creek.
▼ 11.1		SO	Track on right.
0.7 ▲		SO	Track on left.

GPS: N 39°51.82' W 106°58.61'

▼ 11.5		SO	Leave White River National Forest. Cross through gate and leave it as you found it.
0.3 ▲		SO	Enter White River National Forest. Cross through gate and leave it as you found it.
▼ 11.8		SO	Cross over creek.
0.0 ▲		SO	Cross over creek.
▼ 11.8		TR	Cattle guard. Then intersection. Zero trip meter.
0.0 ▲			Continue on FR 611 toward White River National Forest.

GPS: N 39°52.34' W 106°58.16'

▼ 0.0			Continue along road toward Derby Junction.
5.0 ▲		TL	Intersection. Zero trip meter. Sign: Red Dirt Road 611 to Red Dirt Creek and Colorado River Road. Cross cattle guard.
▼ 5.0			End at the stop sign at intersection with County 301, Derby Junction.
0.0 ▲			On County 301 in Derby Junction, turn at National Forest access sign and Conoco sign, and zero trip meter. This intersection is further marked with eight cabins on the left.

GPS: N 39°52.16' W 106°54.28'

Selected
Further Reading

Abbott, Carl, Stephen J. Leonard, and David McComb. *Colorado: A History of the Centennial State.* Niwot, Colo.: University Press of Colorado, 1994.

Aldrich, John K. *Ghosts of Chaffee County.* Lakewood, Colo.: Centennial Graphics, 1992.

Aldrich, John K. *Ghosts of Park County.* Lakewood, Colo.: Centennial Graphics, 1994.

Aldrich, John K. *Ghosts of Pitkin County.* Lakewood, Colo.: Centennial Graphics, 1992.

Aldrich, John K. *Ghosts of Summit County.* Lakewood, Colo.: Centennial Graphics, 1997.

Aldrich, John K. *Ghosts of the Eastern San Juans.* Lakewood, Colo.: Centennial Graphics, 1987.

Aldrich, John K. *Ghosts of the Western San Juans.* Vols. 1 and 2. Lakewood, Colo.: Centennial Graphics, 1991.

Ayer, Eleanor. *Colorado Wildflowers.* Frederick, Colo.: Renaissance House, 1987.

Bancroft, Caroline. *Colorful Colorado.* Boulder, Colo.: Johnson Books, 1987.

Bancroft, Caroline. *Unique Ghost Towns and Mountain Spots.* Boulder, Colo.: Johnson Books, 1961.

Bauer, Carolyn. *Colorado Ghost Towns—Colorado Traveler Guidebooks.* Frederick, Colo.: Renaissance House, 1987.

Beckner, Raymond M. *Along the Colorado Trail.* Pueblo, Colo.: O'Brien Printing & Stationery, 1975.

Benham, Jack. *Ouray.* Ouray, Colo.: Bear Creek Publishing, 1976.

Boyd, Leanne C. and H. Glenn Carson. *Atlas of Colorado Ghost Towns.* Vols. 1 and 2. Deming, N.M.: Carson Enterprises, Ltd., 1984.

Bright, William. *Colorado Place Names.* Boulder, Colo.: Johnson Books, 1993.

Brown, Robert L. *Colorado Ghost Towns Past & Present.* Caldwell, Idaho: Caxton Printers, Ltd., 1972.

Brown, Robert L. *Ghost Towns of the Colorado Rockies.* Caldwell, Idaho: Caxton Printers, Ltd., 1990.

Brown, Robert L. *Jeep Trails to Colorado Ghost Towns.* Caldwell, Idaho: Caxton Printers, Ltd., 1995.

Bueler, Gladys R. *Colorado's Colorful Characters.* Boulder, Colo.: Pruett Publishing, 1981.

Burt, William H., and Richard P. Grossenheider. *Peterson Field Guides: Mammals.* New York: Houghton Mifflin, 1980.

Carver, Jack, Jerry Vondergeest, Dallas Boyd, and Tom Pade. *Land of Legend.* Denver, Colo.: Caravon Press, 1959.

Coombes, Allen J. *Eyewitness Handbooks: Trees.* New York: Dorling Kindersley, 1992.

Crofutt, George A. *Crofutt's Grip-Sack Guide of Colorado.* Omaha: Overland Publishing, 1885. Reprinted, Boulder, Colo.: Johnson Books, 1981.

Cromie, Alice. *A Tour Guide to the Old West.* Nashville, Tenn.: Rutledge Hill Press, 1990.

Crutchfield, James A. *It Happened in Colorado.* Helena & Billings, Mo.: Falcon Press Publishing, 1993.

Dallas, Sandra. *Colorado Ghost Towns and Mining Camps.* Norman, Okla.: University of Oklahoma Press, 1985.

DeLong, Brad. *4-Wheel Freedom.* Boulder, Colo.: Paladin Press, 1996.

Dorset, Phyllis Flanders. *The New Eldorado: The Story of Colorado's Gold & Silver Rushes.* New York: Macmillan, 1970.

Eberhart, Perry. *Guide to the Colorado Ghost Towns and Mining Camps.* Chicago, Ill.: Swallow Press, 1995.

Edrinn, Roger. *Colorado Scenic Wildflowers.* Fort Collins, Colo.: Above the Timber, 1997.

Fisher, Vardis, and Opal Laurel Holmes. *Gold Rushes and Mining Camps of the Early American West.* Caldwell, Idaho: Caxton Printers, Ltd., 1968.

Florin, Lambert. *Ghost Towns of the West.* New York: Promontory Press, 1993.

Folzenlogen, Robert. *Colorado's Year: A Guide to Nature's Highlights.* Littleton, Colo.: Willow Press, 1996.

Foster, Mike. *Strange Genius: The Life of Ferdinand Vandeveer Hayden.* Niwot, Colo.: Roberts Rinehart Publishers, 1994.

Fothergill, Chuck, and Bob Sterling. *The Colorado Angling Guide.* Woody Creek, Colo.: Stream Stalker, 1989.

Gray, Mary Taylor. *Colorado Wildlife Viewing Guide.* Helena, Mont.: Falcon Press, 1992.

Green, Stewart M. *Bureau of Land Management Back Country Byways.* Helena, Mont.: Falcon Press, 1995.

Gregory, Lee. *Colorado Scenic Guide: Northern Region.* Boulder, Colo.: Johnson Books, 1990.

Gregory, Lee. *Colorado Scenic Guide: Southern Region.* Boulder, Colo.: Johnson Books, 1990.

Griffin, Wayne W. *Central Colorado 4-Wheeling Guidebook.* Aspen, Colo.: Who Press, 1994.

Heck, Larry E. *4-Wheel Drive Roads & Ghost Towns of the San Juans.* Aurora, Colo.: Pass Patrol, 1995.

Heck, Larry E. *4-Wheel Drive Roads to Outback Colorado.* Aurora, Colo.: Pass Patrol, 1995.

Heck, Larry E. *4-Wheel Drive Trails & Ghost Towns of Colorado.* Aurora, Colo.: Pass Patrol.

Helmuth, Ed and Gloria. *The Passes of Colorado.* Boulder, Colo.: Pruett, 1994.

Hilton, George W. *American Narrow Gauge Railroads.* Stanford: Stanford University Press.

Jessen, Ken. *Colorado Gunsmoke: True Stories of Outlaws and Lawmen on the Colorado Frontier.* Loveland, Colo.: J. V. Publications, 1986.

Jones, Charlotte Foltz. *Colorado Wildflowers.* Helena, Mont.: Falcon Press, 1994.

Koch, Don. *The Colorado Pass Book.* Boulder, Colo.: Pruett, 1992.

Kruger, Frances, and Carron A. Meany. *Explore Colorado: A Naturalist's Notebook.* Englewood, Colo.: Westcliffe, 1995.

Little, Elbert L. *Audubon Society Field Guide to North American Trees: Western Region.* New York: Alfred A. Knopf.

Litvak, Dianna. *Colorado Travel Smart Trip Planner.* Santa Fe, N.M.: John Muir, 1996.

McLean, Evalyn Walsh. *Father Struck it Rich.* Fort Collins, Colo.: FirstLight, 1996.

McTighe, James. *Roadside History of Colorado.* Boulder, Colo.: Johnson Books, 1984.

Mehls, Steven F. *The Valley of Opportunity: A History of West-Central Colorado.* Denver, Colo.: Bureau of Land Management, 1982.

Noel, Thomas J., Paul F. Mahoney, and Richard E. Stevens. *Historical Atlas of Colorado.* Norman, Okla.: University of Oklahoma Press, 1994.

Norton, Boyd and Barbara. *Backroads of Colorado.* Stillwater, Minn: Voyageur Press, 1995.

Ormes, Robert M. *Railroads and the Rockies.* Denver, Colo.: Sage Books, 1963.

Ormes, Robert. *Tracking Ghost Railroads in Colorado.* Colorado Springs, Colo.: Green Light Graphics, 1992.

O'Rourke, Paul M. *Frontier in Transition: A History of Southwestern Colorado.* Denver, Colo.: Bureau of Land Management, 1980.

Parker, Ben H., Jr. *Gold Panning and Placering in Colorado.* Denver, Colo.: U.S. Geological Survey, Department of Natural Resources, 1992.

Peattie, Donald Culross. *A Natural History of Western Trees.* Boston, Mass.: Houghton Mifflin: 1950.

Pettem, Silvia. *Colorado Mountains & Passes—Colorado Traveler Guidebooks.* Frederick, Colo.: Renaissance House, 1991.

Pettit, Jan. *Utes: The Mountain People.* Boulder, Colo.: Johnson Books, 1994.

Pritchard, Sandra F. *Men, Mining & Machines.* Dillon, Colo.: Summit County Historical Society, 1996.

Reidhead, Darlene A. *Tour the San Juans. Vols. 1 and 2.* Cortez, Colo.: Southwest Printing.

Rennicke, Jeff. *Colorado Wildlife.* Helena, Mo.: Falcon Press, 1996.

Roberts, Harold D. *Mountain Wildflowers of Colorado.* Denver, Colo.: W. H. Kistler Stationery, 1957.

Roberts, Harold and Rhoda. *Colorado Wildflowers.* Denver, Colo.: Bradford-Robinson, 1953.

Russo, Ron. *Mountain State Mammals.* Rochester, N.Y.: Nature Study Guild, 1991.

Rye, David. *Colorado's Guide to Hunting.* Glenwood Springs, Colo.: Mountain Peaks, 1992.

Sinnotte, Barbara. *Colorado: A Guide to the State & National Parks.* Edison, N.J.: Hunter, 1996.

Smith, Duane A. *Colorado Mining: A Photographic History.* Albuquerque, N.M.: University of New Mexico Press, 1977.

Southworth, Dave. *Colorado Mining Camps.* Wild Horse, 1997.

Southworth, Dave. *Gunfighters of the Old West.* Wild Horse, 1997.

Strickler, Dr. Dee. *Alpine Wildflowers.* Columbia Falls, Mo.: The Flower Press, 1990.

Strickler, Dr. Dee. *Forest Wildflowers.* Columbia Falls, Mo.: The Flower Press, 1988.

Swift, Kim. *Heart of the Rockies: A History of the Salida Area.* Boulder, Colo.: Johnson Books, 1996.

Taylor, Colin F. *The Plains Indians.* New York: Barnes & Noble Books and Salamander Books, 1997.

Ubbelohde, Carl, Maxine Benson, and Duane A. Smith. *A Colorado History.* Boulder, Colo.: Pruett Publishing, 1995.

Von Bamford, Lawrence, and Kenneth R. Tremblay, Jr. *Leadville Architecture.* Estes Park, Colo.: Architecture Research Press, 1996.

Waldman, Carl. *Encyclopedia of Native American Tribes.* New York: Facts on File, 1988.

Wassink, Jan L. *Mammals of the Central Rockies.* Missoula, Mont.: Mountain Press, 1993.

Wilkins, Tivis E. *Colorado Railroads Chronological Development.* Boulder, Colo.: Pruett Publishing, 1974.

Wilson, Ray D. *Colorado Historical Tour Guide.* Carpentersville, Ill.: Crossroads Communications, 1990.

Wolle, Muriel Sibell. *The Bonanza Trail.* Chicago, Ill.: The Swallow Press, 1953.

Zim, Herbert S., Ph.D., and Alexander C. Martin, Ph.D. *Trees: A Guide to Familiar American Trees.* New York: Golden Press, 1964.

Zim, Herbert S., Ph.D., Sc.D., and Hobart M. Smith, Ph.D. *Reptiles and Amphibians (A Golden Guide).* Racine, Wis.: Western, 1987.

Index

About the Authors

Peter Massey grew up in the outback of Australia. After retiring from a career in investment banking at the age of thirty-five, he served as a director of a number of companies in the United States, the United Kingdom, and Australia. He moved to Colorado in 1993.

Jeanne Wilson was born and grew up in Washington, D.C. She lived and worked in New York City as a young adult and moved to Colorado in 1993. *4WD Adventures: Colorado* is her second book.

After traveling extensively in Australia, Europe, Asia, and Africa, the authors covered more than 80,000 miles touring the United States and outback Australia in the past five years. They traveled more than 15,000 miles in Colorado to research this book.

The authors are compiling another series of books on 4WD trails. Entitled *4WD Trails,* these books will cover individual regions found in the *4WD Adventures* series.

Further titles in the *4WD Adventures* series will cover other states with four-wheel driving opportunties. Information on all the upcoming books can be found on the Internet at www.4wdbooks.com.

Photograph Credits

Unless otherwise indicated in the following list of acknowledgments (which is organized by section and page number), all color photographs were taken by Peter Massey and are copyrighted by Swagman Publishing Inc., or by Peter Massey.

21 Colorado Historical Society; **22** (upper left) Dick Dixon, courtesy Colorado Historical Society; (lower left) Denver Public Library Western History Collection; (upper right) Denver Public Library Western History Collection; **23** (upper center) William Henry Jackson, courtesy Denver Public Library Western History Collection; **28** Muriel Sibell Wolle, courtesy Denver Public Library Western History Collection; **29** (upper & lower right) Denver Public Library Western History Collection; **30** (upper center) Denver Public Library Western History Collection; **31** Denver Public Library Western History Collection; **32** (upper left) Muriel Sibell Wolle, courtesy Denver Public Library Western History Collection; (lower right) Rose & Hopkins, courtesy Denver Public Library Western History Collection; **34** (upper center) Collier Album, courtesy Colorado Historical Society; (middle left) Denver Public Library Western History Collection; **35** (upper center) William Henry Jackson, courtesy Denver Public Library Western History Collection; **37** Denver Public Library Western History Collection; **38** Alfred Brisbois, courtesy Denver Public Library Western History Collection; **39** Denver Public Library Western History Collection; **41** Jesse L. Nusbaum, courtesy Denver Public Library Western History Collection; **42** Denver Public Library Western History Collection; **45** (upper center) Otto Perry, courtesy Denver Public Library Western History Collection; (lower right) Denver Public Library Western History Collection; **49** (upper center) Colorado Historical Society; (lower right) Denver Public Library Western History Collection; **53** Denver Public Library Western History Collection; **55** (upper left) painting by C. Waldo Love, courtesy Colorado Historical Society; (middle left) Denver Public Library Western History Collection; (lower left) Colorado Historical Society; (middle right) Denver Public Library Western History Collection; (lower right) Huntington Library; **56** (upper left) Denver Public Library Western History Collection; (lower left) Colorado Historical Society, Smithsonian Institute archives; (middle right) William Henry Jackson, courtesy Colorado Historical Society; **57** (left & right) Denver Public Library Western History Collection; **58** (left & right) Denver Public Library Western History Collection; **59** (left) Colorado Historical Society; (right) Denver Public Library Western History Collection; **60** (all) Denver Public Library Western History Collection; **61** (upper & lower right) Denver Public Library Western History Collection; **62** (middle left) Denver Public Library Western History Collection; **63** Denver Public Library Western History Collection; **64** Colorado Historical Society; **65** (upper left) Colorado Historical Society; (lower left) PhotoDisc; (middle right) PhotoDisc; **66 - 67** PhotoDisc; **68** (upper left) PhotoDisc; (lower left) Robert McCaw; (right) PhotoDisc; **69 - 71** PhotoDisc; **72** (top, middle, & lower right) Lauren J. Livo; **73** (upper left) Lauren J. Livo; (lower left) Allen Curickshank, Cornell Lab of Ornithology; (upper right) PhotoDisc; (middle right) Robert McCaw; (lower right) PhotoDisc; **74** (upper left) PhotoDisc; (middle left) Art Biale, Cornell Lab of Ornithology; (middle left) Hawkins, Cornell Lab of Ornithology; (lower left) Ted Wilcox, Cornell Lab of Ornithology; (upper right) D. Robert Franz, Cornell Lab of Ornithology; (middle right) PhotoDisc; (lower right) Helen Fowler Library, Denver Botanic Gardens; **75 - 76** Helen Fowler Library, Denver Botanic Gardens; **77** (upper & middle left, except shrubby cinquefoil) Helen Fowler Library, Denver Botanic Gardens; (lower left) PhotoDisc; (middle right) Helen Fowler Library, Denver Botanic Gardens; **78** (lower left) Helen Fowler Library, Denver Botanic Gardens; (upper right trees) Robert McCaw; (upper right cones) Tim Hogan, University of Colorado at Boulder Herbarium; (middle right cone) Helen Fowler Library, Denver Botanic Gardens; **88** Colorado Historical Society; **97** (lower right) Jesse L. Nusbaum, courtesy Denver Public Library Western History Collection; **123** (lower left) Muriel Sibell Wolle, courtesy Denver Public Library Western History Collection; **185** (upper right) Denver Public Library Western History Collection; **196** Denver Public Library Western History Collection.

Rear cover: (Marsh marigolds) Helen Fowler Library, Denver Botanic Gardens; (Jim Bridger) Colorado Historical Society; (Bighorn sheep) PhotoDisc.

ABOUT THE SERIES OF
swagman guides

The Adventures series of backcountry guidebooks are the ultimate for both adventurous four-wheelers and scenic sightseers. Each volume in the Adventures series covers an entire state or a distinct region. In addition to meticulously detailed route directions and trail maps, these full-color guides include extensive information on the history of towns, ghost towns, and regions passed along the way, as well as a history of the American Indian tribes who lived in the area prior to Euro-American settlement. The guides also provide wildlife information and photographs to help readers identify the great variety of native birds, plants, and animals they are likely to see. All you need is your SUV and your Adventures book to confidently explore all the best sites in each state's backcountry.

71 TRAILS
232 PAGES
209 PHOTOGRAPHS
PRICE $29.95
ISBN: 0-9665675-5-2

4WD Adventures: Colorado gets you safely to the banks of the beautiful Crystal River or over America's highest pass road, Mosquito Pass. This book guides you to the numerous lost ghost towns that speckle Colorado's mountains. In addition to the enormously detailed trail information, there are hundreds of photos of historic mining operations, old railroad routes, wildflowers, and native animals. Trail history is brought to life through the accounts of sheriffs and gunslingers like Bat Masterson and Doc Holliday; millionaires like Horace Tabor and Thomas Walsh; and American Indian warriors like Chiefs Ouray and Antero.

175 TRAILS
544 PAGES
544 PHOTOGRAPHS
PRICE $34.95
ISBN: 1-930193-12-2

Backcountry Adventures: Utah navigates you along 3,721 miles through the spectacular Canyonlands region of Utah, to the top of the Uinta Range, across vast salt flats, and along trails unchanged since the late 19th century when riders of the Pony Express sped from station to station and daring young outlaws wreaked havoc on newly established stage lines, railroads, and frontier towns. In addition to enormously detailed trail information, there are hundreds of photos of frontier towns, historic mining operations, old rail-

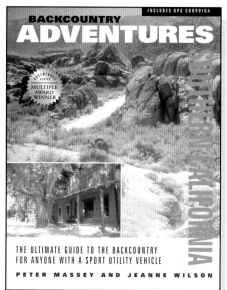

153 TRAILS
640 PAGES
645 PHOTOGRAPHS
PRICE $34.95
ISBN: 1-930193-04-1

157 TRAILS
576 PAGES
524 PHOTOGRAPHS
PRICE $34.95
ISBN: 0-9665675-0-1

road routes, wildflowers, and native animals. Trail history is brought to life through the accounts of outlaws like Butch Cassidy and his Wild Bunch; explorers and mountain men like Jim Bridger; and early Mormon settlers led by Brigham Young.

Backcountry Adventures: Arizona guides you along the back roads of the state's most remote and scenic regions, from the lowlands of the Yuma Desert to the high plains of the Kaibab Plateau. In addition to the enormously detailed trail information, there are hundreds of photos of frontier towns, historic mining operations, old railroad routes, wildflowers, and native animals. Trail history is brought to life through the accounts of Indian warriors like Cochise and Geronimo; trailblazers like Edward F. Beale; and the famous lawman Wyatt Earp, a survivor of the Shoot-out at the O.K. Corral in Tombstone.

Backcountry Adventures: Southern California takes you from the beautiful mountain regions of Big Sur, through the arid Mojave Desert, and straight into the heart of the aptly named Death Valley. In addition to the enormously detailed trail information, there are hundreds of photos of frontier towns, historic mining operations, old railroad routes, wildflowers, and native animals. Trail history is brought to life through the accounts of Spanish missionaries who first settled the coastal regions of Southern California; eager prospectors looking to cash in during California's gold rush; and legends of lost mines still hidden in the state's expansive backcountry.

Additional titles in the series will cover other states with four-wheel driving opportunities. Northern California is scheduled for release during 2002. Information on all upcoming books, including special pre-publication discount offers, can be found on the Internet at www.4WDbooks.com.

order
our award-winning guides

to order

phone	800-660-5107
internet	www.4WDbooks.com
fax	fax this order form to 303-688-4388
mail	mail this order form to Swagman Publishing, Inc.
	PO Box 519, Castle Rock, CO 80104

Backcountry Adventure Series

_____ copies	4WD Adventures: Colorado	(ISBN: 0-9665675-5-2)	Retail: $29.95	$_____
_____ copies	Backcountry Adventures: Utah	(ISBN: 1-930193-12-2)	Retail: $34.95	$_____
_____ copies	Backcountry Adventures: Arizona	(ISBN: 0-9665675-0-1)	Retail: $34.95	$_____
_____ copies	Backcountry Adventures: S. California	(ISBN: 1-930193-04-1)	Retail: $34.95	$_____

4WD Trails Series

_____ copies	4WD Trails: South-Central Colorado	(ISBN: 0-9665675-2-8)	Retail: $14.95	$_____
_____ copies	4WD Trails: North-Central Colorado	(ISBN: 0-9665675-3-6)	Retail: $14.95	$_____
_____ copies	4WD Trails: Southwest Colorado	(ISBN: 0-9665675-4-4)	Retail: $14.95	$_____
_____ copies	4WD Trails: Northern Utah	(ISBN: 0-9665675-7-9)	Retail: $14.95	$_____
_____ copies	4WD Trails: Southwest Utah	(ISBN: 0-9665675-8-7)	Retail: $16.95	$_____
_____ copies	4WD Trails: Central Utah	(ISBN: 0-9665675-9-5)	Retail: $14.95	$_____
_____ copies	4WD Trails: Southeast Utah	(ISBN: 0-9665675-6-0)	Retail: $16.95	$_____

TOTAL PAYMENT DUE $_____
(sales tax and shipping costs will be added)

I understand that I may return any book for a full refund—for any reason, no questions asked

NAME (PLEASE PRINT) _____

COMPANY _____

STREET ADDRESS _____

CITY / STATE / ZIP _____

PHONE _____

Method of payment ❏ CHECK OR MONEY ORDER   ❏ VISA   ❏ MASTERCARD   ❏ AMERICAN EXPRESS

CARD NUMBER _____

EXPIRATION DATE _____

CARDHOLDER'S SIGNATURE _____

call toll free and order now

backcountry adventures series
WINNER OF FOUR PRESTIGIOUS BOOK AWARDS

"The 540-page tome is an incredible resource for getting to, and returning from, almost anywhere in Utah. Concise maps, backed with GPS, make getting lost something you'd have to do on purpose...To borrow a line from a well-known company: Don't leave home without it."

— Truck Trend

"Based on our initial experience, we expect our review copy of *Backcountry Adventures: Arizona* to be well used in the coming months... To say we'd strongly recommend this book is an understatement."

— Auto Week

"*4WD Adventures*...serves as a regional travel guide, complete with glossaries and color photos of wildflowers, animals, famous towns, and natural wonders."

— Four Wheeler Magazine

"Tired of being cooped up in your house because of the weather? This book, designed for owners of SUVs will get you out of the suburbs, off the highways, out of the cities, and into the backcountry..."

— Salt Lake Magazine

"The authors have compiled information that every SUV owner will find handy...Whether you want to know more about four-wheel driving techniques or if you are a snowmobiler or SUV owner looking for places to explore, *4WD Adventures* is the ultimate book...[They] bring the history of these trails to life through their accounts of the pioneers who built them to open up the territory to mining, ranching, and commerce in the 1800s."

— The Denver Post

"[The book]...is a massive undertaking, a textbook-size guide that seems well worth its price. Using this book, SUV owners should be able to explore areas they never knew existed, plus identify plants, animals, ghost towns and Indian history they'll see along the way."

— The Arizona Republic

"Similar to any good history book, once you get started, it's hard to put it down. Not only will it help flesh out your adventures off road, it will also broaden your appreciation of this beautiful country...The wealth of information is second to none, and the presentation makes it a pleasure to read."

— 4 Wheel Drive & Sport Utility Magazine

"This comprehensive book provides over 500 pages of photographs, maps, and detailed information about the trails and sights that make for fun 'wheeling in the Beehive State."

— Peterson's 4Wheel & Off-Road Magazine

"This book is a 10. It contains, in one volume, every kind of information I would want on a 4WD excursion."

— Awards Judge